Lecture Notes in Computer Science

Edited by G. Goos, J. Hartmanis and J. van L

Springer

Berlin
Heidelberg
New York
Barcelona
Hong Kong
London
Milan
Paris
Singapore
Tokyo

Jack Dongarra Peter Kacsuk
Norbert Podhorszki (Eds.)

Recent Advances in Parallel Virtual Machine and Message Passing Interface

7th European PVM/MPI Users' Group Meeting
Balatonfüred, Hungary, September 10-13, 2000
Proceedings

Springer

Series Editors

Gerhard Goos, Karlsruhe University, Germany
Juris Hartmanis, Cornell University, NY, USA
Jan van Leeuwen, Utrecht University, The Netherlands

Volume Editors

Jack Dongarra
University of Tennessee, Innovative Computing Lab.
104 Yres Hall, Knoxville, TN 37996, USA
E-mail: dongarra@cs.utk.edu

Peter Kacsuk
Norbert Podhorszki
MTA SZTAKI Computer and Automation Research Institute
P.O. Box 63, Budapest 1518, Hungary
E-mail: {kacsuk/pnorbert}@sztaki.hu

Cataloging-in-Publication Data applied for

Die Deutsche Bibliothek - CIP-Einheitsaufnahme

Recent advances in parallel virtual machine and message passing
interface : proceedings / 7th European PVM-MPI Users' Group Meeting,
Balatonfüred, Hungary, September 10 - 13, 2000. Jack Dongarra . . .
(ed.). - Berlin ; Heidelberg ; New York ; Barcelona ; Hong Kong ;
London ; Milan ; Paris ; Singapore ; Tokyo : Springer, 2000
    (Lecture notes in computer science ; Vol. 1908)
    ISBN 3-540-41010-4

CR Subject Classification (1998): D.1.3, D.3.2, F.1.2, G.1.0, B.2.1, C.1.2

ISSN 0302-9743
ISBN 3-540-41010-4 Springer-Verlag Berlin Heidelberg New York

Springer-Verlag Berlin Heidelberg New York
a member of BertelsmannSpringer Science+Business Media GmbH
© Springer-Verlag Berlin Heidelberg 2000
Printed in Germany

Typesetting: Camera-ready by author, data conversion by Boller Mediendesign
Printed on acid-free paper   SPIN 10722696   06/3142   5 4 3 2 1 0

Preface

Parallel Virtual Machine (PVM) and Message Passing Interface (MPI) are the most frequently used tools for programming according to the message passing paradigm, which is considered one of the best ways to develop parallel applications.

This volume comprises 42 revised contributions presented at the Seventh European PVM/MPI Users' Group Meeting, which was held in Balatonfüred, Hungary, 10–13 September 2000. The conference was organized by the Laboratory of Parallel and Distributed Systems of the Computer and Automation Research Institute of the Hungarian Academy of Sciences.

This conference was previously held in Barcelona, Spain (1999), Liverpool, UK (1998) and Cracow, Poland (1997). The first three conferences were devoted to PVM and were held at the Technische Universität München, Germany (1996), Ecole Normale Superieure Lyon, France (1995), and University of Rome, Italy (1994).

This conference has become a forum for users and developers of PVM, MPI, and other message passing environments. Interaction between those groups has proved to be very useful for developing new ideas in parallel computing and for applying existing ideas to new practical fields. The main topics of the meeting were evaluation and performance of PVM and MPI, extensions and improvements to PVM and MPI, algorithms using the message passing paradigm, and applications in science and engineering based on message passing. The conference included four tutorials and five invited talks on advances in MPI, cluster computing, network computing, grid computing, and SGI parallel computers and programming systems. These proceedings contain papers on the 35 oral presentations together with 7 poster presentations.

The seventh Euro PVM/MPI conference was held together with DAPSYS 2000, the third Austrian-Hungarian Workshop on Distributed and Parallel Systems. Participants of the two events shared invited talks, tutorials, a vendor session and social events while contributed paper presentations proceeded in separate tracks in parallel. While Euro PVM/MPI was dedicated to the latest developments of PVM and MPI, DAPSYS was a major event to discuss general aspects of distributed and parallel systems. In this way the two events complemented each other and participants of Euro PVM/MPI could benefit from the joint organization of the two events.

Invited speakers of Euro PVM/MPI were Al Geist, Miron Livny, Ewing Lusk, Thomas Sterling, and Bernard Tourancheau.

We would like to express our gratitude for the kind support of Silicon Computers, Microsoft, Myricom, and the Foundation for the Technological Progress of the Industry. Also, we would like to say thanks to the members of the Program Committee for their work in refereeing the submitted papers and ensuring the high quality of Euro PVM/MPI.

September 2000

Jack Dongarra
Peter Kacsuk
Norbert Podhorszki

Program Committee

Vassil Alexandrov   University of Reading, UK
Ranieri Baraglia   CNUCE – Institute of the Italian National Research Council, I
Arndt Bode   LRR – Technische Universität München, G
Shirley Browne   University of Tennessee, USA
Marian Bubak   Institute of Computer Science and ACC CYFRONET, AGH, P
Jacques Chassin-de-Kergommeaux   ID IMAG, F
Jens Clausen   Technical University of Denmark, D
Yiannis Cotronis   University of Athens, G
José Cunha   Universidade Nova de Lisboa, P
Erik D'Hollander   University of Gent, B
Jack Dongarra   University of Tennessee and ORNL, USA
Graham Fagg   University of Tennessee, USA
Al Geist   Oak Ridge National Labs, USA
Wolfgang Gentzsch   GRIDware and Genias, G
Michael Gerndt   LRR – Technische Universität München, G
Andrzej Goscinski   Deakin University, A
Rolf Hempel   C&C Research Labs, NEC Europe Ltd., G
Ladislav Hluchý   Slovak Academy of Science, S
Peter Kacsuk   MTA SZTAKI, H
Gabriele Kotsis   University of Vienna, A
Henryk Krawczyk   Technical University of Gdansk, P
Jan Kwiatkowski   Wroclaw University of Technology, P
Domenico Laforeza   CNUCE – Institute of the Italian National Research Council, I
Miron Livny   University of Wisconsin, USA
Thomas Ludwig   LRR – Technische Universität München, G
Emilio Luque   Universitat Autònoma de Barcelona, S
Tomàs Margalef   Universitat Autònoma de Barcelona, S
Hermann Mierendorff   GMD, G
Benno Overeinder   University of Amsterdam, TN
Norbert Podhorszki   MTA SZTAKI, H
Andrew Rau-Chaplin   Dalhousie University, C
Jeff Reeve   University of Southampton, UK
Yves Robert   LIP – Ecole Normale Superieure de Lyon, F
Casiano Rodríguez   Universidad de La Laguna, S
Wolfgang Schreiner   RISC-Linz – Johannes Kepler University, A
Miquel A. Senar   Universitat Autònoma de Barcelona, S
João Gabriel Silva   Universidade de Coimbra, P
Vaidy Sunderam   Emory University, USA

Additional Reviewers

Table of Contents

1.   Invited Speakers

PVM and MPI: What Else Is Needed for Cluster Computing?   1
A. Geist

Managing Your Workforce on a Computational Grid   3
M. Livny

Isolating and Interfacing the Components of a Parallel Computing   5
Environment
E. Lusk

Symbolic Computing with Beowulf-Class PC Clusters   7
T. Sterling

High Speed Networks for Clusters, the BIP-Myrinet Experience   9
B. Tourancheau

2.   Evaluation and Performance

A Benchmark for MPI Derived Datatypes   10
R. Reussner, J.L. Träff, G. Hunzelmann

Working with MPI Benchmarking Suites on ccNUMA Architectures   18
H. Mierendorff, K. Cassirer, H. Schwamborn

Performance Measurements on Dynamite/DPVM   27
K.A. Iskra, Z.W. Hendrikse, G.D. van Albada, B.J. Overeinder,
P.M.A. Sloot

Validation of Dimemas Communication Model for MPI Collective   39
Operations
S. Girona, J. Labarta, R.M. Badia

Automatic Performance Analysis of Master/Worker PVM
Applications with Kpi   47
A. Espinosa, T. Margalef, E. Luque

MPI Optimization for SMP Based Clusters Interconnected with SCI   56
L.P. Huse

3.   Algorithms

Parallel, Recursive Computation of Global Stability Charts for   64
Liquid Bridges
G. Domokos, I. Szeberényi, P.H. Steen

Handling Graphs According to a Coarse Grained Approach: 72
Experiments with PVM and MPI
I. Guérin Lassous, J. Gustedt, M. Morvan

Adaptive Multigrid Methods in MPI   80
F. Baiardi, S. Chiti, P. Mori, L. Ricci

Multiple Parallel Local Searches in Global Optimization   88
H.P.J. Bolton, J.F. Schutte, A.A. Groenwold

Towards Standard Nested Parallelism   96
J.A. González, C. León, F. Piccoli, M. Printista, J.L. Roda,
C. Rodríguez, F. Sande

Pipeline Algorithms on MPI: Optimal Mapping of the Path Planing   104
Problem
D. González, F. Almeida, L.M. Moreno, C. Rodríguez

Use of PVM for MAP Image Restoration: A Parallel Implementation   113
of the ARTUR Algorithm
G.J. Fernández, J. Jacobo-Berlles, P. Borensztejn, M. Bauzá, M. Mejail

Parallel Algorithms for the Least-Squares Finite Element Solution of   121
the Neutron Transport Equation
E. Varin, R. Roy, G. Samba

4. Extensions and Improvements

GAMMA and MPI/GAMMA on Gigabit Ethernet   129
G. Ciaccio, G. Chiola

Distributed Checkpointing Mechanism for a Parallel File System   137
V.N. Távora, L.M. Silva, J.G. Silva

Thread Communication over MPI   145
T. Nitsche

A Simple, Fault Tolerant Naming Space for the HARNESS   152
Metacomputing System
M. Migliardi, V. Sunderam, A. Frisiani

Runtime Checking of Datatype Signatures in MPI   160
W.D. Gropp

5. Implementation Issues

A Scalable Process-Management Environment for Parallel   168
Programs
R. Butler, W. Gropp, E. Lusk

Single Sided Communications in Multi-protocol MPI   176
E. Mourão, S. Booth

MPI-2 Process Creation & Management Implementation for NT   184
Clusters
H. Pedroso, J.G. Silva

Composition of Message Passing Applications On-Demand   192
J.Y. Cotronis, Z. Tsiatsoulis, C. Kouniakis

6. Heterogeneous Distributed Systems

An Architecture of Stampi: MPI Library on a Cluster of Parallel Computers   200
T. Imamura, Y. Tsujita, H. Koide, H. Takemiya

Integrating MPI Components into Metacomputing Applications   208
T. Fink

7. Tools

PVMaple: A Distributed Approach to Cooperative Work of Maple Processes   216
D. Petcu

CIS - A Monitoring System for PC Clusters   225
J. Astaloš, L. Hluchý

Monito: A Communication Monitoring Tool for a PVM-Linux Environment   233
F. Solsona, F. Giné, J. Lérida, P. Hernández, E. Luque

Interoperability of OCM-Based On-Line Tools   242
M. Bubak, W. Funika, B. Baliś, R. Wismüller

Parallel Program Model for Distributed Systems   250
V.D. Tran, L. Hluchy, G.T. Nguyen

Translation of a High-Level Graphical Code to Message-Passing Primitives in the GRADE Programming Environment   258
G. Dózsa, D. Drótos, R. Lovas

The Transition from a PVM Program Simulator to a Heterogeneous System Simulator: The HeSSE Project   266
N. Mazzocca, M. Rak, U. Villano

Comparison of Different Approaches to Trace PVM Program Execution   274
M. Neyman

8.   Applications in Science and Engineering

Scalable CFD Computations Using Message-Passing and Distributed   282
Shared Memory Algorithms
J. Płażek, K. Banaś, J. Kitowski

Parallelization of Neural Networks Using PVM   289
M. Quoy, S. Moga, P. Gaussier, A. Revel

Parallel DSIR Text Indexing System: Using Multiple Master/Slave   297
Concept
P. Laohawee, A. Tangpong, A. Rungsawang

Improving Optimistic PDES in PVM Environments   304
R. Suppi, F. Cores, E. Luque

Use of Parallel Computers in Neurocomputing   313
Sz. Payrits, Z. Szatmáry, L. Zalányi, P. Érdi

A Distributed Computing Environment for Genetic Programming   322
Using MPI
F. Fernández, M. Tomassini, L. Vanneschi, L. Bucher

Experiments with Parallel Monte Carlo Simulation for Pricing   330
Options Using PVM
A. Rabaea, M. Rabaea

Time Independent 3D Quantum Reactive Scattering on MIMD   338
Parallel Computers
A. Bolloni, S. Crocchianti, A. Laganà

FT-MPI: Fault Tolerant MPI, Supporting Dynamic Applications in   346
a Dynamic World
G.E. Fagg, J.J. Dongarra

ACCT: Automatic Collective Communications Tuning   354
G.E. Fagg, S.S. Vadhiyar, J.J. Dongarra

Author Index   363

PVM and MPI: What Else Is Needed for Cluster Computing?

Al Geist

Oak Ridge National Laboratory,
PO Box 2008,
Oak Ridge, TN 37831-6367
gst@ornl.gov
http://www.csm.ornl.gov/~geist

Abstract. As we start the new millennium, let us first look back over the previous ten years of PVM use (and five years of MPI use) and explore how parallel computing has evolved from Crays and networks of workstations to Commodity-off-the-shelf (COTS) clusters. During this evolution, schedulers, monitors, and resource managers were added on top of PVM and MPI. This talk looks forward and predicts what software besides PVM and MPI will be needed to effectively exploit the cluster computing of the next ten years.

1 The First 10 Years

When the first PVM application was developed back in 1990 to study high-temperature superconductivity, the most common PVM platform was a network of workstations (NOW). This application was the first of several applications to win Gordon Bell prizes using PVM during the last decade. Heterogeneous NOWs were just starting to be exploited in the early 90s. Parallel computer companies came and went with lifetimes of a few years. Computer architectures varied widely from company to company making it difficult to develop scientific applications that did not have to be rewritten for each new architecture. During this period PVM provided a stable middleware layer on which to build parallel applications. PVM even today takes care of the details of a given architecture or NOW while presenting a simple set of functions to the application. In the mid-to-late 90s, MPI was created to provide a common message-passing interface for parallel computers and thus improving the portability of scientific applications.

Neither PVM nor MPI provided for all the needs of the users and system administrators. Soon researchers were developing schedulers, performance monitors, resource managers, debuggers, and performance enhancements for these environments. Once again it became hard for application developers to know what was the best combination of software packages to use for their science. Meanwhile the variability in computer architectures died away and the remaining vendors converged on clusters of commodity computers.

J. Dongarra et al. (Eds.): EuroPVM/MPI 2000, LNCS 1908, pp. 1–2, 2000.

2   Cluster Computing Today

Today the fastest growing market for parallel computers is the cluster of PCs. The key turning point was when PCs became as powerful as workstations. Popularized by the Beowulf project at NASA in the late 1990s, clusters of PCs are much less expensive than their cousins the IBM SP and Compaq Sierra. Once again PVM and MPI are there to provide a standard programming interface, but large PC clusters lack all the software tools needed for system administration, I/O, parallel file systems, etc. Huge gaps exist between the usability of a vendor's cluster and a homegrown cluster of PCs.

At ORNL we have large SP and Sierra systems as well as a 128 processor Pentium III Linux cluster. This talk will describe and demonstrate the latest cluster management software being developed at ORNL. The software is called M3C (Managing and monitoring multiple clusters) and C3 (Cluster Command and Control). In addition the talk will describe an new effort by Intel, IBM, SGI, ORNL, NCSA, and several others to create a Community Cluster Development Kit to be distributed as open source.

3   Next 10 Years

This talk will project forward into the first decade of the 21st century and discuss the future needs and potential directions for cluster computing applications. We will cover three topics: extensible distributed computing environments, fault tolerance with adaptive recovery, and desirable collaboration features in distributed virtual machines.

Collaboration is growing in importance in distributed environments as scientific problems get more complex and experts from around the world are involved in experiments. Projects like Cumulvs at ORNL, which allows remote scientists to dynamically attach, visualize, and steer long running simulations, point out the shortcomings of PVM and MPI. While the APIs in PVM and MPI may still be the standards in the coming years, the distributed environment that supplies these APIs will need to provide the ability for groups of resources (both people and hardware) to be joined together for some period of time and then split back apart afterwards.

The Harness project is a collaboration between the original PVM developers: ORNL, UTK, and Emory University. Building on our experience with PVM, the project goal is to create a fundamentally new heterogeneous virtual machine based on three research concepts: a parallel plug-in environment - extending the concept of a plug-in into the parallel computing world, distributed peer-to-peer control - eliminating single (and multiple) points of failure, and merging/splitting of multiple virtual machines to support advanced collaboration between research teams. An initial prototype of Harness was released this past Spring and plug-ins to provide PVM and a fault tolerant MPI are nearing completion. An update on the status of Harness will conclude the talk.

Links to information about all the projects mentioned in this extended abstract can be found on the author's home page: www.csm.ornl.gov/ geist.

Managing Your Workforce on a Computational Grid

Miron Livny

Computer Sciences Department
University of Wisconsin-Madison
1210 West Dayton St.
Madison, WI 53706
Miron@cs.wisc.edu

Abstract. The Master-Worker distributed computing paradigm has proven to be a very effective means for harnessing the power of computational grids. At any given time, the master of the application controls a collection of CPUs that has been allocated to the application by the resource manager of the grid. Effective management of this dynamic "workforce" of CPUs holds the key to ability of the application to meet its computational objectives. Like in similar real-life situations, the master has to decide on a target size and composition for the workforce, a recruiting strategy and a dismissal policy. It has to decide on who does what and how to deal with workers that do not complete their assigned task on time.

Introduction

Running a Master-Worker application on a Computational Grid resembles managing a real-life factory with human workers and real machines. The master of the application faces almost the same challenges a human factory manager does. All the resources of the grid are potential candidates to join the "workforce" of the application. The availability and properties of these resources are very dynamic and unpredictable. It is up to the master to recruit these resources and integrate them into its workforce. Once a resource joins the workforce, the master has to decide on the work to be allocated to the worker, how to monitor the worker's progress and what to do if the worker quits or does not complete the assigned task on time. Grid resources can very in speed, reliability and cost. Some of them may be available for long time periods while others may only join a workforce for short intervals.

We are currently engaged in a number of efforts that address different aspects of this management problem. These efforts include the development of a framework for dealing with the managing the workforce of grid resources, implementation of tools and a runtime support library for Master-Worker application and experimentation with large-scale applications. Recently, we completed a large Master-Worker computation that consumed almost 12 CPU years of grid resources in less than a week. The grid had more than 2300 CPUs and was actively used by other applications. At one point the workforce of the computation reached 1009 workers.

J. Dongarra et al. (Eds.): EuroPVM/MPI 2000, LNCS 1908, pp. 3-4, 2000.
© Springer-Verlag Berlin Heidelberg 2000

On the average the size of the workforce was 650. This run has demonstrated the strength and the weaknesses of our approach and tools. We are currently working on enhancing our framework and tools to address these weaknesses and to broaden the size and class of applications that can be served by these tools.

Isolating and Interfacing the Components of a Parallel Computing Environment*

Ewing Lusk

Argonne National Laboratory

Abstract. A message-passing library interface like MPI or PVM is only one interface between only two components the complete environment seen be the user of a parallel system. Here we discuss a larger set of components and draw attention to the usefulness of considering them separately. Such an approach causes us to focus on the interfaces among such components. Our primary motivation is the efficient use of large clusters to run MPI programs, and we describe current efforts by our group at Argonne to address some of the interface issues that arise in this context.

1 Introduction

MPI is an example of an *interface*, specifically, an interface between an application (or library) and the portable component of a communication library. MPI has been successful an an interface specification partly because it is *only* and interface; a specific implementation of MPI is a different object. The communication library is only one component (or several) of the overall parallel computing environment seen by a user or parallel program. The desire to make the entire environment more usable, flexible, and powerful motivates us to consider the components of the environment separately and look at the interfaces among these components. In this talk we will focus on the impact of some of these interfaces on the task of implementing MPI, particularly MPI-2. We will conclude with a preliminary proposal for an interface between a communication library and a process manager, and survey some of the tasks that remain to be done.

2 Components and Interfaces

Any list of the components of a parallel environment is bound to be incomplete, but for the sake of our discussion, we need to at least identify the following: a process manager that starts, monitors, and cleans up after processes; a parallel library that implements communication among these processes, and a job scheduler (perhaps nonexistent) that decides when and where to run parallel jobs.

---

* This work was supported by the Mathematical, Information, and Computational Sciences Division subprogram of the Office of Advanced Scientific Computing Research, U.S. Department of Energy, under Contract W-31-109-Eng-38.

J. Dongarra et al. (Eds.): EuroPVM/MPI 2000, LNCS 1908, pp. 5–6, 2000.

The user should perhaps also be considered a component, so that user interfaces (to the scheduler and process manager, for example) can be part of our discussion. These components have subcomponents, resulting in internal interfaces as well, such as MPICH's Abstract Device Interface. In some systems these components are combined, such as in the case of a scheduler/process manager or a parallel library/process manager. When these components are integrated rather than isolated, it becomes difficult to select parts of them for replacement or to interface them to other components.

In this talk we will use the MPICH implementation of MPI as a motivating example, showing how a precise interface to a process manager is necessary in order that a library like MPICH be able to use multiple process managers and that a given process manager support multiple parallel libraries. This is particularly true in the case of MPI-2 implementations, where the job scheduler and resource manager may need to be involved as well.

3   A Library/Process Manager Interface

To allow our new MPI implementation to use a process manager's facilities but be independent of any specific one, even our own, we have designed an interface we call BNR. Requirements for BNR are that it allow a variety of implementations by process managers with quite different architectures, that it be simple enough to encourage implementation by other process managers, and that it be powerful enough to support MPI-2 implementation by the library. We have partially implemented BNR in our MPD process manager, and used the interface in our newly designed MPICH implementation of MPI. The focus on the interface will allow MPICH to be independent of any specific process manager yet take advantage of process manager capabilities where they are available. We will describe the BNR interface and how it is used to support some of the functionality of MPI-2.

4   Future Work

Several other interfaces need to be studied in order to complete the development of a usable, flexible, and powerful parallel environment. One of the most necessary yet most difficult is the interface between the job scheduler and process manager. These are two components that are frequently combined, precisely because of this difficulty, yet scheduling and process management are quite different activities. All parts of the environment will benefit if interfaces are developed that allow components to evolve separately.

Symbolic Computing with Beowulf-Class PC Clusters

Dr. Thomas Sterling

Center for Advanced Computing Research
California Institute of Technology
and
High Performance Computing Group
NASA Jet Propulsion Laboratory

Abstract

Beowulf-class systems are an extremely inexpensive way of aggregating substantial quantities of a given resource to facilitate the execution of different kinds of potentially large workloads. Beowulf-class systems are clusters of mass-market COTS PC computers (e.g. Intel Pentium III) and network hardware (e.g. Fast Ethernet, Myrinet) employing available Unix-like open source systems software (e.g. Linux) to deliver superior price-performance and scalability for a wide range of applications. Initially, Beowulfs were assembled to support compute intensive applications at low cost by integrating a large number of microprocessors primarily for science and engineering problems. But over the last few years, this class of clusters has expanded in scale, application domain, and means of use to embrace a much broader range of user problem. Beowulfs have become equally important as a means of integrating large numbers of disk drives to realize large mass storage support systems for both scientific and commercial applications including data bases and transaction processing and are becoming a major workhorse for web servers and search engines. Yet, Beowulf-class systems are able to assemble together large ensembles of yet another type of resource: memory. This possibility may enable domains of computation so far largely unaddressed by the distributed cluster community.

One such problem domain is symbolic computing which allows the representation and manipulation of abstract relationships among abstract objects. Once the principal tool of artificial intelligence (AI), symbolic computing has received less work than other domains as AI had garnered less attention. In the decades of the 1970s and 1980s, symbolic computation was the focus of significant effort with the development of such languages as Prolog, Scheme, OPS-5, and Common Lisp, as well as special purpose computers such as the Symbolics 3600 series and the TI Explorer. In addition, parallel symbolic computation was explored with such multiprocessor based systems as Concert and Multilisp. However, with the failure of AI to deliver results commensurate with the hype that surrounded it and the advent of more conventional RISC based systems that out performed the slower special purpose microprogrammed controlled systems, the focus on symbolic processing diminished leaving only small pockets of research in natural language processing and robotics among a few such areas. One of the factors that greatly hampered success in this regime was the inadequacy of the memory systems. Symbolic computation is memory intensive,

J. Dongarra et al. (Eds.): EuroPVM/MPI 2000, LNCS 1908, pp. 7-8, 2000.

easily consuming an order of magnitude or more of memory compared to conventional applications. Beowulf-class systems offer an alternative path to achieving large memory systems at moderate cost. A Beowulf today can provide on the order of a thousand times the memory capacity available to symbolic computing problems of the late 1980s with total memory system prices (including PC nodes and networks) of significantly less than $10 per MByte.

The Beowulf Common Lisp (BCL) project is exploring the application of Beowulf class systems to scalable symbolic computation. The motivation is driven both by the opportunity that Beowulf-class systems provide through their large aggregate memory capacities and by the potential application of symbolic computing to knowledge extraction and manipulation in the realm of large scientific applications. BCL is experimenting with a merger of distributed memory hardware and a programming model based on a global name space. The semantics of Common Lisp incorporate a number of intrinsic constructs which are inherently parallel, many of which lend themselves to distributed computing. One class of such constructs is the set of functional or value oriented operators that employ copies of argument structures. Functional semantics is well known for ease of parallelization and work cast in this form can be readily distributed across cluster nodes. Common Lisp incorporates a second set of constructs referred to as mapping functions that are intrinsically parallel permitting data parallel computation across corresponding elements of complex data structures. In addition, many Lisp operators permit out of order evaluation of arguments yielding yet more natural parallelism. Some of these instructions have corresponding operators that impose ordered evaluation (e.g. LET, LET*) providing synchronization where necessary. The CLOS object oriented system is one of the most powerful in language design and provides a natural program representation for parallel distribution, as well as synchronization, and encapsulation. Finally, while not part of the formal Common Lisp language, the "futures" construct developed initially by Hewitt and later by Halstead provides an important semantic tool for distributed coordination of symbolic functions at different levels of abstraction.

There are many challenges to realizing an effective Beowulf Common Lisp. These include a distributed name space directory, movement of structures and processes across system nodes, dynamic memory management with automatic garbage collection, mapping between the Lisp semantics and the MPI to hide the explicit message passing mechanisms from the programmer, and a distributed form of CLOS for BCL. This talk will describe these challenges and the path being pursued along with preliminary results showing both the feasibility and early functionality. It is believed that the availability of a scalable distributed Common Lisp for Beowulf class systems will provide an impetus to the application of symbolic computing to scientific computing and automatic knowledge abstraction extraction.

High Speed Networks for Clusters, the BIP-Myrinet Experience

Bernard Tourancheau

Laboratoire RESAM, Université Claude Bernard de Lyon and INRIA Rhone-Alpes
bernard.tourancheau@inria.fr
http://resam.univ-lyon1.fr/~btouranc

In this talk, we present the evolution of the high speed networks for clusters in the context of on the shelves PC architecture.

We then present our experience in designing an MPI communication system based on the MPICH library and targeted for the Myrinet network using our own firmware called BIP.

The MPI-BIP software layer protocol implementation try to squeeze the most out of the high speed Myrinet network, without wasting time in system calls or memory copies, giving all the speed to the applications. We present the protocols we used for the overall design and its implementation and optimization. The performances obtained are then presented.

SMP architecture offers a very good price/performance ratio. We thus design a special device for SMP communications, called SMP-plug that can follow the network performances in both latency and bandwith. We present its internal design and performances for MPI.

These two open-source software design leads to parallel multicomputer-like throughput and latency on very cheap clusters of PC workstations.

J. Dongarra et al. (Eds.): EuroPVM/MPI 2000, LNCS 1908, pp. 9–9, 2000.
© Springer-Verlag Berlin Heidelberg 2000

A Benchmark for MPI Derived Datatypes

Ralf Reussner[1], Jesper Larsson Träff[2], and Gunnar Hunzelmann[1]

[1] LIIN, Universität Karlsruhe
Am Fasanengarten 5, D-76128 Karlsruhe, Germany.
[2] C&C Research Laboratories, NEC Europe Ltd.,
Rathausallee 10, D-53757 Sankt Augustin, Germany.
skampi@ira.uka.de

Abstract. We present an extension of the *SKaMPI* benchmark for MPI implementations to cover the derived datatype mechanism of MPI. All MPI constructors for derived datatypes are covered by the benchmark, and varied along different dimensions. This is controlled by a set of predefined patterns which can be instantiated by parameters given by the user in a configurations file. We classify the patterns into fixed types, dynamic types, nested types, and special types. We show results from the *SKaMPI* ping-pong measurement with the fixed and special types on three platforms: Cray T3E/900, IBM RS 6000SP, NEC SX-5. The machines show quite some difference in handling datatypes, with typically a significant penalty for nested types for the Cray (up to a factor of 16) and the IBM (up to a factor of 8), whereas the NEC treats these types very uniformly (overhead of between 2 and 4). Such results illustrate the need for a systematic datatype benchmark to help the MPI programmer select the most efficient data representation for a particular machine.

1 Introduction

Derived datatypes in MPI provide a flexible mechanism for working with arbitrary non-contiguous layouts of data in memory. Derived datatypes are fully integrated into MPI, and can be used everywhere a predefined datatype is allowed, in particular as arguments in communication calls. Derived datatypes are useful in themselves, but additionally play an important role in the parallel I/O model of MPI-2 [2, 8]. It is therefore important that use of derived datatypes does not impair performance. Ideally, it should not be significantly more expensive to work with non-contiguous memory described by derived datatypes than it would be to manage such data layouts by hand. On the contrary, derived datatypes provide a handle for an efficient MPI implementation to avoid intermediate packing and unpacking of communication buffers that might otherwise be necessary when working with non-contiguous data manually.

So far, there are no systematic benchmarks for evaluating the performance of derived datatypes with a given MPI implementation (on a given machine). In this paper we present an extension of the *SKaMPI* [7] benchmark for MPI implementations to cover also the derived datatype mechanism of MPI. Benchmarking has always played a particular role in high performance computing. With the

J. Dongarra et al. (Eds.): EuroPVM/MPI 2000, LNCS 1908, pp. 10–17, 2000.

advent of standards like MPI for portable parallel programming, benchmarking of different MPI implementations on different target platforms has become important for ensuring portability of applications also with respect to performance. The *SKaMPI* benchmark is intended as an accurate, detailed MPI benchmark which can be used to guide the design of efficient, portable applications. It can measure (nearly) all communication routines of the MPI standard, as well as all collective operations. Measurements can be selected from a large set of predefined communication patterns, either abstracting common MPI usage, or designed to measure key features of both hardware and implementation (bandwidth, scalability, etc.). Measurement details are controlled by the user who sets up a series of experiments in a configurations file. It should be noted that *SKaMPI* is not intended as a correctness or stress test of MPI.

Often benchmarks for parallel computers are application kernels (see e.g. [1, 6]). Such benchmarks capture the performance of a machine in a more realistic manner than peak performance figures, but application benchmarks can only indirectly guide the development of efficient, portable programs. A widely used MPI benchmark, which is in many respects similar to *SKaMPI*, is `mpptest`, which shipped with the `mpich` implementation of MPI [3, 4]. It measures (nearly) all MPI operations, but is less configurable than *SKaMPI*. A database of implementation/machine results gathered with `mpptest` is not maintained.

2   The *SKaMPI* Benchmark

The goal of *SKaMPI* is to collect performance data of different MPI implementations on different parallel platforms to guide: (1) the optimization of parallel programs in early stages of development, (2) the development of portable programs with good performance on different platforms, and (3) the optimization of a given MPI implementation on a given platform. With this data the developer can take different design alternatives into account already in the design phase to choose the optimum with respect to the considered target platforms. To make performance data available also to developers without access to a specific target platform the data gained with *SKaMPI* can be submitted to the *SKaMPI* performance database: `http://wwwipd.ira.uka.de/~skampi` in Karlsruhe.

Problems of benchmarking parallel computers and MPI in particular were recently discussed in [3, 5]. To provide a reliable, reproducible evaluation of the performance of a given MPI implementation on a given machine, *SKaMPI* makes use of mechanisms for:

automatic control of the standard error: single measurements are repeated until the standard error drops below a user defined threshold (or a maximum number of repetitions is reached). Outliers are discarded, and the mean of the results is taken.

automatic parameter refinement: the arguments where to measure (e.g., the message length) are computed in dependency of previous measurements. This makes it possible to quickly and automatically focus on interesting performance features, without using a too finely grained, uniform scale.

The purpose of these mechanisms is to spend the running time at the "interesting" measurements, e.g. switching points of algorithms, and measurements disturbed by the external environment. As mentioned, *SKaMPI* is controlled by a customizable configuration file, in which the user sets up his measurement suite. *SKaMPI* also includes a report generator, which presents the output in a humanly readable form. These reports can also contain comparisons between different measurement suites. Ideally, new measurements are reported to the *SKaMPI* database in Karlsruhe. The figures in Section 4 were all generated automatically from the database.

3   The Derived Datatype Benchmark

We were faced with two alternatives for how to incorporate derived datatypes into *SKaMPI*. One was to define a reasonable selection of "typical" instances, with the danger of missing out this or that aspect which is important for some particular MPI implementation or user. The other was to give the user of *SKaMPI* the freedom to define the derived datatypes to be measured, with the danger of putting so much burden of definition on the user that the facility will not be used. We opted for the first alternative, which fits well with the overall concept of *SKaMPI*.

The test datatypes are synthetic, but intended to capture typical usage of derived datatypes. All derived datatype constructors of MPI are covered in patterns and combinations that reflect common usage. The suite is completed with instances to probe for special optimizations that might be incorporated in a specific MPI implementation.

A measurement with derived datatypes is described in the configurations file by defining a *base type* over which the selected *send type* and *receive type* are constructed. All communication in the measurement is then done using the receive and send types thus constructed. Each derived datatype specifies the same amount of base type units, so receive and send type can be chosen independently of each other and will always match. The base type is the unit of communication, and can be either of the MPI predefined types. In addition the user can define an MPI structured type to be used as base type. This is done by supplying a list of triples of counts, offsets and predefined types, $(c_1, o_1, t_1), (c_2, o_2, t_2), \ldots, (c_k, o_k, t_k)$. A structure with k blocks is constructed with block i consisting of c_i units of type t_i starting at offset o_i. Each count must be > 0, but negative offsets are allowed. This base type makes it possible to test more complicated instances of nested datatypes.

We classify the *SKaMPI* predefined datatype patterns into *fixed derived types*, *dynamic derived types*, *nested derived types*, and *special derived types*. All of these patterns can be freely combined with the *SKaMPI* communication measurement patterns.

To measure the performance of "computing collectives" like `MPI_Reduce` on derived datatypes an operator must be defined for each derived datatype. This is a delicate issue, since the time spent in performing the operation is counted in the total time of the reduction. How time-consuming is the "typical" user defined operation? How well can the "typical" user defined operation exploit the given machine, e.g. does it have loops that can be vectorized? Letting the *SKaMPI* user fully control the operations to be performed is fair for the individual user/machine, but tiresome for the user, and makes comparison among different machines and implementations difficult. We compromise by taking the "copy first argument" function (also known as `MPI_Replace` in MPI-2), $f(a, b) = a$, as the operation for derived datatypes. The operation is implemented by means of `MPI_Pack` and `MPI_Unpack`. The first (input) argument is packed into an intermediate buffer, and unpacked to the output argument. This solution is general-purpose, fair to the MPI implementations, and does not require user intervention. There is no significant disadvantage to vector-machines; packing and unpacking can be efficiently vectorized as shown in [9].

We now describe the predefined derived datatype patterns, assuming the reader is familiar with the MPI standard terminology for derived datatypes [8]. The parameters `BLOCKS`, `BLOCKSIZE`, and `VECTORSTRIDE` control the data layout, and are set by the user in the configurations file. A length-parameter ℓ is varied by *SKaMPI*. The number of base type units communicated for each derived type pattern is $\ell \times$ `BLOCKS` $\times$ `BLOCKSIZE`.

3.1   Fixed Derived Datatypes

A fixed derived datatype describes a memory layout consisting of a fixed number of units of the base type, independently of the communication volume of a measurement. A fixed datatype is defined for each of the type constructors of MPI-1. Also the new array types introduced in MPI-2 standard can be measured, but we will not comment on the MPI-2 types here.

1. A fixed contiguous type with `BLOCKS*BLOCKSIZE` base type units.
2. A fixed vector or MPI hvector consisting of `BLOCKS` blocks, each of `BLOCKSIZE` base type units and with stride `VECTORSTRIDE`.
3. A fixed indexed or structured type consisting of `BLOCKS` blocks. Even numbered blocks consist of `BLOCKSIZE` base type units, odd numbered blocks of `BLOCKSIZE-1` units, with the last block being large enough for a total number of `BLOCKS` $\times$ `BLOCKSIZE` units. Blocks are spaced one base type unit apart to keep the resulting type non-contiguous.

3.2   Dynamic Derived Datatypes

Instead of sending batches of fixed types, we also measure the performance when sending only one instance of a type. The right amount of data to be sent is controlled by having the length-parameter ℓ be part of the datatype. Three dynamic vectors/structures, where ℓ appears in different positions, are defined:

1. vector/struct with `BLOCKS` blocks, each of $\ell \times$ `BLOCKSIZE` elements
2. vector/struct with ℓ blocks, each of `BLOCKS` $\times$ `BLOCKSIZE` elements
3. vector/struct with ℓ*`BLOCKS` blocks, each of `BLOCKSIZE` elements

For vectors the stride is the proper multiple of VECTORSTRIDE, allowing for non-contiguous as well as contiguous vectors. For structs the blocks are spaced one base type unit apart such that the resulting type does not specify a contiguous segment of memory.

3.3   Nested Derived Datatypes

We have defined both static and dynamic nested derived datatypes, in both cases with two levels of nesting. There are four static nested types: a vector/indexed type of BLOCKS blocks, each consisting of a vector/indexed type of BLOCKSIZE blocks, each of length one and stride two. Three dynamic nested vectors are defined, depending on where the length-parameter appears:

1. BLOCKS vectors, each a vector of BLOCKSIZE blocks of size ℓ
2. BLOCKS vectors, each a vector of ℓ blocks of size BLOCKSIZE
3. ℓ vectors, each a vector of BLOCKS blocks of size BLOCKSIZE

The user can add one extra nesting by setting up a structured base type in the configurations file.

3.4   Special Derived Datatypes

To be able to test for special optimizations in an MPI implementation, like detection of larger consecutive segments, we have defined a special (fixed) MPI struct, which by means of an overlapping vector, an indexed and a struct span a consecutive memory segment. An MPI implementation may detect this and treat the consecutive segment as such.

3.5   Process Local Handling of Datatypes

SKaMPI provides so called simple patterns for measuring MPI operations with local completion semantics. We have extended the benchmark with simple patterns for measuring the costs of defining and committing the derived datatypes discussed above.

4   Example Measurements

We illustrate the use of the *SKaMPI* datatype benchmark with three different platforms: Cray T3E/900, IBM RS 6000 SP, and NEC SX-5. We will not go into the characteristics of these machines here, but comment only on what can be observed from the benchmarks. All three machines run the vendor MPI. **Due to space limitations** we only show the results obtained with the *SKaMPI* send-receive ping-pong pattern, varying over message lengths[1]. The base type is

---

[1] The interested reader should consult either the *SKaMPI* database or the authors for more information

MPI_INT, and the parameters BLOCKS, BLOCKSIZE and VECTORSTRIDE are set
to 10, 7, and 11, respectively. The times reported in the figures are the total
time of an MPI send and an MPI receive operation.

Figures 1, 2, and 3 show the performance of the ping-pong measurement with
all fixed derived types and the special, contiguous type, compared to the performance with contiguous MPI_INT data. None of the MPI implementations detect
that the special type span a contiguous memory segment, but all implementations treat the contiguous derived data type as a contiguous segment (as should
be), obtaining performance similar to non-structured MPI_INT. The NEC SX-5
MPI implementation treat all types roughly equally, with a factor 2 to 4 penalty
over contiguous data. For the Cray T3E the MPI Hvector interestingly seems
to behave better than vector. There is a considerable penalty for the complex
(nested), special type, up to a factor 16. Also the IBM SP has a considerable
overhead for the special type (about a factor 8).

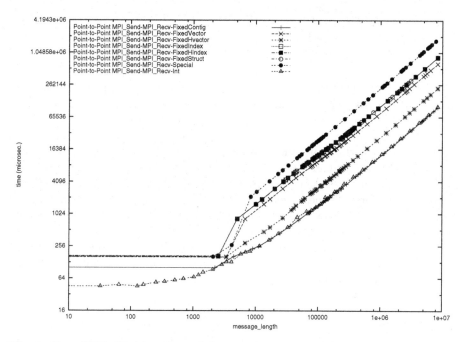

Fig. 1. Cray T3E: Fixed and special types, ping-pong pattern. Message lengths
are in bytes, and the times are the time for a send and a receive operation.

We also investigated the performance of the dynamic structured types with
the reduce pattern (measurement of MPI_Reduce). For all three machines, there
is a noticeable, non-constant overhead for the structured types where the number of blocks is proportional to the length-parameter ℓ. The structure with a
fixed number of blocks (and blocksize proportional to ℓ) is handled well by all

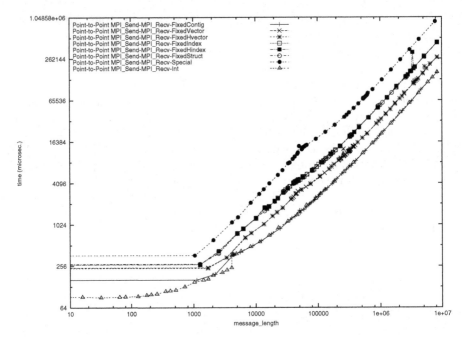

Fig. 2. IBM RS 6000SP: Fixed and special types, ping-pong pattern. Message lengths are in bytes, and the times are the time for a send and a receive operation.

machines, with performance close to that of contiguous `MPI_INT` data. Finally we studied the performance of the nested, dynamic vectors with the ping-pong communication pattern. Here the Cray T3E shows a considerable overhead of a factor up to 8 for the types where the number of vectors at the outermost level are proportional to ℓ, but handles the other extreme very well with performance close to that of contiguous data. The IBM SP also handles the vector where the innermost blocksize is proportional to ℓ well, with an overhead of a factor about 2 for the other cases. The NEC SX-5 handles all cases similarly, with an overhead of a factor about 2.

References

[1] D. Bailey, E. Barszcz, J. Barton, D. Browning, and R. Carter. The NAS parallel benchmarks. Technical Report RNR-94-007, RNR, 1994.

[2] W. Gropp, S. Huss-Lederman, A. Lumsdaine, E. Lusk, B. Nitzberg, W. Saphir, and M. Snir. *MPI – The Complete Reference*, volume 2, The MPI Extensions. MIT Press, 1998.

[3] W. Gropp and E. Lusk. Reproducible measurements of MPI performance characteristics. In *Recent Advances in Parallel Virtual Machine and Message Passing Interface. 6th European PVM/MPI Users' Group Meeting*, volume 1697 of *Lecture Notes in Computer Science*, pages 11–18, 1999.

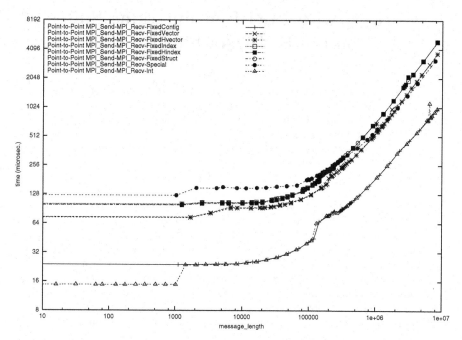

Fig. 3. NEC SX-5: Fixed and special types, ping-pong pattern. Message lengths are in bytes, and the times are the time for a send and a receive operation.

[4] W. Gropp, E. Lusk, N. Doss, and A. Skjellum. A high-performance, portable imlementation of the MPI message passing interface standard. *Parallel Computing*, 22(6):789–828, 1996.

[5] Rolf Hempel. Basic message passing benchmarks, methodology and pitfalls, September 1999. Presented at the SPEC Workshop, slides available at `http://www.hlrs.de/mpi/b_eff/hempel_wuppertal.ppt`

[6] Parkbench Committee. Public International Benchmarks for Parallel Computers. *Scientific Programming*, 3(2):101–146, 1994. Report 1.

[7] R. Reussner, P. Sanders, L. Prechelt, and M. Müller. SKaMPI: A detailed, accurate MPI benchmark. In *Recent Advances in Parallel Virtual Machine and Message Passing Interface. 5th European PVM/MPI Users' Group Meeting*, volume 1497 of *Lecture Notes in Computer Science*, pages 52–59, 1998.

[8] M. Snir, S. Otto, S. Huss-Lederman, D. Walker, and J. Dongarra. *MPI –The Complete Reference*, volume 1, The MPI Core. MIT Press, second edition, 1998.

[9] J. L. Träff, R. Hempel, H. Ritzdorf, and F. Zimmermann. Flattening on the fly: efficient handling of MPI derived datatypes. In *Recent Advances in Parallel Virtual Machine and Message Passing Interface. 6th European PVM/MPI Users' Group Meeting*, volume 1697 of *Lecture Notes in Computer Science*, pages 109–116, 1999.

Working with MPI Benchmarking Suites on ccNUMA Architectures

Hermann Mierendorff, Kläre Cassirer, and Helmut Schwamborn

Institute for Algorithms and Scientific Computing (SCAI)
GMD – German National Research Center for Information Technology
Schloss Birlinghoven, D-53754 Sankt Augustin, Germany

Abstract. Four different benchmarking suites for testing the performance of MPI routines have been considered on an SGI Origin2000. Special properties of these benchmarking suites which are mostly hidden to the user turned out as being of considerable influence on the benchmarking results for ccNUMA systems such as number and location of buffers, warm-up of the cache before running the benchmark, or procedure of measuring the time. In addition, we consider interpretation of results and their approximation by piecewise linear curves.

Key Words: message passing, performance analysis, benchmarking, MPI, ccNUMA architectures.

1 Introduction

There are several possibilities for measuring performance characteristic of MPI message passing routines by the use of existing benchmarking suites. Four of them have been used to achieve reliable performance parameters of an SGI Origin2000: `mpptest` [1], SKaMPI [6], MPBench [4], and PMB [5]. At a glance, all codes were able to deliver a good overview and similar results. A detailed evaluation, however, showed differences among measurements which could not be accepted without analyzing the reasons.

In the present paper, we investigate unexpected properties of the benchmarking suites. We study effects observed on running a single round trip with `MPI_Send/MPI_Recv`. *All performance figures are, therefore, related to a complete round trip.* We mainly consider effects caused by the cache structure and parameters. We leave open the question in which case the results may be of interest for performance evaluation of user programs or what else should be benchmarked for this purpose. For recent numerical results of a great variety of MPI routines, we refer to other publications like [3].

The considered computer architecture is a 4 processor Origin2000 which is a ccNUMA system with R10000 processors and IRIX 6.5 for operating system. For MPI the native SGI implementation release 3.1.1.0 with default parameters was used (i.e. in particular: 16 MPI buffers of 16KB each per process and in addition 16 buffers per host). The considered machine runs at 195 MHz. Each processor has an L1 cache for data only and an L2 cache for data and instructions. The

J. Dongarra et al. (Eds.): EuroPVM/MPI 2000, LNCS 1908, pp. 18–26, 2000.
© Springer-Verlag Berlin Heidelberg 2000

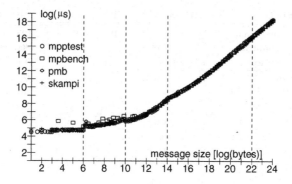

Fig. 1. Overview on Performance values for all message sizes.

L1 cache is a 2-way set associative LRU write back cache of 32 KB with a cache line of 32 bytes. Because of 16KB pages one layer corresponds to a page. The L2 cache is a 2-way set associative LRU write back cache of 4 MB with a cache line of 128 bytes. Memory access needs about 2-3 cycles for the L1 cache, 10 cycles for the L2 cache, and 75-300 cycles for the main memory. All processors are interconnected via a network such that each processor is able to access each part of the global memory. For more details we refer to [2].

Message transmission is always a memory transfer in this system. For benchmarking we only considered pairs of processors residing on different boards (mode ppm1). The SGI implementation of MPI uses always buffering of messages. If we use letters u, m, s, r, b, and b' for *user, MPI, send, receive, buffer in the master process*, or *buffer in the slave process* resp. then a *round trip (ping-pong)* benchmark except for very small messages follows the scheme

$$b_{us} \to b_{ms}, \{b_{ms} \to b'_{mr} \to b'_{ur}, b'_{us} \to b'_{ms}\}, b'_{ms} \to b_{mr} \to b_{ur} \tag{1}$$

We mainly discuss activities of the master process. The activities enclosed by braces are executed by the slave process. A benchmarking routine for message passing routines normally works like the following program:

```
while not_all_sizes_considered do
    select_next_message_size;
    while further_measurement_is_requested do
        initialize_timer;
        for number_of_repetitions do
            execute_test_program;
        enddo;
        save_timing_values;
    enddo;
enddo;
```

Table 1 gives a rough impression which possibilities are provided by the considered benchmarks.

	mpptest	MPBench	PMB	SKaMPI
message sizes	explicit list or automatic selection	mixed geometric/arithmetic sequence	predefined	arithmetic sequence and automatic selection
measurements per size (m)	until standard deviation below error limit	user defined	1	between user limits until std deviation below error limit
repetitions	user defined	user defined	predefined	1
results, μs/transaction or transactions/s	1st to last proc, $min_m(time)$, $max_m(time)$, $av_m(time)$	1st to last proc, transactions, values for all measurements	1st to 2nd proc, $min_{procs}(time)$, $max_{procs}(time)$, $av_{procs}(time)$	max from 1st to any proc in use, $av_m(time)$
buffers	2	2	2	1
buffer address in page	different, 5920 for small msgs.	not considered	not considered	different, $\approx$3400 for small messages

Table 1. Controlling the run of benchmarking Send/Receive and form of results.

2   Overview and Break Points of Runtime Curves

Without considering break points caused by the transfer protocol or by exceeding machine parameters, a precise result cannot be expected for all message sizes from 0 to 16 MB. Figure 1 shows the result of all considered benchmarking tools for round trip with `MPI_Send/MPI_Recv`. About 125 message sizes have been used with increasing distance. The MPBench offers the most convenient way to define the arguments for this first step. The user can start with a sequence 2^i (in our case $i = 0, \ldots, 24$) and can request a certain number of intermediate arguments for all intervals of this sequence. The other tools offer less convenient ways to produce an appropriate list. The automatic selection of arguments turned out to be not useful for this wide range of sizes.

Figure 1 shows that all benchmarking tools deliver similar results. Here we see that MPBench is highly sensitive to unavoidable disturbations in particular for small messages. We see break points at 2^6, 2^{10}, 2^{14}, and 2^{22} bytes. 2^{10}, 2^{14} mark breaks in the transmission protocol and we use these break points to separate intervals of message sizes for discussion in greater detail.

3   Small Messages

Messages below 64 bytes and messages between 64 and 1024 bytes can be studied in common. Messages up to 64 bytes are sent immediately. Up to 1024 bytes the remainder is sent afterwards following a homogeneous protocol. The left part of Figure 2 shows measurements with the four benchmark suites. Values of `mpptest` (minimum values as recommended in [1]) show the clearest timing figures. As PMB and SKaMPI deliver average values and the measurements are not completely free of disturbations, these benchmarks show a little higher values. It was

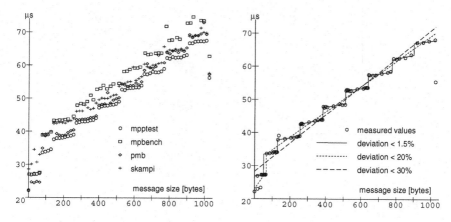

Fig. 2. Performance values for round trip of small message sizes.

a general observation that MPBench is rather sensitive against disturbing activities on the system. Moreover, there is no cache warming run with MPBench and mpptest as for the other tools. Therefore, it is necessary to use a high repetition number (≥ 50) to get reliable values using these benchmarking suites. Though we selected minimum values of measurements for each message size also for MPBench, this tool showed the highest values. There is no explanation of this effect. We only observed that the timer is different.

For the left part of Figure 2, we considered a list of dense arguments as far as possible for providing already a complete curve by the dots alone. In the right part, we considered arguments selected by mpptest automatically. The tool had some problems to distribute its activities evenly over the whole range and the break points are not always clearly defined. Therefore, it is useful to apply an intelligent approximation algorithm for producing a piecewise linear curve. Our algorithm allows to specify a maximum deviation e of values from the curve and to suppress a small number f of subsequent measurements if they are considered erroneous. It executes the following steps:

1. Group values starting at the end of the set into subsets representing linear curves (deviation $\leq e$). Start with 3 points on a straight line and extend the line to smaller arguments as long as no more than f subsequent arguments have to be left out. Repeat this recursively until all points are considered.
2. If there is a non-monotonic part of the curve consisting of a sequence of linear pieces each of which contains two arguments only, try to form a monotonic curve in the following way: suppress the first and the last argument and group the points again in pairs. Remove all single linear pieces showing the wrong direction from a global point of view.
3. Finally try to integrate all single arguments laying between two subsequent linear pieces into one of the neighboring pieces.
4. Define break points in the middle of two subsequent linear pieces.

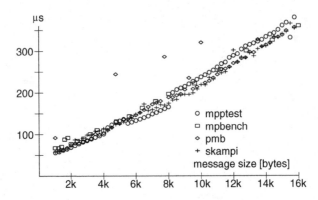

Fig. 3. Performance values for round trip of medium message sizes.

The results of this algorithm can be seen in the right part of Figure 2 for $f = 2$ and different values of the deviation. The algorithm is considered a first step working mostly locally on the set of points. Global operations could improve the result considerably but this has not yet been done. Such an approximation could be used to decide automatically which measurements should be removed at all and where break points of the timing curve can be assumed.

4   Messages of Medium Size and the L1 Cache

Measured values of medium sized messages are summarized in Figure 3. Except for a few mismeasurements the values differ systematically to a certain extent. In particular the values of `mpptest` jump up and down. It turned out that number and location of user buffers explain this behavior. `mpptest` uses 2 subsequent buffers the location of which changes in a complicated way with the message size. Therefore, we developed a test routine which uses a send buffer starting at a well defined offset relative to the beginning of a page and a receive buffer immediately behind the send buffer. Figure 4 shows the results for various offsets. For demonstrating the effects more clearly, we used different scales for each curve by adding offset/40 to the time values.

Considering Figure 4 we can observe two different effects: First there is always a break at 8KB, i.e. the curve is a little steeper above 8KB, and second there are jumps after which the curve continues at higher level for a while.

The break at a size of 8MB is a clear L1 cache effect. The transmission speed depends on the number of cache misses. In the case of *critical overlays* of buffers in a cache (more than 2 different cache lines per set), there are cache misses for each access in this particular region because no data can survive cycle (1) in the cache. In L1 cache, the 2 user buffers (b_{us} and b_{ur}, see (1)) already occupy one line in each set and both lines in an increasing number of sets beyond a size of 8MB. The same is true for the two MPI buffers. Therefore, there is an increasing range of critical overlay.

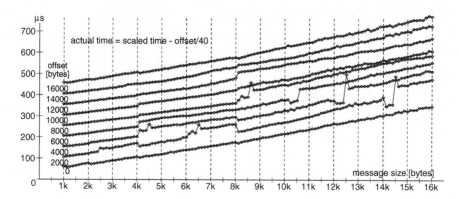

Fig. 4. Shape of time figures for round trip depending on the offset of user buffers.

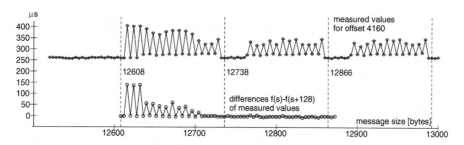

Fig. 5. Shape of jumps in time figures for round trip using offset 4160.

If the location of the second MPI buffer changes after the size of the first buffer has exceeded a certain threshold, the new location might cause a critical overlay in L1 cache for a block of data which was not present before (see Figure 6). Thresholds of this kind have been discovered at 2KB, 4KB and 8KB. We observed indirectly locations of 2KB+ε, 4KB+ε, 8KB+ε, and 0KB+ε relative to the start of a page for b_{mr} and b'_{ms}. The value of ε was around 400 bytes. The size of the critical overlay depends on the location of the user buffers.

If there are 2 user buffers and b_{ur} is located directly behind b_{us} then the starting address of b_{ur} moves ahead with the size of the b_{us}. But the MPI buffer b_{mr} is a little ahead of the b'_{ms}. Therefore, the transfer $b'_{ms} \to b_{mr}$ leaves the b_{mr} unfortunately in the status *least recently used* in the L1 cache for the majority of sets. If the starting address of b_{ur} is also ahead of b_{mr} the store operations of $b_{mr} \to b_{ur}$ destroy the b_{mr} before it can be read. This effect leads to the jumps near message sizes 14776, 12776, 10776, and 8776 KB within the curves for 2000, 4000, 6000, or 8000 bytes offset for b_{us}. If b_{mr} jumps away above a certain message size this effect will disappear again.

In order to better understand the special form of this second kind of jumps, we consider a finer resolution in Figure 5. While the upper curve $t = f(s)$ in Figure 5 shows the time t for certain offsets of b_{us} and message sizes s increasing

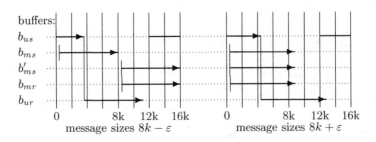

Fig. 6. Overlay in L1 cache in the case of two user buffers and 12k offset

with 4 bytes, the lower curves shows $t' = f(s) - f(s + 128)$. We see that the disturbation is periodic with 128 bytes in size and the first period is overlaid by a special effect. This effect is caused if the normal write back functionality of L1 and L2 caches for the b_{ur} takes place together with reading the b_{mr} from L2 cache after L1 cache misses in the same set of cache lines. The question has to be left open here why the considered effect takes place only if the b_{ur} starts at a double word address (i.e. the address is 0 (mod 8)) or for the first 3 L1 cache lines which lie over an L2 cache line.

If we use j for the message size where a jump of second kind takes place and a for the offset of b_{us} then we observe $a + j = 16776$ for message sizes above 8KB and offsets below 8KB which is 392 (mod 16384). Therefore, we can assume a starting address 384 (mod 16384) of b_{mr}. Similar series of jumps can be found for message sizes above and offsets below 4KB or 2KB.

Figure 6 shows the overlay of buffers in the L1 cache. This is a hypothetical situation which shows the principles for message sizes around 8k bytes. Just at this point, we observed a jump in the timing curve of mpptest in any case but for SKaMPI results in some cases only. Since the exact location of MPI buffers is not completely known, some questions have to be left open.

5   Large Messages and the L2 Cache

According to Figure 1 the time for round trip seems to be a simple curve in the case of messages above 16KB. The bandwidth, however, shows a very complex behavior. Here we use 2*message_size/time_for_round_trip for bandwidth. At the beginning, the bandwidth is increasing with the message size as usual (see Figure 7). Before saturation could be reached, the TLB is exhausted (the TLB contains entries for translation of virtual addresses for 64 pages). In the case of two user buffers, a size of 1/4MB requires 2×16 pages in addition to the 2×16 pages for MPI buffers. If this limit is exceeded, the bandwidth decreases with message size as more and more pages cannot survive the round trip in TLB. Beyond 1/4MB there is an additional break in the transmission protocol above which value messages are moved between user buffers directly. Close to 2MB the L2 cache is no longer able to save two user buffers and the bandwidth

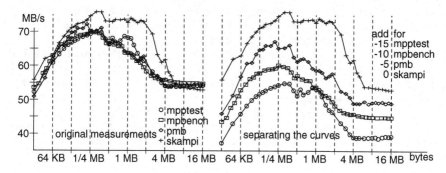

Fig. 7. Performance values for round trip of large message sizes.

decreases until the final level is reached at 4MB which is the size of L2 cache. The SKaMPI results look considerably better between 1/4 and 4MB because SKaMPI uses one user buffer only.

6   Concluding Remarks

Time cost for a round trip with MPI routines depend on the number of user buffers and on their location relative to page addresses. This is particularly important for messages of medium size. Because of the considerable influence of the cache on the speed of message transfer, the user has to decide whether standard benchmarking suites are useful for his purpose or if he should concentrate on test routines which suppress this influence.

The selection of message size where the performance has to be measured is still a problem. Good approximation of resulting curves is required in order to identify points of greatest uncertainty in a time function from a global point of view. We presented a heuristic algorithm for this purpose but the result is not yet satisfactory.

Selection of reliable values out of a collection of measurements for the same size is an open problem. The selection procedure has to decide if differing values represent right and wrong measurements or if they represent different correct values obtained for various possible cases of execution. Average or minimum values as used so far are not satisfying.

References

1. W. Gropp, E. Lusk. *Reproducible Measurements of MPI Performance Characteristics*, in: Dongarra, Luque, Margalef (eds.), Recent Advances in Parallel Virtual Machine and Message Passing Interface, LNCS vol. 1697, Springer, Berlin, 1999, pp. 11-18.
2. J. Laudon, D. Lenoski. *The SGI Origin: A ccNUMA Highly Scalable Server*, Proc. of The 24th Annual Internat. Symp. on Computer Architecture, ACM, Denver, 1997, pp. 241-251.

3. G. Luecke and J. Coyle. Comparing The Performance of MPI on The Cray T3E-900, The Cray Origin 2000 and The IBM P2SC, *Performance Evaluation and Modeling of Computer Systems*, June, 1998.
4. P. J. Mucci, K. London, J. Thurman. *The MPBench Report*, Internal Report, Uni of Tennessee, Knoxville, Nov 1998.
5. PALLAS GmBH. *PMB – Pallas MPI Benchmarks*, PALLAS GmbH, Brühl, 2000, `www.pallas.de/pages/pmb.htm`.
6. R. Reussner, P. Sanders, L. Prechelt, M. Müller. *SKaMPI: A detailed, accurate MPI benchmark*, in Alexandrov and Dongarra (eds.), Recent Advances in Parallel Virtual Machine and Message Passing Interface, LNCS 1497, Springer, 1998.

Performance Measurements on Dynamite/DPVM

K.A. Iskra, Z.W. Hendrikse, G.D. van Albada, B.J. Overeinder, and
P.M.A. Sloot

Informatics Institute, Universiteit van Amsterdam,
Kruislaan 403, 1098 SJ Amsterdam, The Netherlands
kamil,zegerh,dick,bjo,sloot@science.uva.nl

Abstract. The total computing capacity of workstations can be harnessed more efficiently by using a dynamic task allocation system. The Esprit project Dynamite provides such an automated load balancing system, through the migration of tasks of a parallel program using PVM. The Dynamite package is completely transparent, *i.e.* neither system (kernel) nor application program modifications are needed. Dynamite supports migration of tasks using dynamically linked libraries, open files and both direct and indirect PVM communication. In this paper we briefly introduce the Dynamite system and subsequently report on a collection of performance measurements.

1 Introduction

With the continuing increases in commodity processor and network performance, distributed computing on standard PCs and workstations has become attractive and feasible. Consequently, the availability of efficient and reliable cluster-management software supporting task migration becomes increasingly important.

Various *PVM* [5] variants supporting task migration have been reported, such as *tmPVM* [12], *DAMPVM* [3], *MPVM* (also known as MIST) [2], *ChaRM* [4] and CoCheck [11]. For *MPI* [14], task migration has been studied in Hector [8].

Building on earlier *DPVM* work by L. Dikken et al. [7], we have developed Dynamite[1]. Dynamite [1] attempts to maintain optimal task allocation for parallel jobs in dynamically changing environments by migrating individual tasks between nodes. Task migration also makes it possible to free individual nodes, if necessary, without breaking the computations.

Dynamite supports applications written for *PVM* 3.3.x, running under Solaris/UltraSPARC 2.5.1, 2.6, 7 and 8. Moreover, it supports Linux/i386 2.0 and 2.2 (libc5 and glibc 2.0 binaries; glibc 2.1 is not supported at this point).

---

[1] Dynamite is a collaborative project between ESI, the Paderborn Center for Parallel Computing, Genias Benelux and the Universiteit van Amsterdam, partly funded by the European Union as Esprit project 23499. Of the many people that have contributed, we can mention only a few: J. Gehring, A. Streit, J. Clinckemaillie, A.H.L. Emmen.

J. Dongarra et al. (Eds.): EuroPVM/MPI 2000, LNCS 1908, pp. 27–38, 2000.

The principal advantages of Dynamite are its API-level transparency, its powerful, dynamic loader based checkpoint/migration mechanism and its support for the migration of both direct and indirect *PVM* connections. We have found Dynamite to be very stable. Its modular design greatly facilitates the port to *MPI* [14], which is currently underway.

2   Dynamite Overview

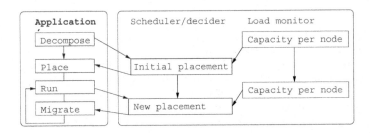

Fig. 1. Dynamite run-time system. An application has to be decomposed into several subtasks already. An initial placement is determined by the scheduler. When the application is run, the monitor checks the capacity per node. If it is decided that the load is unbalanced (above a certain threshold), one or more task migrations may be performed to obtain a more optimal load distribution.

The Dynamite architecture (see Figure 1) is built up from three separate parts:

1. The load-monitoring subsystem. The load-monitor should leave the computation (almost) undisturbed.
2. The scheduler, which tries to make an optimal allocation.
3. The task migration software, which allows a process to checkpoint itself and to be restarted on a different host. Basically, the checkpoint software makes the state of a process persistent at a certain stage.

Parallel *PVM* applications consist of a number of processes (*tasks*) running on interconnected nodes constituting a *PVM virtual machine*. A *PVM daemon* runs on every node and communicates with other daemons using the UDP/IP protocol. *PVM* tasks communicate with each other and with *PVM* daemons using a message-passing protocol. *PVM* message passing is reliable: no messages can be lost, corrupted or duplicated and must arrive in the order sent.

In Dynamite, a *monitor* process is started on every node of the *PVM* virtual machine. This monitor communicates with the local *PVM* daemon and collects information on the resource usage and availability, both for the node as a whole and individually for every *PVM* task. The information is forwarded to a central *scheduler*, which makes migration decisions based on the data gathered. *PVM* daemons assist in executing these decisions.

For migration, first, the running process must be checkpointed, i.e. its state must be consistently captured on the source node. Next, the process is *restored* on the destination node; its execution resumes from the point at which the source process was checkpointed. Typically, the original process on the source node is terminated.

Processes that are part of the parallel *PVM* application present additional difficulties. Every *PVM* task has a socket connection with the local *PVM* daemon. This connection is used for the *indirect routing*. *PVM* tasks can also establish point-to-point *direct* TCP/IP communication channels with each other, to improve the performance. Extra care must be taken when migrating *PVM* tasks to ensure that they do not permanently lose the connection with the rest of the parallel application, and that the *PVM* message protocol is not violated.

In Dynamite robust mechanisms for address translation, connection flushing and connection (re-) establishment have been incorporated that have been demonstrated to survive thousands of consecutive migrations.

For a detailed description of the implementation, the reader is referred to [6].

3   Performance Measurements

In order to evaluate Dynamite's performance, a number of tests have been conducted. Some of these are concerned with the performance of the components of the system, such as the modified *PVM* library. Others attempt to quantify the performance of the Dynamite system as a whole, in a controlled dynamic environment.

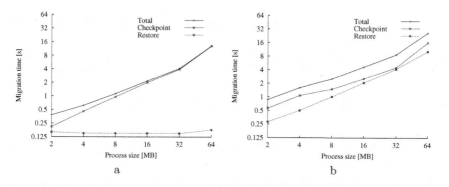

Fig. 2. Migration performance of *DPVM* for (a) Linux and (b) Solaris.

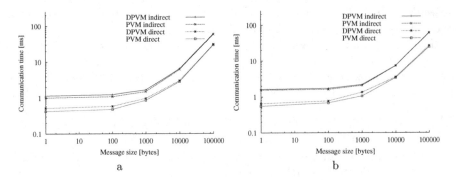

Fig. 3. Communication performance in *DPVM* and *PVM* for (a) Linux and (b) Solaris.

3.1   Performance of System Components

In a system like Dynamite, there are two easily measurable performance factors:

- the time it takes to migrate a task of a given size,
- the difference in communication performance compared to standard *PVM*.

Experiments have been performed to measure these two factors, both under Linux and Solaris. In case of Linux, reserved nodes of a PC-cluster have been used, equipped with PentiumPro 200 MHz CPU and 128 MB RAM, running kernel version 2.2.12. In case of Solaris, idle UltraSPARC 5/10 workstations have been used, equipped with 128 MB RAM and running kernel version 5.6. In both cases, 100 Mbps Ethernet was used. In both cases the NFS servers used for checkpoint files were shared with other users, which could affect the performance to some extent.

Figure 2 presents the performance of migration in *DPVM* for various process sizes. A simple ping-pong type program communicating once a few seconds via direct connection was migrated, process size was set with a single large `malloc` call. Execution time of each of the four migration stages (see [6]) was measured. In general, it was found that the major part of the migration time is spent on checkpointing and restoring, the remaining stages amount to approximately 0.01 – 0.03s, and hence are not shown. The speed of checkpointing and restoring is limited by the speed of the shared file system. On our systems this limit lies at 4–5 MB/sec for NFS running over the 100Mbps network. It can be observed, however, that the restoring phase under Linux takes an approximately constant amount of time, while it grows with process size under Solaris, resulting in twice larger migration times for large processes. This is a side effect of differences in the implementation of `malloc` between the two systems. For large allocations, Linux creates new memory segment (separate from the heap) using `mmap`, whereas Solaris always allocates from the heap with `sbrk`. When restoring, the heap and stack are restored with `read`, which forces an immediate data transfer. However, for the other segments our implementation takes advantage of `mmap`, which uses more advanced *page on demand* technique. Since the allocated memory region is not needed to reconnect the task to the *PVM* daemon, the time it takes to restart the task is constant under Linux. Clearly, delays may be incurred later, when the mmapped memory is accessed and loaded.

In Figure 3, comparison of communication performance between *DPVM* and *PVM* is presented. Both indirect and direct communication performance has been measured. A ping-pong type program was used, exchanging messages between 1 byte and 100KB in size. With *DPVM*, a slowdown is visible in all cases. It stems from two factors:

- signal (un)blocking on entry and exit from *PVM* functions (function call overhead),
- an extra header in message fragments (communication overhead).

The first factor adds a fixed amount of time for every *PVM* communication function call, whereas the second one increases the communication time by a constant percentage. For small messages the first factor dominates, since there is little communication. An overhead from 25% for direct communication under Linux to 4% for indirect communication under Solaris can be observed. While particularly the first difference in speed is significant, it must be pointed out that it represents a worst case scenario. The overhead percentage is larger for direct communication, since the communication is faster while the overhead from signal blocking/unblocking stays the same.

As the messages get larger, the overhead of signal handling becomes less significant, and the slowdown goes down to 2–4% for 100KB messages.

Tests have been made to compare the communication speed in *DPVM* before and after the migration, but no noticeable difference was observed (±1%).

3.2   Stability of the System

Care has been taken to prove the robustness of the environment. Thousands of migrations have been performed both under Solaris and Linux, for processes ranging in size from light-weight, 2 MB processes to heavy, 50 MB and larger. Delays between individual migrations ranged between a fraction of a second and several minutes, in order to test for race conditions. Similarly, different communication patterns have been tested, including tasks using very small and very large messages, using direct and indirect communication, communicating point-to-point and using multicasts. These proved to be very revealing tests.

In one test performed under Solaris, Dynamite was able to make over 2500 successful migrations of large processes (over 20 MB of memory image size) of a commercial *PVM* application using direct connections.

3.3   Performance of the Integrated System

Benchmarks In order to assess the usefulness of the integrated system, reserved nodes of a cluster have been used to run a series of parallel benchmarks under several different conditions. The benchmarks in question originate from the NAS Parallel Benchmarks suite [13]. The individual benchmarks have been adjusted to use four computation tasks each, running for aproximately 30 minutes in an optimal situation. Where necessary, code has been added to provide intermediate information on the execution progress of each task.

Eight nodes of a Linux cluster were reserved, each equipped with PentiumPro 200 CPU and 64 MB RAM, running Linux kernel version 2.0.36. 100 Mbps FastEthernet was used as the communication medium. The number of nodes exceeds the number of tasks, so this is a *sparse* decomposition, and consequently during the execution of the benchmarks some nodes are idle. The Dynamite scheduler works best in such a situation, since it can migrate tasks away from overloaded nodes to idle nodes.

	No	Load	
	load	Dynamite	No Dynamite
cg (smallest eigenvalue approximator)	1795	2226 (+24%)	3352 (+87%)
ep (embarrassingly parallel)	1620	1773 (+9%)	1919 (+18%)
ft (discrete Fourier transform)	1859	2237 (+20%)	2693 (+45%)
is (integer sort)	1511	1758 (+16%)	1688 (+12%)
mg (discrete Poisson problem)	1756	1863 (+6%)	2466 (+40%)

Table 1. Execution times of NAS parallel benchmarks, in seconds.

Table 1 presents the execution times of the NAS parallel benchmarks. The numbers in the *No load* column were obtained by running the individual benchmarks in the ideal situation, when all the nodes were totally idle otherwise. Of course, the results obtained this way are the best. In case of the other two *Load* columns, an external load has been applied. The external load was generated by running a single computationally intensive process for 5 minutes on each node used by the benchmark. One node at a time was overloaded in this way, and the external load program worked in a cycle, going back to the first node when it was done with the last one. Two kinds of measurements have been carried out: one with *Dynamite* running, and one without. In both cases, the benchmarks ran slower than without external load. However, in case of all but one of the benchmarks, the results obtained with Dynamite significantly outperform the other case, reducing the percentage of slowdown by a factor of 2 to 6.

Figure 4 presents the execution progress of the NAS parallel benchmarks (due to space restrictions, only 3 of them could be included). In each case, the data for one of the tasks of the parallel application is shown. The left graph presents the time spent on executing each individual step (ideally, this should be a constant); the right graph presents the total time spent so far.

In Figure 4 (a), results for *cg* benchmark are shown. This benchmark slows down 87% when subjected to external load. Such a significant slowdown is an indication of two things. First, large part of execution time must be spent on

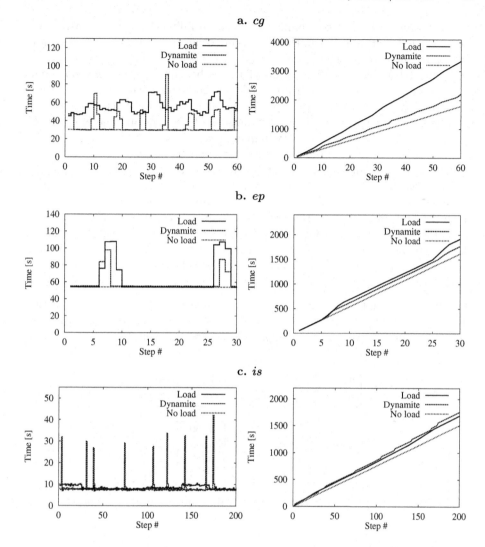

Fig. 4. Execution progress of NAS parallel benchmarks: the time to execute one step (left) and the total time (right).

computation, otherwise the external load would not affect the local task so significantly. Second, the communication pattern of the benchmark (global communication) forces other processes to wait for the one lagging behind, with all the unpleasant consequences to the performance.

The results of *ep* benchmark, as presented in Figure 4 (b), are different. The computation tasks of the *ep* benchmark do not communicate with each other at all, and consequently all of the execution time is spent on computation. In such a case, external load significantly hampers the performance of the affected task, but, due to lack of communication, has no influence on other tasks (the line on the left picture is flat in the area where other tasks of the application are affected by the external load).

Figure 4 (c) shows the execution of the *is* benchmark, the only one that performs worse with Dynamite running. *Is* is in some ways similar to *ep* — they are both only slightly affected by the external load, but the reasons for that are different. Just opposite to *ep*, in *is* most of the execution time is spent on communication: tasks communicate frequently and in large volumes. Therefore, the application progress is limited by the internode communication subsystem, not by the CPU, so an external load has little influence on the local task, and an even smaller one on the remote tasks. The migration decisions of the Dynamite scheduler are not unreasonable, but their gain fails to exceed the migration cost, which is rather high in this case because of large process size (40 MB).

The large process size (30 MB) also affects the result of the *ft* benchmark, where Dynamite reduces the slowdown from 45% to 20%. The reduction would have been significantly larger, had the processes to be migrated been smaller.

Standard Production Code In this test, the scientific application Grail [9,10], a FEM simulation program, has been used as the test application. The measurements were made on selected nodes of a cluster (see Section 3.1).

	Parallel environment	Decomposition	
		sparse	redund.
1	*PVM*	1854	2360
2	*DPVM*	1880	2468
3	*DPVM* + sched.	1914	2520
4	*DPVM* + load	3286	2947
5	*DPVM* + sched. + load	2564	3085

Table 2. Execution time of the Grail application, in seconds.

Table 2 presents the results of these tests, obtained using the internal timing routines of Grail. Each test has been performed a number of times and an average of the wall clock execution times of the master process (in seconds) has been taken. The tests can be grouped into two (decomposition) categories:

- **sparse** — the parallel application consisted of 3 tasks (1 master and 2 slaves) running on 4 nodes,
- **redundant** — the parallel application consisted of 9 tasks (1 master and 8 slaves) running on 3 nodes.

To obtain the best performance, it would be typical to use the number of nodes equal to the number of processes of the parallel application. Neither of the above decompositions does that. In case of the sparse decomposition, one node is left idle (*PVM* chooses to put the group server there, but this one uses only a minimal fraction of CPU time). Such a decomposition would be wasteful for the standard *PVM*. In the redundant case, each node runs 3 tasks of the application (one of the nodes also runs the group server). Although the number of nodes used when running the two decompositions is different, comparing the timings makes sense, since 3 nodes are used at any one time in each case.

In the first set of tests presented in Table 2, standard *PVM* 3.3.11 has been used as the parallel environment. Not surprisingly, the sparse decomposition wins over the redundant one, since it has lower communication overhead.

In the second row, *PVM* has been replaced by *DPVM*. A slight deterioration in performance (1.5-4.5%) can be observed. This is mostly the result of the fact that migration is not allowed while executing some parts of the *DPVM* code. These *critical sections* must be protected, and the overhead stems from the *locking* used. Moreover, all messages exchanged by the application processes have an additional, short (8 byte) *DPVM* fragment header.

In the test presented in the third row, the complete Dynamite environment has been started: in addition to using *DPVM*, the monitoring and scheduling subsystem is running. Because in this case the initial mapping of the application processes onto the nodes is optimal, and no external load is applied, no migrations are actually performed. Therefore, all of the observed slowdown (approx. 2%) can be interpreted as the monitoring overhead.

In the fourth set of tests an artificial, external load has been applied by running a single, CPU-intensive process for 600 seconds on each node in turn, in a cycle. Since the monitoring and scheduling subsystem was not running, no migrations could take place. A considerable slowdown can be observed, although it is far larger for the sparse decomposition (75%) than for the redundant one (19%), actually making the latter faster. This is a result of the UNIX process scheduling policies: for sparse decomposition, the external load can lengthen the application runtime by a factor of 2, while for the redundant decomposition by no more than 33%, since there are already 3 CPU-intensive processes running on each node, so the kernel is unlikely to grant more than 25% of CPU time for the external load process. This shows that sparse decomposition, although faster in a situation close to ideal, performs rather badly when the conditions deteriorate, while the redundant decomposition is far less sensitive in this regard.

The final, fifth set of tests is the combination of the two previous tests: the complete Dynamite environment is running, and the external load is applied. Dynamite clearly shows its value in case of the sparse decomposition, where, by migrating the application tasks away from the overloaded nodes, it manages to reduce the slowdown from 75% to 34%. The remaining slowdown is caused by:

- the time for the monitor to notice that the load on the node has increased and to make the migration decision,
- the cost of the migration itself is non-zero,
- the master task, which is started directly from the shell, is not migrated; when the external load procedure was modified to skip the node with the master task, the slowdown decreased by a further 10%.

Turning to the redundant decomposition, it can be observed that the Dynamite scheduler actually made the matters worse, increasing the slowdown from 19% to 25%. This result, although unwelcome, can easily be explained. The situation was already rather bad even without the external load: not only were all the nodes overloaded, they were also overloaded by the same factor (3). Therefore, the migrator had virtually no space for improvement, and its attempts to migrate the tasks actually worsened the situation. It can be argued that the migrator should have refrained from making any migrations in this case, though.

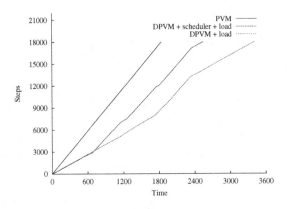

Fig. 5. Execution progress of Grail for sparse decomposition. Note that the performance of plain *PVM* was measured without any load. With a simulated background load it would have been only slightly better than the "*DPVM + load*" performance.

Figure 5 presents the execution progress of Grail for sparse decomposition. For standard *PVM* with no load applied this is a straight, steep line. The other two lines denote *DPVM* with load applied, with and without the monitoring subsystem running. Initially, they both progress much slower than *PVM*: because the load is initially applied to the node with the master task, no migrations take place. After approximately 600 seconds the load moves on to another node. Subsequently, in the case with the monitoring subsystem running, the migrator moves the application task out of the overloaded node, and the progress improves significantly, coming close to the one of the standard *PVM*. In the case with no monitoring subsystem running, there is no observable change at this point. However, it does improve between 1800 and 2400 seconds from the start: that is when the idle node is overloaded. After 2400 seconds, the node with the master task is overloaded again, so the performance deteriorates in both *DPVM* cases.

4 Conclusions and Future Prospects

Concluding, our implementation of load balancing by task migration has been shown to be stable. The use of the Dynamite system results in a slight performance penalty in a well-balanced system, but significant performance gains can be obtained from task migration in an unbalanced system. Improvements can still be made in the scheduling.

Dynamite aims to provide a complete integrated solution for dynamic load balancing. A port to MPI is being implemented, in cooperation with the people from Hector [8]. Dynamite/DPVM can be obtained for academic, non-commercial use through the authors[2].

References

1. van Albada, G.D., Clinckemaillie, J., Emmen, A.H.L., Gehring, J., Heinz, O., van der Linden, F., Overeinder, B.J., Reinefeld, A., and Sloot, P.M.A.: Dynamite — blasting obstacles to parallel cluster computing. HPCN Europe '99, Amsterdam, The Netherlands, in LNCS, n. 1593, 300–310, 1999.
2. Casas, J., Clark, D.L., Konuru, R., Otto, S.W., Prouty, R.M., and Walpole, J.: *MPVM*: A migration transparent version of *PVM*. Usenix Computer Systems, v. 8, n. 2, 171–216, 1995.
3. Czarnul, P., and Krawczyk, H.: Dynamic allocation with process migration in distributed environments. Proceedings of the 6th European *PVM/MPI* Users' Group Meeting, Barcelona, Spain, in LNCS, n. 1697, 509–516, 1999.
4. Dan, P., Dongsheng, W., Youhui, Z., and Meiming, S.: Quasi-asynchronous Migration: A Novel Migration Protocol for *PVM* Tasks. Operating Systems Review, v. 33, n. 2, ACM, 5–14, April 1999.
5. Geist, A., Beguelin, A., Dongarra, J., Jiang, W., Mancheck, R., and Sunderam, V.: *PVM*: Parallel Virtual Machine. A Users' Guide and Tutorial for Networked Parallel Computing. MIT Press, Cambridge, 1994. http://www.epm.ornl.gov/pvm/
6. Iskra, K.A., van der Linden, F., Hendrikse, Z.W., Overeinder, B.J., van Albada, G.D., and Sloot, P.M.A.: The implementation of Dynamite — an environment for migrating PVM tasks. Operating Systems Review, v. 34, n. 3, 40–55, ACM Special Interest Group on Operating Systems, July 2000.
7. Overeinder, B.J., Sloot, P.M.A., Heederik, R.N., and Hertzberger, L.O.: A Dynamic Load Balancing System for Parallel Cluster Computing. Future Generation Computer Systems, v. 12, n. 1, 101–115, 1996.
8. Robinson, J., Russ, S.H., Flachs, B., and Heckel, B.: A task migration implementation of the Message Passing Interface. Proceedings of the 5th IEEE international symposium on high performance distributed computing, 61–68, 1996.
9. de Ronde, J.F., van Albada, G.D., and Sloot, P.M.A.: High Performance Simulation of Gravitational Radiation Antennas. High Performance Computing and Networking '97, in LNCS, n. 1225, 200–212, 1997.
10. de Ronde, J.F., van Albada, G.D., and Sloot, P.M.A.: Simulation of Gravitational Wave Detectors. Computers in Physics, v. 11, n. 5, 484–497, 1997.

---

[2] For commercial use, contact Genias Benelux http://www.genias.nl/

11. Stellner, G., and Trinitis, J.: Load balancing based on process migration for MPI. Proceedings of the Third International Euro-Par Conference, in LNCS, n. 1300, 150–157, Passau, Germany, 1997.

12. Tan, C.P., Wong, W.F., and Yuen, C.K.: *tmPVM* — Task Migratable *PVM*. Proceedings of the 2nd Merged Symposium IPPS/SPDP, 196–202.5, April 1999.

13. White, S., Alund, A., and Sunderam, V.S.: Performance of the NAS Parallel Benchmarks on PVM Based Networks. Journal of Parallel and Distributed Computing, v. 26, n. 1, 61–71, 1995.

14. *MPI*: A Message-Passing Interface Standard, Version 1.1. Technical Report, University of Tennessee, Knoxville, June 1995. http://www-unix.mcs.anl.gov/mpi/

Validation of Dimemas Communication Model for MPI Collective Operations[*]

Sergi Girona[1], Jesús Labarta[1], and Rosa M. Badia[1]

[1] CEPBA-UPC, Mòdul D6 – Campus Nord, c/ Jordi Girona 1 - 3,
08034 Barcelona, Spain
{sergi, jesus}@cepba.upc.es, rosab@ac.upc.es

Abstract. This paper presents an extension of Dimemas to enable accurate performance prediction of message passing applications with collective communication primitives. The main contribution is a simple model for collective communication operations that can be user-parameterized. The experiments performed with a set of MPI benchmarks demonstrate the utility of the model.

1 Introduction

Dimemas [5] has been previously used for performance prediction of message passing programs. In applications were communications are mainly point-to-point it has been demonstrated that is a valuable tool [4]. The next step is to prove its utility for collective operations. It is necessary to develop a collective communication model, as the point-to-point model based on the latency and bandwidth is insufficient.

The second goal is to prove the validity of the tool for point-to-point and collective communications when using communication intensive benchmarks. The results obtained in communication intensive benchmarks will demonstrate the correctness of the models, as they stress the communication.

The paper is organized as follows: section 2 reviews related work. Section 3 presents Dimemas simulator and its point-to-point communication model. The collective operation model is presented in subsection 3.1. Section 4 reports the experiments and results obtained. Finally, in section 5, some conclusions are presented.

2 Related Work

In [2] the LogP, a model of a distributed memory multiprocessor in which processors communicate by point-to-point messages, is presented. The model specifies the performance characteristics of the interconnection network but does not describe its structure. The model is based on the following parameters: L, latency or delay to transmit a message that contains a word; o, overhead, length of time that a processor

[*] This work has been supported by the Ministry of Education of Spain under contract CICYT TIC 98-0511 and by the European Commission under Esprit Project 26276, SEP-Tools

J. Dongarra et al. (Eds.): EuroPVM/MPI 2000, LNCS 1908, pp. 39–46, 2000.

is engaged in the transmission or reception of a message; g, gap, minimum interval between two messages; and P, number of processors. These parameters are not equally important in all situations, and it is possible to ignore one or more parameters depending on the application.

In [8] the authors present the APACHE system, a performance prediction tool for PVM programs. The performance model they use makes difference between computation time and communication time. All nodes are considered to be homogeneous. Their approach is divided in three phases. In the first phase, the compiler constructs a call graph of the PVM program and creates an instrumented version. In the dynamic analysis phase, the instrumented PVM program is executed. It generates a set of equations. With this information and some parameters the prediction phase evaluates the equations and obtains a performance time prediction for the program.

In [10] the authors present a comparison between the performance of collective communication primitives in different systems. The results of these experiments are stored as a database, and are used for performance evaluation. The response time of parallel programs is decomposed in local computation part (LP) and communication part (CP). LP time is predicted by running a program that consists of the local computation part of the program being studied. CP time is derived from the performance database of the communication primitives.

In [7] a parallel simulator for performance evaluation of MPI programs is presented. This simulator uses direct execution to obtain computation time of programs. One of the drawbacks of this system is that host and target processors should be similar to obtain accurate results. Communication and I/O times are obtained by simulation. MPI calls to the MPI library are changed by calls to a library of the simulator, MPI-SIM. Presented results show prediction errors between 5 and 20%.

In [1] the authors present an approach similar to Dimemas. As Dimemas, a trace file obtained from traced execution of the parallel program on a platform different from the one to be evaluated is used as input to a simulator. Previous to this trace execution, a static analysis step is performed. As a result of this step, only one iteration of communication patterns present on the loops appears on the trace. The simulator is oriented to heterogeneous computing environments, and is obtained less accuracy if is used for performance prediction of Massively Parallel Processor systems.

3 Dimemas

Dimemas [5] is a performance prediction tool for message passing programs. It is a trace driven simulator that rebuilds the behavior of a parallel program from a trace file and some parameters of the target architecture. The input trace file characterizes the application. Initially it was developed with the aim of studying the effects of time sharing message-passing programs among several applications [3].

Besides summarized performance data, Dimemas can generate trace files that can be viewed with Vampir [11] and Paraver [5]. Combining a trace driven simulator such as Dimemas with a visualization tool helps understanding the summarized statistics. The user can analyze sensitivity of its program to architectural parameters without modifying the source code and run it again. In a similar way, the effect in global application behavior of a potential improvement in a routine can be observed.

Other significant target in the design of Dimemas is that it should be possible to obtain trace files in a „normal/typical" development environment. By „normal/typical" development environment we understand a single workstation or a time-shared, throughput oriented, parallel machine. Dimemas allows obtaining trace files for performance analysis of message passing programs in one of such environments, without needing a dedicated parallel platform. From this point of view, Dimemas is a tool that avoids the nasty effects of time sharing in trace-based visualization of parallel programs behavior [11]. Dimemas input trace files for MPI programs are generated by VAMPIRtrace, an instrumented MPI library and API [11].

Dimemas models the target architecture (the simulated machine) as a network of nodes. Each node is an SMP connected to the network with a set of links and buses. Every node is composed of one or more processors and local memory.

The model of the target architecture is defined by several parameters: number of nodes, number of processors per node, network bandwidth, communication latency, number of inputs and output links, number of buses, etc. On rebuilding the parallel program execution, Dimemas differentiates between point to point communications and collective communications. Point to point communication time is modeled as:

$$T = L + \frac{S}{B} \qquad (1)$$

where L is the latency, S the size of the message and B the bandwidth. This formula can be applied in a network without contention, with an unlimited number of resources (buses and links). To model the bisection bandwidth of the system, a maximum number of available buses (defined by the user) are considered by Dimemas. Also, to model the injection mechanism, a number of input and output links between the nodes and the network can be defined. Half-duplex link can also be specified.

3.1 A Communication Model for Collective MPI Operations

Many collective operations have two phases: a first one, where some information is collected (fan in) and a second one, where the result is distributed (fan out). Thus, for each collective operation, communication time can be evaluated as:

$$T = FAN\_IN + FAN\_OUT \qquad (2)$$

FAN_IN time is calculated as follows:

$$FAN\_IN = \left(L + \frac{SIZE\_IN}{B} \right) \times MODEL\_IN\_FACTOR \qquad (3)$$

Depending on the scalability model of the fan in phase, the parameter MODEL_IN_FACTOR can take the following values:

Table 1. MODEL_IN_FACTOR possible values

MODEL_IN	MODEL_IN_FACTOR	
0	0	Non existent phase
CT	1	Constant time phase
LIN	P	Linear time phase, P = number of processors
LOG	Nsteps	Logarithmic time phase

In case of a logarithmic model, MODEL_IN_FACTOR is evaluated as the *Nsteps* parameter. *Nsteps* is evaluated as follows: initially, to model a logarithmic behavior, we will have $\lceil log_2\ P \rceil$ phases. Also, the model wants to take into account network contention. In a tree-structured communication, several communications are performed in parallel in each phase. If there are more parallel communications than available buses, several steps will be required in the phase. For example, if in one phase 8 communications are going to take place and only 5 buses are available, we will need $\lceil 8/5 \rceil$ steps. In general we will need $\lceil C/B \rceil$ steps for each phase, being C the number of simultaneous communications in the phase and B the number of available buses. Thus, if steps$_i$ is the number of steps needed in phase i, Nsteps can be evaluated as follows:

$$Nsteps = \sum_{i=1}^{\lceil \log_2 P \rceil} steps_i \qquad (4)$$

For FAN_OUT phases, the same formulas are applied, changing SIZE_IN by SIZE_OUT. SIZE_IN and SIZE_OUT can be:

Table 2. Options for SIZE_IN and SIZE_OUT

MAX	Maximum of the message sizes sent/received by root
MIN	Minimum of the message sizes sent/received by root
MEAN	Average of the message sizes sent and received by root
2*MAX	Twice the maximum of the message sizes sent/received by root
S+R	Sum of the size sent and received root

4 Model Validation

To validate the communication model presented in previous section, several experiments were performed. The experiments were done in 64 processors SGI Origin from CEPBA-UPC with a set of micro-benchmarks that intensively stress some of the MPI communication primitives [6]. Each benchmark was run with dedicated resources and the dedicated elapsed time (DET) was measured. Also, an input trace file for Dimemas for each benchmark was obtained by running them in a loaded system.

The method we follow for the validation of the model is based on the execution of the simulator with different parameters. For all experiments we used ST-ORM, a tool for stochastic optimization, to help us in the specification, execution and analysis of the different experiments [9].

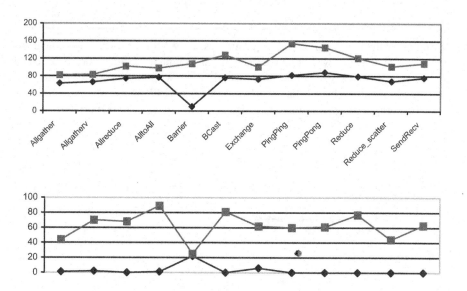

Fig. 1. Up: range of bandwidths (Mbytes/s) that lead to a predicted time between the 10% of error of the dedicated elapsed time; down: Range of latencies (µs) that lead to a predicted time between the 10% of error of the dedicated elapsed time

4.1 General Parameters

A configuration file is used to model the behavior of collective MPI primitives. As we do not know implementation details of the used MPI library, a first set of experiments was performed to fix this file. We found out that a reasonable model would be:

Table 3. Parameters used to model collective operations

Id_op	MODEL_IN	SIZE_IN	MODEL_OUT	SIZE_OUT	Colletive operation
0	LIN	MAX	LIN	MAX	/* MPI_Barrier */
1	LOG	MAX	0	MAX	/* MPI_Bcast */
2	LOG	MEAN	0	MAX	/* MPI_Gather */
3	LOG	MEAN	0	MAX	/* MPI_Gatherv */
4	0	MAX	LOG	MEAN	/* MPI_Scatter */
5	0	MAX	LOG	MEAN	/* MPI_Scatterv */
6	LOG	MEAN	LOG	MEAN	/* MPI_Allgather */
7	LOG	MEAN	LOG	MEAN	/* MPI_Allgatherv */
8	LOG	MEAN	LOG	MAX	/* MPI_Alltoall */
9	LOG	MEAN	LOG	MAX	/* MPI_Alltoallv */
10	LOG	2MAX	0	MAX	/* MPI_Reduce */
11	LOG	2MAX	LOG	MAX	/* MPI_Allreduce */

| 12 | LOG | 2MAX | LOG | MIN | /* MPI_Reduce_Scatter*/ |
| 13 | LOG | MAX | LOG | MAX | /* MPI_Scan */ |

From all collective communication primitives, only MPI_Barrier shows linear behavior. This benchmark was executed changing the number of processors. The results obtained show how the execution time grows linearly with the number of processors. This can be explained by the fact that being the used MPI implementation based in shared memory all processors have to update sequentially a fixed memory position.

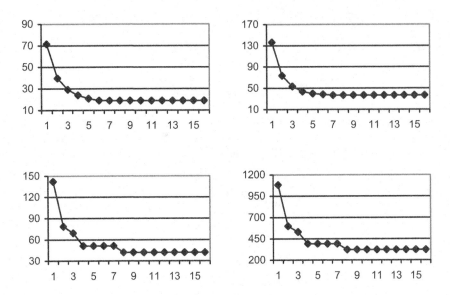

Fig. 2. Influence of the number of buses on the predicted time (in seconds) for the SendRecv (upper-left), Exchange (upper-right), Reduce_scatter (down-left) and Allgather (down-right) benchmarks (BW=87.5, L=25, 1 link HD)

Also this preliminary part of the experiments have shown that setting the number of links of each node to one half-duplex link models better the system than if one full-duplex link is considered. This is also due to the shared memory MPI implementation, where each processor can only be involved in one transfer at a time.

4.2 System Parameters Optimization

A first set of experiments was performed to evaluate the influence of the latency and bandwidth. For each benchmark a set of simulations was performed (between 70 and 110) varying the latency and bandwidth parameters.

For these simulations, the number of buses was set to 10. This number approximates $0.6 \cdot P$, being P the number of processors (P=16 for our case). The value $0.6 \cdot P$ is an approximation to the maximum bandwidth of a crossbar network. The number of links was set to one half-duplex link. For each simulation a predicted (PT) time was obtained. Figure 1 shows the range of bandwidths (in Mbytes/second) such that PT has less than 10% error respect DET and the range of latencies (in μseconds) that complies the same previous condition. From these results we can be concluded that, for example, a bandwidth of 80 Mbytes/s and a latency of 25μs can be used for performance prediction.

A second set of experiments was performed to evaluate the effects of the number of buses. In this case, we set the bandwidth to 87.5Mbytes/s, the latency to 25μs and modeled the connection of the nodes to the network with one half-duplex link, while the number of buses is the parameter that varies. The results obtained for PingPing and PingPong show that these benchmarks are not influenced by the network contention. Predicted time does not change significantly with the number of buses.

Figure 2 (up) shows the results for this experiment for the Exchange and SendRecv benchmarks. We can see that in those cases the predicted time suffers great variation depending on the number of defined buses. As the measured DET for SendRecv is 18,2 secs and for Exchange is 37,4 secs we can conclude that any value between 7 and 16 for the number of buses will model correctly the network contention.

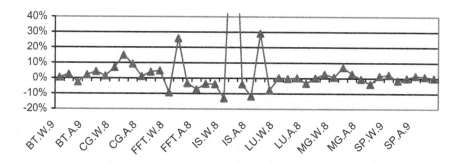

Fig. 3. Error (%) in prediction when simulating with BW=87,5, L=25, 1 HD link, 16 buses

For all collective operations, even MPI_Barrier, the results of the experiment were similar to those obtained for PingPing and PingPong examples, with gaps in most of cases when the number of buses is a power of 2. In figure 2 (down) we can see the results obtained for Allgather and Reduce_scatter benchmarks. Also, the defined number of buses influences the predicted time. As the DET for the Allgather benchmark is 385.1 secs, and for Reduce_scatter is 44.0 secs we can conclude that any value between 8 and 16 can be used to model bus contention for these cases (the same result was obtained for the remaining collective operations).

Given that the bandwidth of the machine we used is wide enough, we can model bus contention with high values. Probably, if a computer with a lower bandwidth had been used, we would have to model bus contention with lower values.

Finally, to validate the correctness of the parameters obtained in the previous experiments, a third set of experiments was performed. For this series of experiments, we run Dimemas for all NAS benchmarks (classes A and B, number of tasks 8-9, 16, 25-32). Figure 3 shows the percentage of error obtained. Most of the benchmarks are predicted with less than a 10% of error. The point out of the graphic takes the value

150% error. This error and those over 10% refer to really short executions (less than five seconds). Thus the real difference between execution and prediction is negligible.

5 Conclusions

In this paper we have presented an approach that takes into account the difference between collective and non-collective message passing primitives. A simple but accurate formulation for the prediction of communication time invested by collective operations has been defined. This formulation has been included in Dimemas.

The experiments developed by using an MPI implementation and communication intensive benchmarks show the validity of Dimemas for performance prediction of message passing programs.

References

1. R. Aversa, B. Di Martino, and N. Mazzocca, „Reducing Parallel Program Simulation Complexity by Static Analysis", Proc. of PDPTA'99, Las Vegas, USA, June 1999.
2. D. Culler, R. Karp, D. Patterson, A. Sahay, K. E. Schauser, E. Santos, and T. von Eicken, „LogP: Towards a Realistic Model of Parallel Computation", in Proc. of the 4th ACM SIGPLAN Symposium on Principles and Practice of Parallel Programming", May 1993.
3. S. Girona, T. Cortes and J. Labarta , „Analyzing scheduling policies using DIMEMAS", Environments and Tools for Parallel Scientific Computing III, Faverges de la Tour, France, August 1996
4. S. Girona and J. Labarta, „Sensitivity of Performance Prediction of Message Passing Programs", Proc. of PDPTA'99, Las Vegas (USA), June 1999.
5. J. Labarta, S. Girona, V. Pillet, T. Cortes and L. Gregoris , „DiP: A Parallel Program Development Environment", Euro-Par'96, Lyon, France, August 1996
6. Pallas MPI Benchmark – PMB, Part MPI – 1. Revision 2.1, Pallas, 1998.
7. S. Prakash, and R. L. Bagrodia, „MPI-SIM: Using Parallel Simulation to Evaluate MPI Programs", Proc. of the 1998 Winter Simulation Conference, pp. 467-474, 1998.
8. M.R. Steed, and M.J. Clement, „Performance Prediction of PVM Programs", in Proc. of IPPS'96, pp. 803-807, 1996.
9. ST-ORM web site, http://www.cepba.upc.es/ST-ORM/
10. Y. Tanaka, K. Kubota, M. Matsuda, M. Sato, and S. Sekiguchi, „A Comparison of Data-Parallel Collective Communication Performance and its application", Proc. of the HPC Asia 97, pp. 137-144, 1997.
11. „Vampir 2.0 - Visualization and Analysis of MPI Programs", http://www.pallas.com

Automatic Performance Analysis of Master/Worker PVM Applications with Kpi

Antonio Espinosa, Tomas Margalef, Emilio Luque

Computer Science Department
Universitat Autonoma of Barcelona
08193 Bellaterra, Barcelona, SPAIN
e-mails: { antonio.espinosa, tomas.margalef, emilio.luque }@uab.es

Abstract. PVM parallel programming model provides a convenient methodology of creating dynamic master/worker applications. In this paper, we introduce the benefits from the use of KappaPi tool for automatic analysis of master/worker applications. First, by the automatic detection of the master/worker paradigm in the application. And second, by the performance analysis of the application focusing on the performance bottlenecks and the limitations of this master/worker collaboration.

1. Introduction

The main reason for designing and implementing a parallel application is to benefit from the potential high performance resources of a parallel system [1]. That is to say, one of the main objectives of the application is to get a satisfying level of performance in the execution. The hard task of building up an application from the use of libraries like PVM[2] or MPI[3] should compensate with the result of obtaining high performance values, like a fast execution or a good scalability, if not a combination of both.

Unfortunately, obtaining a high degree of performance in an application becomes a very hard task. It is necessary to consider many different sources of information like the behavior of the programming model used to select the most adequate primitives for the program, or the actual details of the parallel machine to understand the effect of using certain primitives in the processors and in the communication links.

These requirements, although taken into account in the programming stages of the application, usually require a new stage of performance analysis when the results obtained are far from the desired performance values.

To help in this process of analysing the performance of an application, many tools have been presented. Software tools like Paradyn[4], AIMS [5] and P3T[6] have introduced some techniques that automatize this process of analysis providing information, like, what are the most important performance bottlenecks in the execution, and where they are located in the code of the application.

J. Dongarra et al. (Eds.): EuroPVM/MPI 2000, LNCS 1908, pp. 47-55, 2000.

In this automatic performance analysis effort, Kappa-Pi (Knowledge-based Analyser of Parallel Programs And Performance Improver) was conceived[7]. Kpi tool has been designed for the automatic performance analysis of message-passing parallel programs. Its purpose is to give users some hints about the actual quality of the performance of their applications, together with some suggestions about what changes can be applied to the application to improve the performance.

Kpi tool analyses the execution of parallel applications represented by trace files. These trace files are analysed classifying the inefficiency of the application execution. Those intervals with most important inefficiency found will be analysed in detail looking for the causes of the problem. At the same time, Kpi tool will try to identify any source code reference related to the problem found to build an explanation to the user [8].

Trace files contain all actions happened during the application execution. If traces are the only source of information presented to the user, the programmer will have to understand the low level information (like communication messages sent and received, together with the accumulated times and length); and, from there, abstract the important problems of the application. For this reason, Kpi has an internal rule-based system that identifies common structures in the execution that are closer to programmers' view. The objective of the rule-based system is to relate the recommendations to the actual programming structures used in the application.

A very common structure in PVM applications is the master/worker paradigm. The use of the dynamic process creation and the straightforward use of communication primitives (non-blocking send and blocking receive) together with the use of two clear roles in the computation, master and worker, define a common application structure, rather easy to program in PVM.

Kpi tool will use its rule-based system to recognise master/worker PVM applications. This recognition will allow Kpi tool to analyse the specific performance of such collaborations, suggesting possible changes that will improve the efficiency. Therefore, all applications that fall into this master/worker collaboration paradigm will be specifically studied to obtain suggestions that will specially address the master/worker design of the application.

In section 2 we are going to introduce the principles of the rule-based system used by Kpi to classify the execution performance of a parallel application. Section 3 will explain what are the special characteristics of a PVM master/worker application. In section 4, we give an example of such master/worker applications that will be analysed in detail. Finally, section 5 will present the conclusions of this work.

2. Rule-Based Performance Analysis System

Kappa Pi initial source of information is the trace file obtained from an execution of the application. First of all, the trace events are collected and analysed in order to build a summary of the efficiency along the execution interval in study. This summary is based on the simple accumulation of processor utilization versus idle and overhead time. The tool keeps a table with those execution intervals with the lowest efficiency values (higher number of idle processors). These intervals are saved according to the processes involved, so that any new inefficiency found for the same processes is accumulated.

At the end of this initial analysis we have an efficiency index for the application that gives an idea of the quality of the execution. On the other hand, we also have a final table of low efficiency intervals that allows us to start analyzing why the application does not reach better performance values.

2.1. Automatic Classification of Performance Problems

The next stage in the Kpi analysis is the classification of the most important inefficiencies selected from the previous stage. The trace file intervals selected contain the location of the execution inefficiencies, so their further analysis will provide more insight of the behavior of the application.

In order to know which kind of behavior must be analysed, Kpi tool classifies the selected intervals with the use of a rule-based knowledge system. The table of inefficiency intervals is sorted by accumulated wasted time and the longest accumulated intervals will be analysed in detail. Kpi takes the trace events as input and applies the set of behavior rules deducing a new list of deduced facts. These rules will be applied to the just deduced facts until the rules do not deduce any new fact. The higher order facts (deduced at the end of the process) allow the creation of an explanation of the behavior found to the user.

The creation of this description depends very much on the nature of the problem found, but in the majority of cases there is a need of collecting more specific information to complete the analysis. In some cases, it is necessary to access the source code of the application and to look for specific primitive sequence or data reference. Therefore, the last stage of the analysis is to call some of these "quick parsers" that look for very specific source information to complete the performance analysis description.

This first analysis of the application execution data derives an identification of the most general behavior characteristic of the program. In the case of the example presented in this work, a master/worker PVM application.

The second step of this analysis is to use this information about the behavior of the program to analyse the performance of this particular application. The program, as being identified of a previously known type, can be analysed in detail to find how can it be optimized for the current machine in use.

3. Master/Worker PVM Applications Characteristics

Master/worker applications allow the easy distribution of computational load. Basically, master processes create a data item that must be computed. When this item is created it is send to a worker that carries out some computations with it. Optionally, a result is brought back to the master when the computation finishes.

Normally, workers implement the heavy computation. There are usually some of them calculating in parallel the data items sent by the master. The work carried out by the master usually consists in lighter weight calculations (data item generation) and gathering of final data values. Therefore, the number of running master instances is usually not very high.

Many issues concerning the internal behavior of the master/worker collaboration can be solved in different ways. For example, programmers must choose between different implementation factors when deciding a synchronization mechanism between the master and the workers, number of workers for each master must be decided, etc.

PVM provides a straightforward way of programming a parallel application with this paradigm. Typically, a master process spawns the number of workers it is going to need. Then, it proceeds to calculate and send the data items until there are no available workers (this can be verified using an array of available workers identificators). In this moment, the master can wait for any of the workers to finish to send the new data item generated. Therefore, it must keep control of which workers are idle and which are working.

4. Master/Worker Identification and Performance Analysis

To demonstrate the possibilities of Kpi, we have selected a simple application, called Xfire, to be used as an example to show:
-    How the application is classified as a master/worker collaboration
-    How the performance problems of this application are found and analysed to derive a suggestion to the programmer of the application.

The Forest Fire Propagation application (Xfire)[9] is a PVM message passing implementation of the "fireline propagation" simulation based on the Andre-Viegas model [10] developed for use in any network of workstations. It follows a master-worker paradigm where there is a single master process that generates a partition of the fireline and distributes it to the workers. These workers are in charge of the local propagation of the fire itself and have to communicate the position of the fireline limits back to the master. In the next step, the master collects the new fireline positions and applies the general model with the new local propagation results to produce a new partition of the general fireline (which must be sent to workers to calculate the new propagation interval again).

4.1. Master / Worker Detection

Considering a three-computer cluster, the fireline is divided in two sections, so two workers will be in charge of the local propagation model. Once the instrumented binaries of the application code are generated, the application is executed to get a trace file that serves as an input to the analysis.

The first trace segment is then analysed looking for processor idle or blocking intervals at the execution. A typical processor idle interval is the time waiting for a message to arrive when calling a blocking receive. All these intervals are identified by the ids of the processes involved and a label that describes the PVM primitive that caused the waiting time. For instance, in table 1, we represent the most important efficiency problems found at Xfire execution. In the table, we place the operation that caused the inefficiency and the accumulated processor idle/blocking time (in microseconds). The worst problem found is the accumulated time that the master process (firemaster) was waiting for fireslave 1 in machine 1 to answer back with the local fireline calculation. This inefficiency is the first of those represented in table 1.

Inefficiency caused by:	Accumulated Time (μsecs)
Communication from fireslave1 at machine1 to firemaster at machine3	102.087.981
Communication from fireslave2 at machine2 to firemaster at machine3	53.900.371
Communication from firemaster at machine3 to fireslave1 at machine1	18.833.645
Communication from firemaster at machine3 to fireslave2 at machine2	14.925.344

Table 1. Accumulated time for the most important inefficiencies found in the trace file and the event that produced them.

Once the most important inefficiencies have been found, represented in table 1, it is time to identify them. For this purpose, we are using a rule based knowledge system that, applied to the events produced while the inefficiency was at highest values, will deduce some behavior characteristics that will be useful to analyse the application.

In figure 1, we have shown an example of the sequence of facts deduced to detect a master/worker collaboration. The deduced facts shown above express the way that the rule-based system deduces more general facts at each step. At the beginning, a rather low-level **"communication** between firemaster and fireslave1" is deduced from the send-receive event pairs at the trace file. From the deduced facts, higher level constructions can be deduced. For example, **"dependency** of fireslave1 from firemaster" that reflects the detection of a communication between both processes and a blocking receive at process fireslave1. In this way, similar deductions can be applied to other worker processes. The deduction process is then based on the existence of previous facts and the application of operators like "and" and "or".

The latest fact deduced is the **"master-worker"** relationship between firemaster and fireslave1. This rule depends on the detection of:

- The repeated blocking of the presumed worker process waiting for the master (called **dependency** in figure1).
- The repeated intercommunication between the master and the presumed worker (called **relationship** in figure 1)

A detailed description of the rules and their meaning can be found at [8]. When the facts found lead to the detection of a master/worker application, the analysis concentrates in finding the performance limits of this collaboration.

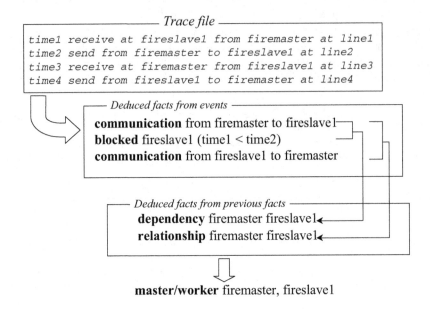

Fig. 1. Deduction steps necessary to identify master/worker collaborations. The first step is based on the trace file events, while the rest use the previously deduced facts.

4.2. Master/Worker Analysis

Once this kind of master/worker collaboration is found, Kpi tool is going to use this paradigm identification to evaluate the performance of the current configuration of master-workers. Kpi attends to their accumulated waiting times and estimates whether it is possible to reduce them in later executions.

To maximise performance, Kpi estimates the ideal number of workers evaluating the ratio between the data generation and the computation rates in a master/worker application, considering the processors and intercommunication links' characteristics.

For each master/worker iteration, Kpi can measure the wasted time at the master. This wasted time is usually spent waiting for the workers to finish their computation, so that they can receive more data.

Wasted time = max (measured computation time per worker) + communication costs

Where the communication costs assume the actual time to send the initial message from the master to the worker and the final message back to the master again.

To build a suggestion to the programmer, Kpi estimates the load of the calculation assigned to each worker (assuming that they all receive a similar amount of work). From there, Kpi calculates the possible benefits of adding new workers (considering the target processor's speed and communication latencies). This process will end when Kpi finds a maximum estimated number of workers to reduce the waiting times.

Figure 2, shows the feedback given to the users of Kpi when the performance analysis is finished. The program window is split in three main areas, on the left hand side of the screen [statistics] there is a general list of efficiency values per processor. On the bottom of the screen [recommendations] the user can read the performance suggestion given by Kpi. On the right hand side of the screen[source view], the user can switch between a graphical representation of the execution (Gantt chart) and a view of the source code, with some highlighted critical lines that could be modified to improve the performance of the application. In the recommendations screen, the tool suggests to modify the number of workers in the application suggesting three as the best number of workers. Therefore, it points at the source code line where the spawn of the workers is done. This is the place to create a new worker for the application.

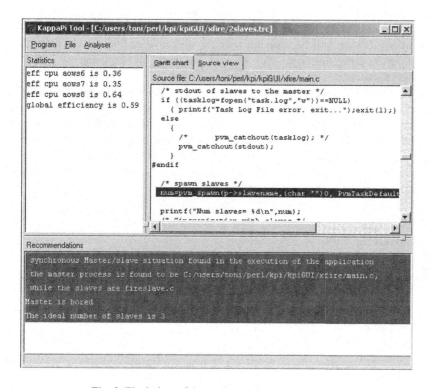

Fig. 2. Final view of the analysis of the Xfire application

Inefficiency caused by	Accumulated time (microsecs)
communication from firemaster at machine3 to fireslave1 at machine1	51.773.801
communication from firemaster at machine3 to fireslave2 at machine2	32.101.666
communication from firemaster at machine3 to fireslave3 at machine4	23.906.561

Table 2. Waiting results with three workers

Following the suggestion shown in figure 2 (suggestion window), we execute the Xfire application including a new worker. As seen in table 2, the accumulated waiting time for the most important performance problems is reduced from the previous execution. Specially, the time wasted in communications arriving at the master (blocking receives).

Additionally, the total execution times have reduced in half from having two workers (383 seconds) to three workers (144 seconds).

5. Conclusions

Kpi is capable of automatically detect a master/worker collaboration from a general PVM application with the use of its rule-based system. Furthermore, the performance of such an application will be analysed with the objective of finding which are their limits in the running machine. This process has been shown using a forest fire propagation simulator.

This process of finding high level programming structures depends very much on the identification of the behavior of a certain code. As there are many different ways to program the same application, this identification process will be much more successful when there are some recognisable operations in the programming of the application. We think that the use of a pre-defined templates, for programming determinate typical structures, could be very helpful for the process of automatic detection and improvement of the application performance.

6. Acknowledgements

This work has been supported by the CYCIT under contract TIC98-0433

7. References

[1] Pancake, C. M., Simmons, M. L., Yan J. C.: Perfonnance Evaluation Tools for Parallel and Distributed Systems. IEEE Computer, November 1995, vol. 28, p. 16-19.
[2] Geist, A., Beguelin, A., Dongarra, J., Jiang, W., Manchek, R. and Sunderam, V., PVM: Parallel Virtual Machine, A User's Guide and Tutorial for Network Parallel Computing. MIT Press, Cambridge, MA, 1994.
[3] Gropp W., Nitzberg B., Lusk E., Snir M.: Mpi: The Complete Reference: The Mpi Core/the Mpi Extensions. Scientific and Engineering Computation Series. The MIT Press. Cambridge, MA, 1998.
[4] Hollingsworth, J. K., Miller, B, P. Dynamic Control of Performance Monitoring on Large Scale Parallel Systems. International Conference on Supercomputing (Tokyo, July 19-23, 1993).

[5] Yan, Y. C., Sarukhai, S. R: Analyzing palallel program performance using normalized performance indices and trace transformation techniques. Parallel Computing 22 (1996) 1215-1237.

[6] Fahringer T., Automatic Performance Prediction of Parallel Programs. Kluwer Academic Publishers. 1996.

[7] Espinosa, A., Margalef, T. and Luque, E., Automatic Performance Evaluation of Parallel Programs. Proc. of the 6th EUROMICRO Workshop on Parallel and Distributed Processing, pp. 4349. IEEE CS. 1998. http://www.caos.uab.es/kpi.html

[8] Espinosa, A., Margalef, T. and Luque E., Relating the execution behaviour with the structure of the application. LNCS 1697. Recent Advances in Parallel Virtual Machine and Message Passing Interface. Springer 1999.

[9] Andre, J.C.S. and Viegas, D.X., "A Strategy to Model the Average Fireline Movement of a light-to-medium Intensity Surface Forest Fire", Proc. of the 2nd Intemational Conference on Forest Fire Research, pp. 221-242. Coimbra, Portugal, 1994.

[10] Jorba, J., Margalef, T., Luque, E., Andre, J., Viegas, D. X. "Application of Parallel Computing to the Simulation of Forest Fire Propagation". Proc. 3td International Conference in Forest Fire Propagation, Vol. 1, pp. 891-900, Luso, Nov. 1998.

MPI Optimization for SMP Based Clusters Interconnected with SCI

Lars Paul Huse

Scali AS, Olaf Helsets vei 6, P.O. Box 70, Bogerud, N-0621 Oslo, Norway
lph@scali.com, http://www.scali.com

Abstract. In this paper, we focus on performance of point-to-point communication and collective operations with multiple processes per node over an SCI network. By careful matching of sending and receiving data, performance close to network peak is achieved for point-to-point communication and a variety of collective operations.

1 Introduction

A *cluster* is a machine that consists of a number of workstations (often low-cost PCs) interconnected with one or more networks adapters to act as a single computing resource. Small *SMPs*(symmetrical multiprocessors) currently have better price-performance than single processor workstations, and is hence attractive as the workhorse for clusters. Solving problems on parallel machines introduce data exchange. The aggregated data volume exchanged for most applications grows with the number of processes. To build scalable clusters, the capacity of the interconnecting network must therefore scale with the number of workstations in the cluster.

SCI (Scalable Coherent Interface) [9] is a standardized high-speed interconnect based on shared memory, with the adapters connected in closed rings. SCI's hardware error-checking mechanisms enable reliable data communication with minimal software intervention, and hence very low latency communication. Dolphin's SCI to PCI bridge family [2], has hardware support for routing traffic between multiple SCI rings connected to the same adapter. Using multidimensional mesh as network topology enables building of large clusters with scalable network performance up to large configurations [1].

MPI (Message Passing Interface) [13] is a well-established communication standard. The collective communication primitives in MPI cover most common global data movement and synchronization primitives. ScaMPI [5] is Scali's thread-hot & -safe high performance implementation of MPI. ScaMPI currently runs over local and SCI shared memory on Linux and Solaris for x86-, IA-64-, Alpha- and SPARC-based workstations. ScaMPI over SCI has a latency of 6.0 μs and a peak bandwidth 90 MByte/s, and 1.7 μs - 320 MByte/s SMP internal (dual 733 MHz Intel Pentium IIIs on an i840 motherboard).

There are two approaches to utilize a multiprocessor in a message passing context. One approach is using threads or a parallelizing compiler, e.g. Posix

J. Dongarra et al. (Eds.): EuroPVM/MPI 2000, LNCS 1908, pp. 56–63, 2000.

threads or OpenMP. A more straightforward approach is to use a one-to-one mapping between processes and processors. Being thread-hot & -safe, ScaMPI can be used with both approaches. This paper focuses on issues regarding multiple MPI processes per SMP. The paper presents the work we have done with ScaMPI to make basic MPI send and receive SMP aware (section 2 & 3). SMP aware algorithms for MPI collective operations are then introduced (section 4) and performance on a 16-SMP cluster is presented (section 4.1, 4.2 & 4.3).

1.1 Used Hardware and Software

The benchmarked cluster consisted of 16 PCs (Intel 440BX) interconnected with Dolphin 32 bit/33 MHz PCI-SCI cards (D311/D312) connected in a 4x4 mesh. Each SMP was equipped with dual 450 MHz Pentium III (Katmai) and 256 MByte memory, and ran Linux 2.2.14-6smp (patchlevel: #1).

The point-to-point test was performed using a modified MPICH perftest [4], and the collective test was performed using Pallas MPI Benchmarks [10]. All tests were compiled with egcs-1.1.2.

2 Synchronizing Multiple Senders on the Same SMP

SCI shared memory is mapped directly into user space and the operating system is only used for connection setup, service and error handling [11]. Since no OS calls are made during normal communication, low latency message passing can be achieved. Data from PCI to SCI are internally buffered on the adapter in one of eight 64 byte *streams* to form longer SCI packets [2]. The streams are direct mapped with respect to the address of its destination. When the highest byte in a stream is written, its content is flushed to the SCI network, and stored in remote memory. A stream is also flushed if the outgoing datum and data already in the stream are from different 64-byte section, or through control registers (to force consistency). Processes writing concurrently to remote SCI memory will therefore cause massive stream usage conflicts, and poor performance.

To provide processes with exclusive access to the adapter a global, pre-initialized *mutex* is offered to all processes. The standard Linux mutex implementations uses 10-30 μs to switch between process - which is high compared to the 6 μs latency of ScaMPI. Scali's own lightweight mutex, using a spinlock, is therefore used. Since this mutex is not registered by the OS, there is no detection if a process terminates while holding the mutex. To avoid deadlock, the SCI driver unconditionally unlocks the mutex when SCI memory is released (which all processes do on termination). Since processes use active waiting, no context switch takes place when the mutex is passed (timing below 1 μs).

Raw (unchecked) SCI traffic have latency below 3 μs and unidirectional bandwidth of 88 MByte/s (bidirectional 97 MByte/s). At MPI level the latency is 6.0 μs and peak bandwidth is 86 MByte/s (bidirectional 90 MByte/s). If two serialized processes on one SMP send to two processes on another SMP the aggregated bandwidth increases to 90 MByte/s, while it drops to 29 MByte/s if the senders are concurrent.

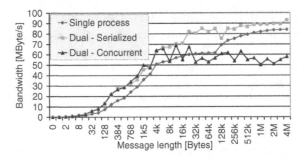

Fig. 1. Aggregated bandwidth for ping-pong communication

Figure 1 shows the aggregated bisection network throughput between two SMPs sending messages in a ping-pong pattern (*mpptest -bisect -roundtrip* [4]). With one process per SMP the throughput for long messages is 84 MByte/s. Throughput increases to 92 MByte/s for two processes with serialized access and drops to approx. 55 MByte/s with concurrent access. As described earlier the concurrent behavior is unpredictable, hence the ragged performance curve.

3   Handling Immediate Communication

Immediate (non-blocking) communication can be implemented in several levels of concurrency:

- Generating separate threads for each call (very resource demanding).
- One separate thread to handle immediate send and receive requests.
- Handling all requests within the context of the application thread.

A dual threaded approach is easy to implement using separate send and receive queues synchronized with semaphores. By combining the functionality of the two operations into one handler, using polling of the request queues and state information, the execution gets less resource demanding. This approach is one of the possibilities for immediate handling in ScaMPI (*threaded*).

A common request, when running on a large machine, is to get acceptable performance with a one-to-one mapping between processes and processors. The default immediate handling in ScaMPI is therefore more *relaxed*. The immediate communication requests are queued and handled; as soon as possible, when the operation is initiated, when another MPI call is made and is eventually forced when MPI_Wait*() is called.

Figure 2 shows the aggregated bandwidth for MPI_Sendrecv() between two SMPs measured with PMB (*PMB-MPI1 -multi 0 Sendrecv* [10]). Relaxed handling with one process per SMP has a latency of 9.4 μs, while threaded handling has 71 μs. The throughput for relaxed handling is higher than threaded, and increases when going from one to two processes per SMP.

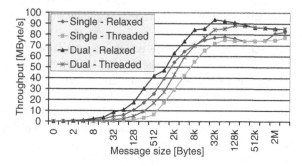

Fig. 2. MPI_Sendrecv performance between two SMPs (threaded and relaxed handling).

4 Algorithmic Adaptations for SMP

There are two ways to reduce network communication time; reducing network traffic and improving network throughput. By rearranging data exchange partners in collective operations, the network data volume can be reduced compared to a naive approach. As illustrated in figure 1, SCI communication throughput improves with increase in message length.

A communication group in MPI is defined by a *communicator*. Each member of a communicator is assigned a unique *rank* from *zero* to *sizeof(comm.)-1*. A communicator can logically be split in two sub-communicators; *global* for traffic between SMPs (one or more) and *local* for SMP internal traffic (one per SMP). Collective communication can generally be performed in the following three steps; Data from all processes are first redistributed (gathered) SMP internally (local). The processes with data then exchange data between the SMPs (global). The resulting data are then finally scattered (broadcasted) within the SMP (local). For certain operations, this approach can reduce the network traffic by a factor equal to the number of processes on the SMP. The number of processes concurrently doing global communication should not exceed the number of network adapters attached to the SMP. For the rest of the paper a single network adapter is assumed.

With current PCI based interconnects, one process (processor) can saturate the bus when sending. Since the data is extracted from the network at the same rate it is injected, the PCI bus on the receiver side will be saturated as well. Three concurrent senders to the same adapter (assuming fair network arbitration and no package rejection) will increase the transfer time by 50% compared to a sequential ordering of the senders! Keeping the sequential algorithms and limiting the number of concurrent senders by a mutex will not reduce this wasted time. Algorithms therefore has to be specially adapted to coordinate network traffic to avoid hot receivers/senders, i.e. matching up senders and receivers in a way that leaves as few network adapters as possible idle at any time. This can be achieved by serializing the receiving in a token-passing approach passing (zero byte messages over the collective communicator) between processes on the same

SMP. By algorithmically adapting sends to match receives from the other SMPs, a smooth data exchange will take place.

Due to different starting time of the collective operation and accumulated timeskew caused by other activity on the SMP, the symmetric data exchange may get disturbed. In eager transfer mode [5], the messages (typically 512 - 64K byte) are posted to buffers on the receiver side beyond the receivers control. As earlier described this can result in loss of performance due to interference from other unrelated transactions. Coordinating the processes to avoid this effect can be done either globally or per transaction. A global coordination can be achieved by splitting each (or every $n'th$) transaction step with a barrier. Performance improvement has earlier been shown with this approach [6], but it have two disadvantages : the exchange can not start until all participants are ready, and barrier is usually a costly operation. A per transaction based synchronization can with ScaMPI either be done explicit or implicit (self-synchronizing). Long messages in ScaMPI are only transferred after a matching receive has been posted (transporter transfer mode [5]), and are hence self-synchronized. A simple protocol to match senders & receivers, is for the receiver to send a `ready-to-receive` token to the sender - which waits for this token before sending, and single sender at all times is assured. This approach is similar to forcing all transfers to use the transporter mechanism. Since ScaMPI latency over an SCI network is only 6 μs, the performance penalty of token passing is acceptable. A send-request is a small message in itself, so synchronizing small messages doesn't reduce concurrency.

4.1   Barrier

Algorithm	PPS	2 Proc.	4 Proc.	8 Proc.	16 Proc.	32 Proc.
Linear gather - scatter	1	11.5	26.2	63.2	137.8	-
Linear gather - scatter	2	5.8	20.6	58.4	141.9	323.1
Binomial tree approach	1	8.9	18.2	29.1	38.2	-
Binomial tree approach	2	3.5	20.9	36.0	51.7	76.2
Binomial SMP approach	1	8.6	17.6	29.8	38.7	-
Binomial SMP approach	2	5.9	15.1	26.2	43.6	61.8
SCI shared memory directly	1	7.5	7.6	9.9	17.7	-
SCI shared memory directly	2	1.3	5.6	6.9	10.0	21.0

Table 1. Performance for synchronization over SCI [μs] (PPS = processes per SMP).

As illustrated in table 1, barrier can be implemented in several ways. The simplest is for one process to `linearly gather` (receive) zero-byte messages from all other and then scatter (send) a zero-byte message to all others to indicate that the barrier is complete. The linear approach can be replaced with hierarchical trees (`Binomial`), with timing $Log2(\#processes)$ [6]. Using one process per SMP to perform the network barrier, with an SMP internal gather (before) and scatter (after) improves performance further (SMP). For the MPI_COMM_WORLD communicator, ScaMPI uses SCI shared memory direct [6] with even better performance (due to a single SCI shared memory commit of all transfers). Table 1 shows that even short messages can benefit from SMP adaption.

4.2 Allgather

In MPI_Allgather() all processes send a chunk of data to all others. Aggregated application throughput is therefore $(\#process^2 * chunksize)/time$. A balanced implementation, using MPI_Sendrecv(), is sending cyclic to upstream neighbor processes and receiving cyclic downstream. For multi-process per SMP, this approach results in multiple senders to each SMP. However, a simple variant of this algorithm reduces the active senders and receivers per SMP to one; One process per SMP gathers all the data from the SMP, and this process exchanges data with gathering processes on the other SMPs, until all data is gathered. The resulting data is then broadcasted within the SMP, and the operation is complete.

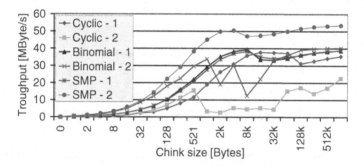

Fig. 3. MPI_Allgather performance between 16 SMPs with 1 or 2 proc. per SMP

Figure 3 shows the throughput per SMP for MPI_Allgather() between 16 dual processor SMPs. With one process per SMP, the binomial has as expected better performance than the linear. Due to lack of priority of SCI response messages in the link-controller [2], an internal livelock may occur under heavy traffic. This is detected by timers and resolved by the device driver, but introduces unproductive timeslots. Running two unsynchronized processes per SMP, some programs get very exposed to this livelock and hence loose additional performance.

A positive side effect of gathering all SMP data in one process is that the messages over the network increase in size. As shown in figure 1 communication performance increases with message size. Since SMP internal communication is much higher than network performance, the increased SMP internal data traffic does not reduce overall performance.

4.3   Alltoall

In all-to-all communication, every process exchange unique chunks of data with all others. As for MPI_Allgather(), an intuitive implementation of this is using MPI_Sendrecv() to cyclicly exchange data. For multi-process per SMP, this approach results in multiple senders to each SMP. Since unique chunks are exchanged between all processes, letting one process do all network communication would result in a lot of extra SMP internal traffic.

A better approach is to coordinate the processes on each SMP by token passing, to let them take terms in sending and receiving. Every send is paired up with its matching receive. To ensure that only one remote process is sending to each SMP, receives are also synchronized, with a ready-to-receive token from the receiver to the sender. By this approach, at most one process sends data to & from each SMP at any time.

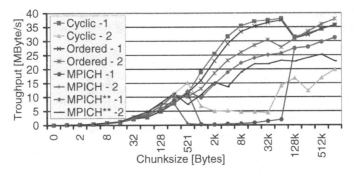

Fig. 4. MPI_Alltoall performance between 16 SMPs.

Figure 4 shows the throughput per SMP for MPI_Alltoall() between 16 SMPs. With one process per SMP the ordered approach outperforms the simple cyclic MPI_Sendrecv(). As in section 4.2 the cyclic approach using two processes per SMP runs into bad performance, while the ordered maintains performance. In MPICH [14] MPI_Alltoall() between N processes is implemented as N immediate sends and receives, followed by a blocking wait for it all to finish. As earlier explained this approach does not perform well with current SCI implementations, but by forcing communication to use transporter mode [5], as shown with the MPICH** curve in figure 4, performance can be improved.

5   Conclusion

Kielmann et al. [8] two rules for high latency networks, seem to have a parallel for high bandwidth, low latency networks, e.g. SCI, given by:

- Concurrent senders to and on the same adapter should be avoided.
- If the network is the limiting factor for data movement, gathering SMP internal data before exchanged over the network may be performance effective.

By synchronizing senders and receivers, performance improvements have been shown for barrier, allgather and alltoall communication.

6 Related Work

Compared to regular binomial tree based communication, [8,7] have shown good performance for wide-area network. This work has been focused on SMPs with a small number of processes, and basic MPI send & receive has been used to broadcast/gather SMP-internal data. For larger number of processes per SMP, internal copying can be improved with techniques a.k.a. [12]. Using user-space to user-space copy without temporal buffering, as described in [3], will improve SMP internal data transfer for long messages. Unfortunately this involves a special patch to be applied to the Linux kernel, which limits the universality of the approach.

References

1. H. Bugge, K. Omang: Affordable Scalability using Multicubes. *SCI. Architecture & software for high-performance compute clusters.* pp 167-175, LNCS 11734 - Springer-Verlag (1999)
2. Dolphin ICS: PCI-SCI Bridge Functional Specification. *Version 3.01* (1996).
3. P. Geoffray, L. Prylli, B. Tourancheau: BIP-SMP: High Performance Message Passing over a Cluster of Commodity SMPs. *Proceedings of Supercomputing 99* (1999)
4. W. Gropp, E. Lusk: Reproducible measurement of MPI performance characteristics. *Proceedings of the 6th Euro-PVM/MPI* pp 11-18 (1999).
5. L.P. Huse, K. Omang, H. Bugge, H. Ry, A.T. Haugsdal, E. Rustad: ScaMPI - Design and Implementation *SCI. Architecture & software for high-performance compute clusters.* pp 249-261, LNCS 11734 - Springer-Verlag (1999)
6. L.P. Huse: Collective communication on dedicated clusters of workstations. *Proceedings of the 6th Euro-PVM/MPI* pp 469-476 (1999).
7. N. Karonis, B. de Supinski, I. Foster, W. Gropp, E. Lusk, and J. Bresnahan: Exploiting hierarchy in parallel computer networks to optimize collective operation performance, *Proceedings of the 14th International parallel and distributed processing symposium* (2000)
8. T. Kielmann, R.F.H. Hofman, H.E. Bal, A. Plaat, R.A.F. Bhoedjang: MagPIe: MPI's Collective Communication Operations for Clustered Wide Area Systems, *Proceedings of the 7th Principles and Practice of Parallel Programming* (1999).
9. IEEE standard for Scalable Coherent Interface IEEE Std 1596-1992 (1993)
10. Pallas MPI Benchmarks *Version 2.2* http://www.pallas.com/ (1999)
11. S.J. Ryan: Efficient Middleware for IO Bus Bridging Cluster Adapters. *Dr.Scient. thesis from Department of Informatics, University of Oslo, Norway* (1998)
12. S. Sistare, R. vande Vaart, E. Loh: Optimization of MPI Collectives on Clusters of Large-Scale SMP's. *Proceedings of Supercomputing 99* (1999)
13. MPI Forum: A Message-Passing Interface Standard. *Version 1.1* (1995)
14. MPICH: Portable MPI Model Implementation. *Version 1.2.0.* Available from http://www.mcs.anl.gov/mpi/mpich (1999)

Parallel, Recursive Computation of Global Stability Charts for Liquid Bridges

Gábor Domokos[1], Imre Szeberényi[2], and Paul H. Steen[3]

[1] Department of Strength of Materials,
domokos@iit.bme.hu
[2] Department of Control Engineering and Information Technology,
szebi@iit.bme.hu
Technical University of Budapest, H-1521 Budapest, Hungary
[3] Department of Chemical Engineering,
Cornell University, Ithaca, NY, 14850 USA
steen@cheme.cornell.edu

Abstract. We investigate the stability of liquid bridges by using a parallel, recursive algorithm. The core of the recursion is the Parallel Simplex Algorithm introduced in [10]. We discuss the PVM implementation of the algorithm and compare our results with earlier published computations.

1 Introduction

A new approach to the computation of global stability diagrams is illustrated on axi-symmetric equilibria of liquid bridges. The computation method is based on a recursive scheme, the core of which is a parallel algorithm. In each successive step of the recursion this algorithm calls itself, decreasing the dimension of the problem by one. The meaning of the trivial, depth-0 recursion is equivalent to the computation of the bifurcation diagram, described in [9]. Computation to stability boundaries requires a depth-1 recursion.

The parallel core algorithm, called the Parallel Simplex Algorithm (PSA) has been developed by [8],[3], [10] with the goal to solve multi-point boundary value problems (BVPs) globally, the parallel implementation under PVM is discussed in [5].

Recently, this method has been applied to the equilibria of liquid bridges [9]. Also recently, the PSA has been generalized in [6] to a depth-n recursive scheme, serving the computation of stability boundaries and other parameter-dependent curves. In the current paper we will combine the results of [9] and [6] in order to obtain global stability curves for liquid bridges.

In section 2 we will briefly describe the PSA, section 3 describes the parallel implementation, section 4 deals with the recursive scheme. Section 5 summarizes the physical background to liquid bridge problems, results are demonstrated in section 6.

J. Dongarra et al. (Eds.): EuroPVM/MPI 2000, LNCS 1908, pp. 64–71, 2000.

2   The Parallel Simplex Algorithm

The PSA can be directly applied of two-point Boundary Value Problems (BVPs) associated with ordinary differential equations (ODEs). Assuming that the latter is of even order (which is most often the case in mechanics), it is equivalent to $\dot{x}(t) = f(x(t), \lambda), x \in \Re^{2n}, \lambda \in \Re, t \in [0,1]$. Let us regroup the equations so that the initial $(t = 0)$ conditions apply to the first n components $(x_i(0) = a_i, i = 1, 2, \ldots n)$ and far-end $(t = 1)$ conditions apply to the those with indices ν_i $(x_{\nu_i}(1) = b_i, \ i = 1, 2, \ldots n)$, where a_i, b_i are given scalars. We denote the remaining initial conditions or *variables* by $v_{i-n} = x_i(0), \ i = n+1, n+2, \ldots 2n$. The $(n+1)$-dimensional space spanned by the variables and the parameter λ is called the Global Representation Space (GRS). Using any convergent forward integrator for the initial value problem (IVP), we can compute the final values $x_{\nu_i}(1), (i = 1, 2, \ldots n)$ as *functions* of v_i and λ: $x_{\nu_i} = g_i(v_1, v_2 \ldots v_n, \lambda)$ and then solve the algebraic system

$$g_i(v_j, \lambda) - b_i = 0; \ i, j = 1, 2, \ldots n, \ v_j \in [v_j^0, v_j^1], \ \lambda \in [\lambda^0, \lambda^1] \tag{1}$$

by the PL algorithm ([1]) in the prescribed $(n+1)$-dimensional domain of the GRS (defined by the constants with superscript in (1)). Geometrically, (1) describes the intersection of n hyper-surfaces in the $(n+1)$-dimensional space, yielding typically (locally) 1-dimensional solution sets, thus branches. These branches will appear as polygons, due to the piecewise linear approximation. (We remark that the variables can have a far more general interpretation in the PSA; however, the above version is sufficient to introduce the most important concepts.)

Application of the method can be visualized without technical details. System (1) can be resolved simultaneously in any sub-domain of the GRS. 'Simultaneous resolution' stands in relation to 'continuation' as photographic imaging stands to free-hand sketching. The pixels of a film negative are developed simultaneously (in parallel) in a chemical bath, whereas the hand-sketch requires a sequence of strokes with each point in a stroke laid down sequentially. Developing this analogy further, bifurcation diagrams obtained by continuation are analogous to hand-sketches where the pencil is not permitted to lift whereas simultaneous resolution can deliver families of equilibria that are unconnected (e.g. isolas), as well. These features make the PSA an optimal candidate for the relatively fast, global understanding of low-dimensional bifurcation problems [8], [3],[17],[10].

3   Implementing the PSA under PVM

A simple BVP involves 3-5 dimensional GRS, however the complexity of the problem grows exponentially with the number of dimensions. In order to solve the equation system with prescribed precision we have to choose sufficiently small grid-size for the PL algorithm. Supposing that the number of points on each coordinate axis is N and the number of dimensions is n, the numbers of points where we have to use the forward integrator will be N^n. Moreover we have to solve $N^n n!$ equations. This means that the CPU and memory requirements of the algorithm grow exponentially with the number of dimensions [6].

Considering that the GRS can divided into smaller domains, and the computation in every domain is independent suggests that the domain partitioning could be the base of the parallelization.

The implemented parallel PVM program is based on a master-slave structure, where the master program distributes the phase space to smaller pieces (domains) and the slaves figure out the equation system in these domains. Since the computation effort inside the domains is by orders of magnitudes larger than the effort for communication, (i.e. the computation/communication ratio is very large) the speedup is almost linear vs. the number of processors, which also defines the scalability of the software. This has been tested in the range between 2-120 processors in different hardware and software environment. The major functions of the master program are: reading the configuration files, creating the domain-list, starting and stopping the slaves, collecting the results from slaves, load-balancing, doing checkpoint restart.

Files are handled only by the master program thus the slaves can run on any network connected machine, and NFS is not required. The slave program essentially contains the serial version of the described Simplex Algorithm and solves the equations in the domain given by the master.

The load-balancing is provided by the master, because the GRS is divided into more domains than the number of processors. When the computation in a domain has been finished, the master assigns the next domain to the next free slave. In this way faster processors will get more jobs then slower ones.

4   Recursive Version of the PSA

The original equation (1) may contain parameters C_i besides the variables v_i and the parameter λ. In this case solution sets emerge as multi-dimensional manifolds rather than 1D-lines. In many applications special, 1D subsets of these multidimensional manifolds are of real interest. We embedded the PSA into a recursive scheme, capable to compute these special lines directly.

The simplest case of such a recursion (depth-1) is when there is one parameter: C_1. In this case one might ask, how do the *extremal points* on the solution branches (1D lines) of the *original problem* vary as we change C_1. The "dumb" approach to this question would be to let the PSA solve the original problem for many values of C_1, select extrema on all diagrams and then connect them. The recursive approach is rather different.

It regards an extended, $n + 1$ dimensional problem. In order to isolate 1D branches, one needs one additional function/constraint: this is delivered by the condition that we are looking for extrema. While the first $n-1$ functions and their evaluation remains identical to the original problem, the evaluation of the last, added function (extremal condition) requires the solution of an n-dimensional problem (in a very small domain). This concept can be generalized to recursion of arbitrary depth (see [6]), however, for the current application the depth-1 recursion is sufficient.

We have modified our PSA implementation for this requirement, resulting in a recursive algorithm, which is a substantial generalization of the original PSA. The key idea is simple (described here for depth-1 recursion):

- enlarge our equation system (1) with a new function which yields the required properties (eg. turning points, local extrema) at the roots of original equation system,
- set the C_1 as a new variable,
- solve this enlarged equation system using the PSA, described in section 2.

We remark that the new function may contain virtually *any* condition on the solution branch of the original, n-dimensional problem, including higher derivatives, singularities, etc. We emphasize that we did not restrict the dimension or recursion depth of the algorithm, so our code is capable of solving a large variety of problems emerging in applications.

5   Liquid Bridges and Stability Boundaries

Liquid equilibria problems are low dimensional; the GRS is only 2-dimensional for a wide range of physical situations. Scientific interest in figures of equilibrium can be traced back to the time of Plateau[20]. Mathematicians have been stimulated by the minimal surface problem and extensions thereof [16]. Physical chemists have made early computations of shapes and families of shapes. Motivation has ranged from improving measurement devices where a meniscus is involved [12] to measuring surface tension using droplet and bubble methods[11,13]. Recent interest from the engineering community has focussed on materials [14,15] and micro-gravity applications [18,19]. The common feature here is that liquid shapes are dominated by surface tension (small capillary length). In these papers, by concentrating on different physical aspects (such as effects of gravity, asymmetric boundary conditions, etc.) unifying features easily recognized in the setting of the GRS have been obscured. Our present goal is to show that the PSA can not only utilize parallel computing resources very efficiently in order to solve such problems but also can help to provide *global* stability diagrams.

Static shapes of surfaces that contain a liquid are governed by the normal stress balance across the surface, called the Young-Laplace equation. In the absence of gravity, this equation can be reduced to the 2-dimensional system

$$\dot{\alpha}(s) = p - \sin(\alpha(s))/r(s)$$
$$\dot{r}(s) = cos(\alpha(s)). \tag{2}$$

where r measures the radius from the axis of symmetry, p is the pressure in the liquid, α is the (counterclockwise positive) tangent angle of the meridian with respect to the r axis, arclength s is the independent variable ($\dot{} \equiv d/ds$). The

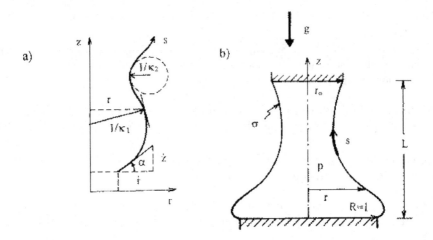

Fig. 1. Definition sketches for axisymmetric figures of equilibrium; (a) IVP: space-curve geometry or 'kinematics'; (b) BVP: liquid bridge

equation $\dot{z}(s) = \sin(\alpha(s))$, yielding the vertical z coordinate is decoupled from (2). We considered pinned boundary conditions (cf. figure 1 with $r_0 = 1$)

$$r(0) = r|_{z=L} = 1. \tag{3}$$

In order to apply the PSA to this BVP, we have to establish the global coordinates spanning the GRS. As described in Section 2, these coordinates (variables) consist of non-specified initial values and parameters. In our case, the only non-specified initial value is $\alpha(0)$ which, with the parameter p, spans the 2-dimensional GRS. Using the coordinates $(\alpha(0), p)$ the physical rz shape can be uniquely reconstructed by forward integration of (2) and the third equation given afterwards. Adopting the general notation of the Introduction, we have $n = 1$; $x_1 \equiv r$; $x_2 \equiv \alpha$, $a_1 = 1$, $\nu_1 = 2$, $v_1 \equiv \alpha(0)$, $\lambda \equiv p$. We are seeking zeroes of the function $f(\alpha_0, p) \equiv \int_0^s \sin(\alpha) - L = z - L$, defining the global bifurcation diagram. Note that L is constant for each separate bifurcation diagram.

The stability of equilibria can be investigated via investigation of the *extremal points* of the bifurcation diagram. If we look for a family of such curves, parametrized by L, we obtain surfaces in the $[\alpha_0, p, L]$ space. We are interested in points where the partial derivative $\frac{\partial p}{\partial \alpha_0}$ vanishes. (We remark that extremas of the *volume* are also of interest and can be obtained by a similar procedure.) Using the terminology of section 4, we have the additional parameter $C_1 \equiv L$ and the additional constraint of the vanishing partial derivative. Added to the original problem we now have a 2D PSA problem, one function of which requires the computation of a 1D PSA (in a small domain). This setting enables us to do *global search* for stability boundaries in the $[\alpha_0, p, L]$ extended GRS.

6   Results and Conclusions

We studied the stability of axi-symmetric liquid bridges in the following domain of the GRS $[\alpha_0, p, L]$: $-1.0 < \alpha(0) < 4.2; -1.5 < p < 3.5; 0.2 < L < 13$. We tested our code on two different hardware environments:

(1) the IBM SP2 supercomputer machine at the Cornell Theory Center (CTC) and

(2) the Intel PIII-based cluster at the Technical University of Budapest, Centre of Information Technology.

In both cases we used "primary" grids with $500 \times 500 \times 500$ subdivisions and refined the results on a secondary grid of triple density. Computation results have been filtered based on errors registered in the two function values, stored together with the three coordinates of the solution points. On both platforms we achieved almost linear speedup factors due to the low communication between the nodes.

We illustrate our results by comparing the result of a typical, 5-hour, 50-processor run with the earlier published data of [21]. As customary, the graphs display the normalized volume versus the length L. Curves ACA and HGJ on the plots, identified by the labels on fig. 2a, should be compared. These are the stability limits to constant pressure disturbances. Curve ACA in fig 2b is cut off for L ¡ 2 because the corresponding extrema in the bifurcation diagrams fall outside the computational window (p and $/alpha$ limits, see above). Note that while our computations show several gaps (due to inadequate meshsize and dense filters), they illustrate the global behavior in accordance with [21] and also predict interesting behavior at $L \approx 9$. The illustrated diagram of [21] has been obtained by a semi-automated procedure, based on the computation of individual bifurcation diagrams and connecting their extrema. Besides providing a fully automated algorithm, our method also yields access to *disconnected* stability curves if they exist.

Acknowledgements

This research was supported for GD and ISz by OTKA grant T031744 and the USA-Hungarian Joint Fund Grant 656/96. PHS thanks NASA grant NAG3-1854 for partial support. The authors thank Chris Pelkie (CTC) for help in the visualization of computational results.

The hardware environment was provided by the Cornell Theory Center (CTC), TUB Dept. of Control Engineering and Information Technology (TUB DCEIT), and TUB Centre of Information Technology (TUB CIT).

The CTC receives funding from Cornell University, New York State, the National Center for Research Resources at the National Institutes of Health, the National Science Foundation, the Department of Defense Modernization Program, and members of the Corporate Partnership Program.

The TUB CIT receives funding from Matav, Compaq Hungary, Hungarian Post, IBM Hungary and Nokia Hungary.

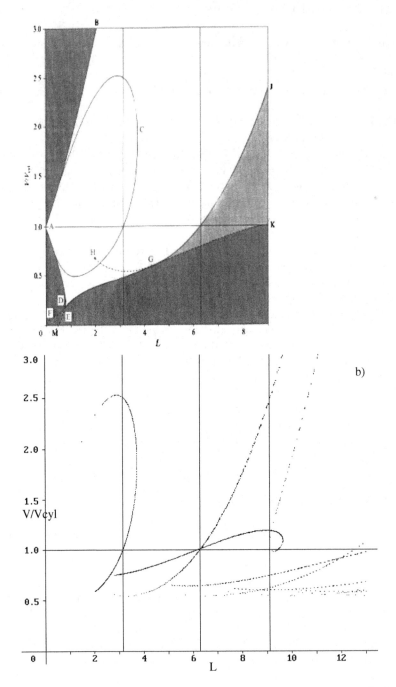

Fig. 2. Global stability chart for liquid bridges (a) as computed in [21], (b) current results

References

1. E.L. Allgower and K. Georg, *Numerical continuation methods: An introduction*, Springer, Berlin, New York, 1990.
2. L. Bieberbach, *Differentialgleichungen*, Springer, Berlin 1923
3. G. Domokos, Zs. Gáspár, *A global direct algorithm for path-following and active static control of elastic bar structures*, J. of Structures and Machines 23 (4), pp 549-571 (1995)
4. A. Geist, A. Beguelin, J. Dongarra, W. Jiang, R. Manchek, V. Sunderam *PVM 3 User's guide and reference manual* Oak Ridge National Laboratory, Oak Ridge TN 37831-6367 Technical Report, ORNL/TM-12187, May, 108pp., 1993.
5. I. Szeberényi, G. Domokos, Zs. Gáspár, *Solving structural mechanics problems by PVM and the simplex algorithm*, Proc. 2nd EuroPVM'95, eds: Dongarra J. et al., Hermes, Paris, 1995., pp 247-252
6. I. Szeberényi., G. Domokos, *Solving generalized boundary value problems by the distributed computing and recursive programming*, Proc. 6th EuroPVM'99, eds: J. Dongarra et al., Springer Lecture Notes in Computer Sci., Vol 1697, pp267-274, 1999
7. P. Holmes, G. Domokos, J. Schmitt and I. Szeberényi, *Constrained Euler buckling: An interplay of computation and analysis*, Comp. Meth. in Appl. Mech. and Eng. 170 (3-4) 175-207 (1999.)
8. G. Domokos, *Global description of elastic bars*, ZAMM 74 (4) T289-T291
9. G. Domokos, I. Szeberényi and P.H. Steen, *Simultaneously resolved bifurcation diagrams: A novel global approach applied to liquid figures of equilibrium*, J. of Computational Physics **159**, 38-57, 2000
10. Zs. Gáspár, G. Domokos and I. Szeberényi, *A parallel algorithm for the global computation of elastic bar structures*, J. Comp. Ass. Mech. Eng. Sci. 4(1) 1997.
11. F. Bashforth, J.C. Adams, *An attempt to test the theories of capillary action*, Cambridge University Press (1883).
12. E. Blaisdell, *The physical properties of fluid interfaces of large radius of curvature*, J. Math. Phys. Inst. Tech. **19** (1940) 186.
13. E.A. Boucher, M.J.B. Evans, *Pendant drop profiles and related capillary phenomena*, Proc. R. Soc. Lond. **A 346** (1975) 349.
14. W.C. Carter, *The forces and behavior of fluids constrained by solids*, Acta Metallurgica **36** (1988) 2283-2292.
15. S.R. Coriell, M.R. Hardy, M.R. Cordes, *Stability of liquid zones*, J. Colloid Interface Sci. **60** (1977) 126.
16. R. Finn, *Equilibrium Capillary Surfaces*, Springer-Verlag, New York (1986).
17. P. Holmes, G. Domokos, J. Schmitt and I. Szeberényi, *Constrained Euler buckling: An interplay of computation and analysis*, Comp. Meth. in Appl. Mech. and Eng. 170 (3-4) 175-207 (1999.)
18. J. Meseguer, *Stability of slender, axisymmetric liquid bridges between unequal disks*, i J. Crystal Growth **67** (1984) 141.
19. A. D. Myshkish et.al, *Low-gravity fluid mechanics*, Springer, New York (1987).
20. J. Plateau, *Statique Experiméntale et Théorique des Liquids soumis aux seules force Moléculaires*, **Tome 1**, Grande et Leipzig, Paris, 1873.
21. B.J. Lowry and P.H. Steen, *Capillary surfaces: Stability from families of equilibria with application to the liquid bridge*, Proc. R.Soc. Lond. A **449** (1995), 411-439.

Handling Graphs According to a Coarse Grained Approach: Experiments with PVM and MPI

Isabelle Guérin Lassous[1], Jens Gustedt[2], and Michel Morvan[3]

[1] INRIA Rocquencourt,
Isabelle.Guerin-Lassous@inria.fr
[2] LORIA and INRIA Lorraine,
Jens.Gustedt@loria.fr
[3] LIAFA and Université Paris 7 and Institut Universitaire de France,
morvan@iafa.jussieu.fr

Abstract. We report on experiments with graph algorithms which were designed for the coarse grained multicomputer (CGM) model. The implementation was based on the message-passing paradigm and uses PVM and/or MPI as communication interfaces.

1 Introduction and Overview

Parallel graph algorithms are a field that had a rich development since the early beginning of parallel computation. But if there are a lot of theoretical studies in this area, relatively few implementations have been presented for all these algorithms that were designed. Moreover most of these implementations have been carried out on specific parallel machines (C90, T3E, CM2, CM5, MasPar, Paragon) using special purpose software (Paris, CMIS, NESL, MPL). As far as we know, few implementations use PVM or MPI and they only concern the minimum spanning tree and shortest paths problems. For a state-of-the-art on the implementations of parallel graph algorithms, see [10].

Two questions coming from a wider framework were the starting point of our work:

1) Which parallel model allows to develop algorithms that are: **feasible** (they can be implemented with a reasonable effort), **portable** (the code can be used on different platforms without rewriting it), **predictable** (the theoretical analysis allows the prediction of the behavior in real platforms) and **efficient** (the code runs correctly and is more efficient than the sequential code)?

2) What are the possibilities and limits of graphs handling in real parallel platforms?

The portability aspect will obviously lead to results less efficient than the use of code fine-tuned for the structure of each machine, but the idea is to obtain results with an acceptable efficiency on each machine by using the same code for a given problem. Most of the actual parallel machines or networks being distributed memory machines, efficient algorithms using message passing-paradigm implemented with portable tools like PVM/MPI should lead to such a compromise.

To give the first answers to these questions, we worked on different algorithmic problems for graphs. For each tackled problem, either we chose an existing algorithm or we proposed a new one if no algorithm had been designed or if the existing algorithm(s)

J. Dongarra et al. (Eds.): EuroPVM/MPI 2000, LNCS 1908, pp. 72–79, 2000.

did not seem adapted to the goals we stated previously. Then, we implemented these algorithms.

In this article we report on the experiences of four studied problems: for each problem, we give a quick state-of-the-art on the algorithms and their implementation (if existing) for this problem and a brief description of the implemented algorithm with its theoretical complexity in time. Then, we present the obtained results from the implementations on PC clusters using PVM/MPI with the main analysis. If each presentation can appear succinct, we prefered to give a survey of our works and an idea of what can be done on graphs with tools like PVM/MPI. For the reader willing to know more detailed studies on the subject, see [10]. Section 2 briefly presents the Coarse Grained Multicomputer (CGM) model that seems well adapted for computations according message-passing paradigm and the experimental framework. Section 3 gives the results obtained for one of the basic problem that is sorting. Section 4 deals with the difficult problem of list ranking. Section 5 shows that it is possible to solve the connected components problem on dense graph efficiently. Section 6 shows that an algorithm with $\log p$ supersteps (p is the number of processors) can be efficient in practise. We give the first answers to the initial questions in Section 7.

2   The Parallel Model and the Implementation Background

The CGM Model Recently, several works tried to provide models that take realistic characteristics of existing platforms into account while covering at the same time as many parallel platforms as possible. Proposed by Valiant , [16], BSP (Bulk Synchronous Parallel) is the originating source of this family of models. It formalizes the architectural features of existing platforms in very few parameters. The LogP model proposed by Culler et al., [3] considers more architectural details compared to BSP, whereas the CGM model initiated by Dehne et al., [4], is a simplification of BSP. We chose CGM because it has a high abstraction that easily enables the design of algorithms and offered the simplest realization of the goals we had in mind.

The three models of parallel computation have a common machine model: a set of processors that is interconnected by a network. A processor can be a monoprocessor machine, a processor of a multiprocessors machine or a multiprocessors machine. The network can be any communication medium between the processors (bus, shared memory, Ethernet, etc).

The CGM model describes the number of data per processor explicitly: for a problem of size n, it assumes that the processors can hold $O(\frac{n}{p})$ data in their local memory and that $1 \ll \frac{n}{p}$. Usually the later requirement is put in concrete terms by assuming that $p \leq \frac{n}{p}$ because each processor has to store information about the other processors.

The algorithms are an alternation of **supersteps**. In a superstep, a processor can send or receive once to and from each other processor and the amount of data exchanged in a superstep by one processor in total is at most $O(\frac{n}{p})$. Unlike BSP, the supersteps are not assumed to be synchronized explicitly. Such a synchronization is done implicitly during the communications steps. In CGM we have to ensure that the number R of supersteps is particularly small compared to the size of the input. For instance, we can ensure that R is a function that only depends on p (and not on n the size of the input).

The Background We have implemented these algorithms on two PC clusters. Note that our code also ran on distributed memory parallel machines. The first cluster[1], called *PF* henceforth, consists of 13 *PentiumPro* 200 PCs with 128 MB memory each. The PCs are interconnected by a 100 Mb/s full-duplex *Fast Ethernet* network. The second cluster[2], called *POPC* consists of 12 *PentiumPro* 200 PCs with 64 MB of memory each. The interconnection network is a *Myrinet*[3] network. The programming language is C++ (gcc) and the communication libraries are PVM and MPI. We began to use PVM release 3.4.2, but our code now runs with LAM/MPI 6.3 and MPI-BIP (developped for the Myrinet network). All the presented results in this article were obtained with PVM except for the results of the list ranking that were obtained with MPI (we explain this fact Section 4). Note that this article does not intend to compare the performances of PVM and of MPI via the graph algorithms but to show the kind of results we can obtain on graphs with the use of message-passing tools like PVM/MPI.

All the tests have been carried out ten times for each input size. The results given are an average of ten tests. All the execution times are in seconds. Each execution time is taken as the maximum value of the execution times obtained on each of the p processors. In all the given figures, the x-axis corresponds to n, the input size and the y-axis gives the execution time in *seconds per elements*. Both scales are logarithmic to make the curves readable. To test and instrument our code we generated input objects randomly. Due to space limitations, we omit this description. See [10] for more details. The time required for the generation of an object is not included in the times as they are presented.

3   A Basic Operation: Sorting

The choice of the sorting algorithm is a critical point due to its widespread use to solve graph problems. In BSP, there are deterministic as well as randomized algorithms. In the CGM setting, all these algorithms translate to have a constant number of super-steps. The algorithm proposed by Goodrich, [8], is theoretically the most performing, but is complicated to implement and quite greedy in its use of memory. We chose the algorithm of [6] because it is conceptually simple and requires only 3 supersteps. It is based on the sample technique which uses $p-1$ splitters to cut the input elements in p packets. The choice of the splitters is then essential to ensure that the packets have more or less the same size. The algorithm is randomized and bounds the packets size by $\left(1 + \frac{1}{\sqrt{\ln n}}\right)\left(\frac{n-p+1}{p}\right)$ with high probability only.

In our implementation, the sorted integers are the standard 32 bit `int` types of the machines. We use counting sort, [2], as the sequential sorting subroutine. To distribute the data according to the splitters, we do a dichotomic search on $p-1$ to find the destination packet of each element. By that we only introduce a $\log p$ factor. Therefore, this sort can be solved with probability $1 - o(1)$ in $O(T_S(\frac{n}{p}) + \frac{n}{p}\lceil \log(p-1)\rceil)$ local compu-

---

[1]   http://www.inria.fr/sophia/parallel

[2]   http://www.ens-lyon.fr/LHPC/ANGLAIS/popc.html

[3]   http://www.myri.com/

tations per processor, $O(n)$ for the total communication cost and with 3 supersteps. T_S is the complexity of the sequential sort.

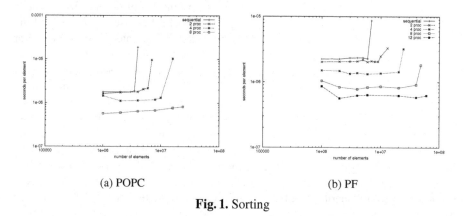

(a) POPC   (b) PF

Fig. 1. Sorting

Figure 1 gives the execution times per element of the program with $1, 2, 4$ and 8 PC for POPC, and with $1, 2, 4, 8$ and 12 PC for PF. The right ends of the curves for the execution times demonstrate the swapping effects. Measures begin at one million elements to satisfy some inequalities required for this sort. The memory of an individual PC in PF is two times larger than the one for POPC, therefore PF can sort two times more data. As expected, we see that the curves (besides swapping) are near constant in n and the execution times are neatly improved when we use $2, 4, 8$ or 12 PC. We see that this parallel sort can handle very large data efficiently, whereas the sequential algorithm is stuck quite early due to the swapping effects. Note that PF can sort 76 million integers with 12 PC in less than 40 seconds.

4   The List Ranking Problem

The list ranking problem frequently occurs in parallel algorithms that use dynamic objects like lists, trees or graphs. The problem is the following: given a linked list of elements, for each element x we want to know the distance from x to the tail of the list. Whereas it is easy to solve sequentially, it seems much more difficult in parallel. The first proposed algorithms were formulated in the PRAM model. In the coarse grained models, several algorithms were also proposed, but none of them is communication optimal, see [5] and [1]. As far as we know, few implementations have been realized, and none of them seems to be portable because they are highly optimized for the target machine, see [14, 15].

We proposed a randomized algorithm that uses the technique of *independent sets*, as described in [12]. It requires $O(\log p)$ supersteps, $O(\frac{n}{p})$ for local computations per processor and $O(n)$ for the total communication cost (see [9] for a detailed analysis).

To not overload the study of the results, we only present the experiments on POPC, but the results on PF are alike. Figure 2 gives the execution times *per element* in function of the list size. p varies from 4 to 12, because the memory of the processors is saturated when we use 2 or 3 PC. All the curves stop before the memory saturation of the processors. We start the measures for lists with 1 million elements, because for smaller size, the sequential algorithm performs so well that using more processors is not very useful. A positive fact that we can deduce from

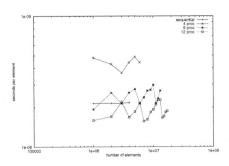

Fig. 2. List Ranking on POPC

the plots given in Figure 2 is that the execution time for a fixed amount of processors p shows a linear behavior as expected. One might get the impression from Figure 2 that it deviates a bit from linearity in n, but this is only a scaling effect: the variation between the values for a fixed p and n varying is very small (less than $1\mu s$). We see that from 9 PC the parallel algorithm becomes faster than the sequential one. The parallel execution time decreases also with the number of used PC. Nevertheless, the speedups are quite restricted (these results are the best we obtained with MPI and are better than those obtained with PVM). We see also that this algorithm performs well on huge lists. Due to the swapping effects, the sequential algorithm dramatically changes its behavior when run with more than 4 million elements. For 5 millions elements, the execution time is a little bit higher than 3000 seconds, whereas 12 PC solve the problem in 9.24 seconds. We see also that we only need 18 seconds to handle lists with 17 millions elements.

5   Connected Components for Dense Graphs

Searching for the connected components of a graph is also a basic graph operation. For a review of the different PRAM algorithms on the subject see [12]. Few algorithms for the coarse grained models have been proposed. In [1], the first deterministic CGM algorithm is presented. It requires $O(\log p)$ supersteps and is based on PRAM simulations and list ranking. According to our experience, it seems that the simulation of PRAM algorithms is complex to implement, computationally complex in practice and hardly predictable. Moreover, this algorithm uses the list ranking that is really a challenging problem as shown previously. On the other hand, the part of this algorithm that is specific to CGM doesn't have these constraints. It computes the connected components for graphs where $n \leq \frac{m}{p}$, that is to say for graphs that are relatively dense, and does this without the use of list ranking. Therefore we implemented this part of the algorithm. It computes the connected components of a graph with n vertices and m edges such that $n \leq \frac{m}{p}$ in $\lceil \log p \rceil$ supersteps, $O(\frac{m}{p} + \lceil \log p \rceil n)$ local computations per processor and $O(\lceil \log p \rceil n)$ for the total communication cost. Each of the p processors requires a memory of $O(\frac{m}{p})$.

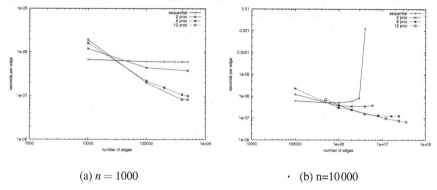

(a) $n = 1000$ · (b) n=10000

Fig. 3. Connected components on PF

We use multi-graphs where two vertices are chosen randomly to form a new edge of the graph. The use of multi-graphs for these tests is not a drawback because the algorithm touches each edge unless it belongs to the spanning tree only once. For this problem, there are two parameters n and m to vary. As the code has the same behavior on the clusters we only show the results for graphs with 1000 and 10000 vertices on PF. Figure 3 gives the execution times in *seconds per item* with $1, 2, 8$ and 12 PC. For $n = 1000$, m ranges from 10000 to 500000. For $n = 10000$, m ranges from 10000 to 36 millions. We see that for a fixed p the curves decrease with m. If we study the results obtained with $n = 1000$ more precisely, we see that when the graph has more than 50000 edges then there is always a speedup compared to the sequential implementation, and the more processors we use, the faster is the execution. With $n = 10000$, we can do the same remark when the graph has more than 1 million edges. Note, that with $n = 10000$ it is possible to handle very large graphs by using several PC. In sequential, the PC begins to swap with about 3.2 millions edges, whereas the connected component computation on a graph with 36 millions edges can be solved in 2.5 seconds with 12 PC.

6 Permutation Graphs

The permutation graph associated with a permutation Π is the undirected graph $G = (V, E)$ where $\{i, j\} \in E$ if and only if $i < j$ and $\Pi(i) > \Pi(j)$. Permutation graphs are combinatorial objects that have been intensively studied. Basic references may be found in [7]. This graph problem can also be translated into a computational geometry problem called the dominance problem that arises in many applications like range searching, finding maximal elements, interval/rectangle intersection problems ([13]). Passing from the permutation to the graph and vice versa is done easily in a sequential time of $O(n^2)$. In parallel, we show how to pass from the permutation to the graph in the PRAM and their approach easily translates to CGM. This leads to a new compact representation of permutation graphs ([11]). The main step of this algorithm is to compute the number of *transpositions* for each value $i = 0, \ldots, n - 1$, i.e. the cardinality of $\{j \mid i < j$ and $\Pi(i) > \Pi(j)\}$. It requires exactly $\lceil \log_2 p \rceil$ supersteps, $O(\frac{n \log_2 n}{p})$ local computations per processor. The overall communication is in $O(n\lceil\log_2 p\rceil)$ and is then smaller than the local computation cost.

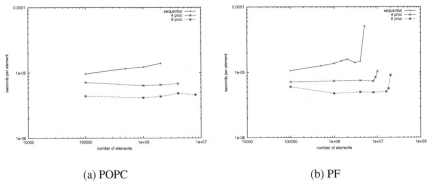

(a) POPC   (b) PF

Fig. 4. A permutation graph algorithm

To simplify the implementation and without loss of generality, we assume that p is a power of 2. The generated inputs are random permutations. The elements are unsigned long integers. Figure 4 shows the execution times in *seconds per element* for 1, 4 and 8 PC. For PF, the size of the permutation ranges from 100 000 to 16 millions, whereas for POPC it ranges from 100 000 to 8 millions (due to the memory size of the PC on each cluster). The right end of the curves show the beginning of the swapping effects. First, the curves have the expected behavior: they are constant in n. The execution time is also lowered when we use more processors, as expected. Again, it is possible to solve this problem on very large data. For PF, one PC begins to swap after 4 millions data, whereas 8 PC do it on a little bit less than 17 millions elements. Note that the local computations time is greater than the communications time, as expected.

7   Answers to the Initial Questions

This work allows us to give some partial answers to the questions we asked at the beginning of this paper.

Question 1) Given the analysis of the results, it seems that coarse grained models are very promising to obtain feasible, portable, predictable and efficient algorithms and code. If there is still a lot of work left over, these first steps go towards practical and efficient parallel computation. These results are in fact a mix of at least three points: a) these models allow to design efficient algorithms based on the message passing-paradigm, b) PVM/MPI provide the main routines to efficiently implement the communication steps needed in the coarse grained algorithms and c) the portable aspect is ensured on one hand by the portability of the software like PVM/MPI and C++ for our experiments and on the other hand by the general structure of the coarse grained algorithms.

Question 2) This work shows that it is now possible to write portable code for graph handling that handles very large data, and that for some problems, this code is efficient. The most challenging problem from the point of view of feasibility and efficiency that we encountered is the list ranking problem. It is possible that this singularity comes from the specific irregular structure of the problem. Nevertheless, it seems obvious that these results can have an impact on many parallel graph algorithms using message-passing paradigm that are based on list ranking.

References

[1] E. Caceres, F. Dehne, A. Ferreira, P. Flocchini, I. Rieping, A. Roncato, N. Santoro, and S. W. Song. Efficient parallel graph algorithms for coarse grained multicomputer and BSP. In *Proceedings of the 24th International Colloquium ICALP'97*, volume 1256 of *LNCS*, pages 390–400, 1997.

[2] T. Cormen, C. Leiserson, and R. Rivest. *Introduction to Algorithms*. MIT Press, 1990.

[3] D. Culler, R. Karp, D. Patterson, A. Sahay, K.E. Schauser, E. Santos, R. Subramonian, and T. von Eicken. LogP: Towards a Realistic Model of Parallel Computation. In *Proceeding of 4-th ACM SIGPLAN Symp. on Principles and Practises of Parallel Programming*, pages 1–12, 1993.

[4] F. Dehne, A. Fabri, and A. Rau-Chaplin. Scalable Parallel Geometric Algorithms for Coarse Grained Multicomputer. In *ACM 9th Symposium on Computational Geometry*, pages 298–307, 1993.

[5] F. Dehne and S. W. Song. Randomized parallel list ranking for distributed memory multiprocessors. In Springer Verlag, editor, *Proc. 2nd Asian Computing Science Conference ASIAN'96*, volume 1179 of *LNCS*, pages 1–10, 1996.

[6] A. V. Gerbessiotis and L. G. Valiant. Direct bulk-synchronous parallel algorithms. *Journal of Parallel and Distributed Computing*, 22:251–267, 1994.

[7] M. C. Golumbic. *Algorithmic Graph Theory and Perfect Graphs*. Academic Press, New York, 1980.

[8] M.T. Goodrich. Communication-efficient parallel sorting. In *Proc. of 28th Symp. on Theory of Computing*, 1996.

[9] I. Guérin Lassous and J. Gustedt. List ranking on PC clusters. Technical Report 3869, I.N.R.I.A., 2000.

[10] I. Guérin Lassous, J. Gustedt, and M. Morvan. Feasibility, Portability, Predictability and Efficiency: Four Ambitious Goals for the Design and Implementation of Parallel Coarse Grained Graph Algorithms. Technical Report RR-3885, INRIA Lorraine, 2000. http://www.inria.fr/RRRT/publications-fra.html.

[11] J. Gustedt, M. Morvan, and L. Viennot. A compact data structure and parallel algorithms for permutation graphs. In M. Nagl, editor, *WG '95 21st Workshop on Graph-Theoretic Concepts in computer Science*, 1995. Lecture Notes in Computer Science 1017.

[12] J. Jájá. *An Introduction to Parallel Algorithm*. Addison Wesley, 1992.

[13] F.P. Preparata and M.I. Shamos. *Computational Geometry: an Introduction*. Springer-Verlag, 1985.

[14] M. Reid-Miller. List ranking and list scan on the Cray C-90. In *Proc. ACM Symp. on Parallel Algorithms and Architectures*, pages 104–113, 1994.

[15] J. F. Sibeyn, F. Guillaume, and T. Seidel. Practical Parallel List Ranking. *Journal of Parallel and Distributed Computing*, 56:156–180, 1999.

[16] L. Valiant. A bridging model for parallel computation. *Communications of the ACM*, Vol. 33(8):103–111, 1990.

Adaptive Multigrid Methods in MPI*

Fabrizio Baiardi, Sarah Chiti, Paolo Mori, and Laura Ricci

Dipartimento di Informatica, Universitá di Pisa
Corso Italia 40, 56125 - PISA (ITALIA)
{baiardi, chiti, mori, ricci}@di.unipi.it

Abstract. Adaptive multigrid methods solve partial differential equations through a discrete representation of the domain that introduces more points in those zones where the equation behavior is highly irregular. The distribution of the points changes at run time in a way that cannot be foreseen in advance. We propose a methodology to develop a highly parallel solution based upon a load balancing strategy that respects the locality property of adaptive multigrid method, where the value of a point p depends on the points that are "close" to p according to a neighborhood stencil. We also describe the update of the mapping at run time to recover an unbalancing, together with strategies to acquire data mapped onto other processing nodes. A MPI implementation is presented together with some experimental results.

1   Introduction

Multigrid methods are iterative methods based upon multilevel paradigms to solve partial differential equations in two or more dimensions. Combined with the most common discretization techniques, they are among the fastest and most general methods to solve partial differential equations [6, 7]. Moreover, they do not require particular properties of the equation, such as the symmetry or the separability and are applied to problems in distinct scientific fields [4, 5, 12].

The adaptive version of multigrid methods, AMM, discretizes the domain at run time by increasing the number of the points in those zones where the behavior of the equation is highly irregular. Hence, the distribution of the points in the domain is not uniform and not foreseeable.

Since the domain usually includes a large number of points, the adoption of a parallel architecture is mandatory. We have defined in [1, 2, 3] a parallelization methodology to develop applications to solve irregular problems on distributed memory parallel architectures. This paper describes the application of this methodology to develop a MPI implementation of the AMM. Sect. 2 describes the main features of AMM, sect. 3 shows the MPI implementation resulting from applying our data mapping technique to the AMM. Sect. 4 describes the technique to gather information mapped onto other processing nodes and the problems posed by the adoption of MPI collective communications. The experimental results on a Cray T3E are discussed in sect. 5.

---

* This work has been partially supported by CINECA

J. Dongarra et al. (Eds.): EuroPVM/MPI 2000, LNCS 1908, pp. 80–87, 2000.
© Springer-Verlag Berlin Heidelberg 2000

2   Adaptive Multigrid Methods

An AMM discretizes the domain through a hierarchy of grids built during the computation, according to the considered equation. In the following, we adopt the finite difference discretization method. For sake of simplicity, we assume that the domain belongs to a space with two dimensions and each grid partitions the domain, or some parts of it, into a set of squares. The values of the equation are computed in the corners of each square. We denote by $g(A, l)$ the grid to discretize a subdomain A at level l. To improve the accuracy of the discretization provided by $g(A, l)$, a finer grid, $g(A, l+1)$, that is obtained by halving the sides of each square of $g(A, l)$, is introduced. In this way, at run time, finer and finer grids are added till the desidered accuracy has been reached. Even if, in practice, the first k levels of the hierarchy are built in advance, to simplify the description of our methodology, we assume that the initial grid is one square, i.e. $k = 0$.

The AMM iteratively apply a set of operators on each grid in a predefined order, the V-cycle, until the solution has been computed. The V-cycle includes two phases: a descending one, that considers the grids from the highest level to the lowest one, and an ascending one, that considers the grids in the reverse order. Two versions of the V-cycle exist: the additive and the multiplicative; we adopt the additive one and briefly describe the involved operators [7]. The *smoothing operator* usually consists of some iterations either of the Gauss-Seidel method or the Jacobi one to improve the current solution on each grid. The *restriction operator* maps the current solution on $g(A, l)$ onto $g(A, l-1)$. The value of each point on $g(A, l-1)$ is a weighted average of the values of its neighbors on $g(A, l)$. The *prolongation operator* maps the current solution on $g(A, l)$ onto $g(A, l+1)$. If a point exists on both grids, its value is copied. The value of any other point of $g(A, l+1)$ is an interpolation of the values of its neighbors on $g(A, l)$. The *norm operator* evaluates the error of the current solution on each square that has not been further partitioned. The *refinement operator*, if applied to $g(A, l)$ adds a new grid $g(A, l+1)$.

Our methodology represents the grid hierarchy through a quad-tree, the H-Tree. A quad-tree is well suitable to represent the hierarchical relations among the squares and it is intrinsically adaptive. Each node N at level l of the H-Tree, hnode, represents a square, $sq(N)$, of a grid $g(A, l)$ of the hierarchy. The squares associated to the sons of N, if they exist, represent $g(sq(N), l+1)$. Because of the irregularity of the grid hierarchy, the shape of the H-Tree is irregular too. The quad-tree has been adopted in [9], while alternative representations of the grid hierarchy have been adopted in [8, 10]. The multigrid operators are applied to $g(A, l)$ by visiting all the hnodes at level l of the H-Tree. All the operators are applied to $g(A, l)$ before passing to $g(A, l+1)$ or $g(A, l-1)$.

3   Data Mapping and Load Balancing

This section describes the load balancing strategies that, respectively, map each square at any level of the hierarchy onto a processing node, p-node, and update the mapping during the computation to recover an unbalancing. Both strategies take into account two locality properties of an AMM: the value of a point on $g(A,l)$ is function of the values of its neighbors $i)$ on the same grid for operators such as smoothing and norm (intra-grid or horizontal locality); $ii)$ on $g(A,l+1)$ (if it exists) and $g(A,l-1)$ for the prolongation, restriction and refinement operators (inter-grid or vertical locality). In the following, we assume that any p-node executes one process and that the np p-nodes have been ordered so that two p-nodes close in the interconnection structure of the considered architecture are close in the ordering as well. P_h denotes the process executed by the h-th p-node.

Our methodology defines a data mapping in three steps: $i)$ determination of the computational load of each square; $ii)$ squares ordering; $iii)$ order preserving mapping of the squares onto the p-nodes. In the AMM the same load is statically assigned to each square, because the number of operations is the same for each point and does not change at run time. To preserve the locality properties of the AMM, the squares are ordered through a space filling curve [11] built starting from the lowest grid of the hierarchy. After a square S in $g(A,l)$, the curve visits any square in $g(S,d)$, $d > l$, before the next square in $g(A,l)$. The recursive definition of the space filling curves preserves the vertical locality. Moreover, if an appropriate curve is chosen, like the Peano Hilbert or the Morton one, the horizontal locality is partially preserved. A space filling mapping has been adopted in [8, 10] too. Since each square is paired with an hnode, any space filling curve sf defines a visit $v(sf)$ of the H-Tree that returns an ordered sequence $S(v(sf)) = [N_0, ..., N_{m-1}]$ of hnodes. To preserve the ordering among squares, $S(v(sf))$ is mapped onto the ordered sequence of p-nodes through a blocking strategy. $S(v(sf))$ is partitioned into np subsequences of consecutive squares; the h-th subsequence includes m/np hnodes and it is assigned to P_h.

The resulting mapping satisfies the **range property**: *if the hnodes N_i and N_{i+j} are assigned to P_h, then all the hnodes in-between N_i and N_{i+j} in $S(v(sf))$, are assigned to P_h as well.* This property is fundamental to exploit locality. The domain subset assigned to P_h, Do_h, includes squares at distinct levels of the hierarchy. To avoid replicate computations, for each square in Do_h, P_h applies the operators of the V-cycle to the rightmost downward corner only.

Our methodology assumes that the whole H-Tree cannot be fully replicated in each p-node because of memory constraints. Hence, each p-node stores two subtrees of the H-Tree: the replicated H-Tree and the private H-Tree. The private H-Tree of P_h includes all the hnodes representing squares in Do_h. Even if, in general, the squares in Do_h may correspond to disjoint subtrees of the H-Tree, for sake of simplicity, we assume that Do_h is represented by one connected private H-Tree only. The replicated H-Tree represent the relation among the private H-Trees and the H-Tree. It includes all the hnodes on the paths from the root of the H-Tree to the roots of each private H-Tree, and it is the same for each process. Each hnode N of the private H-Tree records all the data of the rightmost downward corner of $sq(N)$, while each hnode N of the replicated H-Tree records the position of $sq(N)$ in the domain and the identifier of the owner process.

To determine, during the computation, where the refinement operator has to introduce finer grids, the processes estimates the current approximation error through the norm operator. This requires the exchange of the local errors among all the processes at the end of a V-cycle and the computation of a global error. Any process estimates its local error and the global error is computed through the MPI_Allreduce primitive. At the end of a V-cycle, to check if the creation of finer grids has leaded to a load unbalance, the processes exchange their workloads through the MPI_Allgather primitive. Then, each process computes *max_unbalance*, the largest difference between *average_load*, the ratio between the overall load and *np*, and the workload of each process. If *max_unbalance* is larger than a tolerance threshold $T > 0$, then each process executes the balancing procedure. T prevents the procedure from being executed to correct a very low unbalance. Let us suppose that the workload of P_h is $average\_load + C$, $C > T$, while that of P_k, $h < k$, is $average\_load - C$. The balancing procedure cannot map some of the squares in Do_h to Do_k because this violates the range property. Instead, it shifts the squares involving each process P_i in-between P_h and P_k. Let us define $Prec_i$ as the set of processes $[P_0...P_{i-1}]$ that precede P_i and $Succ_i$ as the set of processes $[P_{i+1}...P_{np-1}]$ that follow P_i. Furthermore, $Sbil(Prec_i)$ and $Sbil(Succ_i)$ are, respectively, the global load unbalances of the sets $Prec_i$ and $Succ_i$. If $Sbil(Prec_i) = C > T$, i.e. processes in $Prec_i$ are overloaded, P_i receives from P_{i-1} a segment S of hnodes. If, instead, $Sbil(Prec_i) = C < -T$, P_i sends to P_{i-1} a segment S of hnodes whose overall computational load is as close as possible to C. The same procedure is applied to $Sbil(Succ_i)$ but, in this case, the hnodes are either sent to or received from P_{i+1}. To respect the range property, if $[N_q....N_r]$ is the subsequence of hnodes it has been assigned, P_i sends to P_{i-1} a segment $[N_q....N_s]$, with $q \leq s \leq r$, while it sends to P_{i+1} a segment $[N_t....N_r]$, with $q \leq t \leq r$. P_i communicates with processes P_{i-1} and P_{i+1} only. All communications exploit the synchronous mode with non–blocking send and receive primitives. Non–blocking primitives overlap communication and computation, while the choice of synchronous mode is due to the MPI implementation on the considered parallel architecture, Cray T3E, that provides system buffering. If the MPI standard mode is used, a deadlock may occur if a large amount of pending non–blocking operations has exhausted the system resources. At the end of the load balancing procedure, all the processes exchange, through MPI_Allgather and MPI_Allgatherv, the roots of their private H-Trees to update the replicated H-Tree. Each process, using MPI_Allgather, declares to any other one how many data it is going to send, i.e how many roots it owns. Then, the MPI_Allgatherv implements the exchange of the roots through a buffer allocated according to the number of roots returned by the MPI_Allgather.

4   Collecting Data from Other P-Nodes

Each process P_h applies the multigrid operators, in the order stated by the V-cycle, to the points in Do_h. While in the most of the cases, any information that P_h needs is stored in the private H-Tree, for some points in the border of Do_h,

P_h has to collect the values of points in squares assigned to other processes. We outline the MPI implementation of our remote data collecting procedure, denoted *informed fault prevention*, where processes exchanges remote data before applying the multigrid operators. This procedure allows P_h to receive any data it needs to apply the operator op without requesting it to the owner processes, before applying op. In this way, when P_i applies op to $g(A, l)$, it can visit the H-Tree in any order because it has already collected the data it needs. The advantages of this technique are discussed in [3].

The *informed fault prevention* technique consists of two steps: the *replicated H-Tree extension* step, executed at the beginning of each V-cycle, and the *fault prevention* step, executed before each operator in the V-cycle. Let us define $Bo_h(op, l)$ as the set of the squares S_i in Do_h at level l, such that one of the neighbors of S_i, as defined by the neighborhood relation of op, does not belong to Do_h. Furthermore, let $I_h(op, l)$ be the set of squares outside Do_h corresponding to the points whose values are required by P_h to apply op to the points in the squares in $Bo_h(op, l)$.

In the replicated H-Tree extension step the processes exchange some informations about their private H-Trees. For each point p_i in $\cup_{op}\cup_l Bo_h(op, l)$ such that one of its neighbors belongs to Do_k, P_h sends to P_k the level of the hnode N where $sq(N)$ is the smallest square including p_i. This information is sent at the beginning of the V-cycle and it is correct until the end of the V-cycle, when the refinement operator may add finer grids. Since the refinement operator cannot remove a grid, if a load balancing has not been executed, at the beginning of a V-cycle each process sends information on the new grids only.

In a fault prevention step, P_k determines $A_k I_h(op, l) \ \forall h \neq k$, i.e. the squares in Do_k belonging to $I_h(op, l)$ by exploiting both the information in the replicated H-Tree about Do_h and the one received in the replicated H-Tree extension step. Hence, P_k sends to P_h, without any explicit request, the values of the points in $A_k I_h(op, l)$. These values are exchanged just before applying op to $g(Do_h, l)$, because they are updated by previous operators in the V-cycle. Notice that P_h can compute $I_h(op, l)$ by simply merging the subsets $A_k I_h(op, l)$ received by its neighbors.

It is worth noticing that, in the case of the refinement operator, $A_k I_h(op, l)$ is approximated. In fact, whether P_h, that owns the square including the point p, needs the value of the point q, in a square owned by P_k, depends not only upon the neighborhood stencil but also upon the value of the points. Since P_h, in the replicated H-Tree extension phase, sends to P_k the depth of the hnodes corresponding to the square in $\cup_{op}\cup_l Bo_h(op, l)$, but not the values of the points in these squares, P_k cannot determine exactly $A_k I_h(op, l)$. To guarantee that P_h receives all the data it needs, P_k determines the squares to be sent according to the neighborhood stencil only, and it could send some useless values.

Both steps are implemented through MPI point to point communications. Collective communications, i.e. MPI_Scatter, have not been adopted, because each process usually communicates with a few other processes. This implies the creation, for each process P_h, of one communicator C_h including any neighbor of P_h. To this aim, P_h should determine the set of the neighbors of each process in MPI_COMM_WORLD, but it has not enough information to do so. Moreover, MPI_Comm_split cannot be exploited because the communicators associated with two neighbors processes are not disjoint. Furthermore, at the end of a V cycle, because of the refinement operator and of load balancing procedure, the neighbors of P_h changes; this requires the elimination of old communicators and the creation of new ones. Also notice that, since the collective communications are blocking, they have to be properly reordered to prevent the deadlock.

In order to overlap a communication with useful computation, in the fault prevention procedure, each process determines the data to be sent to other processes while is waiting for the data from its neighbors. Moreover, data to be sent to the same process are merged into one message, to reduce the number of communications and the setup overhead. This is a noticeable advantage of informed fault prevention and it is implemented as follows: each process P_k issues an MPI_Irecv from MPI_ANY_SOURCE to declare that it is ready to receive the sets $A_k I_h(op, l)$ from any P_k. While waiting for these data, P_k determines the data to be sent to all the other processes, i.e. $\forall h \neq k$ it computes $A_k I_h(op, l)$. When a predefined amount of data to be sent to the same process has been determined, P_k sends it using an MPI_Issend. Subsequently, P_k checks through an MPI_Test the status of the pending MPI_Irecv. If the communication has been completed, P_k inserts the received data in its replicated H-Tree and it posts another MPI_Irecv. In any case, the computation of the data to be sent goes on. This procedure is iterated until no more data has to be exchanged. After sending $A_k I_h(op, l)$ for any h, P_k sends, through np-1 MPI_Isend, a syncronization message to any other process and it continues to receive data from them. Since P_k does not know how many data it will receive, it waits for the syncronization message from all the other processes. Then, P_k begins to apply the op to Do_k. A MPI barrier has not been used to syncronize the processes because it is a blocking primitive; hence, after issuing an MPI_Barrier, P_k cannot collect data from other processes. A data exchange among a pair of processes involves variables with distinct datatypes. In order to merge these values in one message, we have compared the adoption of MPI_Pack/ MPI_Unpack against that of derived datatype; both techniques achieve similar execution times.

5   Experimental Results

We present some experimental results of the MPI parallel version of the AMM. The parallel architecture we consider is a Cray T3E; each p-node includes a DEC Alpha EV5 processor and 128Mb of memory. The interconnection network is a torus. MPI primitives are embedded in the C language.

We consider the Poisson problem on the unit square in two dimensions, i.e. the Laplace equation subject to the Dirichlet boundary conditions:

$$-\frac{d^2u}{dx^2} - \frac{d^2u}{dy^2} = f(x,y) \qquad in \qquad \Omega =]0,1[\times]0,1[$$

$$u = h(x,y) \qquad in \qquad \delta\Omega$$

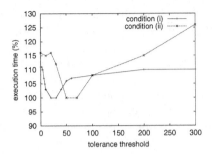

Fig. 1. Load balance

with $f(x, y) = 0$ and two boundary conditions:

$(i)\ h(x, y) = 10$ $\qquad (ii)\ h(x, y) = 10\cos(2\pi(x - y))\dfrac{\sinh(2\pi(x + y + 2))}{\sinh(8\pi)}$

The solution of the Poisson problem is simpler than those of other equations such as the Navier-Stokes one. Hence, the ratio between computational work and parallel overhead is low and this is a significant test for a parallel implementation. The points distribution in the domain in the case of boundary condition *(ii)* is more irregular than the one of *(i)*. In fact, given the same maximum H-Tree depth, the final number of hnodes of H-Tree *(i)* is three times that of H-Tree *(ii)*

In order to evaluate the effectiveness of the informed fault prevention technique, we have measured that, for both the conditions, the data sent in the informed fault prevention are less than 104% than the data required. As previously explained, due to the refinement operator, this percentage cannot be equal to 100%, but the amount of useless data is less than 4%.

Fig. 1 shows the execution time for different values (in percentage) of the tolerance threshold T. The balancing procedure considerably reduces the execution time; in fact, in the worst case, the execution time of an unbalanced computation may be 25% higher than the optimal one. However, if T is less than the optimal value, no benefit is achieved, because the cost of the balancing procedure is larger than the unbalance recovered. Fig. 1 also shows that the optimal value of T depends upon the points distribution in the domain. In fact, the same value of T results in very different execution times for the two conditions; also the lowest execution times have been achieved using distinct values of T for the two equations.

Figure 2 shows the efficiency of the AMM for the two problems, for a fixed initial grid with $k = 7$, see sect 2, the same maximum grid level, 12, and a variable number of p-nodes. The low efficiency resulting in the second problem is due to an highly irregular grid hierarchy. However, even in the worst case, our solution achieves an efficiency larger than 50% even on 16 p-nodes.

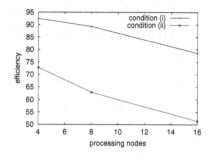

Fig. 2. Efficiency for problems with fixed data dimension

References

[1] F. Baiardi, P. Becuzzi, P. Mori, and M. Paoli. Load balancing and locality in hierarchical N-body algorithms on distributed memory architectures. *Proceedings of HPCN 1998: Lecture Notes in Computer Science*, 1401:284–293, 1998.

[2] F. Baiardi, P. Becuzzi, S.Chiti, P. Mori, and L. Ricci. A hierarchical approach to irregular problems. *Proceedings of Europar 2000: Lecture Notes in Computer Science*.

[3] F. Baiardi, S.Chiti, P. Mori, and L. Ricci. Parallelization of irregular problems based on hierarchical domain representation. *Proceedings of HPCN 2000: Lecture Notes in Computer Science*, 1823:71–80, 2000.

[4] P. Bastian, S. Lang, and K. Eckstein. Parallel adaptive multigrid methods in plane linear elasticity problems. *Numerical linear algebra with appl.*, 4(3):153–176, 1997.

[5] P. Bastian and G. Wittum. Adaptive multigrid methods: The UG concept. In *Adaptive Methods – Algorithms, Theory and Applications*, volume 46 of *Notes on Numerical Fluid Mechanics*, pages 17–37, 1994.

[6] M. Berger and J. Oliger. Adaptive mesh refinement for hyperbolic partial differential equations. *Journal of Computational Physics*, 53:484–512, 1984.

[7] W. Briggs. *A multigrid tutorial.* SIAM, 1987.

[8] M. Griebel and G. Zumbusch. Parallel multigrid in an adaptive pde solver based on hashing. In *Proceeding of ParCo 97*, pages 589–599, 1998.

[9] W.F. Mitchell. Refinement tree based partitioning for adaptive grids. In *Proceedings of the 27th Conference on Parallel Processing for Scientific Computing*, pages 587–592, 1995.

[10] M. Parashar and J.C. Browne. On partitioning dynamic adaptive grid hierarchies. In *Proceeding of the 29th annual Hawaii international conference on system sciences*, 1996.

[11] J.R. Pilkington and S.B. Baden. Dynamic partitioning of non–uniform structured workloads with space filling curves. *Transaction on parallel and distributed systems*, 7(3):288–299, 1996.

[12] Y.N. Vorobjev and H.A. Scheraga. A fast adaptive multigrid boundary element method for macromolecular electrostatic computations in a solvent. *Journal of Computational Chemistry*, 18(4):569–583, 1997.

Multiple Parallel Local Searches
in Global Optimization

Hermanus P.J. Bolton, Jaco F. Schutte, and Albert A. Groenwold

Department of Mechanical Engineering, University of Pretoria,
Pretoria, 0002, South Africa
Albert.Groenwold@eng.up.ac.za
http://vlakvark.me.up.ac.za

Abstract. The unconstrained global programming problem is addressed using an efficient multi-start algorithm, in which parallel local searches contribute towards a Bayesian global stopping criterion.

The stopping criterion, denoted the unified Bayesian global stopping criterion, is based on the mild assumption that the probability of convergence to the global optimum x^* is comparable to the probability of convergence to any local minimum $\tilde{x}_j$.

The combination of the simple multi-start local search strategy and the unified Bayesian global stopping criterion outperforms a number of leading global optimization algorithms, for both serial and parallel implementations. Results for parallel clusters of up to 128 machines are presented.

1 Introduction

Consider the unconstrained (or bounds constrained) mathematical programming problem represented by the following: Given a real valued objective function $f(x)$ defined on the set $x \in D$ in $\mathbb{R}^n$, find the point x^* and the corresponding function value f^* such that

$$f^* = f(x^*) = \min \{f(x) | x \in D\} \tag{1}$$

if x^* exists and is unique. Alternatively, find a low approximation $\tilde{f}$ to f^*.

If the objective function and/or the feasible domain D are non-convex, then there may be many local minima which are not optimal. Hence, from a *mathematical* point of view, Problem (1) is essentially unsolvable, due to a lack of mathematical conditions characterizing the global optimum, as opposed to a strictly convex continuous function, which is characterized by the Karush-Kuhn-Tucker conditions at the minimum.

Optimization algorithms aimed at solving Problem (1) are divided in two classes, namely *deterministic* and *stochastic*. The first class being those algorithms which implicitly search all of the function domain and thus are guaranteed to find the global optimum. The algorithms within this class are forced to deal with restricted classes of functions (e.g. Lipschitz continuous functions with known Lipschitz constants). Even with these restrictions it is often computationally infeasible to apply deterministic algorithms to search for the guaranteed

J. Dongarra et al. (Eds.): EuroPVM/MPI 2000, LNCS 1908, pp. 88–95, 2000.
© Springer-Verlag Berlin Heidelberg 2000

global optimum as the number of computations required increases exponentially with the dimension of the feasible space. To overcome the inherent difficulties of the guaranteed-accuracy algorithms, much research effort has been devoted to algorithms in which a stochastic element is introduced, this way the deterministic guarantee is relaxed into a *confidence measure*. A number of successful algorithms belong to the latter class.

A general stochastic algorithm for global optimization consists of three major steps [1]: a sampling step, an optimization step, and a check of some *global stopping criterion*. The availability of a suitable global stopping criterion is probably the most important aspect of global optimization. It is also the most problematic, due to the very fact that characterization of the global optimum is in general not possible.

Global optimization algorithms and their associated global stopping criteria should ultimately be judged on performance. However, when evaluating global optimization algorithms, the use of *a priori* known information about the objective function under consideration should be refrained from. For example, the termination of algorithms once the known global optimum has been attained within a prescribed tolerance complicates the use of these algorithms, and makes comparisons with other algorithms very difficult.

In this paper a number of very simple heuristic algorithms based on multiple local searches are constructed. A Bayesian stopping condition is presented, based on a criterion previously presented by Snyman and Fatti for their algorithm based on dynamic search trajectories [2]. The criterion is shown to be quite general, and can be applied in combination with any multi-start global search strategy. Since the local searches are independent of each other, they are ideally suited for implementation on a massively parallel processing machine.

2   A Global Stopping Criterion

It is required to calculate $\tilde{f}$, i.e.

$$\tilde{f} = \min \left\{ \tilde{f}^j, \text{ over all } j \text{ to date} \right\} \tag{2}$$

as the approximation to the global minimum f^*. In finding $\tilde{f}$, over-sampling of f should be prevented as far as possible. In addition, an indication of the probability of convergence to the f^* is desirable. A Bayesian argument seems to us the proper framework for the formulation of a such a criterion. Previously, two such criteria have been presented, respectively by Boender and Rinnooy Kan [3], and Snyman and Fatti [2].

The former criterion, denoted the optimal sequential Bayesian stopping rule, is based on an estimate of the number of local minima in D and the relative size of the region of attraction of each local minimum. While apparently effective, computational expense prohibits using this rule for functions with a large number of local minima in D.

The latter criterion is not dependent on an estimate of the number of local minima in D or the regions of attraction of the different local minima. Instead, a simple assumption about the probability of convergence to the global optimum x^* in relation to the probability of convergence to any local minimum $\tilde{x}_j$ is made. In addition, the probability of convergence to f^* can be calculated.

The rule presented by Snyman and Fatti is derived specifically for their dynamic search method, but is in all probability of greater importance and more generally applicable than hitherto realized. In the following, we will show that this rule can be used as a general stopping criterion in multi-start algorithms, albeit for a restricted class of functions. In doing so, we do not consider the region of attraction R_k of local minimum k. Instead, for a given starting point, we simply refer to the probability of convergence α_k to local minimum k.[1] Henceforth, we will denote the rule of Snyman and Fatti the unified Bayesian stopping rule.

2.1   The Unified Bayesian Stopping Rule

Let α_k denote the probability that a random starting point will converge to local minimum $\tilde{x}^k$. Also, the probability of convergence to the global minimum x^* is denoted α^*. The following mild assumption, which is probably true for many functions of practical interest, is now made:

$$\alpha^* \geq \alpha_k \text{ for all local minima } \tilde{x}^k . \tag{3}$$

Furthermore, let r be the number of starting points from which convergence to the current best minimum $\tilde{f}$ occurs after $\tilde{n}$ random searches have been started. Then, under assumption (3), the probability that $\tilde{f}$ is equal to f^* is given by

$$Pr\left[\tilde{f} = f^*\right] \geq q(\tilde{n}, r) = 1 - \frac{(\tilde{n} + \bar{a})! \, (2\tilde{n} + \bar{b})!}{(2\tilde{n} + \bar{a})! \, (\tilde{n} + \bar{b})!} , \tag{4}$$

with $\bar{a} = a + b - 1$, $\bar{b} = b - r - 1$, and a, b suitable parameters of the Beta distribution $\beta(a, b)$. On the basis of (4) the adopted *stopping rule* becomes[2]:

$$\text{STOP when } Pr\left[\tilde{f} = f^*\right] \geq q^* , \tag{5}$$

where q^* is some prescribed desired confidence level, typically chosen as 0.99 - 0.999.

---

[1] Studying simple 1-D search trajectories, we observe that the definition of region of attraction of a local minimum is problematic. Strictly speaking, the region of attraction can only be defined when non-discrete search trajectories (line search or other) are employed.

[2] For the sake of brevity, we refrain from presenting a proof for (4) here. The proof is similar to that presented in [2]. However, we express our proof in terms of the probability of convergence to a local minimum, and not in terms of the region of attraction of the local minimum. Furthermore, no implicit assumption regarding a prior distribution is made.

Table 1. The extended Dixon-Szegö test set

No.	Acronym	Name	No.	Acronym	Function
1	G1	Griewank G1	7	BR	Branin
2	G2	Griewank G2	8	H3	Hartman 3
3	GP	Goldstein-Price	9	H6	Hartman 6
4	C6	Six-hump camelback	10	S5	Shekel 5
5	SH	Shubert, Levi No. 4	11	S7	Shekel 7
6	RA	Rastrigin	12	S10	Shekel 10

3   A Simple Global Search Heuristic

In all probability, the simplest global optimization algorithm is the combination of multiple local searches, combined with some probabilistic stopping criterion. Here, we present such a formulation, and utilize (5). We also provide for a global minimization step. Various sequential algorithms may be constructed using the following framework:

1. **Initialization:** Set the trajectory counter $j := 1$, and prescribe the desired confidence level q^*.
2. **Sampling steps:** Randomly generate $x_0^j \in D$ in $\mathbb{R}^n$.
3. **Global minimization steps:** Starting at x_0^j, attempt to minimize f in a global sense by some preliminary search procedure, viz. find and record some low point $\bar{f}^j \leftrightarrow \bar{x}^j$.
4. **Local minimization steps:** $\bar{x}^j$ is used as the starting point for a robust gradient based convex minimization algorithm, with stopping criteria defined in terms of the Karush-Kuhn-Tucker conditions. Record the lowest function value $\tilde{f}^j \leftrightarrow \tilde{x}^j$.
5. **Global termination:** Assess the global convergence after j searches to date (yielding x^k, $k = 1, 2, \ldots j$) using (5). If (5) is satisfied, STOP, else, $j := j+1$ and goto 2.

Pure multiple local searches are obtained if Step 3 is excluded, with $\bar{x}^j = x_0^j$. We now construct 2 such simple algorithms, namely

1. LLS1: multiple local searches using the bound-constrained BFGS algorithm [4,5], and
2. LLS2: multiple local searches using the unconstrained Polak-Ribiere algorithm [6].

In addition, for both LLS1 and LLS2 we add a global minimization phase (step 3), and denote the respective algorithms GLS1 and GLS2. In the global phase we simulate the trajectories of a bouncing ball (the MBB algorithm, [7]), which is attractive due to it's simplicity. The ball's elasticity coefficient is chosen such that the ball's energy is dissipated very quickly.

Table 2. Number of failures of convergence to the global optimum for 100 (random) restarts of each algorithm for the complete test set. For the problems not listed, the number of failures is 0 for all tabulated values of the prescribed confidence q^*. (Less than 3 failures at $q^* = 0.95$, combined with none at higher values of q^* are not reported)

		Number of Failures			
Algorithm	Function	$q^* = .95$	$q^* = .99$	$q^* = .999$	$q^* = .9999$
GLS1	G1	27	18	6	5
	G2	21	11	4	3
	RA	20	18	6	2
LLS1	G1	39	17	8	4
	G2	12	7	3	2
	RA	54	33	15	4
GLS2	G1	16	12	1	0
	RA	12	8	7	4
LLS2	G1	22	18	7	4
	RA	15	12	7	2
SF [2]	G1	6	2	1	1
	G2	52	29	12	12
	SH	54	43	20	18
	RA	38	18	6	6

4   Parallel Implementation

The search trajectories generated in our algorithms are completely independent of each other. Hence the sequential algorithm presented in section 3 may easily be parallelized. To this extent, we utilize the freely available pvm3 [8] code for FORTRAN, running under the Linux operating system. Currently, the massive parallel processing virtual machine (MPPVM) consists of up to 128 Pentium III 450 MHz machines in an existing undergraduate computer lab.

The distributed computing model represents a master-slave configuration where the master program assigns tasks and interprets results, while the slaves compute the search trajectories. The workload is statically assigned, and no inter-slave communication occurs. The master program informs each slave task of the optimization problem parameters by a single broadcast and awaits individual results from each slave.

4.1   A Measure of Computational Effort

We will assume that our algorithm will ultimately be used in problems for which the CPU requirements of evaluating f is orders of magnitudes larger than the time required for message passing and algorithm internals. (In structural optimization, for example, each function evaluation typically involves a complete

Table 3. Comparison with some other algorithms. For the problems listed, the number of function values N_{fe} for the different algorithms are reported

Problem	GLS1	LLS1	GLS2	LLS2	SF [2]	[10,11]	[12,13]	[14]
G1	2644	10678	2992	7215	5063	1822	396147	3623
G2	1882	1675	2398	1510	86672	10786	828441	16121
GP	454	229	403	471	2069	6775	94587	7450
C6	238	108	275	225	602	579	76293	3711
SH	1715	1626	1363	1485	93204	1443	139087	3788
RA	2893	1487	3119	3161	45273	3420	445711	2051
BR	211	240	552	724	9553	594	71688	4769
H3	289	199	478	462	1695	915	103466	1698
H6	346	266	521	588	3550	3516	106812	9933
S5	315	479	353	607	6563	1772	234654	1915
S7	273	473	417	555	1848	1923	212299	4235
S10	382	508	449	564	1604	2631	330486	4226

finite element or boundary element analysis.) Hence we define a somewhat unconventional measure for the cost of our parallelized algorithm which we denote *apparent visible cost* (N_{vc}). This cost represents the number of function evaluations associated with the random starting point x_0^j which results in the most expensive search trajectory. The time window (in CPU seconds) associated with this search trajectory is denoted the *virtual CPU time*. The virtual CPU time includes the time window associated with initialization and evaluation of stopping criterion (5).

5 Numerical Results

The algorithms are tested using an extended Dixon-Szegö test set, presented in Table 1. The 12 well known functions used are given in, for instance, [9].

Firstly, Table 2 shows the effect of the prescribed confidence level q^* in stopping criterion (5). The decreasing number of failures of convergence to f^* as q^* increases illustrates the general applicability of the unified Bayesian global stopping rule. All of the new algorithms outperform the SF algorithm, for which algorithm the stopping criterion was originally derived.

Table 3 reveals that the simple sequential algorithms presented herein compare very favorably with a number of leading contenders, namely the Snyman-Fatti algorithm [2], clustering [10,11], algorithm 'sigma' [12,13] and the algorithm presented by Mockus [14]. All the algorithms were started from different random starting points, and the reported cost is the average of 10 independent runs. In particular, the results for two very difficult test functions, namely Griewank G1 and Griewank G2 [15], are encouraging: Few algorithms find the solution to G2, (which has a few thousand local minima in the region of interest), in less than some 20000 function evaluations.

Table 4. Apparent visual cost N_{vc} for a 32-node parallel virtual machine and a 128 node parallel virtual machine. N_{vc} may be compared with the number of function evaluations N_{fe} of the sequential GLS1 algorithm. r represents the number of starting points from which convergence to the current best minimum $\tilde{f}$ occurs after $\tilde{n}$ random searches have been started. The probability that $\tilde{f}$ is equal to f^* is given by $q(\tilde{n}, r)$

	GLS1			32-node pvm			128-node pvm		
Prob.	N_{fe}	$r/\tilde{n}$	$q(\tilde{n},r)$	N_{vc}	$r/\tilde{n}$	$q(\tilde{n},r)$	N_{vc}	$r/\tilde{n}$	$q(\tilde{n},r)$
G1	1599	6 / 76	0.9929	90	6 / 96	0.9929	30	7 / 128	0.9965
G2	2122	6 / 50	0.9933	189	6 / 96	0.9928	74	7 / 128	0.9965
GP	341	5 / 12	0.9903	40	18 / 32	1.0000	39	59 / 128	1.0000
C6	163	5 / 9	0.9923	22	19 / 32	1.0000	22	75 / 128	1.0000
SH	1290	6 / 49	0.9933	89	9 / 64	0.9993	50	17 / 128	1.0000
RA	817	6 / 41	0.9935	96	8 / 128	0.9982	26	9 / 128	0.9992
BR	107	4 / 4	0.9921	78	31 / 32	1.0000	76	120 / 128	1.0000
H3	207	5 / 8	0.9932	32	18 / 32	1.0000	32	77 / 128	1.0000
H6	288	5 / 8	0.9932	60	21 / 32	1.0000	59	79 / 128	1.0000
S5	132	5 / 8	0.9932	22	6 / 32	0.9939	52	52 / 128	1.0000
S7	293	6 / 17	0.9953	25	14 / 32	1.0000	37	56 / 128	1.0000
S10	336	6 / 17	0.9953	32	11 / 32	0.9999	39	48 / 128	1.0000

Finally, Table 4 reveals the effect of parallel implementation. For relatively 'simple' problems (viz. problems with few design variables or few local minima in the design space), the probability of convergence to the global optimum becomes very high when the number of nodes is increased. This is illustrated by, for example, the results for the C6 problem. For more difficult problems (e.g. the G1 and G2 problems), the probability of convergence to the global optimum f^* is increased.

Simultaneously, the total computational time, (as compared to the sequential GLS1 algorithm), decreases notably. For the 32-node parallel virtual machine, the virtual CPU time to evaluate all the test functions on average decreases by a factor of 1.93 (not shown in tabulated form). The time associated with message passing is negligible compared to the time associated with the global searches.

When the time associated with a single function evaluations become much larger than the time required for algorithm internals, the fraction N_{fe}/N_{vc} based on Table 4 may be used as a direct indication of the decrease in virtual computational time obtainable as a result of parallelization. For the G2 problem, this would imply a reduction in computational time by a factor of 28.68 for the 128-node parallel virtual machine.

6   Conclusions

We have presented a number of efficient multi-start algorithms for the unconstrained global programming problem, based on simple local searches. A salient point is the availability of a suitable stopping criterion, which we denote the unified Bayesian global stopping criterion.

Parallelization is shown to be an effective method to reduce the computational time associated with the solution of expensive global programming problems. While the apparent computational effort is reduced, the probability of convergence to the global optimum is simultaneously increased.

References

1. Schoen, F. Stochastic techniques for global optimization: A survey of recent advances, *J. Global Optim.*, **1** (1991) 207-228
2. Snyman, J.A. and Fatti, L.P. A multi-start global minimization algorithm with dynamic search trajectories, *J. Optim. Theory Appl.*, **54** (1987) 121-141
3. Boender, C.G.E., Rinnooy Kan, A.H.G. A Bayesian analysis of the number of cells of a multinomial distribution, *Statistician*, **32** (1983) 240-248
4. Byrd, R.H., Lu, P., Nocedal, J. and Zhu, C. A limited memory algorithm for bound constrained optimization, *SIAM J. Scient. Comput.*, **16** (1995) 1190-1208
5. Zhu, C., Byrd, R.H., Lu, P. and Nocedal, J. L-BFGS-B: FORTRAN subroutines for large scale bound constrained optimization, *Tech. Report, NAM-11*, EECS Department, Northwestern University (1994)
6. Gilbert, J.C. and Nocedal, J. Global convergence properties of conjugate gradient methods, *SIAM Journal on Optimization*, **2** (1992) 21-42
7. Groenwold, A.A. and Snyman, J.A. Global optimization using dynamic search trajectories, *Proc., Conf. of Discrete and Global Optimization*, Chania, Crete (1998)
8. Geist, A., Beguelin, A, Dongarra, J., Jiang, W., Manchek, R. and Sunderam, V. Pvm: Parallel Virtual Machine system, `ftp://netlib2.cs.utk.edu/pvm3/`, ver. 3.4 (1997)
9. Törn, A. and Zilinskas, A. *Global optimization: Lecture notes in computer science*, No.350, Springer-Verlag, Berlin Heidelberg (1989)
10. Boender, C.G.E., Rinnooy Kan, A.H.G., Timmer, G.T. and Stougie, L. A stochastic method for global optimization, *Math. Program.*, **22** (1982) 125-140
11. Rinnoy Kan, A.H.G. and Timmer, G.T. Stochastic global optimization methods, Part I: Clustering methods, *Mathemat. Program.*, **39** (1987) 27-56
12. Aluffi-Pentini, F., Parisi, V. and Zirilli, F. Global optimization and stochastic differential equations, *J. Optim. Theory Appl.*, **47** (1985) 1-16
13. Aluffi-Pentini, F., Parisi, V. and Zirilli, F. SIGMA - A stochastic-integration global minimization algorithm, *ACM Trans. Math. Softw.*, **14** (1988) 366-380
14. Mockus, J. *Bayesian approach to global optimization*, Kluwer Academic Publishers, Dordrecht (1989)
15. Griewank, A.O. Generalized descent for global optimization, *J. Optim. Theory Appl.*, **34** (1981) 11-39

Towards Standard Nested Parallelism

J.A. González [1], C. León[1], F. Piccoli[2], M. Printista[2], J.L. Roda[1], C. Rodríguez[1], and
F. Sande[1]

[1] DEIOC. Universidad de La Laguna.
Facultad de Matemáticas. Tenerife. Spain
casiano@ull.es
[2] D. Informática. Universidad Nacional de San Luis
Ejército de los Andes 950. San Luis. Argentina
{mpiccoli, mprinti}@unsl.edu.ar

Abstract. Several generalizations of the flat data parallel model have been
proposed. Their aim is to allow the capability of nested parallel invocations,
combining the easiness of programming of the data parallel model with the
efficiency of the control parallel model. We examine the solutions provided to
this issue by two standard parallel programming platforms, OpenMP and MPI.
Both their expression capacity and their efficiency are compared on a Sun HPC
3500 and a SGI Origin 2000. The two considered architectures are shared
memory and, consequently, more suitable for their exploitation under OpenMP.
In spite of this, the results prove that, under the use of the methodology
proposed for MPI in this paper, not only the performances of the two platforms
are similar but, more remarkably, the effort invested in software development is
also the same.

1. Introduction

Data parallelism is one of the more successful efforts to introduce explicit parallelism
to high level programming languages. The approach is taken because many useful
computations can be framed in terms of a set of independent sub-computations, each
strongly associated with an element of a large data structure. Such computations are
inherently parallelizable. Data parallel programming is particularly convenient for
two reasons. The first, is its easiness of programming. The second is that it can scale
easily to larger problem sizes. Several data parallel language implementations are
available now [2]. However, almost all discussion of data parallelism has been limited
to the simplest and least expressive form: unstructured data parallelism (flat). Several
generalizations of the data parallel model have been proposed which permit the
nesting of data parallel constructors to specify parallel computation across nested and
irregular data structures [1]. These extensions include the capability of nested parallel
invocations, combining the facility of programming on a data parallel model with the
efficiency of the control parallel model in the execution on irregular data structures.
We examine the solutions provided by two standard parallel programming platforms,
OpenMP and *MPI* comparing their expression capacity and their efficiency in two

J. Dongarra et al. (Eds.): EurPVM/MPI 2000, LNCS 1908, pp. 96-103, 2000.
© Springer-Verlag Berlin Heidelberg 2000

shared memory architectures. The first is a Sun HPC 3500 UltraSPARC II based system with 8 processors and 8 Gbytes of shared memory. The second platform considered is an Origin 2000 Silicon Graphics, with 64 MIPS R10000 processors and 8 Gbytes of main memory. The two architectures are shared memory and consequently more suitable for their exploitation under the shared-variable programming model. Despite of this, the conclusion of this work is that, under the use of an appropriate methodology not only the performances of the two platforms are comparable but, more remarkably, the effort invested in software development is also the same.

From the unlimited scope of applications that benefit from nested parallelism, we have chosen the Divide and Conquer technique since it provides an excellent scenario for benchmarking. Both the general technique and the particular case that will be considered all along the paper are introduced in section 2. The two following sections describe in detail the expression of a Nested Parallel Fast Fourier Transform, exploiting both data and code parallelism in MPI and OpenMP. The fifth section presents the computational results in the two mentioned machines. From these results and the comparative study of the codes we elaborated the conclusions in section 6.

2. Divide and Conquer as a Test Bed for Nested Parallelism

Let us consider the special case of the divide and conquer approach presented in Fig. 1 where both the solutions r and the problems x have a vectorial nature. In such case there are opportunities to exploit parallelism not only at the task level (line 7) but also in the divide and combine subroutines (lines 6 and 8). Thus, data parallelism can be introduced by doing every processor in the current group to work in a subsection of the array x in the division phase (respectively a subsection of r in the combination phase).

```
1   procedure pDC(x: problem; r: solution);
2   begin
3     if trivial(x) then conquer(x, r)
4     else
5     begin
6       divide(x, x0, x1);
7       parallel do pDC(x0, r0) || pDC(x1, r1));
8       combine(r, r0, r1);
9     end;
10  end;
```

Fig. 1. General frame for a parallel divide and conquer algorithm

As benchmark instance for this paper we will consider the Fast Fourier Transform (FFT) algorithm. However, the proposed techniques have been applied to other divide and conquer algorithms with similar results. Consider a sequence of complex numbers $a=(a[0], ..., a[N-1])$ of length N. The Discrete Fast Fourier Transform (DFT) of the sequence a is the sequence $A=(A[0], ..., A[N-1])$ given by $A[i] = \sum_{k=0..N-1} a[k] \ w^{ki}$, where $w = e^{2\pi\sqrt{-1}/N}$ is the primitive nth root of the unity in the complex plane. The following decomposition can be deduced from the definition:

$$A[i] = \sum_{k=0..N/2-1} a[2k]\, w^{2ki} + w^i \sum_{k=0..N/2-1} a[2k+1]\, w^{(2k+1)i}$$

From this formula, it follows that the DFT A of a can be obtained by combining the DFT B of the even components and the DFT C of the odd components of a.

3. Nested Parallelism in MPI

The code in Fig. 2 shows a nested implementation of the DFT using MPI [3]. The algorithm assumes that the input vector a is replicated onto the initial set of processors, while the resulting DFT A is delivered block distributed. For simplicity, let also assume that the number of elements N is larger than the number of processors p in the initial set, and that both N and p, are powers of 2. Parameter Np holds the quotient N/p, W is the vector containing the powers of the primitive n-th root of the unity and vector D is used as a temporary buffer during the combination.

```
1    void parDandCFFT(Complex *A, Complex *a, Complex *W, unsigned Np,
2                     unsigned stride, Complex *D) {
3      Complex Aux, *pW;
4      unsigned i, size;
5      if(NUMPROCESSORS > 1) {
6        /* Division phase */
7        size = Np*sizeof(Complex);
8        /* Subproblems resolution phase */
9        PAR(parDandCFFT(A, a, W, Np, stride<<1, D), A, size,
10           parDandCFFT(D, a+stride, W, Np, stride<<1, A), D, size);
11       /* Combination phase */
12       for(i = 0, pW = W+(Np*NAME*stride); i < Np; i++, pW += stride)
       {
13         Aux.re = pW->re * D[i].re - pW->im * D[i].im;
14         Aux.im = pW->re * D[i].im + pW->im * D[i].re;
15         A[i].re += Aux.re;
16         A[i].im += Aux.im;
17       }
18     }
19     else
20       seqFFT(A, a, W, N, stride, D);
21   }
```

Fig. 2. Nested parallel DFT implementation using MPI

The key point in this code is the use of the macro PAR in line 9. The call to macro $PAR(f_1, p_1, s_1, f_2, p_2, s_2)$ is expanded to the code showed in Fig. 3, dividing the current group of processors in two subgroups. Each processor is assigned to a subgroup, and the replicated variable $NUMPROCESSORS$ holds the number of processors in its group. While the first subgroup executes function f_1 (line 7 in Fig. 3), the second one does the same with function f_2 (line 14 in Fig. 3). After that, the two subgroups exchange the results of their computations (lines 8 and 15 in Fig. 3), which are constituted by s_i bytes pointed by p_i. This exchange is done in a pair-wise manner, in such a way that each processor in one of the subgroups sends their results to its corresponding partner in the other subgroup. Variable *ll_partner* indicates the processor in the other subgroup that holds the corresponding elements to be combined with. Variables *NAME* and *LL_NAME* contain, respectively, the logical processor name in the current group and the physical processor name. When this is done, the subgroups rejoin to the original one. This methodology can be straightforwardly expanded for non-binary divisions.

The trivial case in this D&C algorithm is reached when only one processor stays in a group. This case is treated by the procedure *seqFFT* (line 20 in Fig. 2), which is simply the result obtained serializing the code in Fig. 2. While the division phase has been reduced to a simple variable initialization (line 7), the combination phase can be done cooperatively by all the processors in the group. This is possible because partner processors can perform a symmetrical computation using the appropriated subset of elements from the replicated vector *W*. These elements are separated *stride* positions and are pointed by *pW* in the combination loop (line 12).

```
1    #define PAR(f1, r1, s1, f2, r2, s2) {                    \
2    unsigned ll_partner;                                     \
3    MPI_Status status;                                       \
4    NUMPROCESSORS >>= 1;                                     \
5    ll_partner = LL_NAME ^ NUMPROCESSORS;                    \
6    if((NAME & NUMPROCESSORS) == 0) {                        \
7      f1;                                                    \
8      MPI_Sendrecv(r1, s1, MPI_BYTE, ll_partner, NUMPROCESSORS, \
9                   r2, s2, MPI_BYTE, ll_partner, NUMPROCESSORS, \
10                 MPI_COMM_WORLD, &status);                  \
11   }                                                        \
12   else {                                                   \
13     NAME &= (NUMPROCESSORS-1);                             \
14     f2;                                                    \
15     MPI_Sendrecv(r2, s2, MPI_BYTE, ll_partner, NUMPROCESSORS, \
16                  r1, s1, MPI_BYTE, ll_partner, NUMPROCESSORS, \
17                  MPI_COMM_WORLD, &status);                 \
18     NAME |= NUMPROCESSORS;                                 \
19   }                                                        \
20   NUMPROCESSORS <<= 1;                                     \
21 }
```

Fig. 3. Macro *PAR* implementation using MPI

Although the natural way to express nested parallelism in MPI is through the use of communicators and the function *MPI_Comm_split*, it carries a considerable overhead since its execution implies communications. Fig. 4 presents the results of comparing the time taken by *MPI_Comm_split* on a CRAY T3D with different number p of processors (curves labeled *MPI-p*). For each value of p, the experiment consisted in the repetition of N iterations (represented in the horizontal axis) of a loop partitioning the current communicator. The three curves labeled *PAR-p* show the time taken when the division (and reunification) is performed using the alternative division technique proposed above. They appear overlapped in the X-axis since the times they took are negligible compared with the time needed by the *MPI_Comm_split* version.

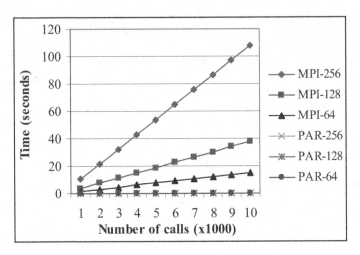

Fig. 4. The cost of *MPI_Comm_split* vs. *PAR*

4.   Nested Parallelism in OpenMP

OpenMP [5] defines a set of compiler directives, library routines and environment variables that extend Fortran API and separately C and C++ API [4] to express shared memory parallelism. Support for nested parallelism is included in the standard. If a thread in a team executing a parallel region reaches another parallel construct, it creates a new team and it becomes the master of that new team. Nested parallel regions are serialized by default. As a result, a team composed of only one thread executes a nested parallel region. The default behavior may be changed using either the runtime library function *omp_set_nested* or the environment variable *OMP_NESTED*, in which case the number of threads in the team is implementation dependent. However, when a nested parallel region is reached, an implementation is always allowed to create a team composed of only one thread. Unfortunately this is the common case for most commercial OpenMP implementations.

Fig. 5 presents an implementation of the DFT algorithm using OpenMP. This algorithm works with the same assumptions that algorithm presented in previous section. In line 17, the directive *parallel* opens a parallel region and the use of the clause *firstprivate* ensures that each thread in the team takes its own initialized copy of the variables *n, B* and *C*, while the rest of the variables are shared by default. Each recursive call to the routine *ompFFT* is enclosed as a section in the work-sharing construct *sections* (lines 19-25). As a result, each of them will be executed once by a thread in the team. In the first call, all available threads will compose the team in the parallel region but in the subsequent nested calls the number of threads in a team is implementation dependent, and following the standard specifications, a compiler is allowed to assign only the current thread to the corresponding team. There is an implicit barrier at the end of the construct *sections* that is needed before performing the combination phase (lines 28-39). The combination is also executed in parallel by the work-sharing construct *for*, which makes a partition in the set of iterations. The clause *schedule(static)* forces a block distribution of equal chunk size among all threads in the team. After that, the parallel region is closed and the execution continues in a sequential way.

```
1    void ompFFT(Complex *A, Complex *a, Complex *W, unsigned  N,
2                unsigned stride, Complex *D) {
3      Complex *B, *C;
4      Complex Aux, *pW;
5      unsigned n;
6      int i;
7      if(N == 1) {
8        A[0].re = a[0].re;
9        A[0].im = a[0].im;
10     }
11     else {
12       /* Division phase */
13       n = (N >> 1);
14       B = D;
15       C = D + n;
16       /* Subproblems resolution phase */
17       #pragma omp parallel firstprivate(n, B, C)
18       {
19         #pragma omp sections
20         {
21           #pragma omp section
22             ompFFT(B, a, W, n, stride<<1, A);
23           #pragma omp section
24             ompFFT(C, a+stride, W, n, stride<<1, A+n);
25         }
26         /* Combination phase */
27         pW = W;
28         #pragma omp for private(Aux)
29                         firstprivate(pW)
30                         schedule(static)
31         for(i = 0; i < n; i++) {
32           Aux.re = pW->re * C[i].re - pW->im * C[i].im;
33           Aux.im = pW->re * C[i].im + pW->im * C[i].re;
34           A[i].re = B[i].re + Aux.re;
35           A[i].im = B[i].im + Aux.im;
36           A[i+n].re = B[i].re - Aux.re;
37           A[i+n].im = B[i].im - Aux.im;
38           pW += stride;
39         }
40       }
41     }
42   }
```

Fig. 5. FFT implementation using OpenMP

Recent works have pointed out the necessity of more flexible control structures that allow OpenMP to handle common programming idioms like recursive control and list or tree data structures. Extensions to the standard have been proposed, as the Workqueuing model [6] and other for groups creation [1]. The Workqueuing model introduces two new directives to OpenMP: *taskq* and *task*. The first causes an empty queue to be created and a single thread executes the code inside the *taskq* block. The second one specifies a unit of work, to be enqueued in the queue created by the enclosing *taskq* block, which can be dequeued and executed by any thread. *Taskq* directives may be nested inside each other, generating a logical tree of queues. On the other hand, in [1] two new clauses are proposed: *groups* and *onto*. *Groups* can be applied to the work-sharing constructs *for* and *sections* and allows creating sets of specified number of threads. The second proposed clause permits to assign each *section* to a previously created group. In this case, nesting of work-sharing constructs could be handled by subgroups creation. Both extensions have available running implementations (http://www.kai.com/parallel/kappro/), (http://www.cepba.upc.es/nanos.html).

Alternatively we can still implement the FFT algorithm using the schedule thread methodology presented in the MPI section.

5. Comparative: Expression Capacity and Efficiency

The experiences were carried out in the Sun HPC 3500 UltraSPARC II based system at Edinburgh Parallel Computing Centre (8 processors and 8 Gbytes of shared memory) and the Origin 2000 Silicon Graphics, (64 MIPS R10000 processors and 8 Gbytes of main memory) at European Center for Parallelism of Barcelona. The OpenMP implementation used in the Sun was the delivered by Kuck and Associated Inc (KAI). The Origin compiler version was the MIPSpro 7.30. Both MPI libraries were the native implementations. Experiments were carried out with different vector sizes. Respectively, Table 1 and Table 2 present the measured time with a vector size of 1 million elements on both platforms.

PROCS	OMP	OMP_LL	MPI
1	-	4.756	4.719
2	-	2.615	2.733
4	-	1.423	1.593
8	-	0.883	0.919

Table 1. FFT. 1 million elements. Sun HPC 3500.

Column labeled MPI corresponds to the code presented in Fig. 2, while columns labeled OMP and OMP_LL respectively correspond to code presented in Fig. 5 and the improved OpenMP implementation using the methodology described in section 3.

PROCS	OMP	OMP_LL	MPI
1	10.772	9.763	9.091
2	9.713	7.214	7.201
4	9.028	5.806	3.604
8	7.173	4.378	2.211

Table 2. FFT. 1 million elements. SGI Origin 2000.

Although the Silicon compiler detects the existence of nested parallelism, it is unable to exploit it. The little improvement observed as processor number increases is due to the data parallelism exploited during the combination phase. Even worse, the KAI compiler does not generate the correct code and the corresponding column in Table 1 is empty.

It can be observed that the MPI and OpenMP_LL times on the Sun Multiprocessor are comparable. Once the macro PAR is encapsulated in a header file, both source codes are almost the same. However, the OpenMP_LL scalability is worse than the MPI one on the SGI Origin. The explicit locality of the MPI version seems to have an impact in a shared distributed architecture.

6. Conclusions

Both the Sun HPC 3500 and the SGI Origin 2000 are shared memory architectures and hence more appropriate for their exploitation under OpenMP. Although OpenMP allows the explicit expression of nested parallelism, the current implementations are unable to take advantage of it. On the other hand, the use of directives to implement work-shared constructs makes OpenMP more suited than MPI to exploit data parallelism. The use of the methodology presented in section 3 for MPI allows the same high level of expression than the exemplified in Fig. 5 without paying any penalties in the performance.

Acknowledgements

We wish to thank to CCCC (Barcelona), CIEMAT (Madrid) and EPCC (Edinburgh) for allowing us the access to their computational resources. This research has been partially supported by CICYT under project TIC1999-0754-C03.

References

1   Ayguadé E., González M., Labarta J., Martorell X., Navarro N. and Oliver J. *NanosCompiler: A Research Platform for OpenMP Extensions.* Proceedings of the First European Workshop on OpenMP, 1999

2   Blelloch G.E., Hardwick J.C., Sipelstein J., Zagha M. and Chatterjee S. *Implementation of a Portable Nested Data-Parallel Lenguage.* Journal of Parallel and Distributed Computing, vol. 21, pp. 4-14, 1994

3   Gropp W., Lusk E., Doss N. And Skjellum A. *A High-Performance. Portable Implementation Of The Mpi Message Passing Interface Standard.* Journal of Parallel Computing, vol. 22, number 6, pp.789-828, Sep 1996.

4   OpenMP Architecture Review Board. *OpenMP C and C++ Application Program Interface.* Version 1.0. October 1998. http://www.openmp.org

5   OpenMP Architecture Review Board. *OpenMP: A Proposed Industry Standard API for Shared Memory Programming.* White paper October 1997, http://www.openmp.org

6   Shah S., Haab G., Peterson P. and Throop J. *Flexible Control Structures for Parallelism in OpenMP.* Proceedings of the First European Workshop on OpenMP, 1999

Pipeline Algorithms on MPI: Optimal Mapping of the Path Planing Problem [1]

Daniel González, Francisco Almeida, Luz Marina Moreno, Casiano Rodríguez

Dpto. Estadística, I. O. y Computacion, Universidad de La Laguna,
La Laguna, Spain
{dgonmor, falmeida, casiano}@ull.es

Abstract. The portability of parallel programs has involved lot of effort during the last decade. PVM and MPI have greatly contributed to solve this drawback and nowadays most parallel programs are portable. However, the portability of the efficiency suffers, in many cases, from inherent effects of the target architectures. The optimal mapping of a parallel program is strongly dependent on the granularity and network architecture. We broach the problem of finding the optimal mapping of pipeline MPI programs. We propose an analytical model that allows an easy estimation of the parameters needed to obtain the mapping. The model is capable to be introduced into tools to produce this mapping automatically. Both the accuracy of the model and the optimal efficiency of the algorithm found are contrasted on a pipeline algorithm for the Path Planning Problem.

1 Introduction

Many pipeline algorithms show an optimal behavior when they are just considered from the theoretical point of view in which so many processors as the number of inputs are available. However, most of them run poorly when they are executed over current architectures. The implementation of pipeline algorithms on a target architecture is strongly conditioned by the actual assignment of virtual processes to the physical processors and their simulation, the granularity of the architecture, and the instance of the problem to be executed. To preserve the optimality of the algorithm, a proper combination of these factors must be considered.

Several software approaches to solve this problem have been provided by different authors. Although HPF is a data parallel language, the version 2.0 [5] approved extensions introduce the constructs to express pipeline parallelism. However, the only existing HPF implementation conforming to the extensions [3] does not deal with the optimal mapping of these algorithms. The same occurs with P3L, an skeleton oriented language allowing the expression of pipelining and its combination with other paradigms as farming, prefixes, etc. [4]. This absence of software contrasts with the amount of theoretical works. Most of them solve the case under particular assumptions. Good solutions are known for the case when the computation occurring between successive communications is constant [1], [2], [9]. The general approach followed in

---

[1] The work described in this paper has been partially supported by the Canary Government Research Project PI1999/122.

J. Dongarra et al. (Eds.): EuroPVM/MPI 2000, LNCS 1908, pp. 104–112, 2000.

those works consists of finding a cost model. This model leads to an optimization problem whose solution for some particular cases can be analytically expressed. Unfortunately, the inclusion of the former methodologies in a software tool is far of being a practicable task.

The *llp* tool presented in [8] allows cyclic and block-cyclic mapping of pipeline algorithms according to the user specifications. Llp is conceived as a macro based library and its portability is guaranteed since is built on top of standard message passing libraries (MPI, PVM). We have provided it with a buffering functionality and it is also an objective of this paper to supply a mechanism that allows *llp* to generate automatically the optimal mapping.

In section 2 we discuss some issues associated to the problem of mapping a virtual pipeline into a physical ring of processors. We introduce the necessities for finding an optimal grain of processes, an optimal buffering of data and an efficient virtualization. In section 3 the Path Planning Problem is formulated and a pipeline dynamic programming algorithm is described. In section 4 we propose an analytical model that allows an estimation of the parameters involved in the optimal mapping. The accuracy of the model is contrasted with the Path Plannning Problem in section 5. According to the computational experience, the numerical approach followed with the estimation of the parameters shows an acceptable error in the prediction. As we conclude in section 6, this numerical approximation is suitable to be introduced in a tool that automatically generates the optimal mapping.

The computational experience has been developed under a Cray T3E. A 3 dimensional torus with distributed memory on shared address space. It has 16 DEC 211164 processors. Each processor has 128 Mb of memory and reaches 600 Mflops.

2   The Problem

The mapping problem is defined as finding the optimal assignment of computations to processors to minimize the execution time. We consider that the code executed by every virtual process of the pipeline is the standard loop of figure 1. In the loop that we consider, $body_0$ take constant time while $body_1$ and $body_2$ depends on the iteration of the loop. The code of figure 1 represents a wide range of situations as is the case of many parallel Dynamic Programming algorithms [6], [10].

The virtual processes running this code must be assigned among the available processors. This is the problem of finding an efficient mapping of

```
void f() {
    Compute(body0);
    While (running)
    {
        Receive();
        Com-
pute(body1);
        Send();
        Com-
pute(body2);
    }
}
```

Fig. 1. Standard loop on a pipeline algorithm.

the virtual pipeline on the actual parallel machine. The classical technique consists of partitioning the set of processes following a mixed block-cyclic mapping depending on the Grain G of processes assigned to each processor. Implementation is achieved on a one way ring topology where the first and last processor are connected through a buffering process.

The straightforward technique to obtain block-cyclic mapping consisting of performing G sequential executions of the f function in each processor is not a good approximation. The delay introduced by each processor produces a parallel algorithm as slow as the sequential one. To obtain an efficient implementation, processors must start to work as soon as possible and they must be fed with data when needed. Efficient implementations are obtained when the context switch between processes is performed every time a process communicates a value.

We can now formulate a first question: *Which is the optimal value for G?*

Another important factor is how data are communicated between processors. It must be taken into consideration that we are dealing with intensive communication applications. According to the granularity of the architecture (the ratio of the time required for a basic communication to the time required for a basic computation) and the grain size G of the computation, it is convenient to buffer the data communicated into the sender processor before an output be produced. When the outputs fill the size of the buffer, data are sent as a single packet. Buffering data reduces the overhead in communications but can introduce delays between processors increasing the startup of the pipeline. The size B of the Buffer is an important parameter to be considered when mapping a pipeline algorithm.

We introduce the second question: *Which is the optimal value for B?*

An experimental analysis of the problem imposes a wide range of executions varying the grain G, the size of the buffer B and the number of processors p. The amount of parameters involved force to the building of tools that simplify the effort invested by the programmer in the development.

La Laguna Pipeline [8], *llp*, is a general purpose tool for the pipeline programming paradigm. The user specifies the code for the first processor, for the last processor and the code for a general processor (code of figure 1) of a virtually infinite pipeline. Llp enrolls the virtual pipeline into a simulation loop according to the mapping policy specified. Llp supports cyclic, blocking and blocking-cyclic policies. The block-cyclic mapping is implemented using the Unix standard library "*setjmp.h*". This library allows unconditional jumps to variable labels. The tool differentiates between internal and external communications of the virtual processors. On every internal communication a context switch is performed using the functions *setjmp()* and *longjmp()* of the former library. Since the context switch is implemented very efficiently, the overhead introduced by the tool on a block-cyclic mapping is minimum.

Llp also provides a directive to pack the data produced on the external communications into a single buffer-packet. The user can specify the number of elements B to be buffered and fits the size of the packet according to the communication parameters (latency and bandwidth) of the network on the target architecture. In [8] we show that the performances obtained with *llp* are similar to those obtained by an experienced programmer using standard message passing libraries.

3   The Path Planning Problem

As an example to illustrate the importance of a good election of the parameters G and B, we are going to consider the Path Planning Problem (PPP). A map is an $m * n$ grid of positions for some positive integers m, n. The eight neighbours of a position p are indicated by the corresponding cardinal point in the compass (fig. 2-a).

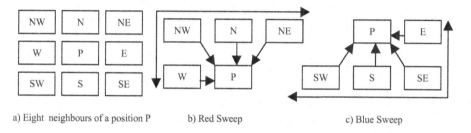

a) Eight neighbours of a position P   b) Red Sweep   c) Blue Sweep

Fig2. Neighborhood dependencies on the PPP.

Each position p is associated with a non-negative real-number $tc(p)$ corresponding to the transversability cost of the position. Given a position p and a neighbour q of p, the edge (p, q) is weighted with a cost $c(p, q) = (tc(p)+tc(q))/2$ if $q \in \{N, S, W, E\}$ and $c(p, q) = (tc(p) + tc(q)) * \sqrt{2}/2$ otherwise: the $\sqrt{2}$ multiplier reflects the added travelling distance due to the diagonal connection. Given a position, called the source, we want to compute the shortest path (or minimum-cost path) from it to every position in the map. A dynamic programming algorithm to solve the problem has been proposed in [7]. The algorithm performs a succession of red and blue sweeps of the map. On the red sweep, a forwarded scan of the map M in the row-major ordering is performed. Each position p is updated according to the red mask depicted in fig 2-b. On the blue sweep, a reversed scan of the map in the row-major ordering is performed. Each position p is updated according to the blue mask depicted in fig 2-c. The best-known cost $f(p)$ in the red and blue sweep is updated according to formula (I) and (II), respectively. The red and blue sweeps are performed alternatively until no values are changed in one sweep. A general stage of the parallel algorithm appears in figure 3.

$$f(P) = min \{f(P), f(W)+c(W, P), f(N)+c(N,P), f(NW)+c(NW, P), f(NE)+c(NE, P)\} \ (I)$$

$$f(P) = min \{f(P), f(E)+c(E, P), f(S)+c(S,P), f(SW)+c(SW, P), f(SE)+c(SE, P)\} \ (II)$$

Fig. 4 presents the running times obtained for G ranging from 1 to 32 and B varying from 1 to 512, on each number of processors. Values for G and B out of these ranges, produce worst running times. The test problem is a 1024*1024 map. When the number of processors increases the product G times B must be reduced to decrease the contention of initialisation while keeping a low latency in communications. The minimum is in a valley that moves depending on the number of processors.

4   The Analytical Model

Given a parallel machine, we aim to find an analytical model to obtain the optimal values of *G* and *B* for an instance of a problem. This problem has been previously formulated by [2] using tiling. The size of the tiles must be determined assumed the shape. However, the approach taken assumes that the computational bodies 0 and 2 in the loop are empty and body 1 takes constant time on each iteration. Also, the considerations about the simulation of the virtual processes are omitted.

Obviously, the analytical model involves both the parallel algorithm and the parallel architecture. The time that elapses from the moment that a parallel computation starts to the moment that the last processor finishes executions has to be modeled. When modeling interprocessor communications, it is necessary to differentiate between external communication (involving physical processors) and internal communications (involving virtual processors).

```
void solve_PPP() {
  int j, x, f[MAX_n];
  for (j = 0; j < n; j++)
    switch (j){
      case 0:
        IN(&x);
        f[0] = cost(N, f[0], x);
        f[1] = cost(NW, f[1], x);
        break;
      case n-2:
        IN(&x);
        f[n - 2] = cost(NE, f[n - 2], x);
        OUT(&f[n - 2], 1, sizeof(int));
        break;
      case n-1:
        f[n - 1] = cost(N, f[n - 1], x);
        f[n - 1] = cost(W, f[n - 1], f[n - 2]);
        OUT(&f[n - 1], 1, sizeof(int));
        break;
      default:
        IN(&x);
        f[j-1] = cost(NE, f[j-1], x);
        f[j] = cost(N, f[j], x);
        f[j] = cost(W, f[j], f[j - 1]);
        f[j + 1] = cost(NW, f[j + 1], x);
        OUT(&f[j - 1], 1, sizeof(int));
        break;
    }
} /* solve_PPP */
```

Fig. 3. Pipeline algorithm for the PPP. llp code of a general stage.

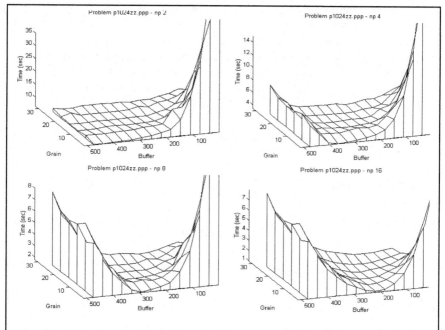

Fig. 4. Running times for the Path Planning Problem. Different values for G and B. np denotes the number of processors.

For the external communications, we use the standard communication model. At the machine level, the time to transfer B words between two processors is given by $\beta+\tau B$, where β is the message startup time (including the operating system call, allocating message buffers and setting up DMA channels) and τ represents the per-word transfer time.

With the internal communications we assume that per-word transfer time is zero and we have to deal only with the time to access the data. We differentiate between an external reception (β^E) without context switch between processes and an internal communication (β^I) where the context switch must be considered.

We denote by t_0, t_{1i}, t_{2i} the time to compute respectively $body_0$, $body_1$ and $body_2$ at iteration i.

T_s will denote the startup time between two processors. T_s includes the time needed to produce and communicate a packet of size B. To generate it, the first B outputs of the G virtual processes must be produced. T_c denotes the whole evaluation of G processes, including the time to send m/B packets of size B.

$$T_s = t_0*(G - 1) + \Sigma_{i = 1, (B-1)}\, t_{1i} *G*B +G*\Sigma_{i = 1, (B-1)}\, t_{2i} +2*\beta^I *(G - 1)*B +\beta^E *B + \beta+\tau*B$$

$$T_c = t_0*(G - 1)+\Sigma_{i = 1, (B-1)}\, t_{1i}*G*m+G*\Sigma_{i = 1, m}\, t_{2i}+ 2*\beta^I*(G - 1)*m+\beta^E*m+(\beta+\tau*B)*m/B$$

The first three terms accumulates the time of computation, the fourth term is the time of context switch between processes and the last terms include the time to communicate packets of size B.

According to the parameters G and B two situations may appear when executing a pipeline algorithm. After a processor finishes the work in one band it goes to compute the next band. At this point, data from the former processor may be available or not. If data are not available, the processor spends idle time waiting for data. This situation arises when the startup time of processor p (the first processor of the ring in the second band) is larger than the time to evaluate G virtual processors, i. e, when $T_s * p \geq T_c$. Then we denote by R_1 the values (G, B) where $T_s * p \leq T_c$ and R_2 the values (G, B) such that $T_s * p \geq T_c$.

For a problem with n stages on the pipeline (n virtual processors) and a loop of size m (m iterations on the loop), the execution time for $1 \leq G \leq n/p$ and $1 \leq B \leq m$, is the

$$T(G, B) = \begin{cases} T_1(G, B) = T_s * (p - 1) + T_c * n / (G * p) & \text{in } R_1 \\[2ex] T_2(G, B) = T_s * (n/G - 1) + T_c & \text{in } R_2 \end{cases}$$

following:

$T_s * p$ holds the time to startup processor p and $T_c * n/(G*p)$ is the time invested in computations after the startup. Note that in R_1, the processors are fed with data and there is no idle time between bands.

$T_s * (n/G - 1)$ is the startup time of the last processor working on the last band. This time includes the idle time that the processors spend between bands.

In the model $T(G, B)$, fixed the number of processors p, the parameters β^I, β^E, β and τ are constants architectural dependent and t_0, t_{1i}, t_{2i}, m and n are variables depending on the instance of the problem. The actual values for these variables are known at running time. An analytical expression for the values (G, B) leading to the minimum, will depend on the five variables and seems to be a very complicated problem to solve. Instead of an analytical approach we will approximate the values for (G, B) numerically.

Note that $T_1(G, B) \leq T_2(G, B)$ in R_2, $T_2(G, B) \leq T_1(G, B)$ in R_1 and $T_1(G, B) = T_2(G, B)$ at the boundary of R_1 and R_2 (i.e., when $T_s * p = T_c$). This fact allows to consider $T(G, B) = max\{\{T_1(G, B), T_2(G, B)\}, 1 \leq G \leq n/p$ and $1 \leq B \leq m\}$.

An important observation is that $T(G, B)$ first decreases and then increases if we keep G or B fixed and move along the other parameter. Since, for practical purposes, all we need is to give values for (G, B) leading us to the valley of the surface, a few numerical evaluations of the function $T(G, B)$ will supply these values.

5   Experimental Results

To contrast the accuracy of the model we have applied it to estimate the optimal grain G and optimal buffer B for the path planning problem considered in section 3. In the pipeline algorithm for this problem (figure 3), bodies 0 and 2 are empties while body 1 depends on the iteration.

The numerical results presented in this section correspond to the running times depicted in figure 4. Table 1 presents the values for grain and buffer *(G-Model, B-Model)* obtained with the model, the running time of the parallel algorithm for this parameters *(Real Time)* and the values of grain and buffer *(G-Real, B-Real)* giving the best running time *(Best Real Time)*. The table also shows the error made ((*Best Real Time - Real Time) / Best Real Time*) when we consider the parameters provided by the tool instead of the optimal values. The model shows an acceptable prediction in both examples with an error not greater than 19 %.

Table 1. Estimation of *G, B* for the PPP.

P	G-Model	B-Model	Real Time	G-Real	B-Real	Best Real Time	Error
2	2	384	7,522	8	384	6,719	0,119
4	2	192	4,080	8	128	3,440	0,186
8	2	96	2,113	8	96	1,788	0,182
16	2	48	1,092	8	32	0,968	0,127

Table 2 presents times and speedup obtained for the cyclic mapping, for the block mapping and for the mapping proposed by the model. Columns are labeled T-*, S-* respectively. Figure 5 illustrates it graphically.

Observe the considerable improvement of the T-model column against the naive cyclic mapping, almost reaching a factor of 10. Although the comparison with the block mapping column may seem not so impressive, it is necessary to notice that the T-block column does not correspond to a pure block mapping but to a block-cyclic assignment with grain 32. The gain against such pure block mapping will be better.

Table 2. Runnig time and Speedup for several mappings.

P	T-Cyclic	S-Cyclic	T-Block	S-Block	T-Model	S-Model
2	78,884	0,061	10,527	0,460	7,522	0,643
4	41,940	0,115	5,323	0,909	4,080	1,186
8	21,020	0,230	2,702	1,791	2,113	2,291
16	10,643	0,455	1,581	3,061	1,092	4,434

6   Conclusions

We have developed an analytical model that predicts the effects of the Grain of processes and Buffering of messages when mapping pipeline algorithms. The model allows an easy estimation of the parameters through a simple numerical approximation. The model is capable to be introduced into tools (like *llp*) that produce the optimal values for the Grain and Buffer automatically. During the execution of the first band, the tool estimates the parameters defining the function *T(G, B)* and carries out the evaluation of the optimal values of G and B. The overhead introduced is negligible, since only a few evaluations of the objective function are required. After this first test band, the execution of the parallel algorithm continues with the following bands making use of the optimal Grain and Buffer parameters.

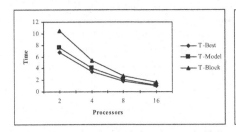 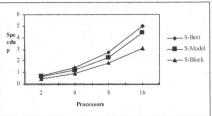

Fig. 5. Running Time and Speedup for the different mappings.

7   Aknowledgments

We thank to the CIEMAT for allowing us the access to their machines.

References

1. Andonov R., Rajopadhye S., Yanev N.. Optimal Orthogonal Tiling. Euro-Par'98 Parallel Processing Lecture Notes in Computer Science, Vol. 1740. Springer-Verlag, (1998) 480–490.
2. Andonov R., Rajopadhye S.. Optimal Orthogonal Tiling of 2D Iterations. Journal of Parallel and Distributed computing, 45 (2), (1997) 159-165.
3. Brandes T.. Exploiting Advanced Task Parallelism in High Performance Fortran via a Task Library. Euro-Par'99 Parallel Processing Lecture Notes in Computer Science, Vol. 1685. Springer-Verlag, (1999) 833-844.
4. Danelutto M., Pasqualetti F., Pelagati S.. Skeletons for data parallelism in p3l. Europar'97. Lecture Notes in Computer Science, Vol. 1470. Springer-Verlag, (1997) 619-628.
5. High Performance Fortran Language Specification Version 2.0
   http://www.ntua.gr/parallel/standards/hpf/
6. Li G., Wah B.. Parallel Processing of Serial Dynamic Programming Problems. IEEE. 1985.
7. Miguet S., Robert Y.. Path Planning on a ring of Processors. International Journal Computer Math. Vol. 32Gordon and Breach Science Publishers. (1990) 61-74.
8. Morales D., Almeida F., García F., González J., Roda J., Rodríguez C.. A Skeleton for Parallel Dynamic Programming. Euro-Par'99 Parallel Processing Lecture Notes in Computer Science, Vol. 1685. Springer-Verlag, (1999) 877–887.
9. Ramanujam J., Sadayappan.. Tiling Multidimensional Iterations Spaces for Non Shared-Memory Machines. Supercomputing'91. (1991) 111-120.
10. Rodriguez C., Roda J., Garcia F., Almeida F., Gonzalez D.. Paradigms for Parallel Dynamic Programming. Proceedings of the 22nd Euromicro Conference. Beyond 2000: Hardware and Software Strategies. IEEE. (1996) 553-563.

Use of PVM for MAP Image Restoration: A Parallel Implementation of the ARTUR Algorithm

Gustavo J. Fernández, Julio Jacobo-Berlles, Patricia Borensztejn,
Marisa Bauzá, and Marta Mejail

Departamento de Computación, FCEyN
Universidad de Buenos Aires
Ciudad Universitaria
1428 Buenos Aires, República Argentina
{gfernand, jacobo, patricia, mbauza, marta}@dc.uba.ar

Abstract. Markov Random Field (MRF) based algorithms used for restoring images affected by blur and noise are generally very effective, but most of them are computationally very heavy. The recently proposed ARTUR algorithm is a deterministic method that belongs to this family. In this work, a parallel implementation of this algorithm is proposed on a PVM environment. Various results are shown and the performance is analysed comparing the proposed parallel implementation against the sequential one.

1 Introduction

The image restoration process we are considering in this work consists in the removal of the additive Gaussian noise that degrades an image. The model for the original non-degraded image consists of uniform regions, separated by abrupt changes in gray level value called edges. P. Charbonnier *et.al.*[1] proposed the Markov Random Field (MRF) based, deterministic algorithm ARTUR that performs a restoration by finding the Maximum a Posteriori (MAP) estimate of the original image, given the degraded one. The contribution of this work is the parallelization of the ARTUR algorithm and the analysis of its performance. ARTUR was chosen because it considers a deterministic approach that allows the use of non-convex potential functions. These functions are known to preserve edges better than the convex ones.

PVM was selected as the framework because it is widely used in network environments for programs based on the message passing paradigm and because it is portable to a great number of computer architectures. A master-slave model was used to implement the aforementioned algorithm.

This article describes briefly the theoretical basis of the image processing involved and the parallel implementation of the algorithm, then it shows the results obtained with different configurations and the derived conclusions. The results show that the parallelization reduces the execution time compared to a sequential implementation of the same algorithm.

J. Dongarra et al. (Eds.): EuroPVM/MPI 2000, LNCS 1908, pp. 113–120, 2000.

2   MAP Restoration by Energy Minimization

The general degradation model consists of a blur operator applied to the original image and the subsequent addition of white Gaussian noise. This is the direct transformation. In order to obtain the original non-degraded image from the degraded one, an inverse problem must be solved . The Maximum a Posteriori criterion estimates the non-degraded original image f as the one that maximizes the *a posteriori* probability, and is given by

$$\widehat{f}_{MAP} = \arg\max_f \Pr(p \mid f) \Pr(f),\tag{1}$$

where p is the degraded image and $\Pr(p \mid f)$ is the likelihood of the degraded image given the original one. $\Pr(f)$ is the 'a priori' probability and represents the hypothesis made over the solution in order to regularize the problem.

If we consider that f is a Markov Random Field [2], this problem can be formulated in terms of the minimization of an energy function $E(f)$, given by

$$E(f) = \sum_s (p_s - (\mathcal{K}f)_s)^2 + \lambda^2 \sum_{<r,t>} \varphi\left(\frac{f_r - f_t}{\delta}\right),\tag{2}$$

where $\mathcal{K}$ is the blur operator and φ is the so called *potential function* [3]. The first summation is carried out over all the positions s in the image and represents the faithfulness to the degraded data p. The second summation is done over all the pairs of adjacent positions $<r,t>$ - called cliques - and represents the 'a priori' probability distribution over all the original non-degraded images. The potential function φ is even, positive and belongs to a family of functions that fulfils a set of conditions that assures edge preservation [1]. The constant λ balances the relative weight of both summations and δ has influence on the discontinuity detection threshold.

It is worth mentioning that, depending on the particular potential function φ chosen, the associated energy may be non-convex in f.

The MAP criterion (1) can then be reformulated as

$$\widehat{f}_{MAP} = \arg\min_f E(f).\tag{3}$$

Several approaches have been proposed to solve this problem [3], [4], [5]. We will consider in this work the deterministic algorithm ARTUR proposed by P. Charbonnier *et.al* [1], which uses a dual energy $E^*(f, b)$ that depends on the original image f and on the set of auxiliary images $\overrightarrow{b} = \{b_h, b_v, b_{ld}, b_{rd}\}$ that represent the edges in the horizontal, vertical, left diagonal and right diagonal directions respectively. This dual energy is defined by

$$E^* (f, b) = \sum_s (p_s - (\mathcal{K}f)_s)^2 + \lambda^2 \sum_{<r,t>} \left(b_{rt} \left(\frac{f_r - f_t}{\delta} \right)^2 + \psi (b_{rt}) \right), \quad (4)$$

where the function ψ is defined such as the condition $\min_b E^* (f, b) = E (f)$ holds (see [3] and [1]). The dual energy E^* has the properties of being quadratic - thus convex - on f for b fixed and of being convex on b when f is fixed. The sought estimator (3) can then be calculated as

$$\widehat{f}_{MAP} = \arg \min_f \min_b E^* (f, b). \quad (5)$$

3   The ARTUR Algorithm

This algorithm is based on the minimization of the aforementioned dual energy and follows a deterministic scheme given by

Algorithm 1 *ARTUR*
    Begin
    $f^0 = 0$
        While *(f^n doesn't converge)*
            $\overrightarrow{b^{n+1}} = \arg \min_{\overrightarrow{b^n}} E^*(f^n, \overrightarrow{b^n})$
            $f^{n+1} = \arg \min_{f^n} E^*(f^n, \overrightarrow{b^{n+1}})$
        End While
    End

It begins with a null estimate of f and proceeds with an alternate minimization of the dual energy E^* with respect to the auxiliary images $\overrightarrow{b}$ and with respect to the unknown original image f, generating a sequence of estimates $f^0, f^1, ..., f^n, ...$ that converges to $\widehat{f}_{MAP}$.
The first minimization in the loop is straightforward and is given by $b^{n+1}_{<r,t>} = \varphi' \left(\frac{f_r - f_t}{\delta} \right) / 2 \left(\frac{f_r - f_t}{\delta} \right)$. The second minimization is done using an iterative method. To do this, we have chosen the Sequential Over-Relaxation (SOR) algorithm.

4   Parallel Implementation

The parallel version of the ARTUR algorithm was implemented within the PVM environment and using a master-slave model [6]. This model allows a master process to take care of all input/output operations and of the distribution and gathering of data. The slaves carry out the calculations with the data received from the master.

The master process reads the whole image, divides it in horizontal strips, and sends each strip to a slave process. Then it waits for the slaves to send back the results, joins the data and writes them back to the disk. Meanwhile, the slaves receive the strips and perform the calculations of the minimization of the energy function. The master process is shown in the blocks diagram on Fig. 1.

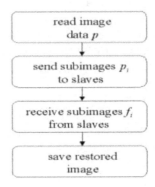

Fig. 1. Master algorithm on parallel adaptation of ARTUR. Master - Slave Model.

Figure 2 shows two instantiations of the slave program. On this figure, points A, B and C indicate the places where data exchange is needed. For each slave, the outer loop corresponds to the main loop in the sequential algorithm and the inner loop corresponds to the SOR algorithm.

Each slave works on a different horizontal strip of the image and exchanges information with the two other processes it shares data with. This is true for all processes, except for those that calculate the minimization for the first and the last strips, which share data with only one process.

The division of the image into strips was done in order to reduce the number of processes each process has to communicate with.

The implementation of the slaves was actually done by fixing the number of iterations in both loops. Enough iterations were allowed in order to let the convergence factor, given by $\left\| f^{n+1} - f^n \right\|^2 / \left\| f^n \right\|^2$, attain a value equal or less than 10^{-8}.

5   Results

On Fig. 3, image a) shows the synthetic original non-degraded image and image b) shows the noisy image obtained by the addition of white Gaussian noise with parameters $\mu = 0.0$ and $\sigma = 20.0$. Images c) and d) show the sequential restoration and the parallel restoration respectively. This restorations have been made with $\lambda = 25.0$ and $\delta = 3.0$ and the potential function used was $\varphi(u) = 2\sqrt{1 + u^2} - 2$.

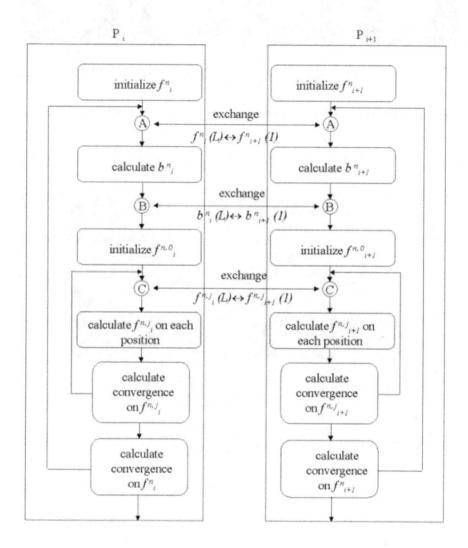

Fig. 2. Slave algorithms on parallel adaptation of ARTUR for two partitions. Master - Slave Model.

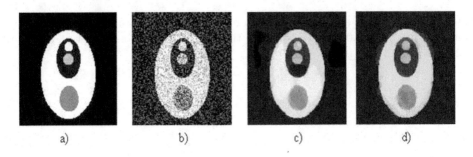

a)   b)   c)   d)

Fig. 3. a) Original image, b) Noisy image, c) Sequential restoration, d) Parallel restoration.

a)   b)

Fig. 4. a) Noisy image, b) Restored image.

The evaluation of the difference between the sequentially restored image f^s and the parallel restored image f^p was made using the relative error between both images, defined as $\varepsilon_{f^s f^p} = \|f^s - f^p\|^2 / \|f^p\|^2$. In order to assess the quality of the restoration, the relative difference between the original image p and the parallel restoration f^p, given by $\varepsilon_{p f^p} = \|p - f^p\|^2 / \|f^p\|^2$, was used. The values obtained were $\varepsilon_{f^s f^p} = 0.0038$ and $\varepsilon_{p f^p} = 0.0392$ respectively.

As an illustrative example, Fig. 4 shows a restoration of a real LANDSAT image of a rural area with several crop fields. In this case, the parameters used were $\lambda = 20.0$ and $\delta = 1.0$ and the potential function used was the same as the one used in the case of the synthetic image.

On Table 1 we present some execution times. These results were obtained using the following configurations:

Size (Pixels)	SUN-S	LINUX-S	SUN-P	LINUX-P
128×128	105	82	69	17
256×256	389	376	290	61
512×512	1445	1456	1114	204

Table 1. Times obtained on sequential and parallell implementations on different machines for various images sizes.

- a uniprocessor SUN Ultra Creator 1 computer, running Solaris 2.7 and PVM 3.4 (named SUN-S and SUN-P for sequential and parallel models respectively), with a processor of 167 MHz and 128 Mb of RAM memory,
- an Ethernet network with UTP 10 Mb/s connecting eight PC machines running LINUX Redhat 6.0 and PVM 3.4 (named LINUX-S for sequential and LINUX-P for parallel model). Each PC has a Pentium processor of 233 MHz and 32 Mb of RAM memory.

All the execution times are measured in seconds and the image sizes are expressed in pixels. The times for the SUN-P and LINUX-P columns were obtained using eight processes.

On Fig. 5 we present the speedup for two, four and eight processors on the above mentioned LINUX machines.

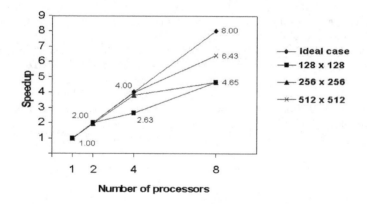

Fig. 5. Speedup for 2, 4 and 8 PCs using PVM under LINUX.

The analysis of the execution times of Table 1, shows that it can be better to run a parallel implementation on a uniprocessor machine than to run a sequential implementation on the same machine (see columns corresponding to SUN-S and SUN-P). The reason for this is that using a parallel implementation, the percentage of time the processor devotes to process the image is greater than in the sequential case.

6   Conclusions

From the results of the execution times on the various configurations considered, it is clear that the parallelization can reduce the execution time both on the uniprocessor architecture as well as on the cluster of computers. The execution times obtained with the cluster of computers are encouraging because they show that, at least for this type of processing, this architecture is a good choice. The parallelization process consisted in the inclusion of data exchange points in the slave processes and in the division of the image by the master process. Also, the model chosen and the use of PVM allow high portability, shown by the use of the same program on different platforms.

7   Acknowledgments

We want to thank P. Charbonnier for the information on his algorithm and for the exchange of ideas. We are also very grateful to M. Bergotto for his assistance.

References

[1] P. Charbonnier, L. Blanc-Feraud, G. Aubert and M. Barlaud, "Deterministic edge-preserving regularization in computed imaging," *IEEE Transactions on Image Processing* **6**(2), pp. 298–311, February 1997.

[2] S. Geman and D. Geman, "Stochastic relaxation Gibbs distributions, and the bayesian restoration of images," *IEEE Trans. Med. Imaging* **PAMI-6**, pp. 721–741, November 1984.

[3] D. Geman and G. Reynolds, "Constrained restoration and the recovery of discontinuities," *IEEE Transactions on pattern analysis and machine intelligence* **14**(3), March 1992.

[4] A. Blake and A. Zisserman, "Visual reconstruction," *The MIT Press series in Artificial Intelligence* , 1987.

[5] D. Geman and C. Yang, "Nonlinear image recovery with half-quadratic regularization," *IEEE Trans. Medical Imaging* , July-1993.

[6] A. Geist, A. Beguelin, J. Dongarra, W. Jiang, R. Manchek and V. Sunderam, *PVM: Parallel Virtual Machine. A User's Guide and Tutorial for Networked Parallel Computing*, 1994.

Parallel Algorithms for the Least-Squares Finite Element Solution of the Neutron Transport Equation

E. Varin[1,2], R. Roy[1], and G. Samba[2]

[1] Ecole Polytechnique de Montréal, IGN-DGM,
P.O. Box 6079, Station Centre-Ville, Montréal H3C 3A7, Canada
{varin, roy}@meca.polymtl.ca
[2] Commissariat à l'Energie Atomique,
BP 12, 91680 Bruyères-Le-Châtel, France
samba@bruyeres.cea.fr

Abstract. The Least-Squares Finite Element Method (LSFEM) is applied to solve the neutron transport equation. Standard parallel algorithms, such as domain partitioning or classical iterative solvers, are developed and tested for 1-D benchmarks on different architectures, the final goal being to select the most efficient approach suitable for realistic 3D problems.

1 Introduction

The neutron transport equation must be solved to know the neutron flux at a specific time and location, moving at a certain speed along a specific direction. Parallel schemes can help with the solution of this equation, which is far too complex for realistic 3D reactor core models. To present such schemes, here a simplified version of the problem is considered (1-D plane geometry, one-speed and steady state):

$$\begin{cases} \mu\frac{d\psi}{dx} + \sigma(x)\psi(x,\mu) = \sigma_s(x)P\psi(x,\mu) + q(x,\mu) \\ P\psi(x,\mu) = \frac{1}{2}\int_{-1}^{1} d\mu'\,\psi(x,\mu') \end{cases} \qquad (1)$$

where σ is the total neutron probability of interaction with its media, σ_s its scattering probability and q a media-independent source of neutrons. The unknown is the flux $\psi(x,\mu)$ defined for $x \in [0,L]$ and for every incident-angle cosine μ, with appropriate boundary conditions at $x = 0$ and $x = L$. Based on the use of linear continuous spatial finite elements, K.J. Ressel[1] has developed a Least-Squares solver where the conditions of existence/unicity of the solution are handled with particular care even in the asymptotic situation (the transport equation becomes singular and can be approximated by a second order diffusion equation).

In this approach, the transport equation is scaled prior to the application of the least-squares method, by a scaling functional $S = P + \tau(I - P)$ $(\tau > 0)$

J. Dongarra et al. (Eds.): EuroPVM/MPI 2000, LNCS 1908, pp. 121–128, 2000.

representing the ratio of diffusion solution part over the transport solution. The least-squares formulation of this scaled neutron equation is: find $\psi \in V$ such that $\forall v \in V$:

$$< S\mathcal{L}\psi, S\mathcal{L}u >=< Sq, S\mathcal{L}u > \tag{2}$$

where the scalar product is defined by $< u, v >= \int_0^L dx \int_{-1}^1 d\mu' \, u(x, \mu')v(x, \mu')$, and the functional $\mathcal{L}$ by $\mathcal{L}\psi = [\mu\frac{d}{dx} + \sigma(x)I - \sigma_s(x)P]\psi$.

The least-squares Eq. 2 is similar to a variational principle and is well suited for the use of spatial finite elements. The incident-angle cosine is represented by a spectral discretization called the P_N method. The flux is then expanded in spherical harmonics[2] as:

$$\psi(x, \mu) = \sum_{l=0}^N p_l(\mu)\phi_l(x) \tag{3}$$

where $\phi_l(x)$ are the flux moments and $p_l(\mu)$ the standard Legendre normalized polynomials. The flux expansion is replaced in Eq. 2 and the $N+1$ flux moments are the actual unknowns of the new equation. The domain $[0, L]$ is split into M cells. Eq. 2 now defines the $(N + 1) \times (M + 1)$ system of equations required to solve Eq. 1.

A penalization technique is used to apply the boundary conditions, leading to the linear system:

$$(S \, IL)^T S \, IL\bar{\Phi} + \lambda E^T E\bar{\Phi} = (S \, IL)^T Sq + \lambda E^T d \tag{4}$$

where IL, S and E correspond to functional, scaling and boundary condition matrices respectively, and λ is a case-dependent constant. Parallel algorithms and communication efforts using PVM [3] or MPI [4] will now be discussed.

2   Different Methods of Resolution

Eq. 4 represents a sparse system written as $\mathcal{A}\bar{\Phi} = \bar{f}$, where $\mathcal{A} = (SIL)^T SIL$ and $\bar{f} = (S \, IL)^T Sq$. The global matrix $\mathcal{A}$ is symmetric and positive definite by the underlying theory of the least-squares method. Moreover, as the finite element method is used to represent a 1-D space variable, the global matrix remains block tridiagonal. At each point, $N + 1$ degrees of freedom represent the flux moments. Each block of $\mathcal{A}$ is then at least $(N + 1) \times (N + 1)$. In fact, these blocks are also sparse because the flux moments form a 3-point stencil prior to the least-squares method. The global system can be expressed as:

$$\begin{bmatrix} \mathbf{B}_1 & \mathbf{C}_1 & & \\ \mathbf{C}_1^T & \ddots & & \\ & \ddots & \mathbf{C}_M & \\ & & \mathbf{C}_M^T & \mathbf{B}_{M+1} \end{bmatrix} \begin{bmatrix} \bar{\Phi}(1) \\ \vdots \\ \bar{\Phi}(M+1) \end{bmatrix} = \begin{bmatrix} \bar{f}(1) \\ \vdots \\ \bar{f}(M+1) \end{bmatrix} \tag{5}$$

The boundary conditions only affect diagonal blocks.

Direct methods can efficiently use the sparsity of $\mathcal{A}$ and a block-tridiagonal solution was implemented. Each block-diagonal $\mathbf{B}$ is LU-decomposed and completely stored in a $(N+1) \times (N+1)$ array. This is acceptable because the number of moments, N, is generally small (under 10) and much smaller than the number of mesh points.

Standard **iterative** methods are also considered. First, block Jacobi iteration $l+1$ can be composed of $M+1$ independent equations that can be written as:

$$\mathbf{B}_i \bar{x}^{(l+1)}(i) = f(i) - \mathbf{C}_{i+1} \bar{x}^{(l)}(i+1) - \mathbf{C}_i^T \bar{x}^{(l)}(i-1) \qquad i = 1, M+1 \quad (6)$$

The Jacobi iterations can be relaxed by applying the parameter w as

$$\bar{x}^{(l+1)} = w \tilde{\bar{x}}^{(l+1)} + (1-w)\bar{x}^{(l)} \tag{7}$$

where $\tilde{\bar{x}}^{(l+1)}$ is the solution of Eq. 6. This parameter is a function of the eigenvalues of the iterative matrix, and is generally < 1.

The block successive over-relaxation (SOR) method follows almost the same algorithm, but in Eq. 6, the unknowns that are already computed are used, such that $\bar{x}^{(l)}(i-1)$ is replaced by $\bar{x}^{(l+1)}(i-1)$. This method converges, if it does, faster than Jacobi. An optimal relaxation parameter $(0 < w < 2)$ can also be used with the SOR method. For both methods, a variational acceleration technique is used.[5] This technique computes a new iterate as in Eq. 7, but a dynamic parameter $w = \alpha_l$ is computed at each accelerated iteration to minimize the residual. Assuming three iterates $\bar{x}_1, \bar{x}_2, \bar{x}_3$, the following expression for α_2 can be used to accelerate $\bar{x}_2$ and $\bar{x}_3$:[6]

$$\alpha_2 = \frac{< r_2, r_3 - r_2 >}{||r_3 - r_2||_2^2} \tag{8}$$

where $r_2 = \bar{x}_2 - \bar{x}_1$ and $r_3 = \bar{x}_3 - \bar{x}_2$ For stability reasons, free and accelerated iterations are often mixed; a cycle of 3 free, 3 accelerated is generally used.

As $\mathcal{A}$ is s.p.d., the Conjugate Gradient (CG) method [7] can also be implemented where iteration k is, beginning with $r^0 = \bar{f} - \mathcal{A}\bar{x}^0$, $\mathcal{M}z^0 = r^0$:

$$\begin{cases} \alpha^k =< r^k, z^k > / < p^k, \mathcal{A}p^k > \\ \bar{x}^{k+1} = \bar{x}^k + \alpha^k p^k \\ r^{k+1} = r^k - \alpha^k \mathcal{A}p^k \\ \mathcal{M}z^{k+1} = r^{k+1} \\ \beta_k =< r^k, z^k > / < r^{k-1}, z^{k-1} > \\ \Rightarrow \text{ Convergence test} \\ p^{(k+1)} = z^{k+1} + \beta_k p^k \end{cases} \tag{9}$$

Preconditionning with $\mathcal{M}$ is considered to accelerate convergence. A block-diagonal preconditioner is used at first because the test cases are often heterogeneous. In this case, the Incomplete Cholesky factorization technique [8] can take advantage of the sparsity of the blocks $\mathbf{B}$ and $\mathbf{C}$.

3   Parallel Algorithms

The direct solver is a LU decomposition version followed by a triangular resolution. Parallel implementation of this direct tridiagonal solver was not done,
because standard parallel schemes would be inefficient for natural ordering.[9] A
domain decomposition method is under development.

The present work is based on iterative methods. The block Jacobi algorithm
is directly parallel even when over relaxed. Partitions of the global matrix $\mathcal{A}$
among the p processors is made simply by assigning $k = (M + 1)/p$ block lines
and communicating the results to the neighboring processors. If p is at least
equal to the number of different regions in the domain, the lines representing
the same region are maintained together so that each processor sees and solves
over a homogeneous domain.

The SOR implementation reorders unknowns forming a Red/Black scheme.
Each SOR iteration is represented in Fig. 1. The implied Jacobi steps are highly
parallel for each colored unknown. An equal number of Red and Black unknowns
are partitioned over the processors. When possible, unknowns corresponding to
the same material region are kept together.

$$
\begin{aligned}
&1.\ \mathbf{B}_R \tilde{\bar{x}}_R^{(l+1)} = f_R - \mathbf{C}_B \bar{x}_B^{(l)} - \mathbf{C}_B^T \bar{x}_B^{(l)} \\
&2.\ \bar{x}_R^{(l+1)} = \omega \tilde{\bar{x}}_R^{(l+1)} + (1 - \omega) \bar{x}_R^{(l)} \\
&3.\ \mathbf{B}_B \tilde{\bar{x}}_B^{(l+1)} = f_B - \mathbf{C}_R \bar{x}_R^{(l+1)} - \mathbf{C}_R^T \bar{x}_R^{(l+1)} \\
&4.\ \bar{x}_B^{(l+1)} = \omega \tilde{\bar{x}}_B^{(l+1)} + (1 - \omega) \bar{x}_B^{(l)}
\end{aligned}
$$

Fig. 1. Red/Black SOR algorithm

The communication effort for partition over regions is limited to the two 1D
interfaces. So each processor sends at most $N + 1$ unknowns to its left and right
neighbors. Each processor computes k blocks of $N + 1$ unknowns with 2 extra
blocks for the neighboring data.

The convergence criteria is based on the L_∞ norm readily available on all
parallel processors:

$$
||(\bar{x}^{(l+1)} - \bar{x}^l)||_\infty < \varepsilon
$$

Special attention is given to select an ε that depends on the solution which is
sought.

In the two previous methods, two inner products are needed for variational
acceleration (Eq. 8), thus increasing the communication effort. However, such
calculations are not needed at every iteration and the more free iterations are
added, the more the inner product calculation effects will be minimized.

The parallel preconditioned conjugate gradient method is also implemented.
Partitions over regions are only used. Two preconditioners are selected, block
diagonal and SSOR preconditioners. For the latter, $\mathcal{M} = (D + L)D^{-1}(D + L^T)$.

As shown in the PCG algorithm (Eq. 9), two inner products are required to evaluate the parameters α and β. The $< r^k, z^k >$ product is used as a first convergence criteria. If $< r^k, z^k > \; < \; \varepsilon$, then the actual residual norm $< r^k, r^k >$ is computed to insure that convergence is reached. The increase in calculations and communication is then limited to the last iterations.

Table 1 summarizes the communication between p processors for the previous methods. In terms of communication effort, standard iterative methods, block Jacobi and block SOR, as well as preconditioned conjugate gradient need almost the same number of exchanges and data size exchanged per iteration.

Table 1. Communication effort per iteration

	$\bar{x}^{l+1}$	α	$\|\cdot\|_\infty$	$\|\cdot\|_2/\beta$	$\bar{x}^{k+1}$
# comm.	$p - 1$	p	p	p	$2 \times p$
# words	$N + 1$	4	1	4	$N + 1$
Methods	SOR only	All	Jac./SOR	PCG only	All

The neighboring exchange labeled $\bar{x}^{k+1}$ depends on the partition and not on the iterative process. The block Jacobi method uses the least communication whereas the block SOR uses the most because of the exchange of new neighboring values as they are computed. It is mostly the number of iterations that will decide the more effective method parallel or not.

4   Numerical Results

Two different test cases are used to evaluate LSFEM discretization of the transport equation in a parallel environment. These test cases are:

- Diffusive heterogeneous domain.[10]
- Heterogeneous domain containing void region. [11]

In diffusive domains, the parameters of Eq. 1 have a particular value: $L >> \frac{1}{\sigma}$ and $\sigma \approx \sigma_s$. The diffusive case, labeled Larsen, is a two-region dimensionless slab using $L = 11.0$ with a fixed incoming source of 1 at $x = 0$ and a free surface at $x = L$. The heterogeneous case, labeled Reed, is a five-region slab using $L = 8.0$ with a perfect reflector at $x = 0$ and a free surface at $x = L$. The properties of the different regions for each case are shown in Table 2.

The direct solution is used as the reference result for every case. First, iterative method results are compared with reference values using a L_∞ norm of the relative error. For this, the Larsen case is chosen for which there are 2230 cells and 16 flux moments, so a total of 35680 unknowns.

All iterative methods give very accurate results with respect to the direct solutions. Optimal over-relaxation parameters were obtained numerically. As

Table 2. Parameters for both test cases

Larsen			Reed			
			ℓ	σ	σ_s	q
			2.0	50.0	0.0	50.0
ℓ	σ	σ_s	1.0	50.0	0.0	0.0
1.0	2.	0.	2.0	0.0	0.0	0.0
10.0	100.	100.	1.0	1.0	0.9	1.0
			2.0	1.0	0.9	0.0

expected, the SSOR preconditioner is more effective for accelerating the GC convergence than the block diagonal one. The Jacobi method converges in 3 times more iterations than SOR or CG does, and these methods show the same order of iterations. In this Larsen case, no source is applied so the only contribution other than 0 in $\bar{f}$ comes from the boundary condition at $x = 0$. This boundary source slowly travels to one new spatial point per iteration.

Parallel calculations are performed with p processors on cluster computers composed of IBM RISC-6000, using PVM 3.4, and on a IBM RS/6000 SP3 computer composed of 4 NightHawk (222MHz Power 3) 8-processor nodes, using MPI.

The Larsen case was first used to benchmark parallel calculations. Partition of the geometry defines the number of unknowns for each processor. Table 3 shows the speed-up for the different methods on the IBM cluster limited by a 10Mbytes Ethernet communication network.

The Red/Black ordering is used for the parallel version of the block Jacobi as well as the block SOR methods. The block Jacobi method is directly parallel and shows a speed-up > 2 for $p = 2$ because the communication effort is really minimum while a total of 17920 unknowns are computing on each processor.

Table 3. Speed-Up for the different methods on the IBM cluster

	# of processors		
	$p = 2$	$p = 5$	$p = 10$
Jacobi	2.41	3.99	3.00
SOR	1.70	2.18	1.65
PCG	1.90	3.58	2.41

Calculation effort is equivalent for the Jacobi and SOR methods, however the speed-up obtained for the latter is less. In fact the 1-dimensional finite element method leads to an almost degenerated parallelism. The Red/Black ordering for the SOR method should be more efficient in speeding up a 2- or 3-dimensional problem.

Speed-up decreases with the number of processors as the communication effort overtakes that required for the calculations. But increasing the number of unknowns by a factor 10, one obtains 8.0 for $p = 10$ when using PGC method.

Calculations were reproduced on the IBM SP3 computer. MPI routines replace PVM ones. Both parallel softwares may be used, but the results are only reported for the MPI version. In fact, this implementation allows the use of the User Space option for inter-node communication through the SPS Switch. For the intra-node exchange, the MP_SHARED_MEMORY flag is set to yes. Table 4 summarizes the results for this computer, speed-up is evaluated in reference to the 2-processor calculations.

Table 4. Speed-Up on the IBM SP3 computer

	# of processors			
	$p = 2$	$p = 4$	$p = 8$	$p = 16$
Jacobi	1.00	1.66	3.33	6.00
PCG	1.00	1.69	3.33	6.10

Efforts has been made to maintain the number of inter-node calculations, so the 2-processor and 4-processor computations use 1 processor per node. But the User Space version is limited to 4 processor per node, so a total of 16 processors. The Red/Black SOR method results in inadequate speed-up due to the 1-D degenerated state. The effectiveness is at most of 6 for an optimal value of 8. Even though, no dedicated session was available, speed-ups are very much acceptable.

The Reed case was used to look into the code scalability. Each processor, from 2 to 16, treats 232 cells for 16 flux moments, so 3712 unknowns. The execution time as a function of the number of processors is flat from 2 to 8 processors. Above that, as the load average of each node was during the tests over 8.0, the results are not significant.

5   Conclusion

The LSFEM is successfully applied to solve the neutron transport equation. The SSOR preconditioned CG method is the most effective iterative method we tested in a parallel context. Both PVM and MPI versions of the code provide similar results on a IBM cluster computer. The speed-up on the IBM SP3 computer is attractive for large problems, providing the use of the User Space option.

Partitions over cells may be used in the future to implement a domain decomposition algorithm coupled with this PCG method. In the 3D implementation, the global matrix will become 7-block diagonals for a regular mesh. The number of moments will increase, but the block will still be sparse. That system may be solved using the Alternated Direction Sweeping (ADS) method. For each direction sweep, the PCG algorithm herein developed can be used.

Acknowledgment. Part of this work was partly supported by the Natural Science and Engineering Council of Canada. The first author (E.V.) wishes to thank the members of Ecole Polytechnique's Computer Centre for their help in setting up the IBM workstation cluster, as well as the IBM support personnel of Bruyères Le Châtel.

References

1. Ressel, R. J., " Least-Squares Finite Element Solution of the Neutron Transport Equation in Diffusive Regimes ", PhD Thesis, University of Colorado at Denver (1994).
2. Lewis, E. E and Miller, Jr., W. F, "Computational Methods of Neutron Transport", ANS, Lagrange Park (1993).
3. Geist A., Beguelin A., Dongarra J., Jiang W., Manchek R., Sunderam V., "PVM: Parallel Virtual Machine. A User's Guide and Tutorial for Networked Parallel Computing", MIT Press (1994).
4. Kropp W., Lusk E., and Skjellum A. "Using MPI: Portable Parrallel Programming with Message Passing Interface", MIT Press (1994)
5. Hébert A., "Variational Principles and Convergence Acceleration Strategies for the Neutron Diffusion Equation", *Nucl. Sci. Eng.*, **91** (1985) 414-427.
6. Roy R., " Méthodes des probabilités de collision ", Report IGE-235,École Polytechnique de Montréal, Institut de Génie Nucléaire" (1998).
7. Hestenes M.R. , and Stiefel E.,"Methods of Conjugate Gradients for Solving Linear Systems", *J. Res. Nat. Bur. Standards*, **49**, 409-436 (1952).
8. Meijerink J. and van der Vorst, H.," An Iterative Solution for Linear Systems of Which the Coefficient Matrix is a Symmetric M-Matrix", *Math. Comp.*,**31**, 148-162 (1977).
9. Kumar V., Grama A., Gupta A. and Karypis G., "Introduction to Parallel Computing", Benjamin/Cummings Publishing Co., Redwood City (1994).
10. Larsen E. W. and Morel J. E. , "Asymptotic Solutions of Numerical Transport Problems in Optically Thick, Diffusive Regimes-II. ", *J. Comp. Phys.*, **83**,212-236 (1989).
11. Reed, W. H.," New Difference Schemes for the Neutron Transport Equation", *Nucl. Sci. Eng.*,**46**,309 (1971).

GAMMA and MPI/GAMMA on Gigabit Ethernet

Giuseppe Ciaccio and Giovanni Chiola

DISI, Università di Genova
via Dodecaneso 35, 16146 Genova, Italy
{ciaccio,chiola}@disi.unige.it

Abstract. The Genoa Active Message MAchine (GAMMA) is a light-weight communication system based on the Active Ports paradigm, originally designed for efficient implementation over low-cost Fast Ethernet interconnects. A very efficient porting of MPICH atop GAMMA as been recently completed, providing unprecedented messaging performance over the cheapest cluster computing technology currently available. In this paper we describe the recently completed porting of GAMMA to the GNIC-II Gigabit Ethernet adapters by Packet Engines. A combination of less than 10 μs latency and more than 93 MByte/s throughput demonstrates the possibility for Gigabit Ethernet and GAMMA to yield messaging performance comparable to the ones from many lightweight protocols running on Myrinet. This result is of interest, given the envisaged drop in cost of Gigabit Ethernet due to the forthcoming transition from fiber optic to UTP cabling and ever increasing mass market production of such standard interconnect.

1 Introduction

The low-cost processing power of clusters of Personal Computers (PCs) can be easily exploited by means of appropriate, high-level, standard Application Programming Interfaces such as, e.g., MPI. Several open-source implementations of MPI (e.g., MPICH [2]) can run on Linux-based Beowulf-type clusters on top of standard TCP/IP sockets. However it is well known that parallel jobs characterized by medium/fine grain parallelism exchange messages of small size (few KBytes) among processors, and that general-purpose protocols such as TCP/IP make very inefficient use of the interconnect for short messages.

On Fast Ethernet, a lightweight messaging system like the Genoa Active Message MAchine (GAMMA) [4, 7] provides far better performance at no additional hardware cost compared to the Linux TCP/IP stack. Started in 1996 as part of a Ph.D. thesis, the GAMMA project was targeted right from the beginning to low-cost Fast Ethernet interconnects. GAMMA implements a non-standard communication abstraction called *Active Ports*, derived from Active Messages, and provides best-effort as well as flow-controlled communication routines. With an end-to-end latency between 12 and 20 μs (depending on the hardware configuration and the NIC used), GAMMA provides adequate communication and

J. Dongarra et al. (Eds.): EuroPVM/MPI 2000, LNCS 1908, pp. 129–136, 2000.

synchronization primitives for tightly coupled, fine-grain parallel applications on inexpensive clusters. A complete yet efficient implementation of MPI atop GAMMA is now available [6, 8].

The link speed offered by Fast Ethernet is insufficient for many communication intensive parallel jobs to scale up. This justifies the interest towards the two most famous gigabit-per-second interconnects, namely, Myrinet and the more recent Gigabit Ethernet. The inefficiency of TCP/IP is exhacerbated here, since the physical transmission time becomes negligible compared to the time spent in the traversal of the protocol stack. Lightweight messaging systems become a key ingredient for an effective use of fast interconnects.

Currently, the per-port cost of a Gigabit Ethernet LAN is too high compared to Myrinet. This is largely due to the current fiber-optic cabling of Gigabit Ethernet. With the forthcoming transition of Gigabit Ethernet from fiber-optic to standard UTP copper cabling, however, we expect a substantial drop in cost which will push this LAN technology into a much larger segment of the marketplace, characterized by competition among different vendors and a potentially very large base of installation; eventually, the per-port cost of Gigabit Ethernet will become negligible compared to the cost of a single PC, in much the same way as it occurred with Fast Ethernet. In our opinion, Myrinet will never enjoy such a large diffusion: its segment of marketplace (system-area networks) will remain narrow compared to LANs.

Moreover, some Gigabit Ethernet NICs are programmable in much the same way as Myrinet is. For instance, the NetGear GA620 NIC, a cheap (300 US dollars) clone of the Alteon AceNIC adapter, comes with as many as two on-board microprocessors and 512 KBytes of on-board RAM, which makes it possible to upload appropriate, possibly self-made custom firmware to the NIC.

The only remaining difference between Myrinet and Gigabit Ethernet is the reliability of the physical medium, especially in case of network congestion which may cause packet losses. Myrinet prevents congestion by using hardware mechanisms for back-pressure, whose practical effectiveness has been demonstrated. Gigabit Ethernet uses hardware-exchanged control packets to block senders in case of congestion hazard, according to the IEEE 802.3x specification; this should in principle avoid congestion, and packet losses thereof, although nobody could assess the effectiveness of this mechanism so far. Another difference, of secondary concern though, is the higher communication latency of current Gigabit Ethernet switches (in the order of 3 to 4 μs), compared to the very low latency of a Myrinet switch (less than 1 μs).

To sum up, in our opinion Gigabit Ethernet is a promisingly successful and cheaper alternative to Myrinet under any respect, and an efficient lightweight protocol is definitely a must to make best use of this technology.

In order to prepare for the transition to inexpensive Gigabit Ethernet, we started developing a prototype of GAMMA for the Packet Engines GNIC-II Gigabit Ethernet adapter. The prototype was ready in September 1999; although Packet Engines discontinued the NIC a few months later, that first prototype of GAMMA was indeed useful to experimentally demonstrate the feasibility and success of a lightweight communication protocol like GAMMA on next-generation inexpensive LANs. Overall, MPI/GAMMA on our GNIC-II Gigabit Ethernet NICs yields excellent performance figures. On two Pentium II 450 PCs networked by a Gigabit Ethernet switch, a MPI user application enjoys 16 μs end-to-end latency and 93.5 MByte/s peak throughput (77 % of the nominal link speed), comparable to if not better than many lightweight messaging systems running on Myrinet.

2   The DBDMA Data Transfer Mode

A NIC is an interface between a host CPU and a network; as such, each NIC must implement suitable mechanisms to cooperate with the host computer, on one hand, and the network, on the other hand. A modern NIC cooperates with the host computer using a data transfer mode called *Descriptor-based DMA* (DBDMA). With the DBDMA mode, the NIC is able to autonomously set up and start DMA data transfers. To do so, the NIC scans two precomputed and static circular lists called *rings*, one for transmit and one for receive, both stored in host memory. Each entry of a ring is called a *DMA descriptor.*

A DMA descriptor in the transmit ring contains a pointer (a physical address) to a host memory region containing a *fragment* of an outgoing packet; therefore, an entire packet can be specified by chaining one or more send DMA descriptors, a feature called "gather".

Similar to a descriptor in the transmit ring, a DMA descriptor in the receive ring contains a pointer (a physical address, again) to a host memory region where an incoming packet could be stored. The analogous of the "gather" feature of the transmit ring is here called "scatter": more descriptors can be chained to specify a sequence of distinct memory areas, and an incoming packet could be scattered among them.

A NIC operating in DBDMA mode allows a greater degree of parallelism in the communication path, according to a producer/consumer behaviour. At the transmit side, while the NIC "consumes" DMA descriptors from the transmit ring operating the host-to-NIC data transfers specified in the descriptors, the CPU runs the protocol stack and "produces" the necessary DMA descriptors for subsequent data transfers. The reverse occurs at the receive side. Since both sides are decoupled from each other, the communication path works like a pipeline whenever traveled by a sequence of data packets, with a potentially high throughput.

However, the Linux implementation of IP forces the NIC device drivers *not* to exploit the "gather/scatter" features. This implies that at least two temporary copies of data are needed, one at the sender and the other at the receiver side, because header and payload of each packet are expected to be contiguous in the same memory area at both sides of communication when control reaches the device driver. A different organization and semantics of the communication protocol could eliminate the memory copy at the sender side by exploiting the "gather" feature: the header could be precomputed and stored somewhere in kernel space, the payload could be pointed to directly in user space, and the NIC would autonomously arrange them contiguous into its on-board transmit FIFO and send the whole packet. However, avoiding the memory copy at the receiver side is impossible: the final destination in user space for the payload of an incoming packet can be determined only *after* inspecting the header, which implies the packet be already stored somewhere, namely, into a temporary buffer. The only way to avoid a memory copy at the receiver side is to run the communication protocol by the NIC itself, and let it inspect the headers when packets are still in its on-board receive FIFO.

To sum up, a lightweight protocol for non-programmable NICs can be zero-copy on send thanks to the "gather" feature, but it must be "one-copy" on receive. Indeed, all the latest prototypes of GAMMA took this very organization, where most of the send overhead is in charge of the NIC and most of the receive overhead is in charge of the host CPU.

3   Maximizing the End-to-End Throughput

The theoretical maximum throughput with Gigabit Ethernet is 125 MByte/s, roughly equivalent to the maximum throughput of the 32 bit, 33 MHz PCI bus where the NICs are plugged. However, a first prototype of GAMMA on Packet Engines GNIC-II adapters yielded a peak end-to-end throughput of only 80 MByte/s. We immediately started investigating the causes for such a low efficiency, using a pair of Pentium II 450 MHz PCs with 100 MHz system bus.

To begin with, we identified the following consecutive stages in the communication pipeline, from sender to receiver, in our opinion accounting for most of the total communication effort:

- stage 1: the "consumption" of DMA descriptors from the transmit ring and the corresponding DMA data transfers from the host RAM to the NIC, operated by the sender NIC;
- stage 2: the physical link;
- stage 3: the DMA transfers from the NIC to the host RAM and the corresponding "production" of descriptors in the receive ring, operated by the receiver NIC;
- stage 4: the "consumption" of DMA descriptors from the receive ring and the related protocol action and data movements, carried out by the receiver CPU.

Measuring the throughput of all the above pipe stages is not necessarily an easy task. Throughput of stage 1 can be measured directly, and throughput of stage 2 is known in advance (125 MByte/s). However, throughput of stage 3 cannot be easily measured by a direct technique. Moreover, we have to evaluate the effect of bus contention between stages 3 and 4 when both try to access the host RAM. Finally, we do not know in advance where the bottleneck is, and the presence of a bottleneck invalidates any direct throughput measurement taken below it in the pipeline.

The throughput of stage 1, directly measured, was 80.8 MByte/s, very close to the end-to-end throughput. This meant that stage 1 was the bottleneck, and also that we could not know much more about stages 3 and 4.

To proceed with our analysis we had to eliminate this bottleneck, even sacrificing the protocol correctness. We suspected that such a slow speed was caused by the "gather" feature: the sender NIC had to "consume" as many as two DMA descriptors for each outgoing packet. In order to prove this, we temporarily switched to a different transmission technique. The sender CPU "produces" only one descriptor for each packet, pointing to a dummy packet of appropriate size but containing only the header, without user data. This way the sender transmits wrong data, but this does not hurt performance measurements. We then observed a much higher throughput of 98 MByte/s for stage 1. The peak end-to-end throughput did not increase as much, though: it only measured 93.8 Mbyte/s, indicating that a second bottleneck was set up somewhere else. Throughput of stage 4, as directly measured, was about 100 MByte/s, therefore stage 3 was the bottleneck with its 93.8 MByte/s. By temporarily disabling the data movements in stage 4 we were able to isolate the performance degradation due to the contention between stages 3 and 4 on the memory bus; indeed, disabling stage 4 led to an increase of the stage 3 throughput from 93.8 to 96 MByte/s.

The lesson is now clear: if we want to maximize the end-to-end GAMMA throughput with the GNIC-II Gigabit Ethernet NICs, we should not use the "gather" feature of the NIC at the sender side. This however forces us to add another stage in the communication pipeline just where it begins, namely:

- stage 0: the copy of the packet payload from the user buffer to a preallocated memory buffer already containing the precomputed header, and the corresponding "production" of one single DMA descriptor into the transmit ring, carried out by the sender CPU.

Indeed we have implemented such an additional pipe stage, which exhibits a throughput of 95 MByte/s. Adding such a temporary copy on send was the paradoxical price we had to pay in order to maximize the end-to-end throughput of GAMMA with our Gigabit Ethernet adapter.

4   Improving Throughput for Short Messages

Fragmenting a message into packets is a need when the total message size exceeds the maximum MTU size of the network. Fragmentation increases the CPU overhead for header processing, and leads to a lower utilization rate of the physical link. However, since the end-to-end communication path is a pipeline, fragmentation also leads to a much better throughput, by exploiting the parallelism among pipe stages. For this reason, message fragmentation has been exploited also with Myrinet, which is not packet oriented. Even with Fast Ethernet, it can be convenient to fragment a message even when it is smaller than the maximum allowed MTU size [5].

To improve the efficiency with short messages, GAMMA can fragment each short message into packets whose size is not necessarily maximal. Of course, this increases the number of packets exchanged. The optimal fragment size depends on the total message size and also depends on the performance profile of the communication hardware. Due to the lack of a satisfactory performance model of the whole communication system, we could only find an empyrical formula for optimal fragmentation, valid only for the GNIC-II adapters: messages up to 512 bytes are fragmented in packets of 128 bytes, messages from 513 to 1664 bytes are fragmented in packets of 256 bytes, messages from 1665 to 5148 bytes are fragmented in packets of 384 bytes, messages from 5149 to 11000 bytes are fragmented in packets of 768 bytes, messages from 11001 to 12000 bytes are fragmented in packets of 896 bytes, and larger messages are fragmented in packets of 1408 bytes.

5   Communication Performance

The measurement platform was a pair of PCs, each with a single Pentium II 450 MHz CPU, 100 MHz system bus, and a Packet Engines GNIC-II NIC. The two machines were connected back-to-back by a fiber-optic cable.

Self-made "ping-pong" microbenchmarks have been run to measure the average end-to-end communication latency of GAMMA, MPI/GAMMA, Linux 2.2.13 TCP/IP sockets, and MPICH atop TCP/IP sockets. The measured one-way latency is 9.5 μs with GAMMA, 12.3 μs with MPI/GAMMA, 132.1 μs with TCP/IP sockets, and 320.9 μs with MPICH. Adding an Intel Express Gigabit Switch in between the two machines results increases the latency by 3.6 μs.

By the same "ping-pong" programs we can estimate the *end-to-end* throughput (not to be confused with the *transmission* throughput as measured by the usual one-way "stream" tests). Figure 1 reports the throughput curves of the following messaging systems: GAMMA using the optimal fragmentation scheme (curve 1), GAMMA with standard fragmentation (curve 3), MPI/GAMMA, based on the optimal fragmentation (curve 2), Linux 2.2.13 TCP/IP sockets (curve 4), and MPICH atop TCP/IP sockets (curve 5). The maximum MTU size with GAMMA is 1408 bytes (1388 bytes of payload plus 20 bytes of GAMMA header), which experimentally provided better performance on our platform (possibly due to a better cache line alignment).

We briefly sketch the main conclusions that can be drawn from the latency numbers and the throughput picture:

- The communication performance of MPI/GAMMA on a Gigabit Ethernet LAN based on Packet Engines GNIC-II adapters is comparable to, if not better than many lightweight implementations of MPI running on Myrinet, even taking into account the additional latency of a switch.
- The efficiency with short messages of Linux TCP/IP, and MPICH thereof, remains too low for running a tightly coupled, fine-grain parallel job on a commodity cluster.

- The performance improvement yielded by the optimal fragmentation technique with GAMMA short messages, as shown by comparing curve 1 against curve 3, is significant (for instance, a 64% improvement in throughput is obtained with 1388 byte messages).
- The performance degradation caused by stacking MPI atop GAMMA, as shown by comparing curve 1 against curve 2, is very modest; the same does not hold with MPI atop TCP/IP sockets (curve 5 is much lower than curve 4). This is obvious, given that the porting of MPICH atop GAMMA was made at the ADI level. The resulting MPI/GAMMA stack is thin compared to the standard MPICH/P4/TCP stack.
- Linux TCP/IP is not able to saturate Gigabit Ethernet: its peak throughput is only 42.4 MByte/s. The scenario is completely different with Fast Ethernet, where Linux TCP/IP is indeed able to almost completely saturate the physical link, thanks to recent improvements with device drivers and protocol.
- The maximum end-to-end throughput achieved by GAMMA is 93.8 MByte/s, and amounts to the measured throughput of the NIC on receive (stage 3 in the communication pipeline, see Section 3). This means that GAMMA is able to saturate the NIC, and that the NIC itself is the communication bottleneck. However, the obtained throughput is a very respectable result, given that the GNIC-II adapter does not support frames larger than 1526 bytes, which is a very small size given the high link speed (the Alteon AceNIC and its clones yield a slightly better throughput but only using a larger MTU size, a non-standard feature called "jumbo frames.").

6   Related Work

Most existing efficient implementations of MPI for clusters presently run on Myrinet (e.g., [9, 10]). To the best of our knowledge, the only attempt of providing an efficient implementation of MPI for Fast Ethernet and Gigabit Ethernet, besides ours, is represented by MVICH [3], the VIA-based implementation of MPI developed in the framework of the M-VIA project [1]. However, little information is available yet on MVICH; the only available performance information is related to MVICH atop Giganet cLAN, an expensive "VIA inside" gigabit-per-second interconnect; MVICH on Giganet yields 13.5 μs latency and 97 MByte/s peak throughput, that is, just slightly better compared to MPI/GAMMA on Packet Engines GNIC-II adapters.

Acknowledgements

We gratefully acknowledge the work of Vincenzo Di Martino and Leonardo Valcamonici (CASPUR, Università "La Sapienza" di Roma), who contributed with useful discussions and helped setting up the cluster environment. We also thank the Istituto Nazionale di Fisica Nucleare (INFN) for sharing their own cluster hardware with our investigation project.

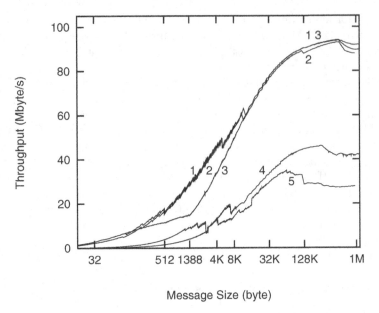

Message Size (byte)

Fig. 1. End-to-end throughput of GAMMA, MPI/GAMMA, Linux 2.2.13 TCP/IP, and MPICH atop TCP/IP, using the GNIC-II Gigabit Ethernet adapters.

References

[1] M-VIA Home Page, http://www. nersc.gov /research /FTG /via/, 1998.
[2] MPICH - A Portable MPI Implementation, http://www. mcs. anl. gov /mpi /mpich/, 1998.
[3] MVICH Home Page, http://www. nersc.gov /research /FTG /mvich/, 1998.
[4] G. Chiola and G. Ciaccio. GAMMA home page, http://www. disi.unige.it /project /gamma/.
[5] G. Chiola and G. Ciaccio. GAMMA: a low cost Network of Workstations based on Active Messages. In *Proc. Euromicro PDP'97*, London, UK, January 1997. IEEE Computer Society.
[6] G. Chiola and G. Ciaccio. Porting MPICH ADI on GAMMA with Flow Control. In *Proc. IEEE - ACM 1999 Midwest Workshop on Parallel Processing (MWPP 1999)*, Kent, OH, August 1999.
[7] G. Chiola, G. Ciaccio, L. Mancini, and P. Rotondo. GAMMA on DEC 2114x with Efficient Flow Control. In *Proc. 1999 International Conference on Parallel and Distributed Processing, Techniques and Applications (PDPTA'99)*, Las Vegas, Nevada, June 1999.
[8] G. Ciaccio. MPI/GAMMA home page, http://www. disi.unige.it /project /gamma/mpigamma/.
[9] M. Lauria and A. Chien. MPI-FM: High Performance MPI on Workstation Clusters. *Journal of Parallel and Distributed Computing*, 40(1):4–18, January 1997.
[10] L. Prylli, B. Tourancheau, and R. Westrelin. The design for a high performance MPI implementation on the myrinet network. In *Proc. EuroPVM/MPI'99*, number 1697 in LNCS, pages 223–230, Barcelone, Spain, 1999.

Distributed Checkpointing Mechanism for a Parallel File System

Vítor N. Távora[1], Luís M. Silva[2], João Gabriel Silva[2]

[1] CISUC / Departamento Engenharia Informática, Escola Superior de Tecnologia e Gestão de Leiria, Morro do Lena – Alto Vieiro, 2401-951 Leiria Apartado 3063, Portugal
vntavora@estg.iplei.pt - Phone: 351 244 820 333 - Fax: 351 244 820310
[2] CISUC - Departamento Engenharia Informática, Faculdade de Ciências e Tecnologia, Universidade de Coimbra - POLO II P
3030 – Coimbra PORTUGAL
{luis, jgabriel}@dei.uc.pt - Phone: 351 239 790 000 - Fax: 351 239 701266

Abstract. Checkpointing techniques have widely been studied in the literature as a way to recover from failures in sequential, distributed and parallel environments. However, most of the checkpointing mechanisms proposed so far focus only on the recovery of the application data. If the application performs some I/O operations to disk files, such schemes may not work correctly, as they do not provide rollback-recovery for the file contents.

In this paper, we present a distributed checkpointing mechanism for a Parallel File System that can be integrated with any of the previous application checkpointing algorithms. Three different file checkpointing schemes will be presented, tested in that mechanism and discussed in detail. The distributed mechanism proposed was integrated in PIOUS - a public-domain parallel file system developed for the PVM distributed computing environment.

Keywords: Fault-Tolerance and Reliability, Checkpointing, File checkpointing, Parallel I/O, Extensions and improvements to PVM.

1. Introduction

In the past decade there has been a considerable effort to develop, provide and support high performance computing systems for solving Grand-Challenge problems. These include climate predictions and control, air and water pollution, combustion dynamics and high-performance aircraft simulation, amongst others [8]. To support intensive computing for different scientific applications several parallel and distributed systems with a large numbers of processors have been developed.

One of the major problems in parallel/distributed systems is the MTBF (Mean Time Between Failures), which tends to decrease significantly with the number of processors. A large percentage of complex scientific codes may take several hours, days or

This work was partially supported by the Portuguese Ministry of Science and Technology (MCT) and the European Union through the R&D Unit 326/94 (CISUC)

J. Dongarra et al. (Eds.): EuroPVM/MPI 2000, LNCS 1908, pp. 137-144, 2000.

even weeks to execute their tasks, so their performance may be strongly affected by the MTBF of the system.

Some problems arise when the system has to be reset due to a crash in the application, or just for maintenance purposes. The application must be restarted from the very beginning, what can be very costly and does not assure a forward progress.

For long-running scientific applications, it is desirable to have the ability to save the state of the computation in order to continue it from that point at a later time. Checkpointing is the solution for this problem: it allows applications to save their state to stable storage at regular intervals. If a failure occurs then the application is restarted from that previous point, without unduly retarding its progress.

Several checkpointing mechanisms have been proposed in the literature [1-6]. However, most of these mechanisms focus only on the recovery of the application data. Most of the scientific computation deals with enormous quantities of data, which exists not only in main memory but also in disk files. This means that checkpointing mechanisms should also include the state of the files, otherwise some inconsistencies may occur in the recovering operation that is performed after the failure.

The checkpointing mechanism proposed in [6] tried to solve part of the problem by saving the position of the file pointer (fp) and the size of the file at each checkpoint operation. It may work for some situations, like when read-only files or write-only files (with write-append operations) are in use. However it is not effective to recover from operations (like write, delete or trunc) that update the file contents. So this mechanism represents only a partial solution to the problem.

First we considered the use of atomic transactions [15] in file access operations, which included a transaction of all file operations done between two checkpoints. However the use of transactions should degrade considerably the performance of scientific parallel applications because it can kill the concurrency between processes.

Then, the solution to assure the consistency of files after a recover operation is to extend data checkpointing mechanisms to files. So, it is necessary to develop file checkpointing mechanisms and integrate them with previous checkpointing schemes.

The main topic of this paper is the study of file checkpointing schemes and its integration in a proposed distributed checkpointing mechanism for a parallel file system. It was integrated in PIOUS [7], a public-domain parallel file system developed for the PVM [11] distributed computing environment.

The rest of the paper is organized as follows: section 2 describes three file checkpointing schemes. Section 3 presents a distributed checkpoint mechanism for a Parallel File System. A performance study is presented in Section 4. A comparison with related work is done in Section 5. Finally, section 6 concludes the paper.

2. File checkpointing schemes

In this section, we analyze in more detail the necessary procedures for checkpointing application files. Basically, the items that should be saved in a checkpoint operation are the position of the file pointer, the size and the contents of the file and some of the file attributes. We developed three file checkpointing schemes:

Shadow – It duplicates the files at each checkpoint. The original copy can be modified in any way by the application. If a failure occurs, the system has only to restore the contents of the files by replacing the original ones with the corresponding shadow files. This version can be very inefficient for most of the cases.

Log Save – It saves in a log file the contents of the files at previous checkpoint (and that were updated by the application). If a failure occurs in the rollback operation, the application has to recover the previous checkpoint, and the files are restored from the log file.

Log Write – It writes in a log file the blocks written by the application in files since previous checkpoint. The physical files are only modified in checkpoint operations. The write append operations are done directly in files. Some read operations are redirected to the blocks stored in log. If a failure occurs, is quite simple to recover the files, as the contents stored in last checkpoint were kept unmodified.

Considering the mode of operation of the file we have introduced some optimizations in schemes, namely in read-only and in write-only files. A comprehensive description of these schemes was presented in [10] and [14]. As described, they can be integrated in any of the previous application data checkpointing schemes. In this situation, to assure the atomicity of the checkpoint operation, a simple two-phase commit protocol should be applied; otherwise, it is possible that a failure occurring during checkpoint time can cause inconsistency between the data checkpoint and the file checkpoint.

3. Distributed checkpointing mechanism

One of the major bottlenecks that affects parallel scientific codes is I/O. When I/O operations are performed exclusively in one disk this becomes a bottleneck. This may cause a significant degradation in application's execution time. Parallel File Systems (Parallel I/O) represents the solution for faster I/O, multiplying the number of physical devices over which a file is stored and therefore increasing the I/O bandwidth. In a parallel I/O system we can make simultaneously accesses to different blocks of a file. Most of Parallel File Systems (Parallel I/O) still lack support for fault-tolerance, namely the assurance of the file's consistency contents after a failure.

Since a Parallel File System splits each file in segments and stores them in multiple I/O servers that reside in different machines, it is necessary to have a distributed file checkpointing mechanism. It must assure that each I/O server has a local file checkpoint support and that all local checkpoints form a coherent distributed checkpoint.

To assure the local file checkpoint in each I/O server we can use one of the three file checkpointing schemes (Shadow, Log Save or Log Write) proposed in Section 2. Therefore, shadow or log files are distributed over several I/O servers.

To avoid inconsistencies, and also to assure the failure atomicity on the distributed checkpoint operation, we propose a coordinated two-phase file checkpointing mechanism. The coordinator of the operation must be a file system process that keeps the information about the parallel files. The checkpoint operation can only start after all previous I/O operations are concluded.

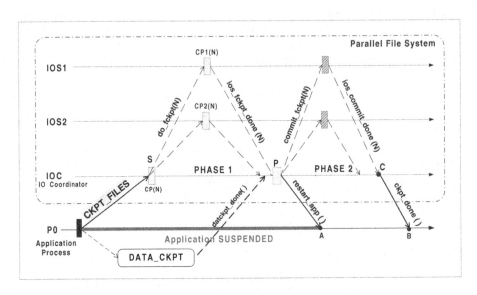

Figure 1: Distributed checkpointing for a Parallel File System

The distributed file checkpointing mechanism that we propose for a Parallel File System is represented in Figure 1. It includes an application process (P0) and a parallel file system formed by a coordinator (IOC) and two I/O servers (IOS1 and IOS2).

An application process (P0) requires a checkpoint operation, which is formed by a data checkpoint (DATA_CKPT) and a file checkpoint. When the IO coordinator receives a message (CKPT_FILES) the two-phase file checkpoint operation is started (point S). In the first phase, to prepare the checkpoint, the coordinator sends a multicast message (*do_fckpt(N)*) to all I/O servers. They store (in stable memory) the attributes of segment files and then send a reply (*ios_fckpt_done(N)*) to the coordinator. After receiving all the replies and a message announcing the successfully conclusion of the data checkpoint (point P), the first phase of the file checkpoint is complete.

In the second phase every I/O server will execute its local checkpoint, using one of the three file checkpoint schemes (Shadow, Log Hold or Log Write). Then a message (*ios_commit_done(N)*) is sent to the coordinator announcing that the operation is completed. After the successful reply of all I/O servers (point C), the coordinator completes the file checkpoint protocol and the whole checkpoint operation.

If, during the first phase, a failure affects an I/O server, the entire operation is aborted. A failure during phase two causes no harm, because the operation will be concluded after the server restart. So, we can conclude that the proposed mechanism warrants the atomicity of the checkpoint operation.

To reduce the overhead introduced by the checkpoint, the mechanism only suspends the application during the first phase of the checkpoint (just to point A), running concurrently with the second phase of the file checkpoint (from point A to point B).

We implemented the distributed checkpointing mechanism in PIOUS [7]. For the sake of portability, we did not use any particular feature of PIOUS unavailable to other systems. Thus, the proposed checkpoint mechanism can be easily ported to any other Parallel File System.

4. Performance Results

In this section we present some performance results that were obtained in a heterogeneous distributed system composed by four workstations: a Sun Sparc 2 running Sun OS 4.1.2 with 64 Mb RAM and 1.05 Gb of hard disk storage (HD), a Sun Sparc 10 running Sun OS 4.1.3 with 64 Mb RAM and 1.05 Gb of HD, and two DEC Alpha 21164 running Digital Unix 4.0b with 128 Mb Ram and 2.1 Gb HD. Workstations were connected via a 10 Mbits Ethernet network.

We used as benchmark a PIOUS (pfbench) distributed application that splits each file in segments and stores them in the four different machines. It also periodically perform read and write operations in segments. Benchmark application was executed using PIOUS 1.2.2 and PVM 3.3.3. All machines were used as I/O servers and the Sun Sparc 10 also was the coordinator of PIOUS file system.

We measured the overhead introduced in read, write and checkpoint operations by each checkpoint scheme (Shadow, Log Save or Log Write) included in the proposed distributed checkpointing mechanism. Due to the lack of space we only present the most important Figures and we refer the interested reader for the [14] document.

Figure 2 represents the overhead when changing the number of write operations performed during the execution of the benchmark: 12, 24, 120 and 240 in each segment. The size of file used was 5760 kb (1440 kb in each I/O server) and each written block has the size of 6 kb. *Pwrite* represents the write operation in original PIOUS version.

As shown in figure 2a, the performance of Log Save mechanism is the most penalized with the increase of the number of write operations done by an application. This is so because that scheme introduces a considerable overhead during each write operation. In Log Save every write operation involves two additional disk accesses, as, before writing the block to the file, the previous contents are read and synchronously written in the log file.

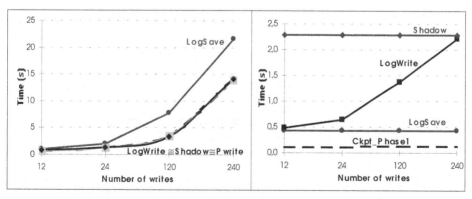

Figure 2: **a)** Overhead in write operations   **b)** Overhead per checkpoint

Figure 2b represents the consequence of the number of write operations performed in the overhead at the checkpoint time. It shows that Log Write and Shadow schemes take more time executing each checkpoint operation because Log Write scheme needs to update the original file and Shadow scheme should duplicate the file. However the overhead introduced by these mechanisms in checkpoint operations can be negligible for the application as it mainly occurs during the phase 2 of file checkpoint. This phase is executed concurrently with the application running. We can also conclude that the first phase (Ckpt_Phase1) of the file checkpoint operation, during which the application must be suspended, introduces an insignificant overhead.

Figure 3 shows the average overhead of a checkpoint operation when changing the size of the file (2880 kb, 5760 kb, 11520 kb and 23040 kb), which was split in four segments with the same size (one for each I/O server). The application performed 60 write operations in each segment with 12 kb blocks.

As expected, when file size increases the Shadow scheme needs substantially more time to conclude the checkpoint operation. This is so because it must replicate the file during that operation. The application is just suspended in phase 1 of the checkpoint, however during the phase 2 some file accesses are suspended while it is replicated.

The shadow scheme can also introduce a significant space overhead due the replication done at each checkpoint and at the first open access to the file. The other schemes (Log Save and Log Write) just store in a log file the portion of data updated since that operation. The file contents updated since previous checkpoint never is bigger than the file size and usually they are much smaller than the entire file.

So, we can conclude that the Shadow scheme can be very inefficient for applications that make use of files with large-size segments.

We have verified that the three schemes introduced a very negligible overhead at the read operation. Their performances were similar at that operation.

We can also conclude that the Log Write is the most effective, especially when the application executes a considerable number of I/O operations (with some writes) and makes use of files with large-size segments.

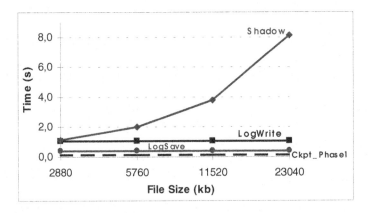

Figure 3: Overhead per checkpoint (file size)

5. Comparison with Related Work

In this section, we give an overview of related work published in the literature and try to compare with the file checkpointing schemes herein presented.

Some authors [12] assume that scientific applications only perform I/O before the computation begins and after it finishes. Since this is not always the case, it means that such scheme does not provide the adequate I/O checkpointing.

Another strategy was followed in [13]: all the files that are open with write or read-write permissions are replicated on several disks. That system provides support for file availability but does not assure file consistency in case of rollback.

The IBM Vesta Parallel I/O file system [16] provides a checkpointing facility for application files. There is a checkpoint function that creates a snapshot of the file's contents. This scheme has some similarities with our shadow mechanism, since the entire file is checkpointed in a synchronous way.

A file checkpointing scheme for UNIX applications has been proposed in [9]. It is based on a lazy-backup approach: it saves the size of the file and the file pointer in each checkpoint operation, and it makes a shadow copy of the file only when it is about to be modified. Despite the "lazy" nature this scheme, it is quite similar to our shadow version. No implementation details or performance results were presented.

The previous file-rollback functionality [9] was optimized later and taken out as a separate file checkpoint library *libfcp* [17]. It is similar to our log save scheme: it uses an in-place update with undo logs approach to checkpoint files. It intercepts all file operations except for read-only ones. When a file is opened for modifications, its size is recorded and an undo log of file truncation is generated. When the portion of the file that existed at previous checkpoint time is about to be modified, an undo log of restoring the pre-modification data is generated. When a rollback occurs, these undo logs are applied in a reversed order to restore the original files.

In [18] it was proposed a file checkpoint scheme similar to our Log Write mechanism: it buffers all modification operations done in user files after the last checkpoint. At the time of the next checkpoint, the buffered operations are flushed from the buffer to the corresponding user files and then the buffer is cleared.

6. Conclusions and Future Work

Checkpointing is extremely important for large and time-consuming applications, as restarting programs from the beginning can be very costly. A solution that supports only checkpointing of the application data but neglects the use of files might be useless in many situations. Supporting file checkpoint is quite important because most of the real applications involve file I/O.

This paper presents a distributed checkpointing mechanism for a Parallel File System that can be integrated with any application data checkpointing algorithm. The mechanism was integrated in PIOUS file system. We introduced and tested three different file checkpointing schemes (Log Save, Log write and Shadow) in that mechanism.

We concluded that the Log Write scheme can be the most effective, especially when the application executes a considerable number of I/O operations (with some writes) and makes use of files with large-size segments. This is due the overhead introduced by the Log Write scheme in each write operation and the inefficiency of Shadow scheme when applications make use of files with large-size segments.

As future work, we plan to improve the performance of Log Write scheme, namely by storing part of the log mechanism in main memory, and by integrating the presented distributed checkpointing mechanism in others parallel file systems.

7. References

1 J.Plank, K.Li. "Performance Results of ickp - A Consistent Checkpointer on iPSC/860", Proc. Scalable High-Performance Computing Conf., Knoxville USA, pp. 686-693, 1994

2 L.M. Silva, J.G.Silva. "Global Checkpoints for Distributed Programs", Proc. 11th Symp. on Reliable Distributed Systems, pp. 155-162, Houston USA, 1992

3 R. Koo, S. Toueg. "Checkpointing and Rollback-Recovery for Distributed Programs", IEEE Transactions on Software Engineering, SE-13(1), pp. 23-31, January 1987

4 E.N. Elnozahi, D.Johnson, W.Zwaenepoel. "Performance of Consistent Checkpointing", Proc. 11th Symp. on Reliable Distributed Systems, pp. 39-47, 1992

5 K.Li , J.F. Naughton , J.S. Plank. "Real-Time, Concurrent Checkpoint for Parallel Programs", Proc. 2nd ACM Symp. on Princ. and Practice of Parallel Programming, pp. 79-88, 1990

6 J.S.Plank, M.Beck, G.Kingsley, K.Li. "libckpt: transparent Checkpointing Under UNIX", Conference Proceedings USENIX Winter 1995 Technical Conference, Jan. 1995

7 S. Moyer, V. Sunderam. "PIOUS: A Scalable Parallel I/O System for Distributed Computing Environments", Proc. Scalable High-Performance Comp. Conf., SHPCC, pp. 71-78, 1994.

8 T.G.Lewis, H.EL-Rewini. "Introduction to Parallel Computing", Prentice-Hall, 1992.

9 Y.M. Wang, Y. Huang, K.P.Vo, P.Y.Chung, C.Kintala. "Checkpointing and its Aplications", Proc. 25th Fault-Tolerant Computing Synposium, FTCS-25, pp.22-31, July1995.

10 L. M. Silva, V. N. Távora, J. G. Silva. "Mechanisms of File Checkpoint for UNIX Applications", Proc. of 14th IASTED Conf. on Applied Informatics, pp. 358-361, Feb. 1996.

11 V. Sunderam. "PVM: A Framework for Parallel Distributed Computing", Concurrency: Practice and Experience, Vol. 2, No. 4, pp. 315-339, December 1990.

12 Y.Tamir, T.M. Frazier."Application-Transparent Process-Level Error Recovery for Multicomputers", Proc. of Hawaii Int. Conf. On System Sciences, Hawaii, January 1989

13 B.Folliot, P.Sens. "GatoStar: A Fault-Tolerant Load Sharing Facility for Parallel Applications", Lecture Notes in Computer Science, 852, Springer-Verlag, pp. 381-398, 1994

14 V. N. Tavora. "File checkpointing Mechanisms", Master Thesis, Computer Science Department, Coimbra University, July 1997.

15 B. Lampson. "Atomic Transactions", Lecture Notes in Computer Science 105, Springer-Verlag, Berlin, pp. 246-265, 1981.

16 F.Bassow. "IBM AIX Parallel I/O File System: Installation, Administration and Use", Document Number SH34-6065-00, IBM, June 1995

17 P. E. Chung et al. "Checkpointing in CosMiC: a User-level Process Migration Environment", Proc. Pacific Int. Symp. on Fault-Tolerant Systems, Taiwan, pp. 187-193, 1997.

18 D. Pei. "Modification Operation Buffering: A Low-Overhead Approach to Checkpoint User Files ", Proc. IEEE FTCS-99, Student Paper, pp. 36-38, June 1999.

Thread Communication over MPI

Thomas Nitsche

Institut für Kommunikations- und Softwaretechnik, Technische Universität Berlin,
Franklinstr. 28/29, Sekr. FR5-13, 10587 Berlin, Germany,
nitsche@cs.tu-berlin.de

Abstract. This paper describes the implementation of a thread communication library on top of MPI. It allows light-weight threads to communicate with each other both locally between threads within the same
process as well as globally between threads on different processors. The
interface is similar to MPI with the use of thread identifiers instead of
processor ranks.

Problems occur in the implementation of global communication operations. Due to limited tag space we are not able to specify source and
target thread identifiers in a call to *MPI_Recv*. As a result we may receive messages from the wrong thread which has to be resolved explicitly.

1 Introduction

MPI, the message passing interface, defines as a standard the communication
between different processors in a parallel machine or different computers in a
network. While in MPI-1 [5] the processors are statically allocated at startup
time, MPI-2 [3] allows similar to PVM the dynamic creation of processes.

Different processes on one processor are used in numerous cases. One reason
is to load-balance tasks of different, statically unknown execution time, where
multiple tasks are allocated to one processor in order to balance the different task
sizes [1]. Another case appears where the work is split into different subobjects,
but their number does not exactly matches the available processors [6, 8].

However, while creating independent processes allows much flexibility in the
program, it is not appropriate in all cases. This is due to the fact that it requires to load another program into the memory, allocate a new process for it
and regularly switch between the different processes which is quite expensive.
Independent processes also cannot communicate with each other via direct memory access but have to use something like sockets.[1] For that reason the use of
(light-wight) threads instead of processes is often desirable. Threads run within
one process allowing them direct memory access as well as thread switches with
very small overhead.

Our aim is to provide a library where different threads can communicate with
each other. This includes both the communication of threads within one process

---

[1] At least a switch to the kernel mode is necessary to access memory of another process.

J. Dongarra et al. (Eds.): EuroPVM/MPI 2000, LNCS 1908, pp. 145–151, 2000.
© Springer-Verlag Berlin Heidelberg 2000

as well as with threads located on another processor. The interface is similar to MPI, such that the thread communication forms a layer on top of MPI.

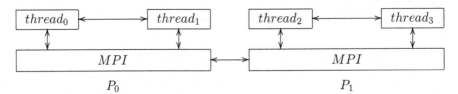

The functions are called TMPI_xxx for thread communication over MPI. Besides that the only differences to MPI within the interface are that the source or target is a thread identifier instead of the processor rank and the MPI communicator is replaced by a thread communicator. This thread communicator internally contains

- the MPI communicator with the group of processors,
- the information where a certain thread is located, i.e. a mapping from thread identifiers to processor ranks,
- as well as some queues of open send and receive operations and MPI requests which will be explained later.

Therefore the threads can communicate in a MPI style, where the difference between local communication between threads within one process and global communication between threads on different processors becomes invisible for the user.

This paper describes the implementation of the thread communication library on top of MPI. The actual implementation is based on OPAL-MPI [7] and communicating agents [4], but the description is independent from that. The local communication is described in section 2, while the global communication is handled in section 3. Section 4 deals with the problems of synchronous and collective operations. Finally, section 5 concludes.

2   Local Communication

While in the case of global, inter-processor communication the matching send and receive operations can in principle be executed simultaneously (on different processors), this is not possible for local communication. Threads run concurrently on one processor, so only one thread can be executed at a certain time.

Therefore a send operation has to store the data such that a following, matching receive operation can fetch them. Analogously, a receive operation stores a receive request such that a following send can directly provide the data. To keep the order of communication operations, i.e. the value that has been sent first has to be received first, we manage queues of open send and open receive operations within the thread communicator.

A local isend operation, i.e. an isend where both source and target thread are allocated within the same MPI process[2], therefore has to distinguish the following two cases. If there exists an open receive request then we remove the first matching request from the open receive queue, put the data there and mark the request as ready. Otherwise we just append a new send request at the end of the open send queue. In order to avoid unnecessary data copying we just store a pointer to the data within the request and not the data itself.

A local irecv operation works analogously. First it checks if there is already data available in the open send queue. If this is the case it stores a new receive request.

The more interesting part happens within the wait operation. If the request is already ready, that means an isend could directly store the data within a matching irecv request or an irecv could immediately read the data from an open isend, then the wait has to do nothing. Otherwise, if we wait for an open isend or irecv operation, the current thread has to be suspended and another active thread has to be chosen by the scheduler. The suspended thread can only become active again if another thread performs a matching communication operation, which will change the mode of the request to ready and awake the thread.

3   Global Communication

3.1   Matching Thread Identifiers to MPI Parameters

For the global communication we want to use the routines provided by MPI. Unfortunately, they cannot be used directly as we have to map the thread parameters to the MPI parameters. In MPI, a communication is described by a communicator, the rank of source and target processors within the communicator as well as a tag. In our thread communication library we have to take care of the fact that on one processor there can be multiple concurrent threads. We therefore have to ensure that a thread only receives that data which was explicitly sent to it and not to any other thread on the same processor.

This means that we have to encode the identifiers of source and target thread within the above mentioned MPI communication parameters. As the processor number is already uniquely determined by the thread running in it, we could only use the MPI communicator or the tag to encode the thread identifiers. Using extra MPI communicators does not make sense due to the large number of communicators needed and therefore the large memory overhead. As the communicator internally contains among other things the list of processors as well as their topology, assigning a MPI communicator for every thread identifier would imply at least $O(P^2)$ memory usage on each of the P processors.[3] Unfortunately,

---

[2] which could be a static processor in case of MPI-1 or a dynamic process in case of MPI-2

[3] If MPI could guarantee that the internal data is shared between communicators containing the same process group, we were able to use a special communicator for every source/target thread-id pair.

we also cannot use the tag to encode the thread numbers, because that would remove the possibility to use different tags for the thread communication. Besides that it would also restrict the number of possible threads.[4]

Therefore we can only map the thread identifiers to the corresponding process ranks and pass the tag and communicator directly to MPI. In order to distinguish the communication from or to multiple threads on one processor, we have to send the identifier of the own as well the the remote thread together with the data. So a call

```
TMPI_ISend(data, ..., target-id, tag, thread-comm)
```

will be mapped to

```
MPI_ISend( [self-id,target-id,data], ...,
           PE(target-id), tag, MPI-comm(thread-comm) )
```

3.2   Receiving Wrong Messages

The problem with that approach is that we cannot fully specify the desired communication operation in MPI. This is unfortunately unavoidable as long as MPI does not provides a richer tagging scheme. Allowing arrays of tags instead of a single integer tag would have been sufficient in our case. For the receive operation we therefore can only specify the communicator, the tag and the remote processor rank but not the thread identifiers of the source and the current thread as target.

As a result, waiting for a receive request can deliver data which are either for a different thread than the current running one, or have been sent from a different thread than the desired one. In that case where we got the *wrong* message we store it in the open send queue for a later receive and make a new call to MPI_IRecv/MPI_Wait until we get the data with the correct source and target thread identifiers. However, in case there exists already an MPI request belonging to a receive operation where source and target thread, tag and communicator matches, then we directly put the data to the corresponding receive request, mark it as ready and use its MPI request for our receive. This is possible, as communicator, tag and processor rank specified within the MPI request correspond to our receive operation.

3.3   Handling MPI_Wait

A second problem occurs if the scheduler switches to another thread only at certain points in the program. Most thread systems avoid the overhead of a time-slicing scheduler used for large-grained processes, as this may result in

---

[4] On a 32-bit computer we could encode approximately 32.000 threads as we have to encode both source and target identifiers, and some values like MPI_ANY_TAG cannot be used. This results on a machine with 2.000 processors to only 8 threads per processor.

interrupts at arbitrary points. Therefore the whole program context consisting of register values, stacks etc. has to be saved. Instead of that light-weight threads are scheduled only on demand. This leads to smaller overheads, but the inability to interrupt calls to external libraries. For this reason we cannot directly execute MPI_Wait if a wait is called, as this may result in deadlocks. Image we have two threads on the same processor where one is sending and the other is receiving data from a third thread on another processor:

P_0		P_1
T_0	T_1	T_2
irecv(T_2,...,Req$_0$)	isend(T_2,...,Req$_1$)	recv(T_1)
wait(Req$_0$)	wait(Req$_1$)	send(T_0)

If now thread T_0 is executed before T_1 then the processor P_0 is locked in the call of MPI_Wait(Req$_0$). As thread switches only occur between different commands and not in a time-sliced manner, process P_0 will stay within the waiting operation and thread T_1 will never be executed. That means that T_2 will wait for T_1 and never send anything to T_0, which is the only way to finish the library call to MPI_Wait.

For that reason we have to delay the execution of MPI_Wait as long as we have other active threads on the same processor. In that case the current thread which calls a wait is suspended and the wait request is stored in a queue within the thread communicator. If there are no active threads anymore, i.e. all threads are suspended, we call MPI_Waitsome with the list of all open MPI requests. Those threads whose MPI requests are finished will be activated again. Note that in the case of finishing a *wrong* receive request, i.e. source or target identifier does not matches, we either exchange the request with that of a matching one and activate the other thread, or we put the data into the open send queue for a later request, initiate another receive request and possible call MPI_Waitsome again. In order to avoid too many open MPI requests we call MPI_Testall with that list at every call to wait.

4   Other Communication Operations

4.1   Synchronous Communication

A synchronous send operation has to wait until the matching receive has been called. For the local, synchronous communication we therefore have to suspend the current thread if we insert a send request into the open send queue and re-activate the thread if a receive operation removes the request from the queue. If, on the other hand, there is already a matching request in the open receive queue, we can immediately continue the sending thread as the receive has already been initiated.

For the global, synchronous communication it is not sufficient to use a synchronous MPI operation, as the transfered message may be received by a *wrong* thread with a non-matching thread identifier. In order to inform the sender that the data has been received by the correct thread we have to send back an explicit acknowledgment message, so a synchronous send operation corresponds to sending the data and receiving the acknowledgment. This acknowledgment is sent in a different communicator such that it cannot interfere with normal data messages, and uses a message counter as tag to enable waiting for different messages at the same time. As the receiver has to know whether he has to send an acknowledgment or not, every message does not only contain the data together with source and target thread identifier, but also the message counter. It has the specific value NO_ACK = -1 in case of an asynchronous operation.

In the current version all global messages between different threads as well as the acknowledgment messages are sent as separate MPI messages. This might be optimized if a message aggregation technique as described in [2] were used, such that messages between different threads but the same processors were sent together as one big message.

4.2 Collective Operations

Due to the presence of local thread communication we cannot use the MPI routines for collective operations but have to re-implement them ourselves.

A direct use of MPI is possible if there is exactly one thread on all processors. In that special case not only the collective operations but also all the other functions are mapped one-to-one to MPI, as dealing with threads is not necessary then.

5   Conclusion

We have described the implementation of a thread communication library on top of MPI. It allows light-weight threads to communicate with each other both locally between threads within the same process as well as globally between threads on different processors. The interface is similar to MPI with thread identifiers instead of processor ranks.

Local communication is realized via open send and receive queues, while global point-to-point communication is mapped to MPI. As MPI only uses the communicator, the processor rank and an integer tag to distinguish different communication requests, we are unable to specify the thread identifiers of source and target that way. Therefore we have to send them together with the actual data. As a result a thread can receive *wrong* messages which should have been received by a different thread, as MPI_IRecv cannot differentiate between them. This has to be resolved explicitly by putting the data which were received *too early* into the open send queue and call MPI_IRecv again until the correct data is received. It also makes it necessary to explicitly send an acknowledgment message in case of synchronous communication, as the synchronization provided by MPI is not sufficient here. If MPI would provide a more flexible tagging mechanism, e.g. a array of tags, this overhead could be avoided and left to MPI.

Performance results demonstrate interesting improvements compared to MPI. A simple ping-pong test executed 20.000 times with 2 threads on one processor takes 12.4 seconds for the thread communication and another second for program start and thread initialization. MPICH needs almost 2 seconds for the program initialization, and the communication phase takes 169.4 seconds. For global communication we have encountered a small overhead, but this is outweighted by the larger process creation time if we generate threads quite often in the program as in [6].

References

[1] Christina Boeres, Vinod E. F. Rebello, and David B. Skillicorn. Static scheduling using task replication for LogP and BSP models. In David Pritchard and Jeff Reeve, editors, *EuroPar'98 Parallel Processing, 4th International Euro-Par Conference, Southampton, UK, September 1-4, 1998, Proceedings*, volume 1470 of *Lecture Notes in Computer Science*, pages 337–346. Springer, September 1998.

[2] Malolan Chetlur, Girinda D. Sharma, Nael Abu-Ghazaleh, Umesh Kumar V. Rajasekaran, and Philip A. Wilsey. An active layer extension to MPI. In Vassil Alexandrov and Jack Dongarra, editors, *Proceedings of Recent Advances in Parallel Virtual Machine and Message Passing Interface, 5th European PVM/MPI Users' Group Meeting, Liverpool, UK, September 7-9, 1998 (EuroPVM/MPI'98)*, volume 1497 of *Lecture Notes in Computer Science*, pages 97–104. Springer Verlag, September 1998.

[3] Message Passing Interface Forum. MPI-2: Extensions to the Message-Passing Interface. Technical report, University of Tennessee, Knoxville, Tenn., July 1997. ftp://ftp.mpi-forum.org/pub/docs/mpi-20.ps.

[4] Thomas Frauenstein, Wolfgang Grieskamp, Peter Pepper, and Mario Südholt. Communicating functional agents and their application to graphical user interfaces. In *Proceedings of the 2nd International Conference on Perspectives of System Informatics, Novosibirsk*, LNCS. Springer Verlag, Jun 1996.

[5] W. Gropp, E. Lusk, and A. Skellum. *Using MPI: Portable Parallel Programming with the Message Passing Interface*. MIT Press, 1995.

[6] Thomas Nitsche. Skeleton implementations based on generic data distributions. In Christian Lengauer, editor, *Proceedings of the Second International Workshop on Constructive Methods for Parallel Programming (CMPP 2000)*, July 2000.

[7] Thomas Nitsche and Wolfram Webers. Functional message passing with OPAL-MPI. In Vassil Alexandrov and Jack Dongarra, editors, *Proceedings of Recent Advances in Parallel Virtual Machine and Message Passing Interface, 5th European PVM/MPI Users' Group Meeting, Liverpool, UK, September 7-9, 1998 (EuroPVM/MPI'98)*, volume 1497 of *Lecture Notes in Computer Science*, pages 281–288. Springer Verlag, September 1998.

[8] Mario Südholt. *The Transformational Derivation of Parallel Programs using Data Distribution Algebras and Skeletons*. PhD thesis, Fachgruppe Übersetzerbau, Fachbereich Informatik, Technische Universität Berlin, August 1997.

A Simple, Fault Tolerant Naming Space for the HARNESS Metacomputing System

Mauro Migliardi[1], Vaidy Sunderam[2] and Arrigo Frisiani[1]

University of Genoa[1], DIST
Genoa, Via Opera Pia 13, 16145, Italy
{om, alf}@dist.unige.it

Emory University[2], Dept. Of Math & Computer Science
Atlanta, GA, 30322, USA
om@mathcs.emory.edu

Abstract. HARNESS is an experimental Java-centric metacomputing system based upon the principle of dynamic reconfigurability not only in terms of the computers and networks that comprise the virtual machine, but also in the capabilities of the VM itself. In HARNESS, as in any other metacomputing systems, providing a consistent naming is a fundamental issue and the naming service is a pillar for any other service provided. HARNESS provides a two level naming scheme that separates virtual machine names from service names. In this paper we describe a simple yet fault tolerant implementation of the naming service dedicated to virtual machine names.

1 Introduction

HARNESS [1] is a metacomputing framework that is based upon several experimental concepts, including dynamic reconfigurability and fluid, extensible, virtual machines. HARNESS is a joint project between Emory University, Oak Ridge National Lab, and the University of Tennessee, and is a follow on to PVM [2], a popular network-based distributed computing platform of the 1990's. The underlying motivation behind HARNESS is to develop a metacomputing platform for the next generation, incorporating the inherent capability to integrate new technologies as they evolve. The first motivation is an outcome of the perceived need in metacomputing systems to provide more functionality, flexibility, and performance, while the second is based upon a desire to allow the framework to respond rapidly to advances in hardware, networks, system software, and applications. Both motivations are, in some part, derived from our experiences with the PVM system, whose monolithic design implies that substantial re-engineering is required to extend its capabilities or to adapt it to new network or machine architectures.

HARNESS attempts to overcome the limited flexibility of traditional software systems by defining a simple but powerful architectural model based on the concept of a software backplane. The HARNESS model is one that consists primarily of a

J. Dongarra et al. (Eds.): EuroPVM/MPI 2000, LNCS 1908, pp. 152-159, 2000.

kernel that is configured, according to user or application requirements, by attaching "plug-in" modules that provide various services. Some plug-ins are provided as part of the HARNESS system, while others might be developed by individual users for special situations, while yet other plug-ins might be obtained from third-party repositories. By configuring a HARNESS virtual machine using a suite of plug-ins appropriate to the particular hardware platform being used, the application being executed, and resource and time constraints, users are able to obtain functionality and performance that is well suited to their specific circumstances. Furthermore, since the HARNESS architecture is modular, plug-ins may be developed incrementally for emerging technologies such as faster networks or switches, new data compression algorithms or visualization methods, or resource allocation schemes – and these may be incorporated into the HARNESS system without requiring a major re-engineering effort.

The generality and the level of dynamicity achieved by the HARNESS framework impose very stringent requirements on the naming service. In fact, in order to be able to manage geographically distributed resources while tracking the evolution of a virtual machine HARNESS needs a global name space that is timely and consistently updated. To limit the level of complexity of naming services HARNESS separates the problem of dealing with a global set of computational resources from the one of tracking the changes of service sets by generating a two level name space. In the first level HARNESS keeps track of all the virtual machines currently active and guarantees the uniqueness of virtual machine names. This level allows nodes willing to join a virtual machine to find out if the virtual machine exists and if this is the case to locate it. Each virtual machine name contained in this space is a key to access a second level name space where uniqueness of service names and timely updating of the set of services available is guaranteed. This level allows applications and services to locate other services inside a virtual machine.

In this paper we will focus on the problem of generating and maintaining the first level name space, i.e. the space containing the names of HARNESS virtual machines.

This paper is structured as follows: in section 2 we begin with an overview of the HARNESS model and implementation; in section 3 we briefly outline the current implementation of HARNESS naming service and we describe our implementation of a fault-tolerant name space for HARNESS; finally, in section 4 we provide some concluding remarks.

2   Architectural Overview of HARNESS

The fundamental abstraction in the HARNESS metacomputing framework is the **Distributed Virtual Machine** (DVM) (see figure 1, level 1). Any DVM is associated with a symbolic name that is unique in the HARNESS name space, but has no physical entities connected to it. **Heterogeneous Computational Resources** may enroll into a DVM (see figure 1, level 2) at any time, however at this level the DVM is not ready yet to accept requests from users. To get ready to interact with users and applications the heterogeneous computational resources enrolled in a DVM need to

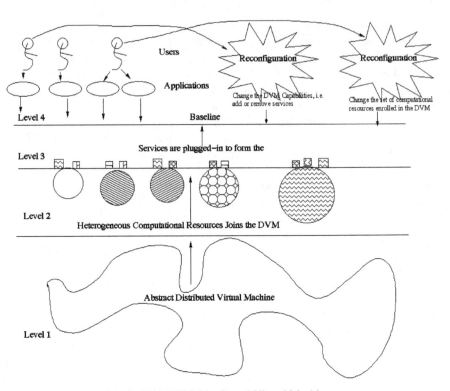

Figure 1   Abstract model of a HARNESS Distributed Virtual Machine

load **plug-ins** (see figure 1, level 3). A plug-in is a software component implementing a specific **service**. By loading plug-ins a DVM can build a consistent **service baseline** (see figure 1, level 4). A service provided by a loaded plug-in is associated with a name that is unique in the DVM name space. Users may **reconfigure** the DVM at any time (see figure 1, level 4) both in terms of computational resources enrolled by having them **join** or **leave** the DVM and in terms of services available by **loading** and **unloading** plug-ins.

The main goal of the HARNESS metacomputing framework is to achieve the capability to enroll heterogeneous computational resources into a DVM and make them capable of delivering a consistent service baseline to users. This goal require the programs building up the framework to be as portable as possible over an as large as possible selection of systems. The availability of services to heterogeneous computational resources derives from two different properties of the framework: the portability of plug-ins and the presence of multiple searchable plug-in repositories. HARNESS implements these properties mainly leveraging two different features of Java technology. These features are the capability to layer a homogeneous architecture such as the Java Virtual Machine (JVM) [3] over a large set of heterogeneous computational resources, and the capability to customize the mechanism adopted to load and link new objects and libraries.

The adoption of the Java language has also given us the capability to tune the tradeoff between portability and efficiency for the different components of the framework. This capability is extremely important, in fact, although portability at large is needed in all the components of the framework, it is possible to distinguish three different categories of components that requires different level of portability. The first category is represented by the components implementing the capability to manage the DVM status and load and unload services. We call these components **kernel level services**. These services require the highest achievable degree of portability, as a matter of fact they are necessary to enroll a computational resource into a DVM. The second category is represented by very commonly used services (e.g. a general, network independent, message-passing service or a generic event notification mechanism). We call these services **basic services**. Basic services should be generally available, but it is conceivable for some computational resources based on specialized architecture to lack them. The last category is represented by highly architecture specific services. These services include all those services that are inherently dependent on the specific characteristics of a computational resource (e.g. a low-level image processing service exploiting a SIMD co-processor, a message-passing service exploiting a specific network interface or any service that need architecture dependent optimization). We call these services **specialized services**. For this last category portability is a goal to strive for, but it is acceptable that they will be available only on small subsets of the available computational resources. These different requirements for portability and efficiency can optimally leverage the capability to link together Java byte code and system dependent native code enabled by the Java Native Interface (JNI) [4]. The JNI allows to develop the parts of the framework that are most critical to efficient application execution in ANSI C language and to introduce into them the desired level of architecture dependent optimization at the cost of increased development effort.

The use of native code requires a different implementation of a service for each type of heterogeneous computational resource enrolled in the DVM. This fact implies a larger development effort. However, if a version of the plug-in for a specific architecture is available, the HARNESS metacomputing framework is able to fetch and load it in a user transparent fashion, thus users are screened from the necessity to control the set of architectures their application is currently running on. To achieve this result HARNESS leverages the capability of the JVM to let users redefine the mechanism used to retrieve and load both Java classes bytecode and native shared libraries. In fact, each DVM in the framework is able to search a set of plug-ins repositories for the desired library. This set of repositories is dynamically reconfigurable at run-time: users can add or delete repositories at any time.

3   Naming Services in the HARNESS System

At present the HARNESS metacomputing framework provides two implementations for the virtual machines name space.

The first implementation is based on IP multicast and adopts a peer-to-peer discovery protocol similar to the one used in the Jini system [5]. This implementation is extremely resilient to failures in fact no component represents a single point of failure. However, the strengths of this implementation are also its limits. In fact while IP multicast works extremely well over a single LAN, it is extremely unreliable and suffer from sever scalability problems over WANs. For these reasons this implementation of the naming service fits only the scenario where the computational resources of a single entity (e.g. an enterprise, a University, etc.) can be dynamically enrolled into HARNESS virtual machines.

The second implementation is based on a naming server residing on a well known host and accepting connections to a well known port. This implementation overcomes one of the limitations imposed by the first implementation, in fact it can easily provide a name space for computational resources distributed over the whole Internet. However, the price of this result is the injection of a single point of failure in the system architecture. In fact, if the name server is not available it is possible neither to enroll additional nodes into existing virtual machines nor to create new virtual machines[1].

To overcome the limitations of the two available implementations we have developed a distributed naming service. Our design is based on some fundamental assumptions:

1. the routing of IP is designed in such a way that the property of a node to be reachable from another node is symmetric and transitive;
2. any situation that negates assumption 1 is transient;
3. it is acceptable for the name space to experience short, temporary splitting as long as the steady state guarantees uniqueness and consistency.

Assumption one means two things. First, the fact that A is reachable from B also implies B is reachable from A; second, the fact that A is reachable from B and B is reachable from C also means that A is reachable from C. To our knowledge, the only non transient situations where this property can be negated permanently are generated by the use of firewalls. However, this does not represent a major limitation of our design, in fact our implementation is based on the TCP protocol and statically configured ports, thus it is possible to configure the firewall so that the packets directed to our naming service are not filtered out. Assumption three allowed us to avoid the large overhead required by a fully distributed, atomically updated naming space.

In our implementation each HARNESS kernel is configured with a list of couples node/port that identify the HARNESS Name space Servers (HNS) that the kernel can inquire. The list is ordered according to the IP addresses of the HNS so that a lower IP will always be contacted before a higher IP. A kernel that needs to contact an HNS will start trying each of the listed servers. If an HNS is not running the kernel will simply time-out and it will try the next one. If an HNS is running the kernel can get two different replies: an acknowledgement that the contacted HNS is the current list master or a redirect reply.

If the kernel gets a redirect it will keep on going through the list. Once the kernel has

---

[1] It is important to notice, however, that existing virtual machines maintain all the remaining functionality, i.e. on the currently enrolled nodes services can still be used, added and removed freely.

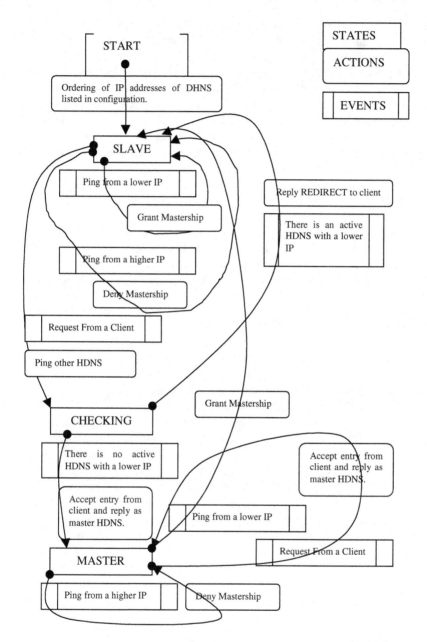

Figure 2 Finite state automaton describing the behavior of each of the HNS

reached the end of the list it will start again from the head up to five times. After five full list scan it will give up and abort.

It is important to notice that the decision about the faulty state of an HNS is not permanent. On the contrary the status of a faulty HNS will be probed again as soon as one of the following two events takes place: a non master HNS is contacted, there as been no probe for a configurable amount of time. This fact guarantees that it is not possible that a transient failure is wrongly assumed to be a permanent failure.

At any given time only one HNS is in charge of the name space, every other HNS will refuse to service kernels and will redirect them. In figure 2 you can see the finite state automata that describes the behavior of each of the HNS. Each HNS bootstraps in the slave status. The reception of a query from a kernel will trigger the process of checking who is the current list-master. This checking consists of pinging the ordered HNS list to see if there is a running HNS with an IP lower than the one that is currently performing the check. If there is one it will remain the list-master and the one currently checking will stay in the slave state. If there is none, the one currently checking will make the transition to master state.

It is possible for the check for the current list-master to require a long time, in fact the worst case is represented by the situation where, with a list of N HNS, the N-1 HNS with the lower IPs are not running. In this situation the Nth HNS needs to time-out on a TCP connect N-1 times in order to get list-master status. However, this check is performed only when an HNS in slave state receives a query from a kernel, thus the overhead required by this process is not injected into each name space query. On the contrary, it is only incurred into at the time of the first query and in the case of list-master faults.

Our scheme does not copy all the HARNESS virtual machine names information to the HNS in the slave state. However, in the case of a list-master fault the refresh mechanism built-into the HARNESS kernel will automatically reconstruct the complete set into the newly elected list-master. This process will take no more than one refresh timeout. During this time frame the HARNESS virtual machines name space is in an inconsistent state, in fact it is possible for a kernel to start a second copy of an existing virtual machine as its existence has not been copied into the new list-master yet. However, this inconsistent, split-brain-like state is strictly transient and it will be automatically removed as soon as the name space is refreshed. In fact, the virtual machine trying to refresh the faulting HNS will detect the fault, contact the new list-master and receive a notification that there is another set of nodes running as the same virtual machine. The nodes enrolled in the original virtual machine will automatically join the new virtual machine and the system will be in a consistent state again. It is important to notice that this sequence of events will be perceived by the services and applications running in the virtual machine only as a growth of the set of nodes enrolled in the virtual machine, thus this process will not prevent the software components from performing the currently ongoing activities.

It is our opinion that in most cases the advantages of a fast, low overhead service in the steady state largely compensate for the problems that can be caused by these transient inconsistencies.

4 Conclusions

In this paper we have described a simple, yet fault-tolerant implementation of the HARNESS naming service dedicated to the tracking and management of virtual machine names. Our implementation overcomes the limitations of the naming space implementations currently available for HARNESS, namely either the presence of a single point of failure or limited usability in WAN connected scenarios, without introducing the large overhead needed by a fully distributed, atomically updated naming service. In fact, when operating in steady state, our implementation has an operational overhead as low as the one introduced by a centralized solution. This result is achieved by relaxing the atomicity constraint and allowing transient inconsistency in the namespace to happen. However, return to a consistent steady state in a finite amount of time is guaranteed as long as there are no asymmetric connectivity patterns such as the ones generated by firewalls configured to filter out HARNESS naming queries. The length of the time period required to return to consistent state is controlled by a configurable time-out.

References

1   M. Migliardi, V. Sunderam, A. Geist, J. Dongarra, Dynamic Reconfiguration and Virtual Machine Management in the HARNESS Metacomputing System, Proc. of ISCOPE98, pp. 127-134, Santa Fe', New Mexico (USA), December 8-11, 1998.

2   A. Geist, A. Beguelin, J. Dongarra, W. Jiang, B. Mancheck and V. Sunderam, PVM: Parallel Virtual Machine a User's Guide and Tutorial for Networked Parallel Computing, MIT Press, Cambridge, MA, 1994.

3   T. Lindholm and F. Yellin, The Java Virtual Machine Specification, Addison Wesley, 1997.

4   S. Liang, The Java Native Interface: Programming Guide and Reference, Addison Wesley, 1998.

5   W. K. Edwards, Core Jini, SUN Microsystems Press, 1999.

Runtime Checking of Datatype Signatures in MPI*

William D. Gropp

Mathematics and Computer Science Division
Argonne National Laboratory
Argonne, Illinois 60439

Abstract. The MPI standard provides a way to send and receive complex combinations of datatypes (e.g., integers and doubles) with a single communication operation. The MPI standard specifies that the *type signature*, that is, the basic datatypes (language-defined types such as int or DOUBLE PRECISION), must match in communication operations such as send/receive or broadcast. Because datatypes may be defined by the user in MPI, there is a limitless collection of possible type signatures. Detecting the programmer error of mismatched datatypes is difficult in this case; detecting all errors essentially requires sending a complete description of the type signature with a message. This paper discusses an alternative: send the value of a function of the type signature so that (a) identical type signatures always give the same function value, (b) different type signatures often give different values, and (c) common cases (e.g., predefined datatypes) are handled exactly. Thus, erroneous programs are often (but not always) detected; correct programs never are flagged as erroneous. The method described is relatively inexpensive to compute and uses a small (and fixed, independent of the complexity of the datatype) amount of space in the message envelope.

1 Introduction

The Message Passing Interface (MPI) [3, 2] provides a standard and portable way of communicating data from one process to another, even for heterogeneous collections of computers. A key part of MPI's support for moving data is the description of data not as a series of undifferentiated bytes but as typed data corresponding to the datatypes natural to the programming language being used with MPI. Thus, when sending C ints, the programmer specifies that the message is made up of type MPI_INT (because MPI is a library rather than a language extension, MPI cannot use the same names for the types as the programming language). MPI further requires that the type of the data sent match the type of the data received; that is, if the user sends MPI_INTs, the user must

---

* This work was supported by the Mathematical, Information, and Computational Sciences Division subprogram of the Office of Advanced Scientific Computing, U.S. Department of Energy, under Contract W-31-109-Eng-38.

J. Dongarra et al. (Eds.): EuroPVM/MPI 2000, LNCS 1908, pp. 160–167, 2000.

receive MPI_INTs.[1] MPI also allows the definition of new MPI datatypes, called *derived types*, by combining datatypes with routines such as MPI_TYPE_VECTOR, MPI_TYPE_STRUCT, and MPI_TYPE_HINDEXED. Because the matching of basic types is required for a correct program, a high-quality development environment should detect when the user violates this rule. This paper describes an efficient method for checking that datatype signatures match in MPI communication.

One reason such error checking is important for MPI programs is that MPI allows messages containing collections of different datatypes to be communicated in a single message. Further, the sender and receiver are often in different parts of the program, possibly in different routines (or even programs). User errors in the use of MPI datatypes are thus difficult to find; adding this information can catch errors (such as using the same message tag for two different kinds of messages) that are difficult for the user to identify by looking at the code.

An additional complexity is that MPI requires only that the basic types of the data communicated match for example, that ints match ints and chars match chars. This ordered set of basic datatypes (i.e., types that correspond to basic types supported by the programming language) is called the *type signature*. The type signature is a tuple of the basic MPI datatypes. For example, three ints followed by a double is

$$(\mathtt{MPI\_INT}, \mathtt{MPI\_INT}, \mathtt{MPI\_INT}, \mathtt{MPI\_DOUBLE}).$$

A type signature has as many types as there are elements in the message. This makes it impractical to send the type signature with the message.

MPI also defines a *type map*; for each datatype, a displacement in memory is given. While the type map specifies both what and where data is moved, a type signature specifies only what is moved. Only the signatures need to match; this allows scatter/gather-like operations in MPI communication. For example, it is legal to send 10 MPI_INTs but receive a single vector (created with MPI_TYPE_VECTOR) that contains at least 10 MPI_INTs. Communicating with different type maps is legal as long as the type signatures are the same. Thus, it isn't correct to check that the datatypes match; only the type signatures must match.

Note that when looking at the type signature, the comparison is made with the basic types, even if the type was defined using a combination of derived datatypes. Thus, when looking at the type signature, any consecutive subsequence may have come from a derived datatype.

Consider the derived type t2 defined by the following MPI code fragment:

---

[1] Two exceptions to this rule are mentioned in Section 4. A third, mentioned in the MPI standard, is for the MPI implementation to cast the type; for example, if MPI_INT is sent but MPI_FLOAT is specified for the receive, an implementation is permitted to convert the integer to a float, following the rules of the language. As this is not required, it is nonportable. Further, no MPI implementation performs this conversion, and because it silently corrects for what is more likely a programming error, no implementation is ever likely to implement this choice.

```
MPI_Datatype t1, t2, types[2];
int          blen[2];
MPI_Aint     displ[2];
types[0] = MPI_INT;        types[1] = MPI_DOUBLE;
blen[0]  = 1;              blen[1]  = 1;
displ[0] = ...;            displ[1] = ...;
MPI_Type_struct( 2, blen, displ, types, &t1 );
types[0] = t1;             types[1] = MPI_SHORT;
blen[0] = 2;
MPI_Type_struct( 2, blen, displ, types, &t2 );
```

The derived type t2 has the type signature

```
( (MPI_INT, MPI_DOUBLE), (MPI_INT, MPI_DOUBLE), MPI_SHORT ) =
( MPI_INT, MPI_DOUBLE, MPI_INT, MPI_DOUBLE, MPI_SHORT ).
```

The approach in this paper is to define a *hashing function* that maps the type signature to an integer tuple (the reason for the tuple is discussed in Section 3). The communication requirement is thus bounded independent of the complexity of the datatype; further, the function is chosen so that it can be computed efficiently; finally, in most cases, the cost of computing and checking the datatype signature is a small constant cost for each communication operation. Since this approach is a many-to-one mapping, it can fail to detect an error. However, the mapping is chosen so that it never erroneously reports failure. Further, for the important special case of communication with basic datatypes (e.g., MPI_DOUBLE), the test succeeds if and only if the type signatures match.

Other approaches are possible. The datatype definitions (just enough to reproduce the signature, not the type map) could be sent, allowing sender and receiver to agree on the datatypes. The definitions could be cached, allowing a datatype to be reused without resending its definition. The special case of (count,datatype) would reduce the amount of data that needed to be communicated in many common cases. Still, comparison of different datatypes in general would be complex, even if common patterns were exploited. Another approach is to send the complete type signature; this is the only approach that will catch all failures (various compression schemes can be used to reduce the amount of data that must be sent to describe the type signature, of course). Such an approach could be implemented over MPI by using the MPI-2 routines to extract datatype definitions, along with the MPI profiling interface. For systems with some kind of globally accessible memory, such as the Cray T3D, it is possible to make all datatype definitions visible to all processes, as in [1]. The approach described in this paper offers several advantages. Perhaps most important, it is simple, requiring very little change to an MPI implementation. Sending the entire datatype signature, even if compressed, requires the MPI implementation to handle variable-length header data. In addition, even with compression, sending the full datatype signature can significantly increase the time to send a message; even in debugging mode, users prefer minimal extra overhead.

2   Datatype Hashing Function

We are looking for a function f that converts a type signature into a small bit range, such as a single integer or pair of integers. The cost of evaluating f should be relatively small; in particular, the cost of evaluating f for a type signature containing n copies of the same type (derived or basic) should be $o(n)$; for example, $\log n$. Because a type signature may contain an arbitrary number of terms, the easiest way to define f is by a binary operation applied to all of the elements of the type signature. That is, define a binary operation $\oplus$ that can be applied to a type signature $(\alpha_1, \ldots, \alpha_n)$ as follows:

$$f(\alpha_1) = \alpha_1$$

$$f((\alpha_1, \alpha_2, \ldots, \alpha_n)) = \bigoplus_{i=1}^{n} \alpha_i.$$

For example,

$$f(int, double) = (int) \oplus (double)$$

and

$$f(int, double, char) = (int) \oplus (double) \oplus (char).$$

In order to make it inexpensive to compute the hash function for datatypes built from an arbitrary combination of derived datatypes, the hash function must be associative. Since we want (`int,double`) to hash to a different value from (`double,int`), we want the operation $\oplus$ to be noncommutative. For this approach to be useful, the hash function must hash different datatypes to different hash values, particularly in the case of "common" errors, such as mismatched predefined datatypes.

3   A Simple Datatype Hashing Function

We need an operation that is both associative and noncommutative. Our approach is to define a tuple (α, n) where α is a datatype (derived or basic) and n is the number of basic datatypes in α. We start with the predefined datatypes, representing, for example, MPI_INT as $(\alpha_{int}, 1)$, where α_{int} is a integer value. The tuple for a derived datatype is then constructed by applying the operator $\oplus$, whose action is given by

$$(\alpha, n) \oplus (\beta, m) \equiv (\alpha + (\beta << n), n + m),$$

where the operators $+$ and $<<$ are chosen to have the following properties:

$$(\alpha << n) << m = \alpha << (n + m) \tag{1}$$
$$(\alpha + \beta) + \gamma = \alpha + (\beta + \gamma) \tag{2}$$
$$(\alpha << n) + (\beta << n) = (\alpha + \beta) << n. \tag{3}$$

One choice for these operators is bitwise exclusive or (xor) for $+$ and circular left shift for $<<$. These operations are often chosen for hash functions because they are very cheap to apply. They have the necessary properties, as can be proven by writing the α and so forth as bit vectors and then applying the operations xor and circular shift to those bit vectors. Another choice of operators is integer addition modulo 2^{32} for $+$ and circular left shift by 3 for $<<$ (that is, $a << 1$ is a, shifted left three bits).

These properties allow us to prove that the operation $\oplus$ is associative:

$$((\alpha, n) \oplus (\beta, m)) \oplus (\gamma, p) =$$
$$((\alpha + (\beta << n), n + m)) \oplus (\gamma, p) =$$
$$((\alpha + (\beta << n) + (\gamma << n + m), n + m + p) =$$
$$((\alpha + ((\beta + (\gamma << m) << n)), (n + (m + p)) =$$
$$((\alpha, n) \oplus (\beta + (\gamma << m), m + p)) =$$
$$((\alpha, n) \oplus ((\beta, m) \oplus (\gamma, p))).$$

The operation $\oplus$ is not commutative:

$$(\alpha, n) \oplus (\beta, m) =$$
$$(\alpha + (\beta << n), n + m)$$
$$(\beta, m) \oplus (\alpha, n) =$$
$$(\beta + (\alpha << m), n + m),$$

but

$$(\alpha + (\beta << n)) \neq (\beta + (\alpha << m))$$

except in special cases.

Note that addition and xor by itself are commutative; the shift operation provides a noncommutative operation.

We will use this operation to build f. Specifically, we will apply $\oplus$ to a type signature where we have replaced every basic type with a tuple containing an integer representing the type and a one, indicating a single basic type. That is,

$$(int, double, char)$$

becomes

$$((int, 1), (double, 1), (char, 1))$$

and

$$f((int, double, char)) = (int, 1) \oplus (double, 1) \oplus (char, 1).$$

3.1   Cost of Evaluating f

Several identities can be used to reduce the cost of computing f. One important case is a type signature containing a large number of the same basic type. This is the signature that represents the most common MPI usage: a send with a basic datatype and a count that is greater than one. Using a method that is very similar to the approach for evaluating integer powers of matrices, we can compute $\bigoplus_{i=1}^{m}(\alpha, n)$ in $O(\log(m))$ time by induction. Let m be 2^k for some k. Then

$$\bigoplus_{i=1}^{m}(\alpha, n) = \left(\bigoplus_{i=1}^{m/2}(\alpha, n)\right) \oplus \left(\bigoplus_{i=1}^{m/2}(\alpha, n)\right),$$

the terms on the right are evaluated by induction. This can be evaluated with $\log_2 m$ evaluations. The generalization to arbitrary m is left to the reader.

Further, note that $v << n = v << (n + wordsize) = v << (n \bmod wordsize)$; this can be used to reduce the cost of evaluating f.

Finally, by exploiting the associative property of $\oplus$, evaluating f for a new derived datatype involves only the values of f for the datatypes that make up the new datatype (with the exception of those containing types MPI_PACKED or MPI_BYTE; see Section 4). Thus, computing f for a datatype has cost proportional only to the number of different datatypes (either user-defined or basic) used in the definition and proportional to the log of the number of instances of each datatype.

3.2   Hash Function Quality

For the hash function to be useful, collisions should be rare. Since in a typical program, MPI type signatures are *not* randomly distributed, it makes the most sense to experimentally evaluate some common datatype patterns. Further, while there are 13 distinct basic MPI datatypes in the C binding, most programs use only a few types, such as MPI_INT and MPI_DOUBLE. Types such as MPI_UNSIGNED_CHAR are rarely used. Thus, for most applications, only a few basic datatypes will appear. To see how likely a collision in the hash function might be, we tested the following patterns:

$$n : \alpha_i \tag{4}$$
$$m : (1 : \alpha_i, \quad (n-1) : \alpha_j) \tag{5}$$
$$1 : \alpha_i, \quad m : (1 : \alpha_i, \quad (n-1) : \alpha_j), \tag{6}$$

where $n : x$ means n copies of x. These correspond to the cases of count (n) of a basic datatype (4), count m of a structure containing n members (5), and a structure containing count m of another structure (6). Various values of n and m were used.

Table 1 shows the results of the tests. Clearly, only the choice of integer addition with medium-sized integers provides an effective hash function; with this choice, only one in one hundred different type signatures hashed to the same value. Further experiments may identify improved hash functions.

Table 1. Results of tests of the hash function. Collisions is the percentage of type signatures whose hash value was the same as a different type signature. Duplicates gives the percentage of hash values that were duplicated. Operand indicates whether the representation for a basic datatype is a small integer (less than 32) or a larger integer (less than 2^{16}). We tested 4625 different type signatures.

Operator1	Operator2	Operand	Collisions	Duplicates
xor	rotate 1	small	57.4	13.4
xor	rotate 3	small	48.9	10.5
+	rotate 1	small	24.9	11.5
+	rotate 3	small	29.4	10.3
xor	rotate 1	medium	45.6	9.8
+	rotate 1	medium	1.2	0.58

3.3   Improving the Type Signature Test

One modification of the approach is to optimize for the special case of count copies of a datatype (basic or otherwise), since this is the fundamental unit in MPI (all MPI communication operations send count copies of a given datatype).

In this case, we send $(count, \alpha, n)$. The modified test is shown in Figure 1. Note that the *count* applied in the receive case is the actual count, not the maximum count that is provided by user in the MPI_RECV call. In addition, we do not need to send the count separately; we can simply use a single bit to indicate that the datatype is basic and the count can be computed, if necessary, from the length of data sent. With this modification, basic datatypes are handled exactly (all errors are detected).

if $(\alpha_{send} \mathrel{!=} \alpha_{recv})$ then
    if $(\alpha_{send}$ and α_{recv} is basic) then error
    else if $(\bigoplus_{i=1}^{count_{send}} (\alpha_{send}, n_{send}) \mathrel{!=}$
            $\bigoplus_{i=1}^{count_{recv}} (\alpha_{recv}, n_{recv}))$ then error
    endif
endif

Fig. 1. Modification to test to provide exact handling of the most common case.

4   Limitations

MPI allows users to send partial datatypes. That is, the user can define a datatype representing, for example, an `int` followed by ten `doubles`, and receive this into a datatype of an `int` followed by fifty `doubles`, as long as the type signature of the data that is sent matches the type signature at the receiver for all of the types that are used. This allows the user to define a maximum-sized datatype on the receive end but an actual sized datatype on the send end.

In MPI, the user can detect this by examining the `MPI_Status` value returned by the receive. If the routine `MPI_GET_COUNT` returns `MPI_UNDEFINED`, then the routine `MPI_GET_ELEMENTS` may be used to determine how many elementary (predefined) MPI datatypes were sent. In the case above, `MPI_GET_ELEMENTS` would return eleven (one `int` plus ten `doubles`). Our test does not handle this. Thus, it must also test for `MPI_GET_COUNT` being `MPI_UNDEFINED`; in that case, the test passes (even if the type signature do not, in fact match). In principle, a corresponding value of f could be constructed by using the same process that is used in an MPI implementation to evaluate `MPI_GET_ELEMENTS`; by integrating the computation of f with this routine, this test can be performed with low additional cost.

The MPI datatype `MPI_PACKED` and `MPI_BYTE` also present special problems whose full discussion would take too long. In short, data sent with `MPI_PACKED` is first packed incrementally into a user-defined buffer using the routine `MPI_PACK`. The function f must thus also be accumulated incrementatlly; one possibility is to use the header of the packed buffer. The more complex case of MPI derived datatypes that contain `MPI_PACKED` can also be handled, though here the function f must be evaluated when the data is sent rather than when the datatype is created. `MPI_BYTE` explicitly turns off type signature matching and is best handled with a reserved hash value (e.g., `0xFFFFFFFF,-1`).

5   Conclusion

We have shown an efficient way to catch many user errors caused by type signature mismatch at run time in MPI programs. The cost is relatively small; consuming only an additional 32 to 64 bits (4 to 8 bytes) of message header and evaluation cost that is bounded by $O(m \log n)$ for derived datatypes containing m different types with repeat count $\leq n$. The most common cases (count of a basic datatype) take constant time. We note that this approach can be used for any system that incrementally packs and unpacks data, such as XDR or PVM.

Acknowledgments

I thank Lloyd Lewins for the suggestion of using a hashing function to support error checking of derived datatypes, and Rusty Lusk for his valuable comments.

References

[1] Jason Hunter. Datatype checking in Cray T3D native MPI. Technical Report EPCC-SS95-07, Edinburgh Parallel Computing Centre, 1995.

[2] Message Passing Interface Forum. MPI: A message-passing interface standard. http://www.mpi-forum.org.

[3] Message Passing Interface Forum. MPI: A Message-Passing Interface standard. *International Journal of Supercomputer Applications*, 8(3/4):165–414, 1994.

A Scalable Process-Management Environment for Parallel Programs*

Ralph Butler[1], William Gropp[2], and Ewing Lusk[2]

[1] University of North Florida
[2] Argonne National Laboratory

Abstract. We present a process management system for parallel programs such as those written using MPI. A primary goal of the system, which we call MPD (for multipurpose daemon), is to be scalable. By this we mean that startup of interactive parallel jobs comprising a thousand processes is quick, that signals can be quickly delivered to processes, and that stdin, stdout, and stderr are managed intuitively. Our primary target is parallel machines made up of clusters of SMPs, but the system is also useful in more tightly integrated environments. We describe how MPD enables much faster startup and better runtime management of MPICH jobs. We show how close control of stdio can support the easy implementation of a number of convenient system utilities, even a parallel debugger. MPD is implemented and freely distributed with MPICH.

1 Introduction

A parallel programming environment may be viewed as comprising three interacting components: a *job scheduler*, which decides what resources a parallel job consisting of multiple processes will run on; a *process manager*, which starts and terminates processes and provides them with a number of services; and a *parallel library* such as MPI, which a parallel application calls upon for communications. Since these components need to communicate with one another, they are often integrated into a single system. An important research question is to what extent they can be separated from one another with well-defined interfaces so that they can be independently developed. A further research question is whether the resulting system can be made scalable to jobs involving thousands of communicating processes. In this paper we focus on the process manager component. We describe a design and an implementation we call MPD (for multipurpose daemon) that provides both fast startup of parallel jobs and a flexible run-time environment that supports parallel libraries.

In Section 2 we summarize related work. In Section 3 we state our explicit design goals, how these goals lead to implementation decisions, and interesting features of the resulting system, including how it can be used to create a parallel debugger out of an existing single-process debugger. Section 4 summarizes

---

* This work was supported by the Mathematical, Information, and Computational Sciences Division subprogram of the Office of Advanced Scientific Computing Research, U.S. Department of Energy, under Contract W-31-109-Eng-38.

J. Dongarra et al. (Eds.): EuroPVM/MPI 2000, LNCS 1908, pp. 168–175, 2000.

preliminary experiments that make us optimistic about the usefulness of MPD as a process manager for large-scale systems. We conclude with a summary of progress to date and a description of our future plans.

The MPD system is in use and is available as open source as part of the MPICH system, obtainable from http://www.mcs.anl.gov/mpi/mpich.

2   Related Work

All parallel computing environments that support execution of truly parallel programs (those in which any two processes can communicate with one another) have had to address at least some of the issues that we address with MPD. Parallel programming systems, such as PVM [10], P4 [7], and implementations of MPI such as MPICH [13] and LAM [6] all provide some mechanism for starting and running parallel programs, often with a specialized daemon process.

Many systems are intended to manage a collection of computing resources for both single-process and parallel jobs; see the survey by Baker, et. al. [3]. Typically, these use a daemon that manages individual processes, with emphasis on jobs involving only a single process. Widely used systems include PBS [17], LSF [18], DQS [8], and Loadleveler/POE [14]. The Condor system [15] is also widely used and supports parallel programs that use PVM [19]. Other, more specialized systems, such as MOSIX [4] and GLUnix [11], provide a form of single-system image support for clusters.

Harness [5, 16] shares with MPD the goal of supporting management of parallel jobs. Its primary research goal is to demonstrate the flexibility of the "plug-in" approach to application design, providing a wide range of services, whereas the MPD system focuses more specifically on the design and implementation of services required for process management of parallel jobs, including high-speed startup of large parallel jobs on clusters and scalable standard I/O management. The book [9] provides a good overview of metacomputing systems and issues.

3   Design of MPD

In this section we describe our goals in constructing MPD and outline the system's architecture.

3.1   Goals

Several explicit goals have governed the design of the MPD system.

Simplicity The persistent (across jobs) part of the system should be simple and robust. In the long run we expect this part to be runnable as root. If its behavior isn't completely transparent, we will never be able to convince system administrators to run the daemons as root.

Speed Startup of parallel jobs should be quick enough to provide an interactive "feel," so that large but short jobs make sense. Large (in number of processes) but short (in time) characterizes system utilities such as those described in [12]. Our immediate target is to start 1000 processes in a few seconds, while still providing a way for such processes to establish contact with one another. Our long-term goal is to support management of 10,000 processes.

Robustness The persistent part of the system should be at least moderately fault tolerant. An unexpected crash of one machine should not bring down the whole system. There should be no single "master" process.

Scalability The complexity or size of any component should not depend on the number of components.

Individual Process Environments It should be possible to start a parallel job in which the executable files, environment variables, and command-line arguments are different for each process. It should be possible to collect return codes individually from processes.

Collective Identity of a Parallel Job It should be possible to treat a parallel job as a single entity that can be suspended, continued (signaled, in general), or killed collectively as if it were a single process. The system should manage `stdin`, `stdout`, and `stderr` in a useful and scalable way and allow them to be redirected as if the parallel job were a single process. An important component of a job's collective identity is its *termination*. All resources allocated for the job, such as files, System V IPC's, other processes, etc., must be reliably freed, even if the job terminates abnormally.

It is explicitly not a goal of the MPD system to provide scheduling services, which we believe to be a separate function from process management.

3.2   Deriving the Design from the Goals

The goals of simplicity and robustness lead us to adopt a multicomponent system. The *daemon* itself is persistent (may run for weeks or months at a time, starting many jobs), typically one instance per host in a TCP-connected network. *Manager* processes will be started by the daemons to control the application processes (*clients*) of a single parallel job and will provide most of the MPD features. The goal of speed requires that the daemons be in contact with one another prior to job startup, and the goals of scalability and "no master" suggest that the daemons be connected in a ring.[1] The services that the managers will provide (see Section 3.3) suggest that they be in contact as well, and the fastest way for them to form these connections is to inherit part of the ring connectivity of the daemons. Separate managers for each user process support the individual process environments. The goal of having a collective identity for a parallel job leads us to treat the `mpirun` or `mpiexec` process as such a representative, and use it to deliver signals and `stdin` to application processes and collect `stdout`

---

[1] While a ring is not ultimately scalable, it is more so than the typical star used in many process management systems, and our experiments have shown it feasible for the 1000-daemon domain.

and `stderr` output from them. This suggests that the `mpirun` process connect first to the daemon ring in order to start the job, and then switch the connection to the manager ring in order to control the job. The goal of speed suggests that these latter connections be restricted to a process running on the same host, either the daemon itself or a persistent gateway process if the daemon is run as root, so that authentication can be through the file system (a Unix rather than a network socket). We refer to all such processes as *console commands*. Finally, in order that this infrastructure be available to support MPI programs or other parallel tools, there needs to be *client library* that each application process may use to interact with its manager.

We do not specify how the daemons are started or connected, since the system provides a number of alternatives, and the process need not be particularly fast. A console command is started by the user, either interactively or under the control of a batch scheduler. The daemons fork and exec the managers, which use information given them by the daemons to connect themselves into a ring, then fork and exec the clients. The startup messages traverse the ring quickly, so most forking, execing, and connecting take place in parallel, leading to fast startup even for large jobs. The situation is then as shown in Figure 1, where the

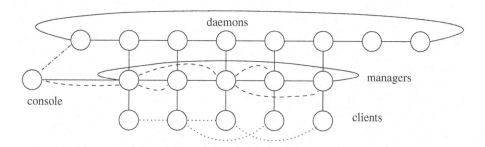

Fig. 1. Daemons with console process, managers, and clients

clients may be application MPI processes. Solid lines represent sockets, except for the vertical ones, which represent pipes. The dashed lines represent the trees of connections for forwarding `stdout` and `stderr`, and the dotted lines represent *potential* connections among the client processes. The dot-dashed line is the original connection from console to local daemon on a Unix socket, which is replaced during startup by the network connection to the first manager.

3.3   Interesting Features

Space restrictions prevent a complete description of all the features and capabilities of the MPD system, but in this section we mention a few highlights.

Security Whenever a process advertises a "listener" socket and accepts connections on it, the possibility exists that an unknown or even malicious process will connect. This is particularly dangerous if the process accepting the connection can start processes as the MPD daemon can. We currently use the "challenge-response" system described in [20]. In the long run, we expect to modify this component of the system to use more elaborate schemes and extend them to other connections such as client/gateway authentication. This will have little impact on the job startup speed since the daemon component startup is separate from job startup.

Fault Tolerance If a daemon dies, this fact is detected and the ring is reknit. This provides a minimal sort of fault tolerance, since the ring remains intact. A new MPD daemon can be inserted in the ring where the old one was, but this process is not (yet) automatic.

Signals Signals can be delivered to client processes by their managers. We currently use this capability in two specific ways. First, signals delivered to a console process are propagated to the clients, so that a parallel application as a whole can be suspended with `cntl-Z`, continued, and killed with `cntl-C`, just as if it were a single process. Second, in the `ch_p4mpd` device in the MPICH implementation of MPI, client processes can interrupt one another with requests to dynamically establish client-to-client connections. Such requests go up into the manager ring from the originating client, around the ring to the manager of the target process, which signals its client.

Support for MPI Implementations Currently MPD provides direct support for the MPICH implementation of MPI. The `ch_p4mpd` device distributed with Version 1.2 of MPICH makes direct calls to the client library component of the MPD system to find out a process's rank, where other processes are and how to contact them, and so forth. In our next major release of MPICH, the support will be indirect, through a general parallel-library-to-process-manager interface we will describe elsewhere.

On clusters of SMPs, it is easy to specify that multiple processes are to be started on the same machine and share memory. Specifically, `mpirun -np 180 -g 2 cpi` starts processes in groups of two and places in their environment a key that can be used to acquire group-attached shared memory and other information needed to set up multimethod communication for an MPI implementation. Other communication mechanisms (such as VIA) will be supported over time.

Handling Standard I/O Mangers capture the `stdout` and `stderr` of their clients, and forward them up a pair of binary trees of socket connections, each manager merging `stdout` and `stderr` from its client with that from each of its two children. A command line option tells the managers to provide a rank label on each line of output from their clients.

Standard input (to `mpirun`, for example) by default is delivered to the client managed by manager 0. This seems to be what most MPI users expect, and what most MPI implementations do. (The MPI standard does not specify.) However, control messages can be used to change this behavior to direct `stdin` to any specific client or broadcast it to all clients.

Client Wrapping The semantics of the Unix `fork` and `exec` system calls provide useful benefits. When a manager forks a client process, for example, it first sets up the manager-client pipes for control messages and standard I/O. The "lower" ends of these pipes are inherited by any process that the client forks. Thus, even though the client is not using any of the client library, managers can manage clients that themselves run the "real" application process. We call this scheme *client wrapping*. Thus `mpirun -np 16 nice -5 myprog` lowers the priority of a parallel job to be run on one's colleagues' workstations, and `mpirun -np 16 pty myprog` can be used when `myprog` needs to be attached to a terminal (otherwise our capture of `stdin` and `stdout` modifies their buffering behavior). (The program `pty` is distributed with the MPD system.)

Putting It All Together The combination of I/O management, especially redirection of `stdin`, line labels on `stdout`, and client wrapping can be surprisingly powerful. We have used these features of the MPD system to add an option to `mpirun` that invokes `gdb` as a client wrapper and dynamically redirects `stdin`. While `mpirun -np 3 cpi` runs `cpi` directly as an MPI job, `mpirun -np 3 -d cpi` runs each `cpi` process under the control of (wrapped by) the `gdb` debugger. (Other sequential debuggers could be used, but are not yet supported.) Thus multiple instances of `gdb` are being run. Output of the `gdb`'s is labeled by process rank. The "(gdb)" prompts are intercepted by the `mpirun` process and counted, so that it can issue an "(mpigdb)" prompt when one has been received from each process. In addition, `mpirun -d` uses the "z" command (one of the few single letters not already claimed by `gdb`) to redirect `stdin` to a specific `gdb` instance or to all processes. Thus processes can be stepped and breakpoints can be set either collectively or individually, and collectively printing a variable will provide all values with rank labels. An example terminal session showing how this works can be seen at http://www.mcs.anl.gov/mpi/mpich/mpd/mpigdb.script.

4 Experiments

Most development of MPD has been on workstation networks where startup of 32-process jobs on five workstations is virtually instantaneous, compared with the approximately 1.5 seconds per process required by the ch_p4 version of MPICH. An early test of the feasibility of using the ring topology showed that a message could make 1024 hops around the ring in less than .4 seconds, which gave us confidence that the ring would not impose scalability limits, at least in the near term. Recently we began experiments on Chiba City, a testbed for parallel computer science research [1]. We performed one set of tests on 211 nodes connected by Fast Ethernet. We were interested only in process startup time, and so tested execution of trivial parallel jobs. Typical experiments included

```
time mpirun -np 211 hostname
time mpirun -np 422 -g 2 hostname
```

We found that starting 211 processes (one on each node) and collecting the `stdout` output of `hostname` took about 2 seconds to execute. Starting twice as many processes (one for each CPU) took about 3.5 seconds, including setting up the relatively complex `stdout` tree and collecting the output. Sending a message around the ring of 211 MPD daemons took only .13 seconds. More experiments are ongoing, and we will soon be able to report on MPI jobs on Chiba City.

5   Future Development

The existing MPD system, consisting of daemons, managers, console commands, and client library, meets our goals of simplicity, robustness, and scalability. It is used for fast startup of MPI jobs and others on systems with hundreds of machines. The flexibility of its `stdio` control mechanism has provided unexpected benefits, such a "poor man's" parallel debugger. It meets our goals for the collective identity of a parallel job. It does not yet meet all of our goals with respect to individual process environments, although that is coming very soon.

In the near term, we expect to use the system to implement the dynamic process creation part of MPI-2 in MPICH. The design presented here, with a simple daemon and a separate manager process providing most of the features needed by user jobs, allows the daemons to be run as root while the managers are run as user processes. We expect to begin running the daemon as root on some large-scale multi-user systems, in order to provide a persistent job management system. This will require increased attention to security issues as well as a precise definition of how MPD will interoperate with a full-featured scheduling system such as the Maui scheduler [2]. We believe that the MPD daemons can also begin to provide more services, such as run-time performance monitoring.

In the long run, as machines grow from hundreds to thousands of nodes, our rings of daemons and managers may have to grow into a more sophisticated structure, such as rings of rings, in order to continue to provide fast startup. We anticipate that this can be done without substantially changing the MPD design presented here. We will also need a more sophisticated output merger in order to provide scalable `stdout`, for example for large-scale parallel debugging.

In summary, we are finding the MPD system already a useful contribution to one's parallel programming environment and expect its applicability to expand in the near future. We also view its design as a valuable starting point for future research into large-scale parallel job execution environments.

References

[1] Chiba City home page. http://www.mcs.anl.gov/chiba.

[2] The Maui scheduler home page.   http://maui-scheduler.mhpcc.edu/new_doc, http://www.mhpcc.edu/maui.

[3] M. A. Baker, G. C. Fox, and H. W. Yau. Review of cluster management software. *NHSE Review*, 1(1), May 1996.

[4] Amnon Barak, Shai Guday, and Richard G. Wheeler. *The MOSIX distributed operating system: Load balancing for UNIX*, volume 672 of *Lecture Notes in Computer Science*. Springer-Verlag, New York, 1993.

[5] Micah Beck, Jack J. Dongarra, Graham E. Fagg, G. Al Geist, Paul Gray, James Kohl, Mauro Migliardi, Keith Moore, Terry Moore, Philip Papadopoulous, Stephen L. Scott, and Vaidy Sunderam. HARNESS: A next generation distributed virtual machine. *International Journal on Future Generation Computer Systems*, 15(5/6), 1999.

[6] Greg Burns, Raja Daoud, and James Vaigl. LAM: An open cluster environment for MPI. In John W. Ross, editor, *Proceedings of Supercomputing Symposium '94*, pages 379–386. University of Toronto, 1994.

[7] Ralph Butler and Ewing Lusk. Monitors, messages, and clusters: The p4 parallel programming system. *Parallel Computing*, 20:547–564, April 1994.

[8] DQS home page. http://www.scri.fsu.edu/˜pasko/dqs.html.

[9] I. Foster and C. Kesselman, editors. *The Grid: Blueprint for a New Computing Infrastructure*. Morgan Kaufmann, 1999.

[10] Al Geist, Adam Beguelin, Jack Dongarra, Weicheng Jiang, Bob Manchek, and Vaidy Sunderam. *PVM: Parallel Virtual Machine—A User's Guide and Tutorial for Network Parallel Computing*. MIT Press, Cambridge, Mass., 1994.

[11] Douglas P. Ghormley, David Petrou, Steven H. Rodrigues, Amin M. Vahdat, and Thomas E. Anderson. GLUnix: A Global Layer Unix for a network of workstations. *Software—Practice and Experience*, 28(9):929–961, July 1998.

[12] William Gropp and Ewing Lusk. Scalable Unix tools on parallel processors. In *Proceedings of the Scalable High-Performance Computing Conference*, pages 56–62. IEEE Computer Society Press, 1994.

[13] William Gropp, Ewing Lusk, Nathan Doss, and Anthony Skjellum. A high-performance, portable implementation of the MPI Message-Passing Interface standard. *Parallel Computing*, 22(6):789–828, 1996.

[14] IBM. *Loadleveler: Using and Administering*, version 2 release 1 edition, November 1998. SA22-7311-00.

[15] M. J. Litzkow, M. Livny, and M. W. Mutka. Condor – A hunter of idle workstations. In *Proc. 8th Intl. Conf. on Distributed Computing Systems*, pages 104–111, San Jose, Calif., June 1988.

[16] M. Migliardi and V. Sunderam. PVM emulation in the Harness metacomputing system: A plug-in based approach. In J. J. Dongarra, E. Luque, and Tomas Margalef, editors, *Recent advances in parallel virtual machine and message passing interface: 6th European PVM/MPI Users' Group Meeting, Barcelona, Spain, September 26–29, 1999: Proceedings*, volume 1697 of *Lecture Notes in Computer Science*, pages 117–124, Berlin, 1999. Springer-Verlag.

[17] PBS home page. http://pbs.mrj.com/.

[18] Load Sharing Facility (LSF). http://www.platform.com.

[19] J. Pruyne and M. Livny. Interfacing Condor and PVM to harness the cycles of workstation clusters. *Future Generation Computer Systems*, 12(1):67–85, May 1996.

[20] Andrew S. Tanenbaum. *Computer Networks*. Prentice Hall, third edition, 1996.

Single Sided Communications in Multi-protocol MPI

Elson Mourão and Stephen Booth

Edinburgh Parallel Computing Centre- Univ. of Edinburgh
E.Mourao@epcc.ed.ac.uk, S.Booth@epcc.ed.ac.uk
http://www.epcc.ed.ac.uk

Abstract. Most of MPI's implementations cope with the different underlying means of communication. More than just providing the ability to send a message through a certain protocol the implementations make use of specific features of a protocol to speed up message exchanging. These different communication protocols are integrated with each other and the MPI user does not and should not need to be concerned about it. However, when it comes to One Sided Communications this integration becomes more complicated. Some protocols, like TCP, do not lend themselves to One Sided Communications, while others, like shared memory, are so similar that implementation is trivial. This paper describes the issues we came across when implementing One Sided Communications for an MPI implementation with multi pluggable protocols.

1 Introduction

MPI [1] has become the de facto standard for message passing in parallel computing. Since its release in 1998 it has increasingly been adopted by both industry and academia. Recently its features have been extended [2] with the release of the "MPI-2 standard"[3]. Amongst its most relevant new features is a chapter on single sided communications, i.e. communication that can be done without requiring explicit calls from all processes involved. This single sided communications chapter is a message passing approach to shared memory.

Implementing single sided communications for a shared memory protocol is a simple task since it just requires mapping MPI's calls to the underlying system's equivalents[4]. Most vendors have single sided communications implemented only for shared memory systems. Implementing shared memory on other communitacion protocols like TCP is not as simple, but it has been topic for research[5] and there are even implementations of shared memory over traditional MPI[6]. In terms of MPI-2 single sided implementations for non shared memory systems the authors are only aware of two: [7] and [8].

However, trying to create an implementation that can cope with both at the same time becomes rather complicated. This paper describes the issues involved in developing and implementing an integration for the pluggable protocols for single sided communications. This work uses the SUN implementation of MPI.

J. Dongarra et al. (Eds.): EuroPVM/MPI 2000, LNCS 1908, pp. 176–183, 2000.

SUN has recently made the source code for SUN-MPI available under a community source licence [9]. We begin by describing the motivations, followed by an overview of the solution we implemented. After that we discuss the issues involved in this solution. Then some benchmark results are presented. Finally section 6 discusses conclusions which include ongoing and future work.

2   Motivations

In order to provide a complete implementation of MPI-2's One Sided Communications one must guarantee that an MPI call can be used by all the processes in MPI_COMM_WORLD. The current implementation from Sun only allows single sided communications between processes that are connected through the shared memory protocol. This is an obvious disadvantage and does not meet one of MPI's goals: portability.

Our implementation overcomes this problem and also integrates the different protocols, thus lifting all previous restrictions to use single sided communications.

Our aim was to implement a generic version of one-sided communications built on top of point to point communications. Ultimately this generic version should be capable of co-existing with optimised protocol specific implementations but provide a fall-back implementation for any protocol that does not implement one-sided communication directly.

One of the examples of the need to use single sided communications with protocols other than shared memory arises when one is intending to use clustered SMPs. Since shared memory cannot be used between the nodes of the cluster the MPI user program would have to be aware of which processes are running on each machine and cope with the fact that some groups of processes cannot use single sided communications between them. Situations like this are what the MPI standard proposes to overcome by making the implementor responsible for dealing with it. Thus it does not specify a way to obtain the information needed to allow the user program to cope with it.

In the following section we present an overview of our approach to solving the problem.

3   The Big Picture

The diagram in figure 1 presents the generic single sided code within the layers of the implementation of MPI we used.

Our generic implementation uses any existing protocol. Whenever the protocol has implemented one-sided functionality this will be used, otherwise our implementation will cover for it. This general purpose implementation's main feature is an asynchronous agent (Request Agent) which handles the RMA requests.

In this first implementation the agent runs in a thread concurrently with the users' code and the normal MPI calls.

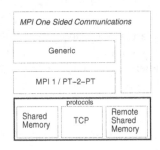

Fig. 1. Single sided layers

The call to the protocol's implementation is done at the highest level possible and the overhead of the integration has been kept to the minimum.

Overcoming the differences between the protocols and providing a way to cope with possibly new protocols brought to light several issues that we discuss next.

4   Issues

This section discusses the main barriers we had to overcome when integrating the different types of protocols. Protocols are designed to provide a certain service. Thus in some cases the strongest feature of one protocol can be the weakest point of another.

4.1   RMA

The remote memory access (RMA) functions only ever utilise a single implementation so no issues arise here. All that is required is to identify the correct implementation based on the rank of the target process. The synchronisation calls are the ones most likely to give rise to conflicts.

4.2   Fence

Out of the three synchronisation calls only the fence is straightforward since it is essentially a barrier. `MPI_Win_fence` completes an exposure epoch and synchronises the processors. Each implementation provides a separate function to complete their own communications, synchronisation is via the normal `MPI_Barrier`

4.3   Lock

If one uses the shared memory protocol or some protocol that provides memory locking then MPI's `MPI_Win_lock` matches the protocol and no extra complexity needs to be added. If the protocol is TCP or similar then some sort of an asynchronous agent is required to provide the lock facility. This agent will process all the requests from remote processes and request the system lock used by the shared memory protocol.

Figure 2 shows the concurrency between local processes, using shared memory, and remote processes using TCP.

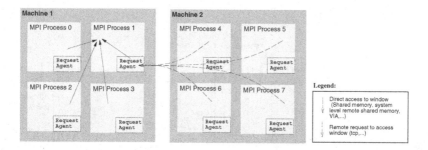

Fig. 2. Lock synchronisation concurrency

Because the request agent is multiplexing requests the remote locks have lower priority relative to true shared memory locks.

The best solution is to implement a lock shared across protocols. This lock allows fairness in the lock acquisition. However it is expected that it will add complexity and subsequently overhead to simple protocols like shared memory. This solution is still under development since the implementation has to cope with the existing protocols and any other protocol that might be added later.

A simple and straightforward solution has been implemented for the time being, resulting in remote locks being at a disadvantage against the local ones.

There are potential deadlock situations if the request agent blocks waiting for the shared memory lock.

1. The request agent needs to continue to process requests if an exclusive lock request cannot be granted immediately. This is essential if some of the current shared locks were made via the Request Agent.
2. The request agent must not attempt to acquire a shared lock if there is an exclusive lock that it made for a different client.

Therefore the request agent should never block while waiting for an exclusive lock. Instead it should re-send the lock request (to itself). Once the exclusive lock has been acquired the request agent only listens to requests from the process that requested the lock. Once the lock is released the Request Agent reverts to listening for any request.

Exclusive lock requests are acknowledged explicitly. Because these requests may be read and then re-queued the originating process must wait for the acknowledge before sending any more requests. Otherwise these requests may be processed before the lock is granted.

Shared locks do not need to be acknowledged as the request (and any subsequent RMA requests) will never be received by the request agent while an exclusive lock is held.

4.4   Post/Start

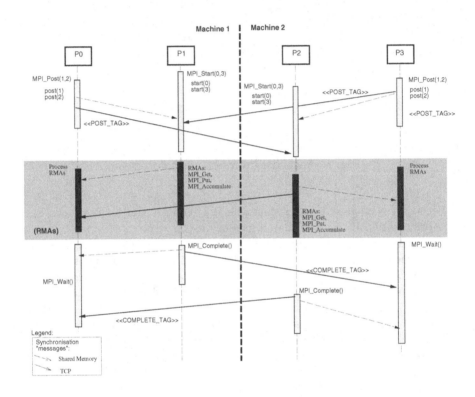

Fig. 3. Start/Post Synchronisation

This synchronisation call also needs special attention, since the call requires a group as a parameter. This group is a subset of the group of processes that are using the same window.

Any combination of processes is possible thus all the protocols must interact to synchronise. However this synchronisation can be partitioned so it is composed by synchronising the subgroups of processes which communicate using the same protocol.

Figure 3 shows an example of the Start Post synchronisation with a shared memory protocol and a TCP protocol. There are two groups of processes using the shared memory protocol because they are running on the same machine. However when they need to synchronise across to the other machine the TCP protocol is used.

The MPI calls are unfolded into similar calls to the underlying protocol. The synchronisation group is decomposed into subgroups where all the members of the subgroup are accessed using the same underlying protocol. Each of these subgroups are then synchronised in turn using the appropriate protocol. The MPI synchronisation call will only return when all the protocols synchronise the subgroups thus synchronising the main group.

5   Performance

The major issue in an integrating implementation such as this is performance, since it ought to add extra complexity with a low overhead. However the integration is still in progress so final benchmarks could not be presented in this paper. This section presents some benchmarks done with a third party application, Pallas' MPI benchmarks[10]. These were taken using a cluster of Sun Ultra5 workstations over a 100Mb Ethernet. All the benchmarks refer to groups of two processes issuing requests to each other.

Since our generic implementation uses MPI's point to point communication we choose to present a comparison between selected Pallas' MPI1 and MPI2 benchmarks. The MPI1 benchmarks chosen are the ones which have message patterns similar to our algorithms.

The graph in figure 4 shows the PingPong benchmark against unilateral single sided operations. On average all the RMAs are implemented with two messages exchanged between the origin and the target. The PingPong benchmark reports the time of a single message between two processes, i.e, half the time of a round trip message.

Figure 4 shows that performance of the single sided operations is not much worse. One can see that the Put times for larger messages are extremely high but this is due to thread switching and the fact that the Put operation is implemented using synchronous send.

Our Request Agent is implemented using threads, which should not have such a visible effect on a workstation network using 100Mb Ethernet since the network latency would nullify any thread context switching overhead. However thread support was added when MPI-1 was extended to MPI-2 and thread concurrency at lower layers has shown an unexpected impact on performance. Thus the strange peaks in the graph of figure 4. This topic is still subject to development.

Figure 5 presents PingPing versus bi-directional RMAs. One can see that the Get was also showing the signs we saw in the previous graph.

Benchmarks taken with more processes have shown these effects at a larger scale since Pallas' benchmarks on single sided operations are done between two processes while all the others wait in a barrier. The processes being benchmarked will receive the barrier's internal messages at the lower levels, which is suffering

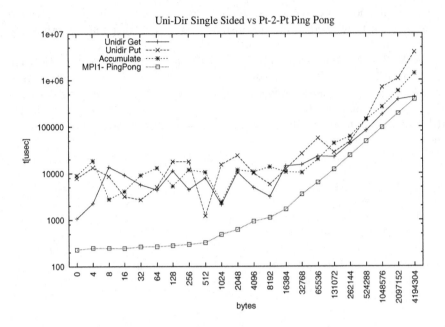

Fig. 4. Unidir-Single sided / Ping Pong

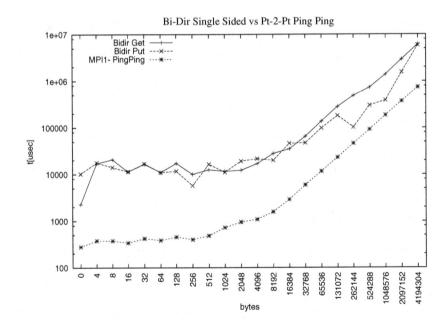

Fig. 5. Bidir-Single sided / Ping Ping

from thread concurrency problems. These extra messages being exchanged have a visible effect in performance and grow with the number of extra processes.

6   Conclusions

An implementation of MPI that restricts the usage of the API calls does not meet the standard in full. On the other hand if the implementation does not impose restrictions but has poor performance then the users will be reluctant to use it. However if one can present the user with an unrestricted library that performs better under certain system configurations then the user will be able to use MPI and take advantage of the system's features whenever possible. This approach is the one we followed to implement a generic single sided library that will use the best protocol whenever possible and revert to a generic MPI 1 based solution otherwise.

Integration work is still undergoing as shown in the performance section. The main issues have been dealt with. The implementation is able to cope not only with the currently available protocols but also with future protocols. Thus the goals of this project have been achieved.

References

1. Message Passing Interface Forum: "Message Passing Interface (MPI)", November 1998, http://www.mpi-forum.org.
2. Minty E., "MPI-2: Extending the Message Passing Interface", EPCC's Technology Watch Reports,
   http://www.epcc.ed.ac.uk/epcc-tec/documents/techwatch-mpi2.
3. Message Passing Interface Forum: "MPI-2: Extensions to the Message-Passing Interface", June 1997 http://www.mpi-forum.org.
4. Cameron K., Clarke L. J., Simth A. G., Wierenga K. J., "Using MPI on the Cray T3D, chapter: Using MPI 2 One-Sided Communications", EPCC, The University of Edinburgh, 6th June 1997.
5. Keleher P.,Cox A.,Dwarkadas S., Zwaenepoel W., "Lazy Release Consistency for Software Distributed Shared Memory", in Proc. 19th Anual Int. Symp. Computer Architectures, 1992, pp. 13-21.
6. Silva L. M., Silva J. G., Chappl S., "Implementation and Performance of DSMPI", in Scientific Programming, vol. 6, pp. 201-214, John Wiley & Sons, Inc, 1997.
7. Mourão F. E., Silva J. G.: Implementing MPI's One-Sided Communications for WMPI, in Proc. of 5th European PVM/MPI Users' Group Meeting, September 1999.
8. University of Notre Dame, "LAM-6.3 release notes" 1999
   http://www.mpi.nd.edu/lam/.
9. Sun Microsystems, "Sun HPC Clustertools" http://www.sun.com/software/hpc/.
10. Pallas GmbH, "Pallas MPI Benchmarks-PMB",
    http://www.pallas.de/pages/pmb.htm,March 2000

MPI-2 Process Creation & Management Implementation for NT Clusters[1]

Hernâni Pedroso and João Gabriel Silva

CISUC
Universidade de Coimbra – Polo II
3030-397 Coimbra
Portugal
{hernani,jgabriel}@dei.uc.pt

Abstract. The second version of the MPI-2 standard introduced new functionality to the Message Passing Interface. The ability of adding new processes to an MPI application at runtime was one of the main new extensions to the existing functionality. This paper presents the first implementation of the Process Creation and Management chapter of the standard for Win32 environments. The implementation of this functionality in generic NT clusters presents challenging problems due to the distributed nature and the considerable difference between each cluster. A description of the problems faced while implementing this new functionality as well as the solutions implemented in the WMPI library are presented this paper.

Introduction

The first version of the Message Passing Interface (MPI) standard [1] was rapidly absorbed by the parallel computation community and became a *de facto* standard. Wishing to use MPI in a wider set of applications, the MPI users requested to the MPI Forum [2] to increase the functionality of the standard. The second version of the standard [3] was released in 1997. In fact, this second version extended the functionality of the standard beyond the message passing. One-sided communication, dynamic process creation and I/O were introduced in the standard. The new API allows the MPI users to create more complete and complex programs that are still portable.

In this paper we present the implementation of the Process Creation and Management chapter of the MPI-2 standard in the WMPI library [4,5]. WMPI, which stands for Windows Message Passing Interface, was the first implementation of the standard available for Win32 environments. Originally based in the MPICH implementation [6], in its last version it was completely redesigned to accommodate new features like simultaneous multiple communication devices and thread safety [7]. The new internal architecture was also designed in order to incorporate the necessary

[1] This work was partially supported by the Portuguese Ministry of Science and Technology through the R&D Unit 326/94 (CISUC) and the project PRAXIS XXI 2/2.1/TIT/1625/95 named ParQuantum.

J. Dongarra et al. (Eds.): EuroPVM/MPI 2000, LNCS 1908, pp. 184-191, 2000.

mechanisms to implement the dynamic creation of processes. This new functionality is the continuation of an effort to fully implement the MPI-2 standard in the WMPI library where one-sided communication [8] and extended collective operations [9] were already implemented.

MPI Process Creation and Management

In the first version of the MPI standard, the MPI Forum created a standard that contained only an API for message passing. How the processes started, how they established communication and managed resources was not addressed. The MPI users felt that the static environment of MPI-1 was too restrictive. Former PVM [10] users found it very difficult to port their existing programs to MPI and constantly run into problems with the lack of process and resource management API. Furthermore some classes of applications (e.g. task farms, client/server applications and serial applications with some parallel parts) can benefit of a process control API.

The second version of the MPI standard included a chapter for process creation and management. It was decided not to include an API for resource management, since no appropriate portable interface was found for a wide range of resource controllers. Although some functionality for process creation and management was introduced, the MPI-2 does not manage the environment were it is running, rather provides an interface to external process managers.

The new functionality can be divided in two different parts: spawning new processes and establishing communication between two different applications. There is also a possibility of disconnecting processes or two joined applications. A brief description of the MPI-2 process creation and management capabilities is presented next.

Spawning New Processes

MPI users have two different functions to create new processes in runtime. The MPI_COMM_SPAWN function allows the creation of one or more processes that will run the same executable with the same arguments. If the users wish to run different executables or to pass different arguments to the several processes they should use the MPI_COMM_MULTIPLE_SPAWN function.

When one MPI's spawn function is executed, the new processes start their own MPI environment. The two environments are immediately connected through an inter-communicator and the users can immediately exchange information between all processes.

The spawning operation is collective over a certain intra-communicator (a subset of the original processes). Only the processes that belong to the intra-communicator will be included in the inter-communicator (the set formed by the intra-communicator plus the group of newly created processes) that connects them to the new processes. A root process, indicated in the function's arguments, is responsible for actually creating the new processes.

Establishing Communication between Separate Applications

Two applications can establish communication to exchange information to cooperatively resolve a problem. The MPI-2 provides functions to establish communication in a Client/Server model. One of the applications opens a MPI port and waits for other applications to connect to it. The MPI port is an implementation dependent entry point that allows the two applications to exchange information about the two environments to create the inter-communicator between the applications. It is opaque to the user, which will simply get a port name that uniquely identifies the port. Using this port name the client application is able to connect to the server application and establish the communication. A name service is also provided, to help clients locate servers by name.

Disconnecting Processes/Applications

When two applications join, they can disconnect without having to terminate. The MPI users have to end every connection between the two sets of processes. A new function to destroy communicators was inserted in the standard: MPI_COMM_DISCONNECT. This function waits for the end of all pending communications in the communicator and ends it.

It is also possible to disconnect and cooperatively terminate processes that were created at runtime. Nevertheless there are some limitations in terminating processes. Since each MPI spawn function creates an MPI environment (i.e. a MPI_COMM_WORLD communicator), a sub-set of the processes that were created with a single spawn function cannot be terminated separately from the others.

MPI-2 Dynamic Environment

In a first overview it might seem that the MPI-2 environment is not really dynamic, because it maintains the new processes connected through an umbilical cord (the inter-communicator) instead of completely merging them. MPI users may find odd the utilization of an inter-communicator instead of an intra-communicator. Although the collective operations have been extended to embrace inter-communicators, they still have different syntax due to the existence of two separated groups.

However, the MPI users can create an intra-communicator that brings together all processes in a single group by using the MPI_INTERCOMM_MERGE function. This way it is possible to completely merge all the processes in a single communicator (though not the MPI_COMM_WORLD). Once the processes can be joined in intra-communicators, the MPI-2 environment is similar to the MPI-1, but dynamic. The MPI-1 becomes a special case of the MPI-2 environment.

The ability of transforming the inter-communicators into intra-communicators allows the users to easily port their static applications into an MPI-2 dynamic environment. Moreover, it enables the users to make any combination of processes from several different joined applications and spawned processes by using the MPI group and communicator handling functions that are included in the MPI-1 version.

The dynamics of the MPI-2 environment is only shadowed by the decision of not changing the concept of communicator introduced in the MPI-1 version. Once created it cannot be changed. This implies that is not possible to remove one single process from one communicator while the others remain communicating. Moreover the MPI_COMM_WORLD remains indestructible. Hence is not possible to terminate a subset of the processes created with a single spawn function or of an application. The termination of processes without ending the whole application is only possible when all the processes of their MPI_COMM_WORLD agree to end.

Process Identification in a Dynamic Environment

The implementation of a dynamic MPI environment imposes considerable changes to most of the existing libraries. As many of the implementations available worldwide, WMPI inherited from MPICH an architecture well adapted for a static environment, but completely inadequate to cope with a dynamic environments. It bases the identification of the processes at low level in their rank in the MPI_COMM_WORLD communicator. Since in MPI-1 every single process of the application belongs to the same MPI_COMM_WORLD communicator, the ranks in this communicator uniquely identifies every process. However, in MPI-2 dynamic environment there are several MPI_COMM_WORLD communicators that can co-exist in the same MPI runtime environment through the execution of MPI spawn functions and the joining of different applications. In this cases the simple MPI_COMM_WORLD rank is not a unique identifier.

It is thus necessary to create an identification form that enables to uniquely represent a process. The system process number would be a good identifier in an MPP (Massively Parallel Processor), however in a distributed environment each node has an independent operating system, hence two processes of a cluster can have the same process number. In a generic cluster environment the data exchange can be done by several different communication media, depending on the cluster configuration. An MPI implementation for such an environment has always to be aware of the processes' addresses in the different communication media used. Since these addresses uniquely represent the process in the communication medium environment (hence the whole cluster), they are used in WMPI to represent the MPI processes inside the library.

Each WMPI process contains information about every other process to which it is connected. The information is placed in a WMPI process object that is kept in memory while there is at least one common group between the two MPI processes. When a process joins a new inter-communicator it compares the addresses of the new processes with the addresses of the processes to which it already has a connection. If it finds a process object containing the same address in the same communication medium it knows that it is the same process. In this situation is not necessary to create another process object, it just increments the number of references to the object.

Spawning Processes in a Distributed System

When an MPI library running on a generic cluster has to spawn new processes it does not know in which machine they should be created. In some systems like MPPs a queuing system able of taking those decisions may be available, in many others not. The MPI Forum was conscious that some environments would require specific information to enable that decision. Hence an extra argument that may contain environment specific information was introduced in the spawn functions. The argument may contain several key-value pairs that the implementation should interpret. Not all the MPI implementations have to consider this argument when executing the functions. In addition, different MPI implementations may require different information, hence different keys. Hence, the usage of such argument reduces the portability of the code. A set of keys reserved by the standard has a specific functionality. This was an effort to minimize the portability problems in using this extra information. However, the MPI implementations are free to interpret these keys or not.

If no extra information is provided to the WMPI implementation when processes are spawned they will be started in the same machine where the operation's root process is running. Nevertheless, WMPI can interpret two of the reserved keys to allow the user to specify where the new processes should run:

- **host**: The user specifies the name of the machine where all the processes should be started.
- file: The user specifies a process group (PG) file that contains all the information about the processes that should be started in the spawning operation. The PG file has the same structure as the one used to launch normal WMPI applications. This file indicates the machine where each process should be executed. The file also identifies the executable and the arguments of the processes

Performance Results

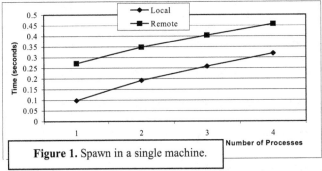

Figure 1. Spawn in a single machine.

The spawn operation implies the execution of many heavy system calls, such as creation of processes. Moreover, the newly created processes have to synchronize and exchange information to setup a new MPI environment and connect to the breeder group of processes. The results presented in this section show the elapsed time to spawn new processes. To get the performance results we used two dual Pentium Pro machines running Windows NT operating system. The machines were interconnected using a non-dedicated Fast

Ethernet network. The time to create a process in any of the machines is approximately 25 milliseconds.

Figure 1 presents the time in seconds to create up to four processes in a local machine and well as a remote machine. The time to create a remote process is around 150 milliseconds slower because it is necessary to contact the remote machine's service and request for the creation of the first process.

Using a third machine (Pentium II 233 MHz), processes were started in both machines simultaneously. Figure 2 presents the time in seconds to create the up to four processes per machine (eight processes). In this case, the spawn time rises because it is necessary to create processes in two different machines. In addition, the created processes have to interact between each other to setup the environment and connect to the creator process.

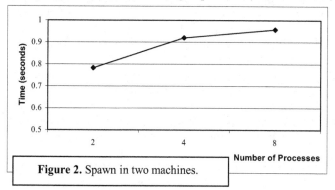

Figure 2. Spawn in two machines.

Connection Establishment

There are many interconnection solutions for Windows clusters. It is impossible to predict, when designing the MPI library, all the possible topologies and interconnection media.

To solve the problem of choosing the best communication medium for each pair of processes, WMPI requires the user to describe the whole cluster in a file, called cluster configuration file, which contains the information about all the machines that might be involved with the application. The file indicates in a simple way the interconnection technologies available, and which communication protocol should be used for communication between each pair of processes.

An additional problem occurs when two applications join (MPI-2 allows two independently launched applications to join at any time), because the first message can come from anywhere in the cluster, and the participants in that communication must agree on the protocol to use. Since TCP/IP is present in practically all environments, WMPI uses it to establish the first connection and exchange the initial information, which includes information about the machines where the processes of both sides are running. Together with the cluster configuration file, each process can then decide which communication medium to use to contact the other processes at the highest possible speed.

WMPI Name Publishing Service

The MPI-2 standard introduced a name publishing service, aimed at enabling MPI applications to easily find the port name where to contact an MPI server application. This functionality has the added value of allowing some MPI applications to work as location transparent service applications. It must be reachable by the server applications (to publish a new name) and by the client applications (to inquire the port name of a service). Once again the implementation of this name serve is quite dependent on the environment of the MPI implementation. In an MPP where MPI implementations are almost always proprietary, the name server might be a process that is waiting on some well-known message queue. However, in a generic distributed environment it can be running on almost any machine and it is impossible for the MPI library to know where the name service is without the user's help.

In the case of WMPI the name server is a separated application that must be running in some machine, whether it is one of the cluster's machines or not. It is only reachable through a TCP/IP connection. Since the TCP/IP protocol is very common in such environments, this decision does not restrict the usability. The MPI process that is publishing the name service or inquiring for a port name of a service can get the name of the machine, as well as the wanting port, where the application is running from an environment variable that must be set by the user. Alternatively the user can pass to the WMPI library the name of the machine that should be contacted through the additional information parameter available in the calls to the name service.

Related Work

Two other implementations we know of have this MPI-2 functionality implemented. LAM/MPI implementation from Notre Dame University [11] implements all the MPI-2 process creation and management functionality. This implementation runs over Unix based systems and is a freely available implementation.

Fujitsu has a full MPI-2 implementation [12] that runs over its proprietary message passing kernel MPlib. This implementation uses the capabilities of the MPLib, which was specially developed for Fujitsu systems, to dynamically spawn new processes.

To the authors best knowledge no other implementation for Win32 environments is available at this time that implements MPI-2 process creation and management functionality.

Conclusions

MPI rapidly became widely used by the high performance community. The MPI users early started to request for more functionality in the MPI standard. One of the requirements was the ability of dynamically add processes to the application. The experience with the PVM library similar functionality helped the MPI Forum to create an interface to dynamically spawn new processes. The introduced interface allows the MPI users to work with a truly dynamic environment where processes can be created and destroyed at runtime as well as applications can join and disconnect without having to finalize.

Although many MPI users required this functionality, its implementation demands a considerable change in the existing MPI-1 implementations. The existence of many MPI_COMM_WORLD communicators removed the possibility of identifying the application processes through their MPI_COMM_WORLD's rank, a widely used technique. Cluster based implementations have additional problems due to the distributed and generic nature of the environment. To overcome these problems, the WMPI library suffered deep changes in its internal design. The process identification is made through the process's communication medium addresses. To allow the newly connected processes to communicate through the fastest communication path a cluster configuration file was introduced. This enabled to produce a library that can run over any cluster and to take full advantage of its capabilities.

Being the first implementation of MPI-2 process creation and management chapter in Win32 cluster environments, this evolution of the WMPI library also shows that it is viable to provide that functionality.

References

1. Message Passing Interface Forum: MPI: A message-passing interface standard. International Journal of Supercomputer Applications, 8(3/4):165-414 (1994).
2. Message Passing Interface (MPI) Forum Home Page, http://www.mpi-forum.org.
3. Message Passing Interface Forum: MPI-2: Extensions to the Message-Passing Interface. (June 1997), available at http://www.mpi-forum.org.
4. Marinho, J. and Silva, J.G.: WMPI – Message Passing Interface for Win32 Clusters. Proc. of 5th European PVM/MPI User's Group Meeting, pp. 113-120 (September 1998).
5. WMPI Homepage – http://dsg.dei.uc.pt/wmpi.
6. Gropp, W., Lusk, E., Doss, N. and Skejellum, A.: A High-Performance, Portable Implementation of the MPI Message Passing Interface Standard. Parallel Computing Vol. 22, No. 6, (September 1996).
7. Pedroso, H., Silva, P., Silva, J.G.: The WMPI Architecture for Dynamic Environments and Simultaneous Multiple Devices. MPIDC2000 - Message Passing Interface and High-Performance Clusters Developer's and User's Conference, Ithaca, NY, USA (March 2000).
8. Mourao, F.E., Silva, J.G.: Implementing MPI's One-sided Communications for WMPI. Proc. of 6th European PVM/MPI User's Group Meeting, pp. 231-238, Barcelona, Spain (September 1999).
9. Silva, P., Silva, J.G.: Implementing MPI-2 Extended Collective Operations. Proc. of 6th European PVM/MPI User's Group Meeting, pp. 125-132, Barcelona, Spain (September 1999).
10. Geist, A., Beguelin, A., Dongarra, J., Jiang, W., Mancheck, B., Sunderman, V.: PVM: Parallel Virtual Machine – A User's Guide and Tutorial for Network Parallel Computing. MIT Press (1994).
11. Burns, G., Daoud, R., Vaigl, J.: LAM: An open cluster environment for MPI. Proc. of Supercomputing Symposium'94, pp. 379-386, Toronto, Canada (1994).
12. Asai, N., Kentemich, T., Lagier, P.: MPI-2 Implementation on Fujitsu generic message passing kernel. Proceedings of Supercomputing'99, Portland, Oregon, USA (November 1999).

Composition of Message Passing Applications On-Demand

J.Y.Cotronis, Z.Tsiatsoulis, C.Kouniakis

Department of Informatics, University of Athens, 157 84, Athens, Greece
{cotronis, zack, ckouniak} @di.uoa.gr

Abstract. Ensemble has been proposed as a methodology for designing and implementing message passing applications by composition of modular and reusable message passing components. In this paper we adapt Ensemble as a mechanism for composing message passing applications in a meta-computing context on demand. Ensemble is particularly effective in the case where users demand different process topologies to be created out of the same components. We demonstrate this case by an application from transaction processing and in particular parallel query execution based on the tree pipelining model.

1. Introduction

We have developed the Ensemble methodology [1,2,3,4] for designing and implementing message passing applications based on the composition of modular and reusable message passing (MP) components. In addition to the general benefits of modular design, Ensemble aims to overcome three problems in the design and implementation of MP applications and in particular those requiring irregular process topologies.

The first is that implementation does not only depend on the application design, but also on the target MP Library (MPL), mainly because of the process management model each MPL adopts. For this reason, some topologies are easier to establish than others on specific MPLs. For example, it is easy to create tree topologies (regular or irregular) in PVM [5] and regular ring or grid topologies in MPI [8], but more difficult the other way round. Topologies not well suited to an MPL may certainly be created, but require specialized programming.

The second problem is that MPLs support regular but not irregular or partially regular topologies. Process topologies are programmed within processes by specifying implicit communication channels, expressed by symmetric calls of send and receive operations. For regular topologies the designer develops functions, which take a process identifier and return the identifiers of its communicating processes. These functions are usually parameterized to return the identifiers of processes in any size of the regular topology. For topologies, which are not globally regular but only partially or locally regular or even altogether irregular, general functions cannot be derived and consequently ad hoc programming methods are used.

The third problem is that reuse of message passing components is limited. The task a designer of a message passing program faces is to express in a source program

J. Dongarra et al. (Eds.): EuroPVM/MPI 2000, LNCS 1908, pp. 192-199, 2000.

(component) the appropriate interactions of all the processes, which will be spawned from it, considering all their possible positions in the topology and additionally, for any size of the topology. Reusability is limited by the use of specific process identifiers (tid or rank) in communication channels or by the functions determining them, which assume specific regular topologies.

The heart of the Ensemble methodology is the design of modular reusable message passing components, which may be used in any topology, whether regular, partially regular or irregular. We have defined simple generic process communication interfaces independent of any topology, which processes use in the parameters of point-to-point and group operations. Topologies are composed by a loader program, which binds process communication interfaces at run time, directed by composition scripts. The components, the scripts, the loader and utility libraries comprise the Ensemble Software Architecture.

In this paper we adapt the use of Ensemble Software Architecture (ESA) as an infrastructure for composing message passing applications in a meta-computing context on demand. ESA is particularly effective in the case where different process topologies need to be created from the same components according to user demand. We demonstrate this case by an application from transaction processing and in particular parallel query execution based on the tree pipelining model [10,12].

The structure of the paper is as follows: In section 2 we present the Ensemble Software Architecture, in section 3 we adapt and demonstrate the use of ESA in a meta-computing context; finally in section 4 we present our conclusions.

2. The Ensemble Software Architecture

Ensemble specifies a software architecture (figure 1) common for all MP applications in any MPL. The design of a message passing application is maintained in the implementation, which is an "ensemble" of reusable executable program components and of composition directives (scripts).

The script specifies the application processes (to be spawned from the reusable executable program components) and their topology (or Process Communication Graph-PCG) independent of any execution environment (MPL or architecture). The script also specifies the allocation of resources of the execution environment (mapping of processes to processors, input and output files, etc.).

The source programs are designed to be independent of any MPL. By compiling and linking with the appropriate MPL and Ensemble libraries the reusable executables (within the specific architecture and MPL) are obtained.

A loader program, universal within an MPL, interprets the script and establishes the topology by creating processes and by setting communication channels. Instead of functions associating processes to their position in a topology, the topology (regular or irregular) is composed directly by binding communication ports of the spawned processes. The loader performs all process and resource management, as specified in the script.

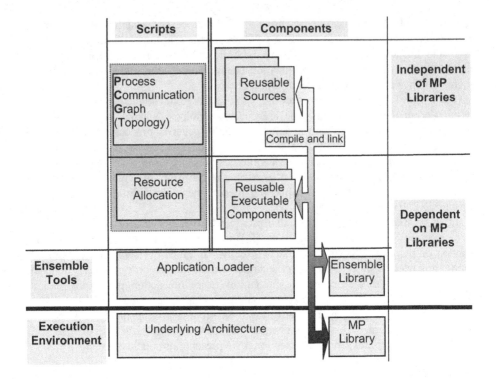

Fig. 1. The Ensemble Software Architecture

2.1 The reusable components

The Ensemble components do not involve any process management nor assume any specific topology in which they operate. Instead they support an unbound interface of communication ports. Ports are implemented as structures holding information of the receiver or the sender process, used respectively by send and receive operations. In PVM3.3 for example, a port is defined as a structure `struct port_struct={int tid, msgtag;}`, which holds pairs of (tid, msgtag) the parameters denoting message destination in send and origin in receive operations, respectively. Ports of the same type form arrays, the number of which is a variable in general and has to be dynamically allocated, defined as a structure `struct port_type {int portcount; port_struct *port;}` which is a header element with two fields, one for holding the actual number of ports (portcount) and a pointer to the actual array of ports of the process to which it belongs. Note that the above declaration is independent of any specific MPL. The differences are hidden in the declaration of a single port. The interface is an array of port_types, defined as `struct *port_type Interface;`

In the body of the components all send and receive operations in processes refer to ports, identified by the appropriate port type and the port index within the type. In

PVM for example, tid and msgtag parameters of pvm_send and pvm_recv routines should refer to tid and msgtag of a port P of type T, i.e. Interface[T].port[P].tid and Interface[T].port[P].msgtag, respectively. Alternatively, the programmer has the option to use abstract communication functions which hide pvm_send and pvm_recv calls within wrapper routines, such as send(T,P,What) and respectively receive(T,P,What), to indicate that message What is sent to, and respectively, received from port P of type T. The same wrapper routines may call MPI routines if the target MPL is MPI, thus hiding all differences and maintaining one source code of components for any MPL. Ports are unbound at compile time as they do not have any values. This way process interfaces are open and scalable and the code that uses them reusable.

A common Main for all program components, which may be seen below has been developed. The application computations for each component are coded in RealMain() function, which accepts the same parameters as function main() in regular C programs, as well as the Interface structure.

```
    void main(argc,argv) int argc; char **argc;
{       MakePorts(Interface);
        SetInterface(Interface);
        RealMain(Interface,argc,argv);}
```

Interface contains all the necessary interfacing information, i.e. the actual number of ports for each port type and is passed by the loader program as command line parameters, and values for port fields. The first call is MakePorts(Interface), which reads these parameters and allocates space for the appropriate number of ports and sets the portcount field to the appropriate value for each port type in array Interface. Processes set actual values to their interface by executing a routine, SetInterface(Interface), which must coordinate with the loader. Each MPL requires its own implementation of the SetInterface routine. In MPI, as process identification (rank) is known at compile time, it is possible to pass it in their command line parameters. In PVM, where process identifiers (tid) are dynamically determined, it is not possible in general to pass to a process at the time of its spawning the tids of its neighbours, as these may have not been spawned yet. In PVM the loader program sends messages with the tids of the neighbouring processes. Symmetrically, the SetInterface receives these messages and updates the interface.

Finally RealMain() is called, which performs the actual application computations.

2.2 The Ensemble script

The script is structured in two main parts. The first part abstractly specifies the Process Communication Graph (PCG) of the application, independently of any MPL or underlying architecture. Here we specify abstractions of the components involved; the processes to be spawned from each component together with their interface parameters; and the communication channels between ports. The second part of the script specifies the resource allocation of the execution environment, process parameters required in the application and information required by specific MPLs and the underlying architectures.

2.3 Composition of applications

The Loader program interprets the script, composes the message passing application by spawning processes from component executables and establishing their communication channels, relieving the programmer of a complex task. There is a universal loader program for all applications in a given MPL. Ensemble tools for PVM [1, 3], Parix [2] and MPI [4] have been developed.

3. Ensemble Software Architecture in Meta-computing

ESA may be used in a meta-computing context to compose applications on demand (figure 2). We assume that the service provider has developed the reusable program components.

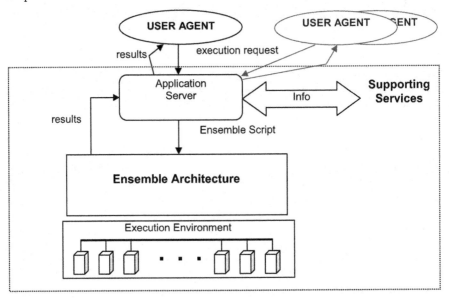

Fig. 2. Using the Ensemble Architecture for composing Applications on Demand

An application server accepts and manages user requests of program executions and from these it produces the PCG part of the script of this request. The application server may consult local information (managed by the service provider) about the availability, policies and permissions of resource allocation and completes the application script, which is then passed in the Ensemble environment. Now the application may be composed and executed as explained in section 2.

In the case of regular SPMD applications topology configuration requires simpler parameters and the use of ensemble scripts are obviously excessive and do not provide any real benefit. But for the class of applications, which need to be configured on-demand, it may prove valuable.

In the next section we demonstrate the above general ideas on a specific application in the domain of transaction processing and in particular parallel SQL query execution.

3.1. Parallel Query Execution on Demand

We first describe the basic model for query execution and then present the implementation architecture.

3.1.1 The Parallel Query Execution Model: Tree Pipelining

In the Tree Pipelining query execution Model (TPM) [10,11,12] an SQL query with a large number of joins, restrictions projections, set operations and aggregates is transformed into a query tree, representing its parallel execution plan (QEP). The query tree is built by a preoptimizer, which performs "unnesting" of nested queries [7], transforms disjunctions into unions and places selection nodes below join nodes on the same relations. Set operations are placed below the root projection and separated from the nodes containing predicates by further projections. So, projections, selections, and joins form "PSJ-zone", in which joins are gathered in a "JOIN-zone". Similarly, set operators are gathered in a zone directly below the root. A parser/preoptimizer producing this tree structure is presented in [11].

This query tree may be used as the Process Communication Graph in Ensemble to compose a message passing application. The nodes of the tree represent relational and set algebra operators and the arcs represent communication of results from children to parent nodes. The query tree is bushy [6], so that nodes in different subtrees can be executed in parallel, while adjacent nodes can be executed in pipeline. The intrinsic parallelism of the tree representation is thus fully utilized: (i) processes on all leaf-processors may start execution immediately, as they have the base relations available, producing tuples of intermediate relations and propagating them to their parent nodes and (ii) processes on inner processor-nodes start execution in pipeline mode as soon as they have sufficient tuples to operate on.

The initial query tree may also be optimized in a parallel way [12]. The optimizer minimizes the execution time of the query by minimizing I/O and communication between processes. It does not take into account processor utilization. A cost model for the estimation of communication and I/O costs in parallel execution spaces according to TPM has been used in exhaustive parallel optimization and in parallelized enhanced iterative improvement.

3.2.2 Parallel Execution of Queries

In such parallel execution scheme, SQL queries demand the creation and execution of distinct "applications". However, these "applications" are all composed out of the same basic components, namely implementations of basic relational algebra primitives, select, project and join and of set operators. We have developed a suite of these primitives as Ensemble reusable components, which may be used to compose any required parallel program as directed by the (optimized) query tree. For the execution of joins we considered the nested loops algorithm and the merge join for sorted input. For equijoins, antijoins and equality outerjoins we also consider a hash algorithm. For restrictions we used two algorithms for sorted and unsorted restriction attributes. For projections we use a merge sort method. The execution algorithms do not support indexing.

In figure 3, we depict the parallel execution of a SQL query on demand. The user sends its SQL query. The Query Server reads the query as well as appropriate information concerning the System Services, the DB schema and the File System, and constructs the initial query tree, the Process Communication Graph. If the initial query tree is small it may be given directly for composition and execution; otherwise it may be optimised before doing so.

Then, the loader interprets the (optimised) query tree and using the reusable executables from the component pool, creates the processes and establishes the appropriate communication channels in the execution environment.

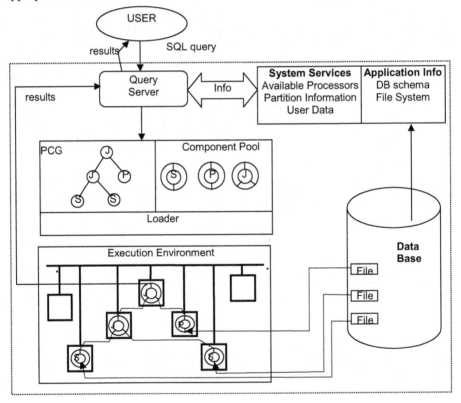

Fig. 3. Parallel Execution of SQL Queries on demand

The Query server as presented above may be relieved of certain duties. A user agent may perform the SQL to query tree transformation locally and send the initial query tree. Concerning the optimization phase there are some options available. The local agent may also optimize the query tree and send an optimized query tree. In this case the Query server is only concerned with the allocation of resources according to its availability and policies. Alternatively, the Query Server may initiate the optimization of the initial query tree as a parallel application and may also be concerned with processor utilization and load balancing issues. We leave these issues open, as in the context of this paper we are mainly concerned with the underlying mechanisms of the on demand composition of message passing applications.

5. Conclusion

In this paper we adapt the Ensemble Software Architecture (ESA) as an infrastructure for composing message passing applications in a meta-computing context on demand. ESA is particularly effective in the case where different process topologies need to be created from the same components according to user demand.

We demonstrated the issues involved on parallel query execution, where all queries ("applications") are composed out of the same relational algebra and set operators and users do not need to know anything about their execution; as far as they are concerned they submit queries and receive the results. All execution aspects are transparent.

References

1. Cotronis, J.Y. (1996) Efficient Composition and Automatic Initialisation of Arbitrarily Structured PVM Programs, in *Proc. of 1st IFIP International Workshop on Parallel and Distributed Software Engineering*, Berlin, 74-85, Chapman & Hall.
2. Cotronis, J.Y. (1996) Efficient Program Composition on Parix by the Ensemble Methodology, in *Proc. of Euromicro Conference '96*, Prague, IEEE Computer Society Press.
3. Cotronis, J.Y. (1997) Message Passing Program Development by Ensemble, in *Proc. of PVM/MPI'97*, Cracow, LNCS **1332**, 242-249, Springer.
4. Cotronis, J.Y. (1998) Developing Message Passing Applications on MPICH under Ensemble, in *Proc. of PVM/MPI'98*, LNCS **1497**, 145-152, Springer.
5. Geist, A. , Beguelin, A. , Dongarra, J. , Jiang, W. , Manchek, R. , Sunderam, V.:PVM 3 User's guide and Reference Manual. ORNL/TM--12187, May 1994.
6. G Graefe, "Query Evaluation Techniques for Large Databases", ACM Computing Surveys", vol.25, no. 2, pp. 73-170, 1993.
7. W .Kim, "On Optimizing an SQL-Like Nested Query", ACM Trans. Database Systems, vol. 7, no. 3, pp.443-469, 1982.
8. Message Passing Interface Forum (1994) MPI: A Message Passing Interface Standard.
9. Parsytec Computer Gmbh.:Report Parix 1.2 and 1.9 Software Documentation.1993
10. G. Philokyprou, C. Halatsis, M. Hatzopoulos, J. Cotronis, D. Nikolos, M. Spiliopoulou, N. Flessas, D. Koutoulas, T. Kalentzos and G. Platanakis. 'Implementation and evaluation of database management systems in parallel environment'. Report SPAN-WP14-6 for 1588-ESPRIT, Univ. of Athens, Dept. of Informatics, Dec. 1989.
11. M. Spiliopoulou, M. Hatzopoulos. Translation of SQL Queries into a graph structure: query transformations and pre-optimization issues in a pipelined multiprocessor environment. Information Systems 17,2, pp 161-170, 1992
12. M. Spiliopoulou, M. Hatzopoulos, J. Cotronis, 'Parallel Optimisation of Large Join Queries with Set Operators and Aggregates in a Parallel Environment Supporting Pipeline'. IEEE-TKDE, Vol.8, No. 3, pp 429-445, June 1996.

An Architecture of Stampi: MPI Library on a Cluster of Parallel Computers

Toshiyuki Imamura, Yuichi Tsujita, Hiroshi Koide, and Hiroshi Takemiya

CCSE, Japan Atomic Energy Research Institute
2-2-54 Nakameguro, Meguro-ku, Tokyo 153-0061, Japan
{imamura, tsujita, koide, takemiya}@koma.jaeri.go.jp

Abstract. In this paper, we present a communication library which extends an MPI application on a single parallel machine to a cluster of parallel machines. Stampi provides some functionality which are required for constructing distributed applications and environments based on the MPI2 standard with a focus on dynamic process management. Since the mechanism of communication bridge is transparent for users, it is very useful to assemble and link MPI applications on meta-computer systems. Furthermore Stampi supports novel functions; one is the communication between a Java applet to the backend parallel computer. Another is supporting remote file-IO. Both give us a framework of distributed resource management based on an MPI communication infrastructure. This paper covers the architecture of Stampi.

1 Introduction

Recent progress of computer and network technology allows us a high-speed and large scale scientific simulation. By using several parallel computers, we can treat a huge problem heretofore impossible. Such computing, called *metacomputing*, is greatly desired from the realm of computational science and engineering. To construct the environment in which the users handle such computing with ease, it is significant to support seamless use for any users (here 'seamless' has various meanings). One can easily imagine communication is one of core parts for such environment, and it should be highly developed and flexible to support various kinds of services.

Users need many existing applications to be processed on such a seamless environment and to inherit their know-how for distributed computing. From the standpoint of scientific computing, both speed-up and scale-up are indispensable for the developed code so as to gain a profit of distributed computing. In addition cost-performance with regard to running or porting is an important factor for scientists who are not experts in this area. Fortunately almost existing applications are developed in consideration of portability on various platforms, and ported with MPI[1,2]. This means that if common communication layer and process management system work over distributed machines, the MPI applications also run on a virtual parallel computer system in which each machine becomes a computational element. Thus we recognized that utilizing the MPI standard is the best way for distributed parallel computing, and adopted it as a communication infrastructure in our metacomputing environment. This was the first objective of developing Stampi.

J. Dongarra et al. (Eds.): EuroPVM/MPI 2000, LNCS 1908, pp. 200–207, 2000.

Many efforts have been done in the implementations of MPI which extend functionality for heterogeneous computing. PACX-MPI[3], MPICH-G[4] MPI_Connect[5] and LAM(version 6.4)[6] are well-known, and many experiments of distributed computing are reported. Especially PACX-MPI was developed as a part of global wide-area application testbed, and it demonstrated transatlantic computing in SC97, 98 and 99. MPICH-G is one communication infrastructure in Gridware[7], which integrates MPICH and globus toolkit, nexus. Both intend to process global or wide are computing spread across several countries, and support static process management and network routing. Stampi[8] was originally developed on local-area network, wherein several small parallel computers work.We are going to expand this to wide-area network. Stampi supports from dynamic process management to MPI-IO[9] for effective use of limited computational resources in a LAN.

2 Outline of Stampi's Features

The basic concept of Stampi is to remove a barrier of heterogeneity in communication in distributed computing, and to provide all communication functionality in the MPI semantics. We focused on utilizing applications developed in the MPI2 standard with minimal modification. Stampi realizes distributed computing in which a virtual super-computer comprises any parallel computer connected via LAN or WAN. The minimum configuration of Stampi is illustrated in Fig.1. Stampi library is linked to the user's parallel application, the vendor's supplied MPI library and message routers bridging the gap between two user applications on the different machines. Here we assume that parallel machine A and B are managed in interactive and batch(NQS) mode respectively. In addition to the basic configuration shown in Fig.1, it is assumed that NQS commands (qsub, qstat, etc.) are available on only the frontend node of machine B. All nodes in a cabinet including the frontend are IP-reachable on the private address and separated in global IPs.

To establish real distribute computing, we should introduce common rules to share the distributed heterogeneous resources. They involve to remove or hide the difference in various version of software or handling of data and application caused by hetero-

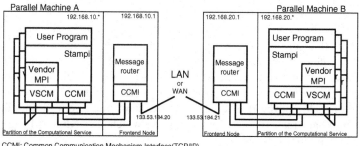

CCMI: Common Communication Mechanism Interface(TCP/IP)
VSCM: Vendor Supplied Communication Mechanism

Fig. 1. Schematic view of Stampi basic architecture

geneity. In the above mentioned configurations, we considered communication layer, segmenting in private addresses, execution mode(interactive and batch), handling of remote processes, compile and link (commands, options etc.), data formats and so on.

Achieving distributed executables without modification to the MPI applications, Stampi uses a profiling interface shift in its implementation. Therefore users only need to recompile their codes before they run the application. Stampi manages hosts and the local rank internally by Stampi-communicator, and when it detects a communication, it chooses the best way of inter- or intra- communication mechanism. In the current implementation, Stampi uses a TCP-socket for inter-communication and the vendor supplied communication mechanism for intra-communication. Introducing such a hierarchal mechanism lighten the disadvantages in a common usage of communication.

Common data representation is also considerably most important in a heterogeneous environment. Stampi adopted **external32** format defined in the MPI2. Stampi hooks a converting procedure on the subroutines, MPI_Pack and MPI_Unpack, also in the external communication layer.

Other term, especially the handling of remote processes is significant, and it was realized by introducing a router process and new API, which are described in the next section. Although optimization of routing and control of load balance are indispensable for distributed computing, they are located on the upper layer of Stampi and we do not exploit them in this paper (please see the related work[13]).

3   Technical View of the Stampi Library

3.1   Router Process

The message router processes are routing from internal-private IP address to the global IP address (and other way round). Though VPN and NAT are effective ways to resolving private networks, introducing them on parallel super computer has problems in management and supports. Because of it, we introduced the router process in Stampi.

The router process runs on the frontend node, and makes connection between the internal nodes and the counterpart. Since some parallel computers MPI applications cannot run on the frontend, it was developed as non-MPI application. Another function of the router is starting-up a remote MPI application. Since a startup requirement of the remote application cannot arrive at the remote machine directly, the router issues a remote procedure call.

To avoid the disturbance of introducing router processes, users can change the number of routers statically in the current version of Stampi. For the case that all nodes in parallel computer have global IP addressing, the router process is not required and all MPI processes can communicate directly. If one parallel machine has global IP and another has private IPs, one router will be created on the frontend node of the system with private IPs. Moreover, if parallel computers have multi network interface cards (NIC), the user can create several routers on nodes which have NICs and will take care of parallel network routing (Fig. 2).

Next we would like to present performance of the router. Since redundant memory copies must occur in the internal process, throughput becomes no more than the harmonical average of that in the connected networks. From a preliminary measurements,

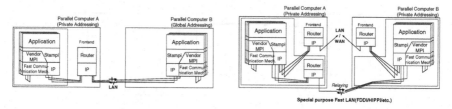

Fig. 2. Examples of router configuration (*one router* and *multi-network routing*)

sustained performance did not exceed the estimation (see Table 1). Here, a Fujitsu VPP-300 requires a router process and an SGI ONYX and as NEC SX-4 need no routers, and all machines were connected via HIPPI (peak 100MB/s). For the case in the long message, Stampi performed about 94% (at VPP inside–VPP frontend–ONYX) and 95% (at SX-ONYX) of the raw TCP-socket, therefore the loss of introducing the router was at least 1% of the communication performance. These results show that Stampi fully uses the performance of TCP-socket and it is an effective tool in a large scientific application. On the contrary for the short message, it reached quite a half performance of the estimation derived from the sustained throughput. It can be interpreted that; communication overheads such as checking header, protocols and data conversion became outstanding in the short communications, but it was only a few millisecond per a Stampi packet and it was neglectable in the long communications.

Table 1. The performance results in a ping pong communication

	latency	throughput [MB/s]			
		length of message [Byte]			
	[ms]	8000	$8*10^4$	$8*10^5$	$8*10^6$
VPP frontend–ONYX(raw TCP)	1.71	3.49	13.3	14.6	14.7
VPP frontend–VPP inside(raw TCP)	1.00	6.05	26.7	39.2	40.9
VPP inside–VPP frontend–ONYX(estimation)	2.71	2.21	8.87	10.6	10.8
VPP inside–VPP frontend–ONYX(Stampi; one router)	5.89	1.45	5.67	9.34	10.2
SX–ONYX(raw TCP)	0.92	6.75	20.3	20.7	21.2
SX–ONYX(Stampi; no routers)	2.60	3.54	14.3	19.0	20.2

3.2 Dynamic Process Management

Dynamic process management is one of the most important function of Stampi. This function and APIs were adopted in MPI2 and the user can write a manager-worker type process creation with calling `MPI_Comm_spawn` or `MPI_Comm_spawn_multiple` functions. In the semantics of MPI2 standard, these functions create new child MPI processes on the specified host and establishes a connection between them. A new inter-communicator is obtained and it enables inter- communication. Thus this functionality provides an ability to rebuild a virtual-computer world at run-time with user's intention.

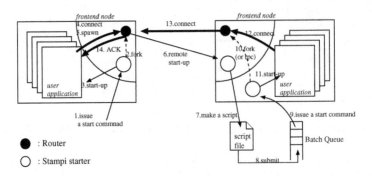

Fig. 3. Spawn operation under the batch mode

As described in the last subsection, this function requires a message router for creating a remote process. The router relays start-up commands and information, like connected network, allowed socket number, program name, user-id, the number of processors to be used, working directory. These specification are given by setting an MPI_info object, which lists a pair of information (key,value). Stampi originates some infokey, user id, node, partition, batch queue name and so on. Furthermore the router issues a remote program with help of a remote shell command.

Stampi supports both interactive and batch mode. Though batch requests of other users violates the connection between batch and interactive jobs, it was introduced for common usage of both jobs in heterogeneous environment, wherein batch job is only permitted. Fig.3 shows the sequence of the remote process creation using the batch mode. When user code calls the `MPI_Comm_spawn` function, the router process starts a Stampi-startup command (starter) and generates a script file which is submitted to a batch queue. Next the starter written in the script file kicks off the user MPI application and the router process. Finally connection between machine A and B is established, and ACK returns. The interactive mode is simpler than the batch mode; initiation command starts the remote application and forks the router directly. All other operations are similar as in the batch mode.

A client-server type connection is also supported; `MPI_Open_port`, `MPI_Comm_connect`, `MPI_Comm_accept`. This type of connection supports constructing client-server applications. In addition, it supports to establish the complete connection of more than three applications, because the spawn function only provides the connection between parent and children and there is no way to make a connection in the same generation or between child and grandparent. Since its mechanism is very similar to TCP-socket model, its detailed implementation is omitted.

The dynamic process creation requires users to modify or insert the functions into their codes so as to control a remote MPI application. Stampi also has a command-line option whereby Stampi spawns the distributed applications and make one `MPI_COMM_WORLD` when the `MPI_Init`s complete. For example next command:

'`jmpirun -np 1 foo : -np 4 -host B -nqsq classC foo`'

initiates up a process (foo) on localhost and 4 processes (foo) on machine B with an NQS submit command and creates a united `MPI_COMM_WORLD`. From the viewpoint of application user, this option provides a flat MPI world spread over parallel machines, and it clears the way for increasing the number of processors. But we would like to point out here that it only removes a communication barrier of distributed computer resources. It will give rise to a penalty in computing because of problems of load imbalance and varying inter-communication speed. If users expect better performance, they should be considered investing some effort in tuning their code for the distributed environment.

3.3 MPI I/O

MPI I/O is another significant feature of the present Stampi. Stampi provides distributed I/O, which is similar to ROMIO[9], and this function removes a manual file transfer and temporary disk spaces for handling the large amount of data. The user initially enters the function, MPI_File_Open, and then Stampi creates an I/O server on the specified machine. The basic architecture of MPI-I/O is shown in Fig. 4. The I/O server acts as an MPI application and talks with the client processes about I/O operations. A typical I/O operation corresponding to an MPI_File_read follows the next procedures. (This function of MPI2 standard is using blocking data access with individual file pointers.)

1. send a read request, '(read command, data type, count, file position, ...)',
2. prepare a buffer area on the IO-server,
3. read data from remote disks,
4. return a status code of data read by the IO-server, and finally
5. if status is 'SUCCESS', then data transfer to the client.

In this read operation, firstly the client sends requests of file manipulation which is then processed by the server on its local disk. As shown in the figure, implementation of MPI-IO is based on 3-way connection process. One might feel that it is a costly design, but data transfer of mage-byte order will hide these overheads and assurance of buffer area is important in the real I/O operation. Other operations, such as MPI_File_sync, collective access (MPI_File_read_ all and MPI_File_write_all) and nonblocking

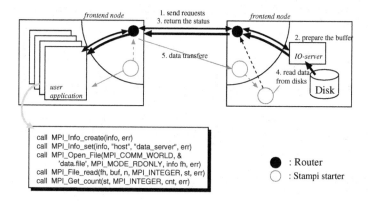

Fig. 4. The architecture of MPI-IO in Stampi (descriptions in this view present a read operation)

versions, are processed in a similar way. As described in the previous subsection, user application can talk with the IO-server directly if direct communication is available.

3.4 Stampi/Java

Java is a portable programming language which is available in a wide range of platforms. Many users hope to access metacomputing resources from their local terminal with user-friendly interface like the Web browser. Stampi/Java provides function to connect MPI applications (developed in Fortran or C) and Java applets. This extension is not a part of the MPI-standard, but similar implementations were proposed[10]. Stampi/Java implementation supports the functionality of point-to-point communication, process creation and client-server connection to the backend machines. Relaying a message between Java-socket layer and Stampi-communication is realized by introducing a Stampi/Java server (SJ), which runs on the web server. SJ talks with both applets and Stampi-application, and relays the received messages. The architecture is presented in Fig. 5. In the Stampi class layer, message objects are marshaled and translated to the intermediate format.

A preliminary test was carried out using the following configurations; the Web server, the web client and the backend supercomputer are a Sun enterprise, a note-PC and an SGI ONYX2 respectively, and all connected with 100Base-TX. Latency was less than 1 millisecond and throughput reached 530KB/sec. The result implies that java applets cannot perform high speed communication between the supercomputers. But it can conduct a program controller, whereby users determine a dynamic assignment of resources in a metacomputing environment.

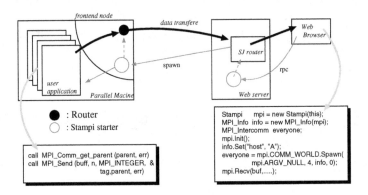

Fig. 5. The architecture of Stampi/Java

4 Summary

We have presented an outline and architecture of Stampi, which provides some extension to vendor MPI libraries and the world of distributed parallel computing. Implementing dynamic process control, MPI-IO and bridging to Java platform extend its usability, and we believe that it will contribute towards the progress of metacomputing.

Currently Stampi is ported on several platforms, for example MPPs (Hitachi SR2201, IBM SP, Intel Paragon, Fujitsu AP3000, etc.), vector parallel computers (Fujitsu VPP300, NEC SX-4 and Cray T90), SMP servers (SGI Origin, etc.), WS / PC cluster (Solaris, HP, Alpha, Linux and FreeBSD) and so on. We installed Stampi on a parallel computer cluster, COMPACS (COMplex PArallel Computer System), introduced in the Japan Atomic Energy Research Institute, and use it as a testbed for metacomputing. Several results in distributed parallel computing, fluid/structure couple simulation for airplane[11] and hybrid plasma simulation[12], were reported, and the number of supported function and platform are increasing. The latest progress and distributions of Stampi are obtained from following URL; http://ssp.koma.jaeri.go.jp/en/stampi.html.

Finally, the authors would like to thank reviewers for their valuable comments, and Toshiya Kimura, Hironori Kasahara and Michael M.Resch for their helpful discussion.

References

1. Message Passing Interface Forum: MPI: A Message-Passing Interface Standard, University of Tennesee (1995)
2. Message Passing Interface Forum: Extensions to the Message Passing Interface, University of Tennesee (1997)
3. Beisel, T., Gabriel, E., Resch, M.: An Extension to MPI for Distributed Computing on MPP's, in *Recent Advances in Parallel Virtual Machine and Message Passing Interface*, Lecture Notes in Computer Science, Springer (1997)
4. Foster, I. and Karonis, N.: A Grid-Enabled MPI: Massage Passing in Heterogeneous Distributed Computing System, Proc. 1998 SC Conference (1998)
5. Fagg, G.E., London, K.S, and Dongarra, J.J.: MPI_Connect Managing Heterogeneous MPI applications Interoperation and Process Control, in *Recent Advances in Parallel Virtual Machine and Message Passing Interface*, Lecture Notes in Computer Science, Springer (1998)
6. Squyres, J. M. et. al.: The Interoperable Message Passing Interface (MPI) Extensions to LAM/MPI, Proc. the MPI Developer's Conference, MPIDC (2000)
7. Foster, I., Kesselman, C. (eds.): The Grid: Blueprint for a New Computing Infrastructure, Morgan Kaufmann Pub. (1998)
8. Imamura, T., Koide, H., Takemiya, H.: Stampi: A Message Passing Library for Distributed Parallel Computing, –User's Guide, 2nd Edition, JAERI-Data/Code 2000-002, JAERI (2000)
9. Thakur, R. Gropp, W., Lusk, E.: On implementing MPI-IO portably and with high performance, Proc. 6th Workshop on I/O in Parallel and Distributed Systems, ACM press (1999)
10. Carpenter, B., Gotov, V. Judd, G., Skjekkum, T., Fox, G.: MPI for Java: Position Document and Draft API Specification, Technical report JGF-TR-03, Java Grande Forum (1998)
11. Kimura, T. and Takemiya, H.: Distributed Parallel Computing for Fluid Structure Coupled Simulations on a Heterogeneous Parallel Computer Cluster, International Journal of High Performance Computing Applications, Vol. 13, No. 4 (1999)
12. Imamura, T., Tokuda, S.: A hybrid computing by coupling different architectural machines, a case study for Tokamak plasma simulation, Proc. 11th IASTED Conference Parallel and Distributed Computing and Systems, PDCS99 (1999)
13. Takemiya, H., Imamura, T., et al.: Software Environment for Local Area Metacomputing, Proc. 4th international conference on Supercomputing in Nuclear Applications, SNA2000 (2000)

Integrating MPI Components into Metacomputing Applications

Torsten Fink

Freie Universität Berlin, Dept. of Computer Science,
Takustr. 9, 14195 Berlin, Germany
tnfink@computer.org

Abstract Metacomputing applications can often be composed from sub-applications written for parallel, but not wide-area distributed systems. For these systems tools like MPI or PVM are well known and many legacy applications exist. This paper describes the usage of such sub-applications as components for a metacomputing application. The approach is based on two ideas: First, abstract data objects encapsulate the binary executables and potentially the source code. Second, the compilation and execution of MPI components is provided as an abstract service type. This approach is implemented as prototype in the metacomputing infrastructure Amica using Java and CORBA.

1 Introduction

Metacomputing adds new challenges for the application development regarding heterogeneity, security, reliability, and many more aspects. Therefore, several infrastructures exist which support the development of metacomputing applications. Well known examples are Globus [3] and Legion [5].

These complex infrastructures require the application developer to learn new tools and new programming models. However, many developers of parallel applications are not willing to invest the time for learning another complex proprietary system. They want to use their acquired knowledge which usually includes an imperative language like Fortran or C++, and a middleware based on the message passing paradigm, like MPI or PVM. Furthermore, developers often rely on legacy software systems which are not compatible with the new infrastructure.

One solution to the problem is to build a metacomputing infrastructure which represents a global batch system, e.g. [8]. The application developer builds its "usual" program and gives it to the infrastructure. The infrastructure transfers the program to free computation resources, executes it there, and returns the results. The disadvantage of this solution is that only the computation resources of one computation domain can be used for the application.

Often an application can be broken into several sub-applications which can be executed concurrently in different domains. Using the global batch system approach, the application developer himself has to do the distribution and co-ordination of the sub-applications. Additionally, it is hard to implement two concurrent sub-applications which exchange information.

J. Dongarra et al. (Eds.): EuroPVM/MPI 2000, LNCS 1908, pp. 208–215, 2000.

Therefore this paper introduces a different new approach. An abstract data object stores the executable and potentially the source code of a parallel MPI sub-application. The application developer can then use a service type to execute this sub-application on the computer with the least load in a location-transparent way. This service type is encapsulated in a component which can be *glued* together with other components to form a metacomputing application.

This paper is structured as follows. In the next section the metacomputing infrastructure Amica is introduced, which serves as a testbed for our approach. In Sec. 3 the integration of the MPI support into the infrastructure is described. Then, this approach is compared to related work. Finally, the last section gives conclusions and outlines future work.

2   Overview of Amica

Amica[1] is an experimental metacomputing infrastructure to research some new approaches. Applications are built from predefined components and connectors by adapting them and gluing them together. This is done in the architecture description language Acme [4]. An introduction to this programming model is provided in the next section.

An application is compiled into a light-weight code format. An interpreter executes this code as a distributed application using the computation and storage resources of the metacomputer. The computation resources are modeled as service providers. This will be described in Sec. 2.2. An application access storage resources using abstract data objects, which are only accessible using CORBA interfaces. For a more detailed description see [2].

2.1   Structure and Semantics of Applications

In the programming model of Amica, applications are built out of components attached to connectors. Components represent application data and application functionality while connectors represent data and control flow. Figure 1 shows a visualization of an example application which performs concurrent simulations.

Components are depicted as rectangles with their type printed in the top segment and internal parameters in the bottom. They have named ports which can be used for data access. Connectors glue components together. They are depicted as oval boxes. Bold arrows specify the control flow while the dotted lines specify the flow of data.

The example application starts with the activation of a *UserBrick*, a component for the integration of Java code. This allows support for graphical user interfaces and formatting of application data so that it fits the needs of the computation services. In the application a class is instantiated to load and edit an executable file which performs the simulation.

Components representing data objects have two important properties: a type and a name. The executable file is stored in a data object named `simulationExe`.

---

[1] **A**bstract **M**etacomputing **I**nfrastructure for **C**oarse Grained **A**pplications

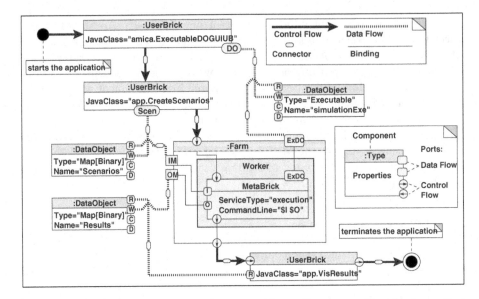

Fig. 1. Graphical representation of an example application written in Acme that performs concurrent simulation runs

All data objects have four ports for read and write access and for creation and deletion. If the creation port is not connected the data object is automatically created at startup time of the application.

When the first UserBrick terminates, another UserBrick containing the Java class `CreateScenarios` is activated, which loads some scenarios for simulation into a data object named `Scenarios` with the type `Map[Binaries]`. This means each scenario is stored as a sequence of bytes under a unique key.

In the next step a farm connector is activated. For every element of the map connected to its port `IM`, it creates a replicate of its worker. A worker is a component itself with an internal representation consisting of an arbitrary number of connected components. *Bindings* connect the internal representation to the application by propagating the data flow.

In the example, the worker consists only of one *MetaBrick*. This is a component which provides access to the computation resources. The functionality is described in the following section. It is parameterized with the service type `execution` and with attachments to data objects with the input data and for the output data and to the data object containing the executable. The actual semantics of this special service type and the format of the attached data objects are described in Sec. 3.

Now for every scenario a simulation is computed and the results are stored in a data object named `Results`. A UserBrick is activated to visualize the results and, finally, the application terminates.

2.2   Computation Subsystem

As shown in the previous section the computation resources are modeled as service providers. In the Amica infrastructure there are three main classes to support distributed computing:

- A *brick factory* can generate a service provider for a given service type and a computer architecture. This can be done in arbitrary ways, e.g., by compiling a substituted source code template or simply by using a library.
- A *brick* provides a service for a fixed service type and computer architecture.
- A *computation unit* manages the actual resources. It is the only instance which provides access to the resources. Additionally it gives information about the current load.

Figure 2 shows the interaction of these classes. A MetaBrick directs a brick factory to generate a brick. After generation, the brick is registered at the computation unit along with its demands on resources. Demands are specified as a potentially open interval (minimum, maximum) of processors and the need for disk space.

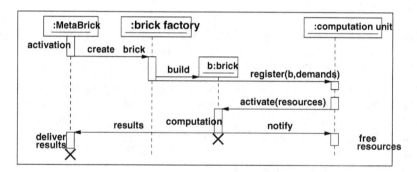

Fig.2. Interaction of the main computation classes

When the resources are available and a scheduling strategy chooses this brick to run, it is activated. With this activation comes a specification of resources the brick can use for its computation. The format of this specification depends on the concrete environment. For a workstation cluster, the Internet addresses of the assigned workstations are transmitted plus an NFS directory. After the computation the results are delivered to the MetaBrick and the computation unit is notified that the used resources are free.

3   Integration of MPI Support

As stated in the introduction, many parallel applications are developed using portable infrastructures for local-area networks like, e.g., MPI or PVM. In the following these applications are called sub-applications.

To investigate how these sub-applications can be smoothly integrated in a metacomputing framework, we designed a general framework but concentrated on MPI for a practical evaluation of the concept. The integration is based upon the introduction of a new service type for executing sub-applications and a new data object type for storing them.

The sub-application is given as source code. For execution on a given platform it is automatically configured, compiled, and finally executed. Because configuration and compilation depends strongly on the application, scripts provided by the application developer are used. If the sub-application was already compiled for the given platform the old binary code can be reused to save the compilation and link time. Input and output data are automatically transferred to the sub-application.

Figure 3 shows the CORBA interface `ExecutableDO` of the new data object type `Executable` introduced to store executable binaries along with their source code. Two binary types exist, specified by the union `BinaryType`. One is for single, directly executable programs and the other is for archives containing several programs. Archives are first unpacked and then the program with the name `mainProg` is started.

The structure `Executable` consists of a binary type, a binary executable as sequence of bytes, and the required run time support. Currently only MPI is supported as special runtime environment. For every computer architecture, specified by the structure `CUArchitecture`, an executable structure can be stored.

The source code is stored as an attribute of type `SourceCode`. It contains an archive, i.e., a gzipped tar file, the commands to build the executable from the archive and to configure the build process, and the type and required runtime support of the produced executable. Figure 4 shows a user interface to edit an executable data object. This user interface is also used by the example application in Fig. 4 to edit the executable data object.

To make the executables available to an application the service type *execution* is added to Amica. Figure 5 shows a flowchart specifying the semantics of this new service type using the elements of an executable data object. If an executable exists for a given architecture it is put into the local file system. If it is an archive it is first unpacked. Then the input data is copied from the data objects to the file system and the program is started. After termination the results are copied to the data objects and the file system is cleared. In addition to files it is also possible to use the standard input and output streams as interfaces to the executable.

If the executable does not exist but source code is provided, the executable is built using a configuration and a compilation phase. The result is inserted into the executable data object and executed as described above. If the build process or the execution of the MPI sub-application failed the locally used resources are freed and the execution is retried on another computation resource. Therefore failures of the MPI system do not effect the Amica application.

We implemented two implementations for this service type in Java. One utilizes multiprocessor workstations with shared memory, while the other utilizes

```
interface ExecutableDO : DataObject {
 /* type of the executable binary */
 union BinaryType switch (char)
 { case 's': boolean single; /* empty union elements are invalid */
   case 'a': struct  BinaryArchive { string mainProg;  } archive ;
 };
 enum RuntimeSupport {NONE,MPI};

 struct Executable
 { BinaryType binaryType;
   OctetSeq    binary;
   RuntimeSupport runtimeSupport; };
 struct SourceCode
 { string      compileCommand;  /* build executable*/
   string      configureCommand;/* configure build process*/
   string      execFileName;    /* name of the executable */
   BinaryType execType;         /* type of the executable */
   RuntimeSupport execRuntSupp;
   OctetSeq   archive; };
 attribute SourceCode sourceCode;

 /* returns true iff a binary exists for a given architecture. */
 boolean existsForArchitecture(in computation::CUArchitecture arch);

 /* adds a new executable. */
 void addExecutable(in computation::CUArchitecture arch,
                    in Executable prog);
 /** returns an executable for a given architecture. */
 Executable getExecutable(in computation::CUArchitecture arch); }
```

Fig.3. The CORBA interface for data objects of type Executable

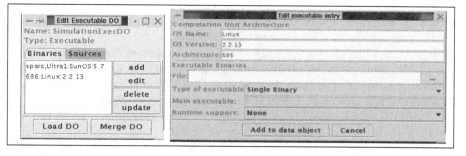

Fig.4. Screen shots of the user interface for editing an executable data object

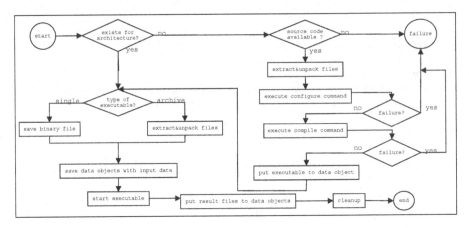

Fig.5. A flowchart specifying the usage of the executable data object

clusters of multiprocessor workstations. The MPI runtime support is built on MPICH.

To measure the management overhead we built an application that compiles and starts a small C program ($\approx 5KB$). The Amica infrastructure and the application were started on the same computer (Pentium III-450 MHz). Omitting the compilation time it took 529 $msec$ from the activation of the MetaBrick to the start of the compiled program. This is clearly a negligible amount of time if the sub-application runs at least one minute.

4   Related Work

WebFlow [6] provides a high-level programming environment for the Globus [6] system. Applications are graphically composed from components which encapsulate services of the infrastructure. Currently, an in-depth knowledge about the resource management system of Globus is needed for application development. Additionally the programming model concentrates on functional components without providing a sophisticated data model. Therefore the transparent usage of MPI components as data objects is not possible.

GIS [9] uses data flow graphs instead of the more general task graphs. Unlike Amica, GIS aims at the manipulation of geographical data and is specialized in the manipulation of streaming data. It uses DISCWorld [7], which is also based on service types. However, it does not support abstract data objects.

UNICORE [1] provides abstract job objects which are represented as directed acyclic graphs. The nodes resemble tasks of specific classes (e.g., compile task, transfer task) and are thus more restricted than the general service nodes of Amica. The integration and local execution of Java code is not supported by UNICORE. Application data is explicitly loaded and transferred by special file tasks. UNICORE offers the composition of an application from sub-applications, such as MPI programs, but it uses a very explicit approach. The user must perform load balancing and file transfers on his own, whereas our approach is location-transparent.

Summarizing, all related approaches lack support for abstract data objects. This is essential for our approach because it accommodates transparency of location and heterogeneity by hiding dynamic compilation. Furthermore, it offers efficiency by automatically reusing precompiled code.

5   Conclusions and Future Work

This paper introduces a new approach to integrate general MPI applications into a metacomputing application using an intuitive programming model based on components and connectors. This approach facilitates reuse of programming knowledge and of legacy systems for the creation of wide-area distributed applications. We have implemented a prototype of this approach using the Amica metacomputing infrastructure. The prototype offers location transparency, heterogeneity by dynamic compilation, and efficiency by reusing precompiled code.

Currently, we are enhancing the infrastructure to support authentication and accounting. We then plan to test our approach on high performance computers. We are also working on the support of pipe parallelism in the programming model to broaden the class of supported applications. After the programming model is fixed a visual editor will be implemented to ease the application development.

References

[1] J. Almond and D. Snelling. UNICORE: Secure and uniform access to distributed resources via the world wide web. Technical report, Forschungszentrum Jülich, October 1998.

[2] T. Fink and S. Kindermann. First steps in metacomputing with Amica. In *Euromicro-PDP 2000*, pages 197–204. IEEE Computer Society, 2000.

[3] I. Foster and C. Kesselman. Globus: A metacomputing infrastructure toolkit. *The International Journal of Supercomputer Applications and High Performance Computing*, 11(2):115–128, 1997.

[4] D. Garlan, R.T. Monroe, and D. Wile. Acme: An architecture description interchange language. In *Proceedings of CASCON '97*, 1997.

[5] A.S. Grimsaw and W.A. Wulf. Legion-a view from 50,000 feet. In *Proc. of the 5th IEEE Int. Symp. on High Performance Distributed Computing*, August 1996.

[6] T. Haupt, E. Akarsu, and G. Fox. WebFlow: A framework for Web based metacomputing. In *HPCN Europe '99*, number 1593 in LNCS. Springer, 1999.

[7] K.A.Hawick, H.A.James, C.J.Patten, and F.A.Vaughan. DISCWorld: A distributed high performance computing environment. In P.M.A. Sloot, M. Bubak, and L.O. Hertzberger, editors, *High Performance Computing and Networks Europe*, number 1401 in LNCS, Amsterdam, 1998.

[8] D. Tavangarian, P. Eschholz, M. Koch, C. Pitz, and S. Preuß. Hypercomputing: A concept for a network-based computer architecture. In *PDPTA '98*. CSREA Press.

[9] D. Webb, A. Wendelborn, and K. Maciunas. Process Networks as a High-Level Notation for Metacomputing. In *IPPS '99, workshop on Java for Distributed Computing*, April 1999.

PVMaple: A Distributed Approach to Cooperative Work of Maple Processes

Dana Petcu

Western University of Timişoara, B-dul V.Pârvan 4, 1900 Timişoara, Romania,
petcu@info.uvt.ro,
http://www.info.uvt.ro/~petcu

Abstract. We study the issue of interconnecting computer algebra system Maple and the message passing environment PVM. A prototype system, namely PVMaple, is presented. The system allows to create concurrent tasks and have them executed by Maple kernels running on different machines of a network.

1 Introduction

Recent developments in parallel distributed systems have resulted in increased use of suitable environments, like PVM, which make the message-passing programming to solve complex problems easier and faster for users. PVM framework allows the user to write his applications as a collection of cooperative tasks.

Computer algebra systems (CAS) can be successfully used in prototyping sequential algorithms for symbolic or numeric solution of mathematical problems. Maple, widely used environment for scientific computing, is such a CAS. Constructing prototypes for parallel algorithms in Maple is an actual challenging problem.

Several attempts have been made to combine Maple with parallel or distributed computation features. ||Maple|| [10], developed at the beginning of the 1990s, is a portable system for parallel symbolic computations built as an interface between the parallel declarative programming language Strand and the sequential CAS Maple. Sugarbush [2] combines the parallelism of C/Linda with the Maple V Release 3 kernel. In [1] porting Maple kernel to the Intel Paragon family of massively parallel distributed memory machines is described. A number of Maple kernels running on different machines of a local network can communicate also by a simple mechanism based on reading and writing on shared files in a global network file system [11]. FoxBox [3] provides an MPI-compliant distribution mechanism that allows for parallel and distributed execution of FoxBox programs; it has a client/server style interface to Maple. The most recent Distributed Maple ([8] and [9]) is a portable system for writing parallel programs in Maple, which allows to create concurrent tasks and have them executed by Maple kernels running on different machines of a network. The system can be used in any network environment where Maple and Java are available. It provides message passing facilities via a global heap.

J. Dongarra et al. (Eds.): EuroPVM/MPI 2000, LNCS 1908, pp. 216–224, 2000.

We present a prototype system allowing to study the issue of interconnecting PVM and Maple, namely Parallel Virtual Maple (shorter PVMaple). Its aim is to interface the flexible process and virtual machine control from the PVM system with several Maple processes thus allowing Maple applications the ability to inter-operate transparently across multiple heterogeneous hosts. It provides facilities for post-execution analysis of the behavior of a session. The design principles are very similar to that of Distributed Maple.

2   PVMaple Inside

PVMaple system proposes an extension of Maple capabilities to distributed computations for workstations grouped into a Parallel Virtual Machine. The user interacts with the system via the text oriented Maple front-end. PVMaple can be used in any network environment where Maple and PVM are available. The necessary packages are enumerated in Table 1.

Table 1. PVMaple components and dependencies

Component	Format	Machine	Restrictions
Package pvm.m	Maple	local	to be readed before any pvm[ ]
Command messenger	Binary	local	to be started after pvmd
File with binary paths	Text	all	in the same path
Maple V	Binary	all	at least Release 4
Pvmd	Binary	all	at least version 3.4

Figure 1 indicates the active processes on each machine of the PVMaple system. The communication routes are represented by arrows. The command-messenger ensures the inter-communication between the Maple processes via the PVM environment. Initialization of a Parallel Virtual Maple session, creation of Maple processes and inter-processes communications are provided by pvm.m package.

Table 2 enumerates the functions and constants which are currently included in the pvm.m package. Four separate issues are here specially addressed: process start-up facilities, Maple process identifiers, transparent message passing, and post-execution analysis of Maple session behaviour. A Maple process is identified by a tuple pair [machine_name,processes_id]. A process can communicate with another one by using his tuple and via the package's function calls pvm[send] and pvm[receive]. Note that the Maple processes cannot communicate directly. A Maple send command is registered by the associated command messenger which will send a message (via pvmds) to the destination command messenger which at his turn informs the associate Maple process about the incoming message.

Figure 2 shows the time sequence in which the processes are activated when PVMaple is started and also the effects of different commands from the pvm.m package (via pvmd and pvm-functions implemented in the command messenger).

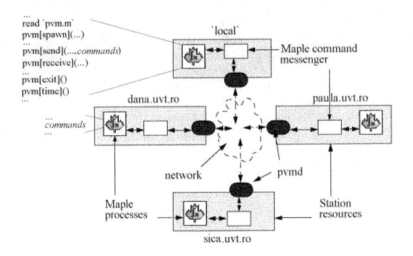

Fig. 1. Processes and inter-communication routes

Table 2. Functions and constants

Function	Synopsis	Meanings/Parameters
spawn	pvm[spawn](*sequence*)	create Maple processes;
		sequence is a sequence of elements
		like [*station_name,processes_no*]
send	*int*:=pvm[send](*destin,message*)	send Maple commands;
		int is the message identifier,
		destin can be 'all' for all processes
		or [*station_name,process_id*]
		message: a string with Maple commands
receive	*list*:=pvm[receive](*mesid,source*)	receive processes results;
		list store results returned by each process,
		mesid is the *int* given by a send or 'all'
		source: 'all' for all processes
		or [*station_name,process_id*]
exit	pvm[exit]()	return a success or fail message
settime	pvm[setttime]()	start time registration
time	pvm[time]()	show a time graphic
version	pvm[version]()	version message

Constant	Synopsis	Meaning
ProcId	*integer*:=pvm[ProcId]	process identifier on a particular station
MachId	*integer*:=pvm[MachId]	station number into the virtual machine
TaskId	*integer*:=pvm[TaskId]	process identifier into the virtual machine
Tasks	*list*:=pvm[tasks]	list of process identifiers [*station_name,process_id*]

In Distributed Maple communications between the Java scheduler and the
Maple processes are based on pipes; the corresponding Unix functions are not

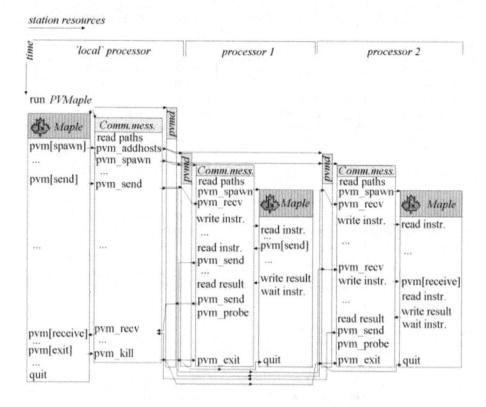

Fig. 2. Communications and components inter-dependencies

available under Microsoft Windows (a Maple V Release 4 problem). In PVMaple package currently available for PC's running Microsoft Windows a communication between Maple and its associated command messenger uses text files.

3   Examples

In this section we evaluate the behaviour of our prototype. The tests have been run in a network composed of five identical PC Pentium 250 MHz with 64 MB of RAM running Windows '95. The PVM 3.4 version for Windows '95 [4] was used for message passing.

Table 3 presents three examples of command sequences written in Maple using the pvm.m package. In the first one we can see two kind of a message send command: between the main Maple process (local process) and a remote Maple process (located on machine dana); and between a remote Maple process (located on machine dana) and another remote Maple process (located on machine paula). The Maple command sequences which will be executed on remote processes are those included between pairs of back quotes (Maple commands starting with M

Table 3. Examples of distributed commands wrote in Maple

Example 1: communication between processes

> restart; read 'pvm.m';	*load the PVMaple functions*
> pvm[settime]();	*start time chronometer*
> pvm[spawn]([dana,1],[paula,1]);	*start two tasks*
Tasks: [['local', 1], [dana, 1], [paula, 1]]	*result: pvm[tasks] values*
> mess1:='pvm[send]([paula,1],"global S;	*prepare a message to be sended*
S:=2"); S:=5;':	*and finish with an assignation*
> M:=pvm[send]([dana,1],mess1):	*send command to the first task*
pvm[receive](M,[dana,1]);	*receive last command's result*
[5]	*1st task last command's result*
> mess2:='S:=3; pvm[receive]([dana,1],'all');	*prepare receive from task 1*
S+10;';	*and finish with an addition*
> N:=pvm[send]([paula,1],mess2):	*send command to the second task*
pvm[receive](N,[paula,1]);	*receive last command's result*
[12]	*2nd task last command's result*
> pvm[exit]();	*kill the tasks and stop the time*
PVMaple quitted	*PVMaple stopped*
> pvm[time]();	*show the time graph*

Example 2: matrix-vector multiplication

```
> restart: with(linalg): read 'pvm.m': pvm[settime] ():
> pvm[spawn] ([dana,1],[sica,1],[bubu,1],[paula,1]):
                Tasks: [['local', 1], [dana, 1], [sica, 1], [bubu, 1], [paula, 1]]
> # pvm[spawn] ([dana,4]]): variant for 4 tasks on the same processor
> # prepare the matrix and vector
> n:=500: p:=5: r:=n/p: x:=randmatrix(n,1): X:=mat2str(x):
> # prepare the commands for remote tasks
> message:='with(linalg): r:='.r.': n:='.n.': x:='.X.':':
> message:= ".message.' A:=randmatrix(r,n): multiply(A,x);':
> # send the commands to all remote tasks
> s:=pvm[send] ('all',message):
> # compute the local part of the product
> z:=array(1..n): A:=randmatrix(r,n): u:=multiply(A,x):
> # receive the remote parts of the final vector
> v:=pvm[receive] (s,'all'):
> for i from 1 to n-r do z[i]:=v[iquo(i-1,r)+1][irem(i-1,r) +1,1] od:
> for i from n-r+1 to n do z[i]:=u[i-n+r,1] od:
> pvm[exit](): pvm[time] ();
```

Example 3: parallel ODE method implementation (one iterative step)

```
> parallel_Runge_Kutta_method_onestep_pvm:=proc(y,h,t) local message,L,R;
> for i to q do # number of stages
>     message:=prepare_fsolve_stage(h,y,n,t,i,L,R);
>     S[i]:=pvm[send] (['all',1],message): # to all p(i) − 1 processors
>     L[i]:=fsolve(message[1]) # solve local stages
>     R[i]:=pvm[receive] (S,['all',1]); od: # receive remote task results
> K:=assembly(R,S); y:=update(y,K); end: # new solution approximation
```

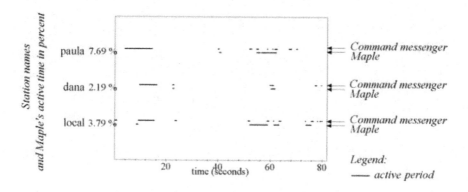

Fig. 3. Result of pvm[time] command from Example 1, Table 3

and N). The graphical result of the pvm[time] command is presented in Figure 3. The active time periods of Maple processes and auxiliary command messengers are indicated by horizontal lines. The total active time (between a pvm[settime] and a pvm[exit] command) of a Maple process is expressed in percent, so that the user can easily estimates the load balance of the distributed algorithm, the delays and the idleness sources.

Example 2 from Table 3 presents a distributed variant of a square matrix-vector multiplication. A randomly generated 500-dimensional vector x, send to five different processors, is multiplied with local randomly generated $100{\times}500$ matrices, and the multiplication results are assembled into a final 500-dimensional vector z. The high usage percent reported in Figure 4.(a) as results of settime command indicate a possible efficient implementation of a distributed multiplication algorithm. Indeed, comparing the time necessary to obtain the result of multiply(A, x) command with A a $500{\times}500$ matrix and the time depicted in Figure 4.(a) (between send commands and eexit), we get a speed-up of 4.02 (using 5 processors).

The third sequence of commands presented in Table 3 is a part of a largest program generating numerical solutions of initial value problems for ordinary differential equations of the form $y'(t) = f(t, y(t))$, $y(t_0) = y_0$, $f : [t_0, t_0 + T] {\times} R^n \rightarrow R^n$. A short description of parallel solving strategies for such a problem is presented in [5]. One step of a particular solving strategy, namely using parallel Runge-Kutta method (iterative method), involves the solution of a nonlinear system in the unknown n-dimensional vectors $k_j, j = 1 \ldots s$, computed in $q < s$ stages using in each stage $p(i)$ processors $i = 1 \ldots s$ (ideally $s = qp$). Maple's function fsolve is used in this case. When n is large the processes intercommunications are insignificant relative to the time requested by fsolve calls. Figure 4.(b) indicates how the time is spent in applying four steps of a particular Runge-Kutta method, Hammer's method [6], to a nonlinear initial value problem (convection-diffusion problem [6]) with $n = 40$ differential equations. The speed-up in this case is 1.59 (2 processors). More details about ODE integration using PVMaple are presented in [7].

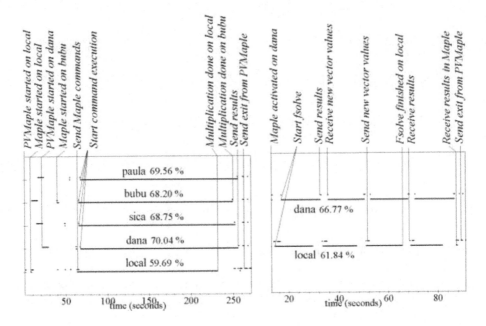

Fig. 4. Time diagrams and Maple's usage percent for (a) matrix-vector multiplication ($n \times n$, respectively n-dimensional objects, with $n = 500$) and PVMaple starting overhead (Example 2 from Table 3) (b) four steps of Hammer's method applied to an initial value problem of dimension $n = 40$ and PVMaple stopping overhead (Example 3)

4   Proposed Improvements and Perspectives

PVMaple not pretends to be better or more complex than the tools mentioned in the first section. It is designed for the common user which cannot afford to bye a parallel computer or another high-performance computer, but who has access to a workstation of a local network (a PC for example) with Maple, and who want to solve a problem requesting a large amount of computer resources. The system intends to be a public domain tool (unlike ‖Maple‖). Based on PVM functions, it is faster than those systems using shared files for communications. Like Distributed Maple it provide an environment where parallel programming is possible within Maple.

PVMaple will be ported soon to Unix platforms. The command-messenger, written in C, must be recompiled when it is ported to a new operating system. The next step consists in extending the system by introducing new functions with equivalents in the PVM library. We estimate that at the end of this year, a beta-version of PVMaple will be available for freely download from the author's web page. Future implementation activities will follow two directions: experiments with applications of PVMaple and command-messenger rewriting for interfaces with Mathematica and Matlab. Apart from extending PVMaple, our planes for future include prototyping parallel algorithms for initial value problems (project D-NODE [6] based on Distributed Maple and also PVMaple).

5   Conclusions

This document described the basic concepts behind the Parallel Virtual Maple package for cooperative work of Maple processes on networks. We showed that by mapping Maple onto PVM we can get an efficient and extensible environment. This was realized through the use of PVM inter-communications which are handles to Maple inter-communications. The current prototyped system proved its usefulness from the software's point of view in solving large mathematical problems. Due to its relatively low communication/computation ratio it can be implemented in local networks. Large sets of small (PC class) workstations can be used as a virtual machine with quite high computational power.

Acknowledgments. The author would like to express her appreciation to Wolfgang Schreiner, the creator of Distributed Maple, and to thank him for the fruitful discussions and precious references.

References

1. Bernadin, L., Maple on a Massively Parallel, Distributed Memory Machine. In *PASCO '97: Second International Symposium on Parallel Symbolic Computation*, eds. M. Hitz, E. Kaltofen, ACM Press, New York (1997), 217-222.
2. Char, B.W., Progress Report on a System for General-Purpose Parallel Symbolic Algebraic Computation. In *ISSAC '90: International Symposium on Symbolic and Algebraic Computation*, ACM Press, New York (1990), 96-103.
3. Diaz, A., Kartofen, E., FoxBox: a System for Manipulating Symbolic Objects in Black Box Representation. In *ISSAC '98: International Symposium on Symbolic and Algebraic Computation*, ed. O. Gloor, ACM Press, New York (1998), 30-37.
4. Markus Fisher, PVM 3.4 port to Microsoft's Win32 Architecture, http://www.markus-fischer.de/win32project.htm.
5. Petcu, D. Implementation of Some Multiprocessor Algorithms for ODEs Using PVM. In *LNCS* **1332**: *Recent Advances in Parallel Machine and Message Passing Interface*, eds. M. Bubak, et al., Springer-Verlag, Berlin (1997), 375-382.
6. Petcu, D., Numerical Solution of ODEs with Distributed Maple, Technical Report 00-09 (2000), RISC-Linz, submitted to *Second Conference on Numerical Analysis and Applications*, Rousse, June 11-15 2000.
7. Petcu, D., Experiments with PVMaple and Parallel Methods for ODEs, submitted to Cluster'2000: International Conference on Cluster Computing, Chemnitz, Germany, 28-30 November 2000.
8. Schreiner, W., Distributed Maple – User and Reference Manual. Technical Report 98-05 (1998), RISC-Linz, and http://www.risc.uni-linz.ac.at/software/distmaple.
9. Schreiner, W., Developing a Distributed System for Algebraic Geometry. In *Euro-CM-Par'99: 3rd Euro-conference on Parallel and Distributed Computing for Computational Mechanics*,ed.B.Topping, Civil-Comp Press, Edinburgh (1999), 137-146.

10. Siegl, K., Parallelizing Algorithms for Symbolic Computation Using ∥Maple∥. In *4th ACM SIGPLAN Symposium on Principles and Practice of Parallel Programming*, ACM Press, San Diego (1993), 179-186.
11. Wang, D., On the Parallelization of Characteristic-Set-Based Algorithms. In *LNCS* **591**: *Parallel Computation - 1st International ACPC Conference*, ed. H.P. Zima, Springer-Verlag, Berlin (1991), 338-349.

CIS - A Monitoring System for PC Clusters

Ján Astaloš and Ladislav Hluchý*

Institute of Informatics, Slovak Academy of Sciences, Bratislava, Slovakia
{astalos,hluchy}.ui@savba.sk

Abstract. PC clusters are still more popular platform for high performance computing. But there is still lack of freely available tools for resource monitoring and management usable for efficient workload distribution. In this paper, a monitoring system for PC clusters called Cluster Information Service (CIS) is described. Its purpose is to provide clients (resource management system or application scheduler) with information about availability of resources in PC cluster. This information can help the scheduler to improve performance of parallel application. CIS is designed to have as low intrusiveness as possible while keeping a high detail of monitoring data.

The possibility of improving the performance of PVM/MPI applications is also discussed.

1 Introduction

PC clusters gain still more popularity, mainly because they can deliver supercomputer performance at far lower cost than commercial supercomputers. Unlike clusters of workstations (CoW), computing nodes in PC clusters often consist only of main board, CPU, memory and network card which allows to dramatically reduce the price/performance ratio. Moreover, whole cluster acts as single entity (from management point of view), therefore node availability does not depend on node owners and thus is more predictable.

Most of existing PC clusters are based on Linux operating system and clustering is done using message passing environments, usually MPI or PVM. Although there is still more freely available software, there is still lack of tools for resource monitoring and management. For embarrassingly parallel application it is possible to use some of available queuing systems with integrated load balancing. However, for communication-intensive application it is very important to balance network load as well. Since dynamic optimization problem is NP-hard, many different heuristics were proposed [1]. They are mostly designed for special type of parallel algorithm and they have various needs for information about resources. While random task placement strategy uses no information at all, preemptive methods with process migration [8] need to know detailed information about

* This work was supported by the Slovak Scientific Grant Agency within Research Project No.2/7186/20

J. Dongarra et al. (Eds.): EuroPVM/MPI 2000, LNCS 1908, pp. 225–232, 2000.

process (size, communication dependencies, CPU requirements) as well as information about capacity of network links, and, of course, an estimated node performance.

To minimize the impact of wrong decisions, the scheduler must predict availability of resources in the future [11]. For this, it needs to know not only current state but also dynamic changes in the past. This imposes high requirements on monitoring system. In general, the level of information detail depends on the intrusiveness of monitoring.

In this paper, a low-intrusive monitoring system for PC clusters is presented. Next section gives an overview about its design and features. Section 3 is devoted to short term CPU performance prediction, built in the information server. Resource management extensions of the PVM environment as well as the possibility to use monitoring information in PVM/MPI applications are addressed in section 4. Section 5 gives a brief description of the other monitoring systems usable in PC clusters. Finally, section 6 concludes the paper.

2   Cluster Information Service

As mentioned above, the detail of monitoring data depends on intrusiveness of monitoring system. Thus, the main design goal of CIS was to reduce the overhead of monitoring as much as possible, mainly by its structure, data transfer and data acquisition techniques.

The architecture of high performance PC clusters used for scientific computations consists, in general, of a set of computing nodes connected by high speed network and one or more front-end nodes usually not used for computations. CIS structure follows this architecture (Fig.1). CIS server is running on a head node and collects information from monitors running on computing nodes.

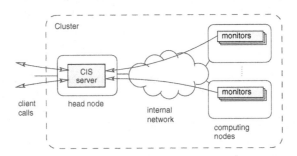

Fig. 1. Structure of Cluster Information Service

Monitors are designed to be as simple as possible. They check monitored objects in regular time intervals and inform the server about the changes. The overhead of data acquisition is reduced using special kernel probes instead of standard (textual) kernel interface. Probes provide monitors with monitoring data in binary form and all objects at once. Moreover, they are able to detect monitored events and notify the monitor. The events (object creation/termination) are sent to the server immediately, thus reducing server data inconsistency. Instrumenting OS kernel also make it possible to measure the activity of communication endpoints (sockets). This information is essential for identification of communication dependencies between tasks. The messages from monitors are sent using UDP protocol (Fig.2) reducing the overhead of data transmission.

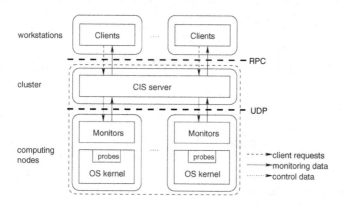

Fig. 2. Data transfer

Clients can obtain monitoring information from CIS server via RPC calls. Unlike most of fully distributed monitoring systems designed for CoWs, the requests are not propagated to monitors. CIS server keeps up-to-date view about whole cluster and provides clients with requested information. Therefore the load imposed on internal network does not depend on frequency of client requests. It only depends on monitoring interval, number of objects and their activity. System administrator can adjust the monitoring interval and thereby can control the level of monitoring system intrusiveness. This structure was selected considering possible integration of clusters into large computational grids where the number of requests for information about resources availability can be quite high. Client RPC calls are encapsulated in API library included in CIS package.

The information provided by CIS is listed in Tab.1.

Table 1. The information provided by CIS

system	memory, swap, number of processes, average load, CPU availability
processes	identification, owner, priority, start time, used memory, CPU usage, disk transfer rates
sockets	source and destination addresses, owner, transfer rates
network devices	name, status, transfer rates, collisions

Monitoring information can be viewed using visual client called xcis (Fig.3). Like the top utility it provides user with an ongoing look on monitored objects. One instance of xcis running on user workstation is able to display the data from multiple CIS servers. In host list folder with system information the user can select the hosts to be viewed in the other folders (processes, communication links, network devices, CPU availability and network usage history).

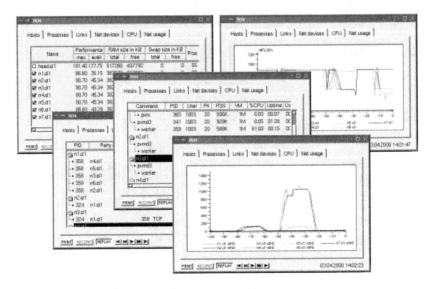

Fig. 3. Xcis screenshots

Monitoring information can be saved to a file for later processing either using xcis or background daemon. Archived information can be used for long term analysis of dynamic behavior of parallel applications. CIS package includes also tools for processing of record files (cutting, merging, printing in text form). And, of course, xcis is able to visualize the data from the record files.

The overhead of CIS monitors measured on Pentium III 550 MHz with 384 MB of RAM, 100Mbit network interface and monitoring interval set to one second is shown in Tab.2. For comparison the table contains also the overhead of top utility.

In the empty state there were 13 system processes on the node. In loaded state there were 10 additional user processes computing and communicating in cycle. Since standard Linux kernel is not able to count time slices shorter than one clock tick (usually 10ms) and monitors were consuming less than one tick, for correct measurement it was necessary to modify time accounting code in the kernel.

Table 2. The overhead of CIS monitors and the top utility

	interval	sysmon		procmon		sockmon		netmon		top	
	s	%CPU	B/s	%CPU	B/s	%CPU	B/s	%CPU	B/s	%CPU	B/s
empty	1	0.01	67	0.01	49	<0.01	119	<0.01	46	1.5	1743
loaded	1	0.01	75	0.01	96	<0.01	272	<0.01	45	1.66	1647
empty	0.1	0.11	750	0.13	491	0.05	1289	0.05	402		
loaded	0.1	0.12	750	0.18	904	0.08	2021	0.06	402		

3   CPU Performance Prediction

Main goal of an application scheduler is to achieve the shortest possible run time. Since the resources in PC clusters are usually shared and their usage varies in time, the scheduler must predict their availability in the future. Wrong decisions may lead to performance degradation.

For estimating the CPU availability most of the schedulers use load average values provided by UNIX operating systems. They represent average number of processes waiting in run-queue for 1, 5 and 15 minutes. Main drawbacks of load average are slow reaction on changes and no sensitivity to process priorities. In Network Weather Service [11] the authors tried to overcome the problem with priorities using special probe process that measures real CPU availability for tuning the estimation algorithm. This approach imposes additional overhead on monitoring.

CIS server contains a simple algorithm for short term CPU performance prediction, based on simulation of Linux process scheduler. Having information about CPU usage for all processes, idle time and priorities, it can estimate how much CPU time could be allocated to a new process (response time). CPU usage of process is computed from last three changes in order to include also processes with period larger than the monitoring interval. The algorithm for estimating the CPU availability is based on elimination of processes with lower CPU consumption than they can have (non CPU-bound). The rest of available CPU time is divided between CPU-bound processes and virtual new process (according to their priority).

The result can be used by application scheduler along with maximal performance the scheduled task can have to estimate current node performance. Since process start/exit is reported immediately, reaction of predicted CPU performance on these events is immediate as well.

Mean error of estimation and benchmark (linpack) measured with multiple CPU bound processes with various priorities was 1.73%, though for more realistic workload the error may be higher. Especially if there will be higher cache contention.

Client can, however, obtain the information needed for prediction and predict the performance itself. It is therefore possible to build an advisory system with more sophisticated prediction techniques on top of CIS.

4   Dynamic Optimization of PVM and MPI Applications

CIS was developed as a part of Dynamic Load Balancing (DLB) system for PVM [4], mainly for dynamic process creation [5]. To avoid multiplying of the overhead by collecting the same information by multiple applications, we decided to separate monitoring subsystem and make it independent from PVM. Another reason for doing this was to allow to use monitoring information also in data parallel applications.

Our DLB system is based on semi-distributed approach, in which the nodes in virtual machine are grouped into so called spheres. Each sphere has one scheduler that manages the sphere according to a centralized strategy and when needed, it can transfer tasks into a less loaded sphere. At the level of spheres, load balancing works on fully distributed principle. This approach is a compromise between centralized and fully distributed strategies and it is well suited for multi-cluster environments. Since PVM has no built-in support for transparent process migration, our DLB system uses non-preemptive load balancing algorithms. In the future, we plan to experiment with PVM extensions for process migration (e.g. Condor, Dynamite or MOSIX).

The implementation is based on the ability of PVM to forward the requests for spawning new tasks to a special process called resource manager (an example of such plug-in process called *srm* is distributed along with PVM source code). The interconnection between our DLB system and CIS is shown in Fig.4.

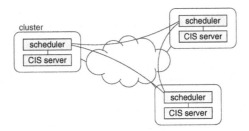

Fig. 4. Semi-distributed dynamic load balancing

Srm uses very simple load balancing algorithm based on task number, but it is quite easy to enhance it with more sophisticated strategy. Modified *srm* (centralized) which distributes tasks according to the information provided by CIS server can be downloaded from CIS homepage.

In MPI, process creation is different for each implementation and the state of their support for MPI 2 functions for process management is under examination. However, scheduling using the information from CIS can be integrated into an application (PVM or MPI).

5   Related Work

Most of existing monitoring tools are designed for performance analysis of an application (e.g. for detection of bottlenecks). There are only a few monitoring tools that can provide information for dynamic optimization.

Monitoring systems differ by purpose, architecture, provided information and also data acquisition mechanisms. General model of monitoring system for distributed systems can be found in [7]. A system for monitoring of heterogeneous workstations called Node Status Reporter is presented in [9]. It consists of a set of daemons (one per host) communicating on client-server principle. It provides clients with static and dynamic information about hosts. In [2] commercial object-oriented monitoring system PARMON that provides information about hosts, processes, network devices and kernel activities is presented. The information is accessible via Java interface. Another Java based monitoring system for large clusters of workstations called ClusterProbe is presented in [6]. It is designed to be open, flexible and scalable. Monitoring information can be accessed through multiple adaptors (including CORBA, SQL and HTTP). Monitoring of large computational grids is addressed in Network Weather Service [11]. Along with monitoring of hosts and networks, it contains also performance forecasting techniques.

The monitoring systems mentioned above are not (yet) freely available. One of the freely available monitoring systems for PC clusters (except very simple bWatch for displaying average load on nodes) is SMILE Cluster Management System [10] which contains also monitoring subsystem and API for accessing monitoring information. It provides quite rich information about nodes including network statistics. Its overhead is affected by client-server access to monitoring information on computing nodes. Monitoring just CPU information, load average, memory and swap usage on the system described in section 2 with monitoring interval set to one second has CPU overhead around 1.75% and network overhead around 7 kB/s. This overhead is multiplied by the number of clients.

In February 2000, the SGI company released a monitoring infrastructure of the "Performance Co-Pilot" as open source. Unfortunately, at the time of writing this paper their visualization tools were not freely available.

CIS differs from the monitoring systems mentioned above by its structure and data acquisition techniques. Using kernel instrumentation it is able to monitor also parameters not provided by standard kernel interface. On the other hand, CIS has no means for managing monitored objects.

6   Conclusions and Future Work

Cluster Information Service presented in this paper can provide application schedulers with the information about availability of resources in PC cluster. The overhead of data acquisition is reduced using special probes in OS kernel. Unlike most of other monitoring systems based on client-server principle, CIS provides continuous monitoring of computing nodes. Thus, its intrusiveness is relatively stable. Knowing the history of CPU usage, CIS server can make short term prediction of CPU availability.

The information provided by CIS can be useful not only for application schedulers but also for cluster management system or system for providing Quality of Service (QoS).

Releasing it as open source (http://ups.savba.sk/parcom/cluster/cis.html) we hope that it will evolve to best fit to the requirements of wide range of users of PC clusters. In the future we plan to implement CORBA and HTTP interfaces and to connect CIS to the information system of the Globus project [3].

References

1. K. Baumgartner and B. W. Wah, Computer Scheduling Algorithms: Past, Present, and Future, Information Sciences, vol. 57 & 58, pp. 319-345, Elsevier Science Pub. Co., Inc., New York, NY, Sept.-Dec. 1991.
2. R. Buyya, K. Mohan, B. Gopal, PARMON: A Comprehensive Cluster Monitoring System, Proceedings of the Australian Users Group for UNIX and Open Systems Conference and Exhibition, AUUG98 - Open Systems: The Common Thread, Sydney, Australia, 1998.
3. I. Foster, C. Kesselman, Globus: A metacomputing infrastructure toolkit, International Journal of Supercomputer Applications and High Performance Computing 11 (2) (1997) 115-128.
4. L. Hluchy, M. Dobrucky, J. Astalos: Hybrid Approach to Task Allocation in Distributed Systems. Computer and Artificial Intelligence, Vol.17, No.5, 1998, pp. 469-480, ISSN 0232-0274.
5. P. Kacsuk, G. Dozsa, and T. Fadgyas: Designing parallel programs by the graphical language GRAPNEL, Microprocessing and Microprogramming 41 (1996) 625-643.
6. Z. Liang, Y. Sun, and C.-L. Wang, ClusterProbe: An Open, Flexible and Scalable Cluster Monitoring Tool, 1st IEEE Computer Society International Workshop on Cluster Computing, Melbourne, Australia, December 1999.
7. M. Mansouri-Samani, M. Sloman, Monitoring Distributed Systems (A Survey) Imperial College Research Report No. DOC92/23, Imperial College of Science Technology and Medicine, London, 1992.
8. M. Nuttall and M. Sloman, Workload characteristics for Process Migration and Load Balancing, Proc. of the 17th Int. Conf. on Distributed Computing Systems, pp.133-140, May 1997.
9. C. Roder, T. Ludwig, and A. Bode, NSR - A Tool for Load Measurement in Heterogeneous Environments. In A. Bode, A. Ganz, C. Gold, S. Petri, N. Reimer, B. Schiemann, and T. Schneckenburger, editors, Anwendungsbezogene Lastverteilung – ALV'98, number TUM-I9806, SFB-Bericht Nr. 342/01/98 A, pages 133-144. Technische Universitat Munchen, February 1998.
10. P. Uthayopas, S. Phaisithbenchapol, K. Chongbarirux, Building a Resources Monitoring System for SMILE Beowulf Cluster, Proceeding of the High Performance Computing Conference ASIA,Singapore,September 1998.
11. R. Wolski and N. Spring and C. Peterson, Implementing a Performance Forecasting System for Metacomputing: The Network Weather Service, Proceedings of the 1997 ACM/IEEE SC97 Conference in San Jose California, November, 1997.

Monito: A Communication Monitoring Tool for a PVM-Linux Environment*

Francesc Solsona[1], Francesc Giné[1], Josep Lérida[1], Porfidio Hernández[2], and
Emilio Luque[2]

[1] Departamento de Informática e Ingeniería Industrial, Universitat de Lleida, Spain.
{francesc,sisco,j.lerida}@eup.udl.es
[2] Departamento de Informática, Universitat Autònoma de Barcelona, Spain.
{p.hernandez,e.luque}@cc.uab.es

Abstract. In this paper a new tool for monitoring the different queues
of messages in a PVM environment is presented. The main aim of implementing this facility is to provide a means of capturing the bottlenecks
and overheads of the communication system in a PVM-Linux cluster.
Also, it will allow to know the communication pattern of a distributed
application. Its good behaviour has been proved experimentally.

1 Introduction

Nowadays, one of the most important goals in distributed computing and specially in PVM [4] environments is performance evaluation such as Paradyn [7],
Aims [10] and XPVM [6]. To study this, some questions must be answered: such
as how good the message passing libraries of the distributed environment are or
where there is room for improving their performance and so on.

We are interested in knowing what the relevant factors are and how far
these influence system performance, focusing the study on the communication
related ones. With this purpose in mind, a monitoring tool named *Monito* [9]
was developed, which samples the state of the communication buffers (composed
of messages, fragments, packets and frames) of a PVM-Linux system, from top
(PVM), through the kernel (sockets and logical network device) to bottom (physical network device).

The */proc* Linux file system [1] offers much information about the communication subsystem, but this information is insufficient to obtain a global view
of its behaviour on each instant (bottlenecks, saturations, reasons for crashing
in distributed applications, and so on). The *Monito* tool was designated to provide a means of investigating and localizing these phenomena. Other tools like
netperf [2], *Paragraph* [5] and so on, give global statistical performance, but do
not provide information about the state of each communication buffer.

This paper is organized as follows. Section 2 describes the main buffers and
structures of the communication subsystem. *Monito* implementation and operation details are presented in section 3. In section 4, Monito behaviour is
evaluated. Finally, the conclusions and future work are detailed.

* This work was supported by the CICYT under contract TIC98-0433

J. Dongarra et al. (Eds.): EuroPVM/MPI 2000, LNCS 1908, pp. 233–241, 2000.

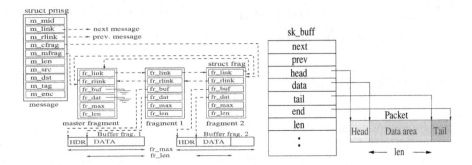

Fig. 1. (left) PVM message structure (*pmsg*) and (right) sk_buff and packet structures. The packet Data area contains the information to be transmitted. *next* and *prev* links sk_buff structures.

2   Analysis of the Communication System

In this section the main queues involved in the communication process are analyzed, from the PVM to the physical network device layer.

2.1   PVM Layer

PVM allows the execution of distributed applications in two different communication modes: *RouteDirect* and *DontRoute*. In DontRoute mode, all communication between tasks is done through the *pvmd* daemon. In this way the daemon-daemon communication is through UDP protocol and the task-daemon communication is by means of TCP or UNIX Domain protocol. On the other hand, in RouteDirect mode, communication between remote tasks uses the TCP protocol.

The PVM transmission unit is the *message* (with variable length). Every message has an associated *pmsg* structure, which is divided into fixed lengths *fragments* (= 4096 bytes). Initially, a head fragment called *master* is created, then every time that a new fragment is filled up, another one is initialized and linked to the previous one and so on. Fig. 1(left) shows the structure of a PVM message made up of a master fragment and two data fragments (the first is full).

Every PVM task has an associated dynamic list called *pvmrxlist*, which stores the received messages, waiting for such a task. On the other hand, all the messages sent by a PVM task are stored in a static queue called *txlist*, which has a maximum capacity of 100 messages.

The pvm daemon (*pvmd*) converts fragments into *packets* and vice versa. A *packet* is a fragment with additional control information. It maintains two different queues, *locltasks* and *hosts*, for packet delivery to all the local tasks and to other hosts respectively.

2.2   Socket and Protocol Layer

The fragment sent by the PVM layer is decomposed into MTU (*Maximum Transmission Unit*) size *packets*. A structure called *sk_buff* will be associated with every packet. This structure is used by Linux for passing data through the TCP/IP protocol layers [8]. In emission/reception of packets, every protocol will add/extract control information to/from its reserved Head and Tail space (see Fig. 1(right)).

In the emission/reception of packets to/from the logical network device, the socket layer creates/receives a new *sk_buff* and stores it in the *write_queue/ receive_queue*, both with a max. capacity of 65535 bytes.

2.3   Logical Network Device Layer

In transmission, the *sk_buff* structures, coming from the protocol layer are stored in one of three buffering queues (with a max. capacity of 100 elements per queue). The choice of the queue will depend on the priority of the packet, *interactive* (highest priority), *normal* (PVM messages) and *background* (lowest priority). The head of every queue is stored in an array called *buffs*. On the other hand, the packets received from the physical device are stored in a list called *backlog*, which has a maximum length of 300 buffers.

2.4   Physical Network Device Layer (Driver)

Our communication board is an Intel EtherExpress 10/100 Mbps, which has an i82558 microprocessor. The i82558 communicates with the kernel by means of a shared memory mechanism. This memory is divided into two different packet (named frame in this layer) sk_buff queues, *CBL*, for sending packets to/(and *RFA*, for receiving packets from) the network. The maximum number of elements in both queues is 16.

3   Monito: The Monitoring Tool

Based on the previous section, the most interesting transmission/reception queues to be analyzed in each layer are *hosts, locltasks and txlist/pvmrxlist* in the PVM, *write_queue/receive_queue* in the socket, *buffs/backlog* and *CBL/RFA* in the logical and physical device respectively.

The set of implemented utilities are: two PVM services, *pvm_getpvmdstats* and *pvm_getaskstats*, the *stadsoc, stadque* and *staddev* modules, the *dev_queues* system call and finally *Netmon*, an application that monitors and collects information about these utilities.

Table 1. Netmon arguments.

$Netmon -d$sp$ -tmt [-s -f] [Interface]
-dsp : sampling period (sp) in milliseconds
-tmt : monitoring time (mt) in seconds
-s : output to display
-f : output to file Netmon.dat
[Interface] : sampling interface, default eth0

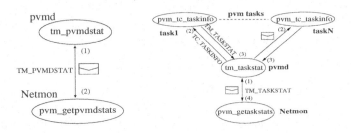

Fig. 2. (left) *pvmd* monitoring; (right) pvm tasks monitoring.

3.1   Netmon

The *Netmon* arguments are: the sampling period (sp), the total monitoring time (mt) and sample storage file. The format of the Netmon invocation call is shown in table 1. Netmon does the following operations in every *sampling period*:

1. Obtain PVM information
   (a) Obtain *pvmd* (PVM daemon) statistics. This is carried out by the pvm call *pvm_getpvmdstats* (see Fig. 2(left)). The function *pvm_getpvmdstats* sends a TM_PVMDSTAT message to the daemon and waits for a response from it (1). In the daemon a new function, *tm_pvmdstat* was implemented to reply *to Netmon* with another TM_PVMDSTAT message containing the information of the *hosts* and *locltasks* structures (2), such as, for example, the packets to deliver to remote hosts (in *hosts*) and packets to deliver to the local tasks (in *locltasks*).
   (b) Obtain PVM tasks statistics. This begins in the new pvm call *pvm_getaskstats* (see Fig. 2(right)). The function *pvm_getaskstats* sends a TM_TAS-KSTAT message to the daemon and waits for a response from it (1). In the daemon a new function for dealing with this kind of messages was implemented, named *tm_taskstat*. This function sends a TC_TASKINFO message to all the pvm tasks (2). Next, this function waits for the reply from all the pvm tasks through a new *pvm_tc_taskinfo* function (3) and then sends a TM_TASKSTAT message to *Netmon* (4). The information obtained is the number and size of the buffered messages, waiting for sending in *txlist* (or to be taken in *pvmrxlist*) queue.

Table 2. stadsoc, stadque and staddev information.

stadsoc	stadque	staddev
protocol type (tcp, udp, raw)	# of queues	received collision packets
@IP and port Source	max. queue length	pending packets in RFA
@IP and port Target	Interactive queue	delayed transmission packets
sk_buff's in recv_queue	Normal queue	one trans. collisions
sk_buff's in write_queue	Background queue	multiple trans. collisions
total bytes in recv_queue	backlog sk_buff's	pending packets in CBL
total bytes in write_queue		
retransmissions		

2. Obtain Linux information

   (a) Obtain the sockets statistics. Netmon reads the file */proc/net/stadsoc*, created and maintained by the *stadsoc* module for storing *write_queue* and *receive_queue* information. The stadsoc column in table 2 shows the information provided by *stadsoc*. Note that this information is also supplied by the kernel in three different files but the overhead in reading these can be unacceptable in small sampling periods. This is the reason for implementing this function.

   (b) Obtain logical device statistics. The method used to get information about the *backlog* and *buffs* queues of the logical device is the same as in the previously explained module, *stadsoc*. The module is named *stadque* and its associated file is */proc/net/stadque* (see stadque column in table 2). There is no known utility that gets this kind of information.

3. Obtain network device information. To capture information about the physical network device (see table 2 column staddev), not supported in the */proc/net* file system and also to sample its RFA and CBL queues, another module, *staddev* was implemented. Its associated file is */proc/net/staddev*.

Note that the PVM data is collected by message passing. This can produce some overhead in the monitor. When it finalizes, Netmon displays the additional *Netmon* execution, the percentage of samples which overlapped the *sampling period* and the maximum extra time required in a *sampling period*.

4 Experimentation

The trials were performed in a PVM distributed environment, a cluster made up of a 100 Mbps Fast Ethernet network and four PCs with the same characteristics: a 350Mhz Pentium II processor, 128 MB of RAM, 512 KB of cache, Linux o.s. (kernel v. 2.0.36) and PVM 3.4.0.

The good behaviour of *Monito* is checked by means of a synthetic benchmark. Next, two kernel benchmarks from the NAS suite [3] are run in order to show an example of Monito's use for evaluating the performance (and finding the bottlenecks) of the communication system in a PVM-Linux cluster.

Table 3. Sampling period overlap. Fault means *sintree* crash due to lack of memory.

N	M	%Overlap in DontRoute	N	M	%Overlap in RouteDirect
32	8KB	0%	25	8KB	0%
32	4MB	Fault	25	2MB	48%
750	8KB	4%	25	4MB	Fault
1000	8KB	Fault	32	8KB	Fault

4.1 Monito Evaluation

The benchmark implemented, called *sintree*, works on a communication pattern of one to vary, and vary to one. *sintree* accepts two arguments, the number of composing processes (N) that continuously send sized (M) messages by multicasting (by default $N = 25$ and $M = 8$KB). In the trials the two PVM operating modes *(RouteDirect* and *DontRoute* [4]) and notation processes/size_of_messages were used. For example 32/8K means that *sintree* arguments are N = 32 processes and M = 8KB. The default *Netmon* arguments were $sp = 100\mu s$ and $mt = 200s$.

Table 3 shows the percentage of times that the sampling period was overlapped while monitoring the *sintree* application. This table informs us of the critical values for N and M in each PVM operation mode; note that a more precise search should be done but this is out of the scope of this article.

Fig. 3 shows the main results obtained in the physical and socket layers. The figure on the left reports the results obtained for the physical layer in the DontRoute 32/2MB case. The CBL queue is filled due to the great number of fragmented packets transfered from higher levels. Remember that the maximum CBL and RFA capacity is 16 packets, but for security reasons, the driver keeps two CBL elements in reserve. For this reason the maximum number that appears in Fig. 3(left) is 14. Fig. 3 (right) shows the socket layer statistics for the DontRoute 750/8K case. Note that the reception queue is saturated (the maximum capacity is 65535 bytes). There is no buffer saturation or relevant events in the other cases in these layers and thus the results obtained are not shown.

Fig. 4 reports the most representative values obtained from the pvm layer queues. Monito gives the size of every queue in bytes or packets as can be seen in Fig. 4 (a), where *locltasks* statistics of the PVM daemon in bytes/(packets) are reflected. Note that the size of the *pvmd* packets is 4032 Bytes (equal to, for example, 3689280 Bytes from Fig. 4 (a) divided by 915). Fig. 4 (b) shows the reception queue (*pvmrxlist*) in the parent task of the *sintree* benchmark. Observe the result of dividing the max. *pvmrxlist* capacity reached (= 46137344 Bytes) by the number of packets (= 22) is 2097152 Bytes (the sending message size); this also demonstrates the good behaviour of *Monito*.

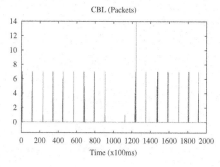
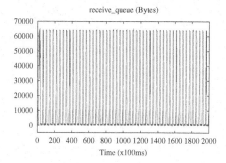

Fig. 3. DontRoute (left) buffered packets in transmission (CBL queue) for 32/2MB and (right) *pvmd* socket buffer in reception (*receive_queue*) for 750/8K.

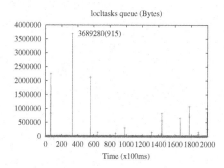
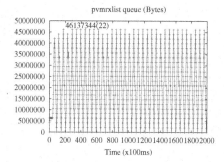

Fig. 4. (left) DontRoute *locltasks* queue in bytes 32p/2MB; (right) RouteDirect *pvmrxlist* queue 25p/2MB.

4.2 NAS Benchmarks

In order to reflect the use of Monito for evaluating the performance of the communication system, two kernel benchmarks, *MG* and *IS*, for class A problem size of the NAS suite are run. The execution time for *IS* and *MG* with one process per node are 156s and 103s respectively. The main transmission queues from the PVM layer to the driver layer are shown in the Fig. 5.

In the CBL queue the maximum capacity is hardly reached. Also, in the same queue the number of iterations of every benchmark (10 in IS and 4 in MG) is displayed as their respective number of impulses. The extreme communication required in the IS benchmark is revealed overall in the hosts queue, although the saturation isn't reached (its max. capacity is determined by the remaining memory). However, more accurate research is required in order to determine exactly which level the main bottlenecks and overheads of the communication system are in in a PVM-Linux cluster.

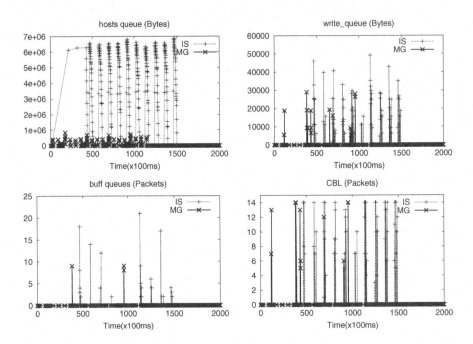

Fig. 5. Main transmission queues from the PVM layer until the device layer.

5   Conclusions

Monito, a tool for measuring the state of all the message queues in a PVM-Linux communication environment is presented. The analysis goes from the PVM queues, through the kernel queues, to the physical network device ones. By executing some benchmarks and comparing different data collected with the expected results, the correct behaviour of Monito was shown. This tool will allow in-depth study of communication bottlenecks and their correction.

Future work is directed towards new algorithms to decrease overhead in sampling data (in the current implementation, the sampling period often overlapped). Another goal is to expand *Monito* for also evaluating MPI communication performance.

References

[1] R. Card, E. Dumas, and F. Mevel. *The Linux Kernel Book*. Wiley, 1998.
[2] Information Networks Division. HP Co. Netperf: A network performance benchmark. *http://www.netperf.org/netperf/NetperfPage.html*, 1996.
[3] Parkbench Committe. Parkbench 2.0. *http://www.netlib.org/park-bench*, 1996.
[4] A. Geist, A. Beguelin, J. Dongarra, W. Jiang, R. Manchek, and V. Sunderam. *PVM: Paralell Virtual Machine - A User's Guide and Tutorial for Networked Parallel Computing*. The MIT Press, 1994.

[5] M.T. Heath and J.A. Etheridge. Visualizing performace of parallel programs. *IEEE Software*, 8(5):29–39, September 1991.

[6] J.A. Kohl and G.A. Geist. Xpvm 1.0 user's guide. *Technical Report ORNL/TM-12981, Computer Science and Mathematics Division, Oak Ridge National Laboratory*, April 1995.

[7] B.P. Miller, J.K. Hollingsworth, and M.D. Callaghan. *Environments and Tools for Parallel Scientific Computing*. J.J. Dongarra and B. Tourencheau (eds.), SIAM Press, 1994.

[8] J. Postel. Rfc 791 - internet protocol: Protocol specification. September 1981.

[9] F. Solsona, F. Giné, J.L. Lérida, P. Hernández, and E. Luque. Monito v1.0. *http://www.eup.udl.es/diei*, 2000.

[10] J.C. Yan, M. Schmidt, and C. Schulbach. The automated instrumentation and monitoring systems (aims) - version 3.2 user's guide. *NAS Technical Report NAS-97-001*, January 1997.

Interoperability of OCM-Based On-Line Tools

Marian Bubak[1,2], Włodzimierz Funika[1], Bartosz Baliś[1], and
Roland Wismüller[3]

[1] Institute of Computer Science, AGH, al. Mickiewicza 30, 30-059 Kraków, Poland
{bubak,funika}@uci.agh.edu.pl, balis@icsr.agh.edu.pl
phone: (+48 12) 617 39 64, fax: (+48 12) 633 80 54
[2] Academic Computer Centre – CYFRONET, Nawojki 11, 30-950 Kraków, Poland
[3] LRR-TUM – Technische Universität München, D-80290 München, Germany
wismuell@in.tum.de

Abstract. In the course of a parallel application development, the use
of supporting tools for debugging, performance analysis or visualization
is indispensable. Since the services provided by the tools usually com-
plement one another's, it is necessary to enable the tools to cooperate
with each other. This cooperation, often referenced as interoperability,
is feasible by means of the OCM universal monitoring system. This paper presents some issues of interoperability of two OCM-based tools, the
DETOP debugger and the PATOP performance analyzer. An insight
into the tool environment based on the OCM is also provided.
Keywords: monitoring, on-line tools, interoperability, OMIS.

1 Introduction

Tools for parallel programming support are important components of parallel
application development. Each type of tools for parallel programming support
has a well-defined functionality, therefore, in order to achieve a complex set of
services in a tool environment, the *interoperability* of tools is highly desirable,
which is meant as the capability to run concurrently and be applied to the same
application with possible synergetic effect [5]. Ideally, we would like to enable
interoperability between two tools coming from different vendors. However, such
tools are likely to be incompatible with each other and it might be even not
possible to run them concurrently due to low-level conflicts, or, event if the tools
are able to run concurrently, further conflicts may occur at higher levels.

On-line tools need a specialized module for observing and possibly manipulating of a parallel program state, which is called *monitoring system*. Sometimes
this module is integrated with a tool but it is much more profitable to have
a separate facility to provide information on parallel application processes and
mediate in controlling the application. One benefit of this approach is modular-
ity: the tool development is separated from the monitoring system development.
The most important benefit, however, is that multiple tools are enabled to use
a single monitoring system, which not only reduces the overhead induced by
running multiple tools, but also gives prerequisites for tools interoperability.

J. Dongarra et al. (Eds.): EuroPVM/MPI 2000, LNCS 1908, pp. 242–249, 2000.

This paper presents how interoperability of on-line tools is enabled in a tool environment based on the OCM (OMIS-Compliant Monitor) universal monitoring infrastructure.

2   Interoperability

The term *interoperability*, in the context of monitoring, refers to on-line tools, and means their capability to run concurrently and be applied to the same application [6]. Moreover, a cooperation between tools is possible to provide additional functionality to the tool environment. For example, if a performance analyzer runs concurrently with a load balancer, and the latter migrates a process , the former should visualize the migration on its displays. And vice versa, a process migration may be forced manually via the peformance analyzer.

The first basic requirement for interoperability concerns the possibility to run different tools concurrently. In case of tools coming from different vendors, supplied with their own monitoring modules, *structural conflicts* between different portions of the monitors may occur, which may even prevent tools from concurrent running. As multiple tools may request an operation on a single object (e.g. writing into a process address space) at the same time, an infrastructure must exist to handle the multiple requests. For these reasons, unless tools form a monolithic, integrated environment being dependent on each others' implementation, interoperability of tools based on distinct monitoring systems is hardly possible due to likely structural conflicts or conflicts on exclusive objects among the monitoring modules [5].

Further problems may occur at the user level and manifest in *logical conflicts*. For example, if a debugger and a visualizer work concurrently, and a process is stopped by the former, the latter might not show it on its displays unless it is notified of the event. This results in inconsistencies in representation of the monitored system state, which we call *consistency problems*.

The next two sections describe a universal monitoring system OCM and provides an insight into the interoperability support within the OCM.

3   OCM - A Universal Monitoring System

3.1   General Structure

The OCM is an implementation of the OMIS (On-line Monitoring Interface Specification) [3] specification, being a centralized distributed system, composed of a central module, called NDU (Node Distribution Unit), which is interfaced to a tool, and a collection of modules, called local monitors, which are interfaced to the application. The operation of the OCM is thoroughly presented in [8].

In accordance with the OMIS specification, the target parallel system is viewed by the OCM as a hierarchical set of objects. The specification defines 5 types of objects: nodes, processes, threads, message queues and messages, with a collection of services to operate on objects. The services fall into three categories: *information services* to obtain information about an object, *manipulation services* to change the state of an object and *event services* to trigger an action list whenever a specified event occurs.

The OCM is currently adapted to support PVM [2] and MPI [4] applications. In the course of the TOOL-SET [7] project development, several tools were adapted to work on top of the OCM: the DETOP debugger, the PATOP performance analyzer and the VISTOP visualizer.

3.2   Interoperability Support in the OCM

The OCM provides some coordination features to address low-level conflicts in accessing shared objects by multiple tools [6]:

- requests referring to a single object are mutually exclusive,
- requests operating on more than one node are distributed to local monitors via an atomic multicast operation, to provide their execution in the same order on each node.
- requests can be locked to prevent any other requests on any node from execution while the locked requests is being executed.

Furthermore, the concept of events, as defined by the OMIS specification, allows to address higher level conflicts. These issues are described in the following sections.

4   OCM-Based Tool Environment

In this section, we focus on the interoperability of two tools, DETOP and PATOP. An insight into the structure of an OCM-based tool environment and some its components is provided. Also covered is the startup "protocol" of the environment.

4.1   General Structure of an OCM-Based Tool Environment

General structure of an OCM-based tool environment composed of DETOP and PATOP is shown in Fig. 1. The OCM is a layer between the application and tools. In fact, the tools communicate with the OCM indirectly through a high level routine library, called ULIBS [1].

OCTET is a newly developed tool to provide a management of the environment. It will be described in the next subsection.

4.2   The OCTET Tool

The OCTET (OCM-based Tool Environment top-level Tool) tool was created to work on top of the tool environment. OCTET performs two tasks, the first of them being the start-up of the tool environment, which includes spawning the

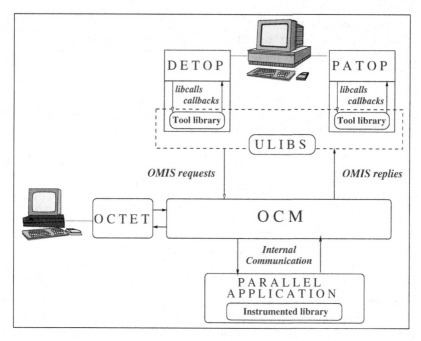

Fig. 1. OCTET in the tool environment.

application processes and running the tools, while the second is to provide tools with information to resolve consistency conflicts.

OCTET is a console application that provides a simple interface for setting up a number of parameters like the name of a parallel environment (PVM or MPI), paths to the application and tools' executables, number of processes to be run (in case of MPI only). A sample session with OCTET is shown in Fig. 2. The **set** command is used to set up the environment including the parallel library type (PVM or MPI), path to the application executable and possibly other parameters. The **run** command schedules the specified tool to be run. The tools as well as the application are actually run after the **go** command is invoked. Commands which are not recognized by OCTET are considered as explicit requests to the monitoring system, hence are sent to the OCM and replies to them are printed to the standard output.

4.3   Startup Mechanism in the Tool Environment

The startup of the tool environment is managed by OCTET. Time dependencies at the tool environment startup are shown in Fig. 3.

First, OCTET establishes communication with the monitoring system, which typically means start of of the OCM. Next, basing on the information provided by the user, OCTET orders the OCM to start the application. This process may

```
octet> set mode MPI
application type set to MPI
octet> set app-path "$HOME/MPI/cpi"
application path set to /home/balis/MPI/cpi
octet> run patop
PATOP has been scheduled to run
octet> run detop
DETOP has been scheduled to run
octet> go
starting the tool environment...

    [tools and the application are being started]

octet> :mpi_get_proclist()
```

Fig. 2. A sample session with OCTET.

vary depending on the parallel environment[1]. In the next step, OCTET starts the
tools and provides them with a list of application process tokens. The tools are
supposed to attach to each of the application processes. Finally, OCTET provides
the tools with information on the environment to enable possible interactions
between them (see Subsection 5.2).

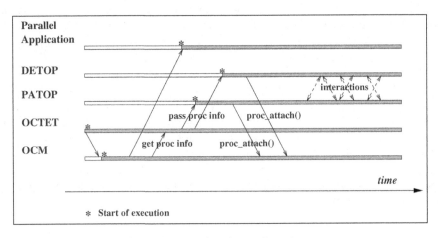

Fig. 3. Time dependencies for the tool environment startup.

---

[1] In the current implementation, this pattern is actually reversed in case of an MPI
application: the application itself is started prior to the OCM.

5   Interoperability of DETOP and PATOP

5.1   Possible Benefits of DETOP and PATOP Cooperation

Let us consider a long-time running parallel application. PATOP, as a performance analysis tool, can be used to monitor and visualize the application execution. Suppose the application reveals an unexpected behaviour, observed via PATOP performance displays. We would like undoubtedly to localize the application's point of execution to find the cause of the behaviour. This is what DETOP helps with, as it works at the source code level. After having suspended the application execution with DETOP and a possible examination of proper variables, DETOP is used to resume the application execution.

5.2   Direct Interactions

PATOP and DETOP cooperation reveals consistency problems (section 2). The incorrect behaviour occurs in two cases:

- When the application is started with PATOP, it starts reading the performance data from the OCM and updates performance displays to visualize the execution. However, when the application is suspended by DETOP, PATOP proceeds reading data and updating displays, while the expected behaviour is that, PATOP hangs up monitoring while the application is being suspended. This is only possible if PATOP is notified whenever DETOP suspends the application execution.
- Once the application is started with DETOP, PATOP does not start monitoring. Again, a notification that the application processes has been continued is necessary. Similarly, when the application is resumed by DETOP after having been breaked, the notification is also needed.

Fortunately, the notion of events provided by the OMIS specification help resolve these problems [3]. Basically, PATOP needs to "program" a reaction to each event of thread suspension or continuation. It can be achieved if PATOP issues two following conditional requests to the OCM:

```
thread_has_been_stopped([]): print([$proc])
thread_has_been_continued([]): print([$proc])
```

The semantics of these requests is as follows: *whenever a process to which PATOP is attached has been stopped (continued), the process identifier of the stopped (continued) process is returned.* The events are handled by means of a callback mechanism. The process' identifier is actually passed to the appropriate callback function, which is invoked on every occurrence of the event. This callback function performs actions to stop (or resume) the measurements.

The succeeding questions are:

1. PATOP can program reactions to various scenarios of tools' cooperation. However, how can PATOP learn the actual configuration of the tool environment (which tools are running) so that it can perform appropriate actions?

2. Where should the above requests be implemented? We might decide to insert the appropriate code directly to PATOP, however, this would be an intrusion into the tool implementation, which contradicts the principal ideas of a universal monitoring environment, where tools are independent.

In [6], the second problem is resolved by dynamically inserting and calling the necessary code in the tool via machine-level monitoring techniques like dynamic instrumentation. A drawback of this approach is its complexity and the resulting poor portability. The approach presented in [6] is currently implemented only for PVM on Sparc/Solaris. For our environment, we thus chose a more high-level approach. For each tool, a specific library is provided in which every possible scenario of tools' cooperation would be handled.

One might get the impression that in this approach tools actually know about each other, thus it is arguable whether they remain independent of each other. However, all the interoperability related code is implemented as a new module in ULIBS which might be considered as an independent component of the tool environment (Fig. 1), although it is implemented as a library being linked to the tools' executables. Thereby the tools themselves are not really affected. It should be stressed, that the new module is designed to provide a general support for interoperability of any combination of tools, not only DETOP and PATOP. Although at present only the case of DETOP-PATOP interoperability is implemented, the other scenarios can easily be added.

Note that with the implementation described above, the tools have to be provided with information on which tools are running in the environment. The component which possesses *de facto* knowledge on the whole system, in particular, which tools are running is the OCTET tool. OCTET can pass the information to all the tools, which would cause a part of the interoperability module to be activated, which is appropriate to the given scenario. For example, if OCTET knows that it would run PATOP and DETOP, it can pass to PATOP the information that DETOP is running. This information would actually be processed by the startup module in ULIBS and passed to the interoperability module, in which, as a result, the two requests described earlier would be issued.

6   Concluding Remarks

Interoperability of on-line tools for parallel programming support is a key feature to build a powerful, easy-to-adapt tool environment. With the interoperability support lying in the environment infrastructure, not in the tools themselves, the user is enabled to customize its environment by picking tools which best fit his needs.

A system that supports interoperability must meet a number of requirements. First of all, the tools must be able to run concurrently. Next, a way to enable interactions between the tools must be provided. Finally, there must be a control mechanism to coordinate access requests to the target system objects.

The OCM monitoring system provides mechanisms that are enough to meet these requirements. Tools adapted to the OCM are enabled to run concurrently and operate on the same object. Moreover, a definition of tools' interactions, which leads to effective tool cooperation is possible without intrusion into their implementation.

Future work will be concentrated on the problem of direct interactions between tools. The current implementation is just the most basic implementation of the idea presented in Section 5.2. Further development will be focused on extending the role of OCTET in "programming" the interactions. Currently, OCTET just provides the basic information, while the whole rest is up to ULIBS. In future, OCTET can even provide general directives on how to "program" the interactions of tools.

Acknowledgements. This work has been carried out within the Polish-German collaboration and supported, in part, by KBN under grant 8 T11C 006 15.

References

1. Bubak, M., Funika, W., Iskra, K., Maruszewski, R., and Wismüller, R.: Enhancing the Functionality of Performance Measurement Tools for Message Passing Applications. In: Dongarra, J., Luque, E., Margalef, T., (Eds.), Recent Advances in Parallel Virtual Machine and Message Passing Interface. Proceedings of 6th European PVM/MPI Users' Group Meeting, Barcelona, Spain, September 1999, Lecture Notes in Computer Science 1697, Springer-Verlag Berlin-Heidelberg, pp. 67-74 (1999)
2. Geist, A., et al.: PVM: Parallel Virtual Machine. A Users' Guide and Tutorial for Networked Parallel Computing. MIT Press, Cambridge, Massachusetts (1994)
3. Ludwig, T., Wismüller, R., Sunderam, V., and Bode, A.: OMIS – On-line Monitoring Interface Specification (Version 2.0). Shaker Verlag, Aachen, vol. 9, LRR-TUM Research Report Series, (1997)
   http://wwwbode.in.tum.de/~omis/OMIS/Version-2.0/version-2.0.ps.gz
4. MPI: A Message Passing Interface Standard. In: Int. Journal of Supercomputer Applications, **8** (1994); Message Passing Interface Forum: MPI-2: Extensions to the Message Passing Interface, July 12, (1997)
   http://www.mpi-forum.org/docs/
5. Trinitis, J., Sunderam, V., Ludwig, T., and Wismüller, R.: Interoperability Support in Distributed On-line Monitoring Systems. In: M. Bubak, H. Afsarmanesh, R. Williams, and B. Hertzberger, editors, High Performance Computing and Networking, 8th International Conference, HPCN Europe 2000, volume 1823 of Lecture Notes in Computer Science, Amsterdam, The Netherlands, May 2000. Springer.
6. R. Wismüller. Interoperability Support in the Distributed Monitoring System OCM. In R. Wyrzykowski et al., editor, Proc. 3rd International Conference on Parallel Processing and Applied Mathematics - PPAM'99, pages 77-91, Kazimierz Dolny, Poland, September 1999, Technical University of Czestochowa, Poland.
7. Wismüller, R., Oberhuber, M., Krammer, J. and Hansen, O.: Interactive Debugging and Performance Analysis of Massively Parallel Applications. *Parallel Computing*, **22**, (1996), 415-442
8. Wismüller, R., Trinitis, J., and Ludwig T.: OCM - A Monitoring System for Interoperable Tools. In: Proceedings of the 2nd SIGMETRICS Symposium on Parallel and Distributed Tools SPDT'98, Welches, OR, USA, August 1998.

Parallel Program Model for Distributed Systems[*]

Viet D. Tran, Ladislav Hluchy, Giang T. Nguyen

Institute of Informatics,
Slovak Academy of Sciences
Email: viet.ui@savba.sk

In this paper, we present a new model for parallel program development called Data Driven Graph (DDG). DDG integrates scheduling to parallel program development for cluster of workstations with PVM/MPI communication. DDG API library allows users to write efficient, robust parallel programs with minimal difficulty. Our experiments demonstrate the new parallel program model with real applications.

1. Introduction

Advances in hardware and software technologies have led to increased interest in the use of large-scale parallel and distributed systems for database, real-time, and other large applications. One of the biggest issues in such systems is the development of effective techniques for the distribution of tasks of a parallel program on multiple processors. The efficiency of execution of the parallel program critically depends on the strategies used to schedule and distribute the tasks among processing elements.

Task allocation can be performed either dynamically during the execution of the program or statically at compile time [7]. Static task allocation and scheduling attempt to predict the program execution behavior at compilation time and to distribute program tasks among the processors accordingly. This approach can eliminate the additional overheads of the redistribution process during the execution. On the other hand, dynamic task scheduling is based on the distribution of tasks among the processors during the execution, with the aim of minimizing communication overheads and balancing the load among processors. The approach is especially beneficial if the program behavior cannot be determined before the execution.

Although scheduling has been intensively studied from the beginning of parallel and distributed processing, its applications for real programs are still difficult. Message-passing libraries like PVM/MPI provide little support for DAG generation, task migration, etc., which are necessary for scheduling. Therefore developing a program model, which integrate scheduling to message-passing systems is very important.

---

[*] This work was supported by the Slovak Scientific Grant Agency under Research Project No. 2/7186/20

J. Dongarra et al. (Eds.): EuroPVM/MPI 2000, LNCS 1908, pp. 250-257, 2000.
© Springer-Verlag Berlin Heidelberg 2000

2. Message-Passing Libraries and Scheduling

Parallel program development can be divided into two steps. In the first step, the parallel program is divided into a set of interacting sequential sub-problems, often called as tasks, which can run in parallel. In the second step, the tasks are assigned to processors and scheduled in such a way that program can best use the system. The parallel program is often written using message-passing libraries like PVM/MPI.

2.1 Message-Passing Libraries

Typical message-passing libraries are Parallel Virtual Machines (PVM) and Message-Passing Interface (MPI). These libraries allow programmers to write portable and efficient parallel programs in programming languages C or Fortran.

The largest disadvantage of PVM/MPI is that it cannot match corresponding send() and recv() routines at compilation time. The result of this disadvantage is that almost all programming errors in communication, from simple errors like wrong addresses, unmatched data format, etc. to more complex errors like race condition, deadlocks, etc. cannot be detected at compilation time. Run-time testing and debugging is well known as one of the most exhaustive and boring work of software development. Furthermore complex errors like race conditions are not easy to detect; they may appear only in very specific condition. Such an error is very dangerous because it may not appear during testing process and appear when the users do not expect it.

For proper understanding of PVM/MPI, they can be compared with assembler languages in sequential programming. Both are used to write the most efficient programs. However, programs in both environments are not structured, most of errors cannot be detected at compilation time and testing and debugging them are time-consuming. Finding a higher level model for message-passing programs, which is easier to write programs and has comparable efficiency is imperative.

2.2 Scheduling

Scheduling can be static or dynamic. In static scheduling the behavior of the parallel program is predictable before its execution. Therefore static scheduling is often done before execution so it does not require run-time overhead. In dynamic scheduling the behavior of the parallel program is not known in advance so scheduling has to be performed at run-time.

Almost all of static scheduling algorithms are based on Directed Acyclic Graph (DAG) [5]. Each node of the DAG represents a task when edges represent communication and precedence relationship among tasks.

The largest problem of static scheduling is how to get a DAG from a parallel program. Some scheduling tools provide a graphical environment for drawing DAG [2]. However, drawing a DAG of a large parallel program is exhaustive work. Other provide some functional or descriptive languages for generating DAG. However, most of parallel programs are written in C/C++ or Fortran, using PVM/MPI and mixing functional languages with them is not welcomed.

Dynamic scheduling algorithms often require moving tasks from a processor to another in order to balance the loads of processors [6]. In PVM/MPI, tasks are running in preemptive mode, so task reallocation requires suspending the migrating task, saving current state of the task, transferring the task with its state to the target processor, restoring the state of the task and resuming the execution of the task on the target processor. Therefore task migration is complex and costly process; it also requires large supports from operating systems and/or programmers.

3. Data Driven Graph

Data Driven Graph [1] is a new program model that integrates scheduling to parallel program development. The basic properties of DDG are as follows:

- It is a *parallel* program model: DDG allows specifying tasks, data dependence, parallelism, etc.
- It is a parallel program for *High Performance Computing*: DDG is a program model for computation-intensive application. The additional overhead of DDG is low enough for developing efficient program.
- It is a parallel program model with *scheduling*: DDG allows generating DAG, static and dynamic task scheduling, run-time task reallocation. Scheduling algorithms can be integrated to DDG.
- It is a parallel program for *development*: Unlike many program models that are only for theoretical analysis, DDG is a program model for software development. DDG Application Programming Interface (API) provides a simple way to write robust, efficient programs with minimal difficulty.

3.1 Basic Ideas

Fig. 1 shows the steps of parallel program development. DAG is the basis of many scheduling algorithms therefore DAG generator is one of the primary aims of DDG. DAG generator requires data dependence among tasks. In order to get the data dependence among tasks, DDG has to know for each task which variable the task uses and which variable the task modifies. It can be done by tracing the code of the task, however it is time consuming. Furthermore, as many C/C++ programmers use pointers to data in their programs, it is very difficult to get which data a pointer refers to by tracing code. Therefore, in DDG each task must declare which variable it uses and modifies.

Data dependence is also the basis for data synchronization. As discussed in Section 2.1, data synchronization is the source of potential errors in parallel programs and programmers spend a large part of time for synchronizing data, testing and debugging communication errors. It is requisite if the data synchronization is done automatically and programmers can concentrate on coding tasks.

Data use declaration of a task has to be consistent with its code. However, the codes of tasks change during parallel program development and using separate data use declaration is not welcomed. In DDG, the input and output data of a task are referred to in its code as formal parameters and the real variables are passed to the code as parameters during task creation. By wrapping task creation routine, DDG can determine which data the task uses without separate declaration.

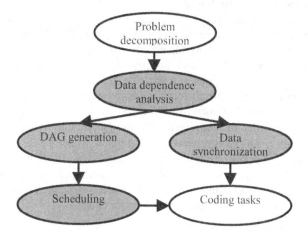

Fig. 1. Parallel program development in DDG

Fig. 1 shows the steps of parallel programming development. The steps with dark background are done by DDG. There are only two steps left to programmers: program decomposition and task coding. Program decomposition is the most critical step; the performance of the parallel program strongly depends on this step so it is left to programmers. On the basis of the knowledge of the solving problem and of target hardware environment, programmers can choose the best way to divide the solving problem to a set of tasks. Coding tasks, of course, cannot be done automatically. It is shown in Fig. 1 that DDG can do most of the work for programmers.

3.2 Task and Data Definition

```
void code_of_task1(int x)
{ . . . }
void code_of_task3(int x, int y)
{ . . . }
main()
{ int a, b, c;
  create_task(code_of_task1, wo(a));
  create_task(code_of_task1, wo(b));
  create_task(code_of_task3, ro(a), rw(b));
}
```

Fig. 2. Task and data creation in DDG.

Tasks in DDG are created by calling `create_task(code, parameter,...)` where `code` is a function/procedure/subprogram in High Level Languages (HLL), and parameters are variables with access right (read-only (ro), read-write (rw), or write-only (wo)). Because the code of a task contains no information about which real data it uses, several tasks can have the same code, but different variables as parameters. An example of task creation can be found in Fig. 2.

Tasks in DDG, which are assigned to the same processor, can share variables. In order to remove anti-dependence and output dependence, variables in DDG may have multiple value: each task that writes to a variable creates a new copy (version) of the variable. Versions that are not used by any unfinished tasks are automatically removed from memory. Number of versions of a variable depends on the number of threads of tasks. Fig.3 shows an example of multi-version variables. For simplicity, the tasks in Fig.3 contain only one command line and task creation is not shown. If the tasks are executed in the order they are created, only one version of variable a exists at a moment. If task7, task8 are executed in parallel with task1, task2, version 3 and version 1 exist simultaneously in memory. If multi-version variables were not used, task7 and task8 would have to be executed sequentially after all other tasks. DDG remembers internal data dependence structures similar to the scheme in Fig. 3 and always provides correct versions for tasks.

```
1.  a = 10;
2.  b  = a + 5;
3.  c  = a * 3;
4.  a = a + 5;
5.  d  = a / 2;
6.  e  = a - 1;
7.  a = 7;
8.  f  = a3 + 2;
```

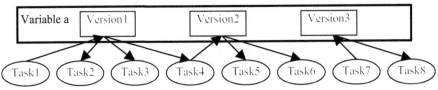

Fig. 3. Multiple-version variable in DDG

3.3 DAG Generation

DDG can generate the DAG graph of a parallel program directly from the structures in Fig. 3. It is easy to see that a DAG graph can be generated by connecting the arrows that go to and from the same version in Fig. 3. The DAG graph contains only true data dependence; anti-dependence and output dependence are removed by using multi-version variables.

3.4 DDG Communication Module

DDG communication module is very simple: it contains only two variables: ddg_proc_num, which gives the number of processors, and ddg_my_proc, an integer from 0 to ddg_proc_num-1 giving the identification number of the current processor. Four functions are implemented in communication module: `ddg_init_comm()`, which initializes communication, sets values for `ddg_proc_num` and `ddg_my_proc`; `ddg_send()` and `ddg_recv()`, which send and receive data in DDG buffers; and `ddg_finish_com()`, which is called when the program finishes. DDG communication can be based on PVM or MPI library. An example of DDG communication module based on PVM is in Fig. 4. As the communication module of DDG is very simple, porting to MPI or other communication libraries can be done in some minutes.

```
int ddg_proc_num;
int ddg_my_proc;
ddg_init_comm()
{   pvm_config(&ddg_proc_num, &narch, &hi);
    ddg_myproc= pvm_joingroup(ddg_group);
}
ddg_send(int dst, ddg_buffer &buffer)
{   pvm_initsend(PvmDataInPlace);
    pvm_pkbyte(buffer.data, buffer.size(), 1);
    pvm_send(pvm_gettid(dst), 1);
}
ddg_finish_com()
{   pvm_exit();
}
```

Fig. 4. DDG communication in PVM

4. Case Study

For demonstration of DDG capability, we applied DDG for Gaussian elimination algorithm, which has static behavior, nested loop and data parallelism. The study does not only show performance of DDG, but also introduces DDG Application Programming Interface (API), because detailed describing DDG API cannot be included to this article. All experiments are performed on a PC cluster of 6 Pentium 500 connected by 100Mb Ethernet.

```
1.   #define N 1200
2.   main()
3.   {    float a[N][N];
4.        init(a);            // initial the values of a
5.        for (int i = 0; i < N-1; i++)
6.            for (int j = i+1; j < N; i++)
7.            {   coef = a[j][i] / a[i][i];
8.                for (int k = i+1; k < N; k++)
9.                    a[j][k] = a[j][k] - coef*a[i][k];
10.           }
11.       print(a);           // print the result values of a
12.  }
```

Fig. 5. Sequential Gaussian elimination algorithm.

The sequential Gaussian elimination algorithm (GEM) is described in Fig. 5. We concentrate only on GEM, the input and output functions (init() and print()) are not considered. The tasks are defined from the lines inside two outer loops, (line 7, 8 and 9 in Fig. 5). Before defining task, the code of the tasks has to be moved to a function (Fig. 6). Finally, the task is created from the code (Fig. 7). In order to use DDG multi-version variables, ddg_var<T>, where T is standard or user-defined type in C/C++, is used instead of T. For simple type T, ddg_var<T> can be automatically converted to T, otherwise ddg_var<T>.get() has to be called explicitly. The access rights of variables are defined by function ddg_ro() (read-only) ddg_rw() (read-write) and ddg_wo() (write-only). All DDG API function and variable names have the prefix ddg_. It is easy to see that the programs in Fig. 6 and Fig. 7 have the same structures. DDG API using PVM library for communication.

```
1.   #define N 1200
2.   main()
3.   {    float a[N][N];
4.        init(a);
5.        for (int i = 0; i < N-1; i++)
6.            for (int j = i+1; j < N; i++)
7.                compute(i, a[i], a[j]);
8.        print(a);
9.   }
10.  void compute(int i, float i_line[N], float j_line[N])
11.  {    coef = i_line[i] / j_line[i];
12.       for (int k = i+1; k < N; k++)
13.           j_line[k] = j_line[k] - coef*i_line[k];
14.  }
```

Fig. 6. Intermediate step of DDG task definition

```
1.   #include "ddg.h"
2.   #define N 1200
3.   typedef float vector[N];
4.   void ddg_main()
5.   {    ddg_var_array<vector> arr(N);
6.        init(a);
7.        for (int i = 0; i < N - 1; i++)
8.            for (int j = i+1; j < N; j++)
9.                ddg_create_task(compute, ddg_direct(i),
                                 ddg_ro(arr[i]), ddg_rw(arr[j]));
10.       print(a);
11.  }
12.  void compute(ddg_var<int> line, ddg_var<vector> i_line,
                  ddg_var<vector> j_line)
13.  {    coef = j_line.get()[line] / i_line.get()[line];
14.       for (int k = line + 1; k < N; k++)
                j_line.get()[k] = j_line.get()[k] -
                                  i_line.get()[k]*coef;
16.  }
```

Fig. 7. DDG version of GEM

Execution times (in milliseconds) of DDG and equivalent PVM version of GEM are shown in Table 1. We can calculate the computational overhead of DDG program by executing it on a single processor. The percentage of DDG overhead is (12874-12789)/12874 = 0.0066, it means that DDG overhead is smaller than 1%. The speedup of DDG version on 6 processors is about 3.6. In comparison with PVM version, DDG version is less than 1% slower but the source code of DDG version is much shorter, easier to understand. It is very similar to the source code of the sequential program so porting existing sequential programs to DDG is done with minimal difficulty.

Table 1. DDG performance for GEM

Processor	DDG version	PVM version	Sequential version
1	12874	12804	12789
6	3576	3542	

5. Conclusion

Data Driven Graph, a new model for parallel program development, provides a new approach for parallel programming in message-passing systems with integrated scheduling. DDG API allows programmers to write robust, efficient parallel programs in DDG with minimal difficulties. Experiments with DDG on PC clusters with PVM communication showed that programs in DDG are simple, efficient and with minimal overheads.

References

1. V. Tran, L. Hluchy, G. Nguyen: Parallel Programming with Data Driven Model. Proc. Eight Euromicro Workshop on Parallel and Distributed Processing, Jan. 2000, Greece, pp. 205-211.
2. P. Kacuk, J. Cunha, G. Dosza, J. Lourenco, T. Fadgyas, T. Antao: A graphical development and debugging environment for parallel programs. Parallel Computing 22, 1997, pp. 1747-1770.
3. C. Coroyer, Z. Liu: Effectiveness of Heuristics and Simulated Annealing for the Scheduling of Concurrent Tasks – Am Empirical Comparison. Proc. Parallel Architectures and Languages Europe, Jun 1993, Germany, pp. 452-463.
4. Y. Wang, R. Morris: Load Sharing in Distributed Systems. IEEE Trans. on Computers, vol. 34, no. 3, Mar. 1985, pp. 204-217.
5. H. El-Rewini, T. Lewis: Distributed and Parallel Computing. Manning 1998.
6. B. Sharazi eds.: Scheduling and Load Balancing in Parallel and Distributed Systems. IEEE Computer Society Press 1995.
7. D. V. Tran: Static Task Scheduling in Distributed Systems, Proc. International Scientific Conference Electronic Computers & Informatics, pp. 228-233, Slovakia 1998.

Translation of a High-Level Graphical Code to Message-Passing Primitives in the GRADE Programming Environment*

Gábor Dózsa[1], Dániel Drótos[2], and Róbert Lovas[1]

[1] MTA SZTAKI, Computer and Automation Research Institute,
Hungarian Academy of Sciences, Hungary,
{dozsa,rlovas}@sztaki.hu
[2] Department of Automation, University of Miskolc, Hungary,
drdani@malacka.iit.uni-miskolc.hu

Abstract. To provide high-level graphical support for developing message passing programs, an integrated programming environment (GRADE) is being developed. GRADE provides tools to construct, execute, debug, monitor and visualise message-passing based parallel programs. GRADE provides a general graphical interface that hides low-level details of the underlying message-passing system thus, it allows the user to concentrate on really important aspects of parallel program development such as task decomposition.

The current paper describes the translation mechanism that is applied in GRADE to generate the executable message-passing code from the high-level graphical description of the user application.

1 Introduction

The message-passing paradigm for implementing applications on distributed systems (including network of workstations and massively parallel computers) closely corresponds to the way in which data are actually moved around in a distributed memory computer. Thus, message-passing libraries can be implemented very efficiently in such systems. Moreover, with the advent of PVM and MPI the portability level of such applications has been raised significantly. Nevertheless, the lack of real user-friendly support for development of such applications prevents most of the potential users from dealing with concurrent programming at all.

To cope with the extra complexity of parallel programs arising due to interprocess communication and synchronization, we have designed a visual programming environment called GRADE (Graphical Application Development Environment). Its major goal is to provide an easy-to-use, integrated set of programming tools for development of message-passing applications that can run either on a

---

* This work was partially funded by Mexican-Hungarian Intergovernmental S&T project MEX-1/98 and by the Hungarian Science Research Fund (OTKA) Contract No.: T032226.

J. Dongarra et al. (Eds.): EuroPVM/MPI 2000, LNCS 1908, pp. 258–265, 2000.

real parallel computer or on a heterogeneous cluster of workstation. Most important features of GRADE can be summarized as follows:

- All process management and inter-process communication activities are defined visually in the user's application. Graphics assist to better understand the complex structure and run-time behaviour of the distributed program even for users not familiar with parallel programming.
- Low-level details of the underlying message-passing system are hidden. GRADE generates all message-passing library calls automatically on the basis of the visual code. This approach has two basic advantages: the programmer is not required to know the syntax of the MP library and the same user application is able to run in different MP environments provided that GRADE can generate the code for those environments. Currently, GRADE can generate code for PVM and MPI.
- Local computations of the individual processes can be defined in C (or in FORTRAN in the future) independently from the visually supported message-passing related activities. Thus, GRADE provides a comfortable environment for parallelizing existing sequential applications.
- Compilation and distribution of executables of user's processes are performed automatically in the heterogeneous environment.
- A distributed debugging [2] and an execution visualisation tool [4] are provided that are fully integrated into the common graphical user interface of the system. Debugging and monitoring information is related directly back to the user's graphical code during on-line debugging and visualisation.

Graphical notation used in GRADE is called GRAPNEL (GRAphical Process NEt Language) [3]. The current paper explains how the high-level GRAPNEL applications are translated into pure text code by the system.

Rest of the paper is organised as follows. Various layers of GRAPNEL applications are described in the next section followed by some words about the persistent (i.e. text) representation of the graphical code. Actual translation of GRAPNEL code into C files is explained in Sect. 4. Finally, the paper ends with some conclusions.

2   Layers of **GRAPNEL** Programs

GRAPNEL programs can be represented at several layers. In the current section we summarize the role of the various layers and the transformation mechanisms between the layers.

2.1   **GRAPNEL** Layer

GRAPNEL provides the top layer of the GRADE system where the user can construct his/her parallel program by a graphical editor called GRED. At this layer the program is represented graphically as described in [5] in detail. The basic idea behind this graphical representation is the following. Two hierarchical level of the graphical code is distinguished: *application* level and *process* level. At the application level, the communication graph of the whole application is defined graphically, where processes are represented as nodes connected by communication channels. At the process level, communication operations (i.e. send and receive actions) are defined by visual means for each process. In fact, the top-level control-flow of each process is defined as a graph containing every message transfer operation as various nodes.

For illustration purpose, Fig. 1 depicts a sample Application and Process window of GRADE. They are explained in detail in Sect. 4.1.

This representation is easy to understand for the program developer but it is difficult to interpret by programs like parsers. Because of this difficulty GRED editor saves the graphical program in a plain text file, called GRP file, which is used by the programs and utilities of the GRADE system. GRED is also able to read back GRP files and restore graphical representation on the screen. The GRP file is an internal form of the GRAPNEL program containing information on both the graphical and textual parts. Brief description of the GRP file is given in Sect. 3.

2.2   C-Source Layer

The GRP file is translated into C-source by the GRAPNEL pre-compiler called GRP2C. The goal of this translation is that all the graphical information which represent C code should be replaced with the equivalent C source code. However, those graphical information that are relevant only for drawing the GRAPNEL graphs on the screen without representing any C code (for example X-Y coordinates of graphical nodes) are omitted during this translation. Notice that, meanwhile the GRP file is completely equivalent with the original GRAPNEL code, the C-source generated by the GRP2C pre-compiler is not.

2.3   GRAPNEL API Layer

Because the communication layer upon which GRAPNEL programs run can be implemented by different kinds of message passing systems, an other software layer is required which hides dependencies of the communication layer. This layer is an Application Programming Interface and because its physical representation is a C library, it is called as GRAPNEL Library. This API layer can support any kind of message passing system, e.g. PVM, MPI, or an operating system directly. This API consist of GRAPNEL (or shortly: GRP) functions and higher layers of the GRADE system and particularly, the generated C-sources use these GRP functions to start processes and sending messages.

GRAPNEL API is the lowest layer which is really included into the GRAPNEL system and is developed by the GRADE team. An API for PVM and MPI is already available and support for other systems such as QNX [6] operating system is under development.

2.4   Message Passing Layer

This layer should be a widely used communication system. PVM or MPI is a good choice because they are ported to many operating systems. Because this layer hides operating system dependencies the GRADE system can be hardware and operating system independent.

3   Persistent Representation of **GRAPNEL** Applications: GRP Files

GRAPNEL applications are represented by mixed graphical icons and textual code segments on the screen. In order to store such applications on the disk or to produce the executable code of them they are saved into the so called GRP files. GRP files are plain text files that contain all necessary information about GRAPNEL programs. The exact syntax of a GRP file is defined in BNF form (that serves as input data for the UNIX *yacc* tool used to generate the parser of such files).

GRP files have human readable format. Information are stored in a well structured hierarchical way in them. The top level structure is the "Application" that consists of two main parts: "HeaderPart" and "ProgramPart". They are used for storing information related to the whole application and to the individual processes, respectively. The "ProgramPart", in fact, is a list of "Process" sections describing each individual process of the application separately.

The next subsections give a brief summary about how GRAPNEL applications are stored in GRP files and what are the real contents of those files.

3.1   Separation of Information with GRP Files

GRP files are interpreted by a parser that is integrated into all components of the GRADE environment need to extract information from them (e.g. GRED editor and the GRP2C code generator). This parser enables a GRAPNEL application to be split into several GRP files. Thus, different parts of the same application can be stored in separate files. According to the two distinct levels of the graphical code, information that must be saved into GRP files can be divided into two main groups. The first one concerns the global view of the application including the application level GRAPNEL code while the second one deals with local information about individual processes.

In order to support easy re-use of processes across different applications, GRAPNEL code of each process is saved into an individual GRP file separately from application level information. In these GRP files, "HeaderPart" section is left empty and the process is described as the only one element of the process list in the "ProgramPart" section. On the other hand, all application level information is stored in the "HeaderPart" section of a separate GRP file in which "ProgramPart" section contains no data.

As a result, the user can open individual process files belonging to other GRAPNEL application to insert those processes into the program being developed. Furthermore, it is also possible to save the code of any process individually, e.g. to store it in a "process warehouse" directory for later use in other applications.

4   Translating the Graphical Code into C Source Files

After defining the structure of the GRP files, we show how the GRP2C pre-compiler generates standard C source code from the GRP files. The programs generated by the pre-compiler can be compiled with any standard C compiler and can be executed in the usual way[1].

In order to explain the translation mechanism of GRP2C we show the graphical representation (application layer) of a simple example in Fig. 1. There are two processes ("slave1" and "slave2") computing subtasks and sending the result to the third process ("master") that collects the results and send new subtasks.

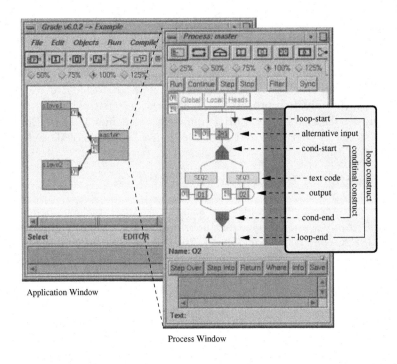

Fig. 1. Simple GRAPNEL Application

---

[1] Compilation and distribution of executables are carried out automatically by GRADE even in case of heterogeneous distributed execution environment.

4.1   C Files Generated by the Pre-compiler

The GRP2C pre-compiler generates one C source file for every process based on a general template and on the GRP description of the particular process. Every such source file starts with include section. It depends on the information located in the *HeaderSection* of the GRP file. Next part is the definition part of the global variables. This part and the beginning part of the main function —where local variables and the channels are defined— are included to the template by the pre-compiler. After variable definitions, the pre-compiler inserts C instructions into the template.

Several GRAPNEL Library calls will be inserted in front of the code defined by the user. These system calls register the start of the process and initialize the channels used by the process.

The functionality of a process is defined by the programmer and it is represented by the different nodes of the process graph. These nodes are called graphical blocks. Every block represents a small piece of the executable code and the connections between the blocks define the order of execution. The blocks must be translated into C code in the appropriate order. There are several types of the graphical blocks and some of them must be processed recursively.

Let us see as an example the *master* process of Fig. 1. Its user-defined graph structure is depicted in the *Process Window* in the figure. It consists of a loop, an alternative input operation (IA1) inside the loop and a conditional execution of two sequential blocks (SEQ2 and SEQ3) followed by two output operations (O1 and O2). Code generated for the various graphical symbols by GRP2C is explained as follows.

The C code of loop_start and loop_end must be attached by the programmer to "loop begin" and "loop end" blocks, respectively. Thus, GRP2C simply substitutes loop_start and loop_end in the pseudo code above with the appropriate user supplied C code segments. Nested loops are kept track by the code generator using an internal stack. Codes of blocks between "loop begin" and "loop end" are placed in a compound statement after the code of loop_start.

Communication operations such as input, output, and alternative input blocks require several GRAPNEL API function calls to be included into the generated file. GRAPNEL API provides three different communication operations independently from the underlying low-level message-passing layer: SEND, RECEIVE and ALTERNATIVE RECEIVE both in synchronised and not synchronised forms.

The GRP2C pre-compiler places different functions in the generated programs in order to compose messages, and to send and receive them. Composing a message means picking up all the required data and packing them together into a message. To produce proper API calls, the pre-compiler must know the type and name of the variables which the programmer would like to use as source or destination of the data to be transferred. So, the user must attach the type of messages being sent through a channel and the name of the variables taking part in the communication operation to the appropriate port icon and communication block, respectively. Communication blocks in the graphical code are connected to one or more of the available ports by the user thus, the pre-compiler can put all the required information together.

[SEND] For send operation the pre-compiler produces one or more *pack* API function calls to pack variables into the message. The next function call generated by the pre-compiler is the *send* function which sends the prepared message to the addressed process. This function call accepts a parameter which specifies if the process should be blocked on this send operation or not.

[RECEIVE] For receive operations GRP2C produces one function call which receives the message and one or more *unpack* API function calls to pick up data fragments from the message and place them in variables.

[ALTERNATIVE RECEIVE] The alternative receive operation is similar to the simple receive one but it accepts a message selectively via more than one ports. The pre-compiler generates different *unpack* API function calls for different ports but they are placed in a *switch* instruction and the right one is selected based on the number of port on which the actual message arrived in.

Conditional block represents a conditional (i.e. `if()`) statement. Any of the TRUE or FALSE branch can be empty. The C code of the `if()` statement must be attached to block "cond begin" by the programmer, and the pre-compiler includes it into the generated file. The pre-compiler then generates both non-empty branches as compound statements. Nested conditionals are handled using the internal stack mentioned earlier at loop construct.

SEQ Translation of sequential blocks is simple. The pre-compiler simply includes the source code attached to the block SEQ by the programmer into the generated file. Any source code except communication can be placed in a sequential block. Size of the attached code is unlimited and it can contain calls to any existing library written even in languages different from C (for example FORTRAN). The syntax of the GRP file enables the graphical editor to store large source code fragments in a separate file and to mention only the file name in the GRP file.

GR1 There is a special kind of block called graph block which is not shown in our simple example. It can be used in more complex programs to simplify graphical representation of the process control flow. A graph block represents a sub-graph, i.e., any subpart of the process graph can be packed and hidden by a graph block. In the graphical editor it can be opened and edited by the user. When the pre-compiler finds a graph block it simply starts to generate code of list of blocks represented by the graph block.

5   Conclusions

Availability of powerful programming environments for heterogeneous networks is getting more and more important. GRADE provides an integrated programming environment where the programmer can concentrate on high level abstractions without worrying about the low level details of communication primitives. Through its graphical user interface, GRADE provides efficient support for the most important and time consuming phases of parallel program development: rapid prototyping and correctness/performance debugging.

Comparing it with other visual programming environments have been developed so far (e.g. TRAPPER [7], CODE and HeNCE [1]), GRADE exhibits significant advantages discussed, for instance, in [5].

Currently the GRADE environment supports PVM and MPI as target systems and it runs on UNIX hosts. GRAPNEL Compiler generates C source files from graphical representation of the program. Graphical symbols are language independent so it is possible to modify the translator tool to generate source files for other programming languages. The development team is going to support Fortran language which is still very important in high performance computing business. New GRAPNEL API implementations are going to be developed as well to support more message passing systems for example QNX [6] operating system. Supporting QNX operating system can be important for industrial real-time applications.

References

1. J. C. Browne, S. I. Hyder, J. Dongarra, K. Moore, and P. Newton.: Visual programming and debugging for parallel computing. IEEE Parallel and Distributed Technology **3(1)** (1995)
2. P. Kacsuk, J. C. Cunha, G. Dózsa, J. Lourenço, T. Fadgyas, and T. Antao.: A graphical development and debugging environment for parallel programs. Parallel Computing **22** (1997) 1747–1770
3. P. Kacsuk, G. Dózsa, and T. Fadgyas.: Designing parallel programs by the graphical language GRAPNEL. Microprocessing and Microprogramming **41** (1996) 625–643
4. P. Kacsuk, G. Dózsa, and T. Fadgyas.: A graphical programming environment for message passing programs. In Proc. of 2nd International Workshop on Software Engineering for Parallel and Distributed Systems, Boston, USA (1997) 210–219
5. P. Kacsuk, G. Dózsa, and R. Lovas.: The GRED graphical editor for the GRADE parallel program development environment. Future Generation Computer Systems **15** (1999) 443–452
6. QNX Software Systems Limited: QNX Operating System, System Architecture
7. S. Scheidler and L. Schafers.: TRAPPER: A graphical programming environment for industrial high-performance applications. In Proc. of PARLE'93: Parallel Architectures and Languages Europe, Munich, Germany (1993)

The Transition from a PVM Program Simulator to a Heterogeneous System Simulator: The HeSSE Project

N. Mazzocca[1], M. Rak[1], and U. Villano[2]

[1]DII, Seconda Universita' di Napoli, via Roma 29, 81031 Aversa (CE), Italy
n.mazzocca@unina.it , maxrak@iol.it
[2]Universita' del Sannio, Facolta' di Ingegneria, C.so Garibaldi 107, 82100 Benevento, Italy
villano@unisannio.it

Abstract. This paper describes HeSSE, a research project whose objective is the development of a simulator of heterogeneous systems starting from an existing simulator of PVM applications. After a discussion on the main issues involved in dealing with a wider class of applications, the devised simulator design is described. Finally, the state of the art of the project is presented.

1 Introduction

Thanks to the availability of high speed networks and reliable run-time supports, almost the totality of the computing systems currently used for message-passing applications is heterogeneous. As far as the design and development of applications targeted at these systems is concerned, the main problem is the absence of any consolidated technique or tool. As a matter of fact, the approaches followed for development in the small, homogeneous environments mainly used in the past are totally inadequate to tame the complexity of contemporary computing environments. Moreover, the subtle effects of computer resource and network heterogeneity further complicate the traditionally difficult task of application performance evaluation and tuning [1]. Therefore, performance evaluation techniques that are more sophisticated and cost-effective than those currently available are needed.

In the last few years, our research group has been active in the performance analysis and prediction field, developing PS [2], a simulator of distributed applications executed in heterogeneous systems using the PVM run-time system [3]. This experience led us to discover the high potential of simulation tools for application development [4], performance prediction and tuning. In particular, among the three customary approaches to performance analysis, namely monitoring, analytical models and simulation, only the third seems able to provide reliable performance predictions of complex systems. We think that the possibilities to get reasonable information on application behavior and response time even at the earliest stages of the development process (possibly in the absence of a fully-developed program), to compare different algorithms and workload sharing policies on real, fictitious or unavailable target machines, are worth the effort to learn to use a new and relatively unusual development environment.

J. Dongarra et al. (Eds.): EuroPVM/MPI 2000, LNCS 1908, pp. 266-273, 2000.

Being unsatisfied of the friendliness and ease of use of PS, at the end of 1998 we decided to develop a new version of the simulator. PS was heavily dependent on the Ptolemy graphical simulation environment [5], whose powerful facilities were not used at a great extent. Its second fundamental drawback was the lack of a module modeling the computing node scheduler, hence the impossibility to simulate applications with more than one task per processor and to take easily into account the effect of the load due to external processes. We studied the possibility to widen the range of systems that could be successfully simulated. The result was the decision to develop, instead of a new version of PS, a modular, extensible simulator of the hardware and software objects making up current heterogeneous distributed systems, with support for the most commonly used programming environments (PVM, MPI, socket-based).

However, the transition from a parallel program simulator as PS to a complete distributed heterogeneous system simulation environment was not just a matter of developing new simulation objects modeling additional hardware or software agents. In simulators, speed is obtained at the expense of accuracy. The developer of a simulation environment has to choose which characteristics of the phenomena to be modeled are fundamental (in that they have a direct influence on system response), and which can instead be neglected without a significant loss of simulation accuracy. Of course, this choice is tied to the particular class of applications to be simulated. In other words, it is not possible to develop a general-purpose simulator, but rather one where an optimal trade-off between simulation speed and accuracy has been made for a particular (albeit wide) class of applications.

PS was developed with scientific applications made up of coarse tasks running over relatively slow networks in mind. As a consequence, such details as the timing behavior of the underlying operating system, TCP/IP stack and I/O devices, the effect of message forwarding through daemons (typical of the PVM environment) were systematically ignored, being "hidden" behind long CPU and message transmission bursts. If the objective is the simulation of more finely grained applications, namely applications where computing and message transmission time do not systematically hide O.S., I/O and TCP/IP times, different choices have to be made.

We will discuss hereunder these and other issues linked to the transition from the existing PS simulator to the new simulation environment, which has been named HeSSE (**He**terogeneous **S**ystem **S**imulation **E**nvironment). The paper is structured as follows. First we discuss the motivations and the design issues of the HeSSE simulator. Then its structure is sketched, showing one of its most peculiar characteristics, the dynamic environment configuration capability. Finally, the state of the art of the project and the objective of our future research are presented.

2   Design Issues for a Heterogeneous System Simulator

Upgrading the design of PS to a (almost) general-purpose simulator of heterogeneous distributed systems is not just a case of developing objects modeling new hardware and software components not available in the old simulation environment. Below we will consider some of the involved issues, whereas the adopted solutions are discussed in the next Section, where HeSSE structure is described. We will not instead describe the structure of the old simulator, which was presented in [2,4].

Probably the first question that must be answered is what to preserve of the old simulator design. As compared to other last-generation simulators [6-8], the distinctive features of PS are the use of input traces collected through a preliminary execution in a software development host, and the production of output in the form of simulated execution traces, which can be post-processed to get performance indexes or summaries of program behavior. Several years of use of the various PS prototypes have shown the substantial validity of this approach. A trace is essentially a sequence of snapshots of one particular program execution, the traced one. Therefore, traces can hardly ever be useful for debugging purposes, not to mention detailed analysis of non-deterministic programs. They are instead fully satisfactory for performance evaluation, as performance behavior is not at a great extent dependent on the particular program execution or path followed in the code. The trace-based simulation cycle has proven to be simple, friendly and easily understood by simulator users.

As for the tradeoff between accuracy and simulation speed, it should be noted that PS simulation is based on a very simplified view of program execution, which is modeled by predicting in a reasonable (but not particularly accurate) way the duration of CPU bursts, i.e., of the intervals of time spent computing between two successive interactions with the PVM run-time support. PS converts the CPU-time intervals extracted from the traces into the (predicted) duration of the corresponding CPU bursts *in the target machine*. The method used relies on a simple analytical model of the target computing system, which essentially takes into account the difference between the processing speeds of the host and the target for the given problem, evaluated beforehand by running suitable benchmarks [2]. Whereas, all process interactions through the network, data exchanges included, are fully simulated. This modeling structure, represented graphically in Fig. 1, has turned out to be successful for the simulation of most PVM applications, making possible to obtain fairly accurate results (errors typically less than 5%) with modest computational effort.

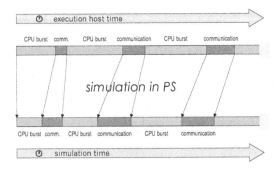

Fig. 1. Conversion from traced timing to simulation time in PS

In light of this experience, there no good reason to adopt different solutions for the new simulator. The problem with PS is that it models monoprogrammed nodes, where exactly one PVM task is executed per node with the support of PVM daemon and operating system. Daemon and O.S. are not actually simulated, as all the times spent in system activities (PVM daemon, O.S. support, TCP/IP) are modeled as a whole. Only simulators targeted exclusively at coarse-grained, computation-intensive processes can get reasonable accuracy without a simulation model of operating system services, I/O and interrupt processing. Looking at existing simulators, we find at one end of the range of possible design choices simulators as PS and Dimemas [6], which ignore (or model very roughly) all CPU time not spent in application processing. At the opposite end, there are simulators as SimOS [9] which, instead, perform a complete emulation of the entire operating system and any attached I/O device. In the first case, reasonably high simulation speed can be obtained, but accuracy can be satisfactory only for CPU-intensive application. In the latter, accuracy can be fairly high for any type of application, including I/O intensive ones, but simulation is very slow, even if a single computing node is simulated. In practice, at the state of the art, the latter solution is not applicable for the simulation of large complex systems. As will be shown in the Section that follows, HeSSE is based on an intermediate approach, as it adopts a simplified model of system node activities.

3   The HeSSE Simulator Structure

In order to be relatively light-weight and highly portable, HeSSE does not rely on the use of a complete graphical simulation environment as PS, but is based on a fast simulation library written in C++. The simulator software has been designed in order to make it easy to develop new components, or even to use existing simulators as components modeling new objects and networks. To boost as much as possible the modifiability, reusability and extensibility of the simulator design, the software system has been developed by using an object-oriented paradigm.

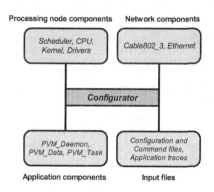

Fig. 2. HeSSE schematic structure

In each simulation session, a suitable simulator configuration has to be set up using as building blocks the components corresponding to the objects making up the real hardware/software system. This task is carried out by the *Configurator*, which, as shown by the H-like diagram chosen for the project logo (Fig. 2), is the "heart" of the simulator. Our experience in the PS project, where the configuration was set up "by hand" using the Ptolemy graphical interface, helped us to understood the fundamental role played by the configurator in the simulation of large, complex systems. In HeSSE, the configurator reads all simulation input data, using a *Configuration* and a *Command* file. The first describes all the components that are to be used and their interconnections, whereas the latter contains the names of the trace application files and the temporal parameters for the configurable components (e.g., relative node processing speed, network bandwidth, ...). The traces are to be produced beforehand by running the fully-developed program on any possible sequential or parallel hardware configuration (most typically, on a single workstation), or built synthetically by means of a program skeleton and the expected times spent in every section of sequential code [2]. The *Configurator* instances all the required objects communicating them any required temporal parameter, and starts the simulation run. It is important to note that the target configuration can be dynamically altered, in that the *Configurator* can set up all the components to be used and their interconnections without recompilation (nor even relinking) of the simulator code.

A simulation session in HeSSE is represented graphically in Fig. 3. The trace files of the events relative to each task are used to drive the simulation engine. The duration of each CPU burst, extracted from the trace file, is processed in order to derive the duration on the final target, thus taking into account the effect of different machine speeds. As mentioned before, task interactions with O.S., run-time supports, I/O devices and networks are instead dealt with by simulation. The events and the timestamps representing the (simulated) execution of the program on the target environment are written to an output trace file. This file can be filtered and converted into the format required by virtually any program visualization tool. Subject to time resolution constraints, the availability of a trace file of the simulated execution allows any possible performance index to be evaluated with small effort.

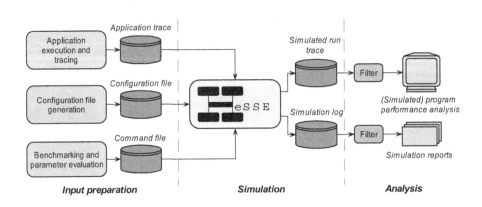

Fig. 3. A HeSSE simulation session

To understand how the HeSSE simulator works, it is worth to sketch its internal structure, showing which are its main modules and how the simulation task is shared among the various simulation components. In general, the simulation of a heterogeneous system requires the simulation of processing nodes, network and application software. In HeSSE, this is carried out by the *Node, Network,* and *Application* components, respectively, as shown in Fig. 2. Below we will orderly examine each of these tasks.

3.1   Processing Node Simulation

As far as the node activities modeling is concerned, HeSSE is based on an approach halfway between the one of PS (no O.S. and I/O simulation) and that of SimOS (full O.S. emulation). O.S. service times and I/O devices are not taken into account by complete emulation, but using a simplified model of the node activities. The temporal parameters used by this model (e.g., the times spent in O.S. calls) are to be measured beforehand on the particular combination of hardware and O.S. to be simulated. The objective is to obtain reasonable accuracy for the majority of heterogeneous system applications, while retaining a simulation structure of tractable complexity.

The node activities simulated in HeSSE can be logically divided into three groups: *Process, Interrupt* and *Message-exchange Management.* As regards the first group, the *Node* is a sort of macro-component which includes all the hardware/software components available in a processing node. It can be used by the simulated application processes to ask the Operating System for services. In fact, the *Node* is essentially an interface to three internal components which simulate processor (*CPU*), pre-emptive scheduler (*Scheduler*) and operating system kernel behavior (*Kernel*), respectively. Among other things, the *Node* provides the processes with a function that makes it possible to create a new process, registering it with the *Scheduler* and *CPU* objects.

The Interrupt Management activities rely on a *Driver* object that is used as base class to implement the components that allow O.S. interaction with I/O Peripherals. *Driver* components are used as follows. An I/O device can register with a *Node* component for a given interrupt. At registration (which is carried out in the initialization phase by the *Configurator*), the *Driver* associated with the I/O device is also connected to the *Node.* From that moment onwards, the *Driver* will be able to accept "interrupt" signals on a mailbox. Upon reception of such a signal, the *CPU* object stops its activities, changes processor mode to supervisor and executes an *ISR* defined by the *Driver.* At *ISR* completion, another signal awakes the *CPU*, which enters once again user mode and resumes (simulated) processing.

The *Message-exchange Management* module is used to allow coordination and communication among applications processes. This is obtained through a fairly simple message-exchange support relying on a non-blocking *Send* and a blocking *Receive* primitive. These primitives are only used to coordinate the (simulated) process execution, not to simulate real interprocess communications.

3.2   Network Simulation

At the state of the art, the only networks that can be simulated by HeSSE are single-bus Ethernet or Fast Ethernet. Components that will allow the simulation of Routers, Myrinet and ATM networks are under development. As far as Ethernets are concerned, a first component (*Cable802_3*) simulates the behavior of a Ethernet cable at 10 or 100 Mb/s, making it possible to connect multiple stations and to detect collisions. A second component (*Ethernet*) simulates the behavior of the network interface card, implementing the CSMA/CD transmission protocol and the reception of the packets sent to its own Ethernet address or to all receivers. Every *Ethernet* is associated with a *Driver*, which acts as interface to the *Kernel* and moves data in transit between the network and the destination process (in the two directions).

3.3   Application Process Simulation

Our objective in the development of the very initial version of HeSSE has been to mimic the functionality offered by PS (with higher simulation accuracy, of course). At application level, the only (distributed) process interaction that can currently be simulated is the one offered by the PVM run-time support. We hope to implement soon the components needed to simulate other supports (in particular, MPI) and the data exchange through sockets typical of network applications. By the way, it is worth pointing out that PVM is probably the most complex of all the three mentioned cases, since it is the only one where messages (unless explicitly directly-routed) are forwarded to their final destination through daemon processes.

The simulation of PVM processes relies on three components: the PVM daemon (*PVM_Daemon*), a manager of the physically-distributed data common to the whole network of PVM daemons (*PVM_Data*), and a component representative of PVM application tasks (*PVM_Task*). *PVM_Daemon* is connected to the *Node*, to *PVM_Data* and to all the PVM application tasks running in the same computing node. During the initialization phase, the *PVM_Daemon* component asks the O.S. for the creation of a daemon process, which sleeps until it is scheduled for execution following up the reception of a PVM message directed to that node.

The *PVM_Task* component models one application process. Each *Node* can be connected to one or several instances of this component, which are scheduled along with other possible user processes. During the simulation, all *PVM_Tasks* loop reading records from the trace files of the corresponding processes. These records may correspond to CPU bursts or to interactions with the node O.S.. In the first case, *PVM_Task* asks the *Node* for CPU time (more detailed, for a CPU time equal to the duration of the CPU burst converted to the expected duration on that node). In the latter, an O.S. service is requested and simulated by the *Node* sub-components.

4   Conclusions

This paper is essentially a preliminary report on the HeSSE simulation project. We have described the main reasons behind the decision to develop a new simulation environment, instead of upgrading an existing one targeted at coarse-grained PVM applications. An important point dealt with here is that a simulator design should match the class of applications that can be successfully simulated, making an optimal tradeoff between speed and simulation accuracy.

We have described some of the features of the old simulator we have decided to preserve in the new design, and discussed the design constraints linked to the necessity to simulate a wider class of systems and applications. Then we have shown the structure devised for HeSSE, describing the functionality of the main simulation components and discussing its dynamic configuration capabilities.

At the state of the art, an alpha version of the simulator targeted exclusively at PVM applications has been implemented and it is currently under testing. We are trying to ascertain how wide is the class of applications that can be simulated with reasonable accuracy. This process should give us the feedback required to evaluate the validity of the simulator design, making it possible to revise promptly any possible unsatisfactory choice.

References

1. Special joint issue of IEEE Computer **28** (Nov. 1995) and IEEE Parallel and Distributed Technology (Winter 1995) on Parallel Performance Evaluation Tools
2. Aversa, R., Mazzeo, A., Mazzocca, N., Villano, U.: Heterogeneous System Performance Prediction and Analysis using PS. IEEE Concurrency **6** (July-Sept. 1998) 20-29
3. Geist, A., Beguelin, A., Dongarra, J., Jiang, W., Manchek, R., Sunderam, V.: PVM: Parallel Virtual Machine. MIT Press, Cambridge, MA (1994)
4. Aversa, R., Mazzeo, A., Mazzocca, N., Villano, U.: Developing Applications for Heterogeneous Computing Environments using Simulation: a Case Study. Parallel Computing **24** (1998) 741-761
5. Buck, J. T., Ha, S., Lee, E. A., Messerschmitt, D. G.: Ptolemy: A Framework for Simulating and Prototyping Heterogeneous Systems. Int. Journal of Computer Simulation **4** (1994) 155-182
6. Labarta, J., Girona, S., Pillet, V., Cortes T., Gregoris, L.: DiP: a Parallel Program Development Environment. Proc. Euro-Par '96, Lyon, France (Aug. 1996) Vol. II 665-674
7. Davis, H., Goldschmidt, S. R., Hennessy, J.: Multiprocessor Simulation and Tracing using Tango. Proc. 1991 Int. Conf. on Parallel Processing (1991) Vol. II 99-107
8. Brewer, E. A., Dellarocas, C. N., Colbrook, A., Weihl, W. E.: Proteus: a High-performance Parallel-architecture Simulator. MIT Tech. Rep. MIT/LCS/TR-516, Cambridge, MA (1991)
9. Rosenblum, M., Herrod, S. A., Witchel, E., Gupta, A.: Complete Computer System Simulation: The SimOS Approach. IEEE Parallel & Distributed Technology **3** (Winter 1995) 34-43

Comparison of Different Approaches to Trace PVM Program Execution

Marcin Neyman

Technical University of Gdańsk
Narutowicza 11/12, 80-952 Gdańsk, Poland
marcinn@pg.gda.pl

Abstract. Distributed application suffer from nondeterminism thus may behave in a different way for subsequent executions with the same input. To be able to ensure determinism of replay the sequence of received messages should be recorded for each process. The paper deals with comparison of various strategies for tracing PVM programs. It concerns centralised and distributed approach for tracing as well as techniques with and without race detection.

1 Introduction

Rapid growth of distributed applications employment caused vast demand on development of mechanisms supporting this type of computing. The very important area is recovery in a broad aspect covering not only dependability problems like fault tolerance, testing and debugging [6,7,8] but also visualisation [5] and modification of computations as well as application of control procedures (e.g. in financial systems).

This article addresses development of strategies of tracing distributed applications in PVM. Finding a proper strategy of tracing application behaviour is critical in reducing the recovery overhead, especially storage and time overhead [10]. In the previous work [13] an approach to trace PVM applications involving a race detection procedure was presented. This paper continues that research. Other tracing strategies are compared to the one mentioned in the earlier article. The stress is put on the time and storage efficiency. Term "recovery of computations" is used here paper as a generalisation of execution replay. It covers two areas:

- backward state recovery techniques,
- re-execution mechanisms.

State recovery as well as re-execution depend on mechanisms of tracing application execution in order to log information needed by recovery procedures. This paper concerns tracing techniques supporting re-execution. Checkpointing techniques supporting roll-back procedures are well-defined by other authors [11] and will not be discussed in this work.

J. Dongarra et al. (Eds.): EuroPVM/MPI 2000, LNCS 1908, pp. 274–281, 2000.

DEFINITION 1 (RECOVERY OF COMPUTATIONS)
Let E_{ij} be an execution of a distributed application from its state $S(\tau_i)$ to $S(\tau_j)$, and $S(\tau_k)$ be an intermediate state of this execution ($\tau_i < \tau_k \leq \tau_j$). Recovery of computations is defined as a transformation of $S(\tau_j)$ into $S'(\tau_k)$ by rolling the application back to $S'(\tau_i)$ and re-executing it.

$$R_{jk} : S(\tau_j) \rightarrow S'(\tau_k) \qquad R_{jk} = (S_{ji} + E'_{ik}) \tag{1}$$

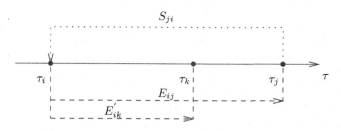

Fig. 1. Recovery of computations R_{jk}

According to this definition, three phases of recovery of computations may be distinguished (see figure 1):

- primary execution E_{ij},
- roll-back S_{ji},
- re-execution (replay) E'_{ik}.

Each of these phases incorporates its own recovery procedure. For the primary execution this is a *tracing procedure*. For the second phase this is a *roll-back procedure*, while for the re-execution this is a *replay management procedure*. However the tracing procedure precedes the recovery itself, it plays very important role when overhead is concerned. Overhead caused by the tracing procedure should be very carefully analyzed not only because additional cost of execution but also because of influence on replayed application behaviour what is very important especially in testing of distributed software [4,5,12].

2   Problem of Nondeterminism

The basic problem of replaying distributed applications is their nondeterministic behaviour. An application is said to be nondeterministic if its behaviour may be different for subsequent executions with the same input.

Nondeterminism is caused by interactions with the environment. Its sources may be some system calls (e.g. `random()`), non-initialized variables, interrupts and signals [2]. Distributed applications also suffer from nondeterminism caused by message exchanges. While methods of dealing with nondeterminism caused by sources that affect also sequential programs are well known [1], the problem concerning distributed applications is much harder to solve. This article addresses logging information during primary execution in order to ensure deterministic replay. Only the problems specific to distributed applications are considered in this work.

Typical method of achieving determinism of replay is recording the order of receiving messages by logging their control data during primary execution. Logging sender *tid* and *tag* of each received message is sufficient in PVM environment [7,13]. In case of nonblocking receive (`pvm_nrecv()`, `pvm_trecv()`) the data is recorded provided that a message was successfully received. During replay parameters of receive functions (`pvm_recv()`, `pvm_precv()`) are substituted with the data recorded in the log [7,13]. The nonblocking receive functions (`pvm_nrecv()`, `pvm_trecv()`) are replaced by the blocking `pvm_recv()` in case of successful reception of a message in the primary execution. In the opposite case, the nonblocking function is ignored.

In the next section various tracing strategies are analysed with respect to the PVM characteristics.

3   Tracing Strategies

There are two general strategies of tracing execution of PVM program: centralised and distributed. The idea is either to create one centralised log file or a collection of files distributed over the virtual machine. The advantage of the centralised approach is the opportunity to perform on-line analysis of the recorded data. However this strategy increases communication overhead due to sending data to a centralised log manager. On the other hand distributed logging does not introduce communication overhead while the recorded data needs to be merged before it may be analyzed. Volume of time overhead in both strategies is subject to analysis. In case of distributed logging it depends on the hardware (hard disk technology, type of interface, etc.) and operating system mechanisms (disk caching). Considering parameters of present systems and relatively small size of portions of recorded data, expected time overhead should not be very significant. In section 4 results of experimental comparison o the two strategies will be presented.

As stated in section 2, to achieve determinism during replay, we need to record the order of receiving messages. However it is not necessary to trace all the messages. The storage and time overhead may be reduced by tracing receive functions accepting messages from any process. Only those receives may cause races. This approach is called *optimistic*. However log generated with optimistic approach may still be redundant for the reason that not every wild-card receive generates a race. To reduce amount of recorded data to the racing messages only a race detection procedure should be used. A tracing strategy based on race detection is called *pessimistic*. Netzer and Miller [10] propose an elegant solution to detect races "on the fly". But their method based on tracing the second message involved in a race cannot be easily adopted in PVM. In this work an alternative method based on tracing the first racing message was used. This approach was described in [13]. Applying a race detection procedure we can limit size of the log file. On the other hand we increase time overhead. In section 4 experimental results will be presented to compare overhead introduced by different variants of the tracing procedure.

As mentioned in [13] race detection mechanism should be implemented with centralised tracing. This allows on-line identification of processes and proper initialisation of vector clocks, necessary to perform a race detection procedure.

4   Experimental Results

Two series of experiments have been performed to compare time overhead introduced by tracing procedure. The first one compared optimistic tracing in centralised and distributed strategy. The other one concerned centralised strategy with optimistic and pessimistic approach. Three small applications[1] were selected to perform the tests:

INT – numerical integration,
LIN – linear recurrence,
HQS – quick sort in hypercube topology.

All those applications have been implemented in *master-slave* model. Each one contains receive races either in communication between *master* and *slave* processes or among *slaves*. The intensity of communication between *slave* processes is different in each application. INT does not involve any message exchange between *slaves* while for LIN the communication among them is moderate and for HQS is intensive.

The tests were performed on a switched 10 Mbps CSMA/CD network of SUN Sparc 4 machines with Solaris 2.6. To reduce influence of the environment on the obtained results, all of the measures were performed 100 times and average execution time was calculated. Time overhead $\overline{ovrt_t}$ was defined as a ratio of difference between average execution time of application with tracing procedures $\overline{t_p}$ and pure application $\overline{t_a}$ to average execution time of pure application $\overline{t_p}$ [3].

$$\overline{ovrt_t} = \frac{\overline{t_p} - \overline{t_a}}{\overline{t_a}} = \frac{\overline{t_p}}{\overline{t_a}} - 1 \tag{2}$$

Figure 2 presents time overhead of tracing procedures executed on a virtual machine consisting of four hosts. The points show measured results while the lines show approximated trends. Time overhead of tracing for all three applications in case of distributed strategy is small (less than 5%) and may be assumed constant (the deviation is within the measuring error). Overhead caused by centralised tracing linearly grows with number of processes in an application. The growth is faster for communication intensive applications. This is justified

---

[1] The applications originally developed by Roy Pargas and John N. Underwood were retrieved from an Internet site and adopted by the author.

by larger number of messages sent over the network to the log manager process. There is a significant difference between optimistic and pessimistic tracing. It is caused by the race detection procedure, especially by timestamping the application messages. Detecting races "on the fly" requires implementing vector clocks [9] that are attached to every message sent. PVM applications use two kinds of communication functions. Along with the basic pvm_recv() and pvm_send() their p-versions may be used (pvm_precv() and pvm_psend()). The difference in their interfaces makes development of generic piggybacking mechanism impossible. That is why vector clocks are sent as separate messages significantly increasing the time overhead.

Figure 3 presents the number of messages traced with optimistic and pessimistic approach compared to the number of all processed messages. The difference in sizes of log files produced with optimistic and pessimistic tracing procedures strongly depends on an application and programming characteristics. Figure 3 shows that for the three test programs applying the optimistic tracing strategy significantly reduces number of logged messages while pessimistic strategy compared to the optimistic one does not introduce such a big difference.

5   Conclusions

Basic strategies of tracing an application behaviour were compared both in theoretical and experimental way. The results show that distributed tracing introduces small overhead while centralised tracing allows to implement a race detection procedure that reduces size of the recorded data. However use of race detection procedure seem to be justified only in case of long running applications where the size of recorded data may be a critical problem.

The ongoing work will focus on development of hybrid techniques based on distributed tracing with centralised logging of process creation information that allows to apply a race detection procedure. Also mechanism for attaching vector timestamps to messages will be analysed in order to reduce time overhead.

References

1. K. M. R. Audenaert, L. J. Levrouw. Interrupt replay: A debugging method for parallel programs with interrupts. *Microprocessors and Microsystems*, 18(10):601–612, 1994.
2. J. Chassin de Kergommeaux, K. De Bosschere, M. Ronsse. Efficient execution replay for ATHAPASCAN-0 parallel programs. Technical Report 3635, INRIA, 1999.
3. A. Fagot, J. Chassin de Kergommeaux. Systematic assessment of the overhead of tracing parallel programs. E. L. Zapata, ed., *Proceedings of 4th EUROMICRO Workshop on Parallel and Distributed Processing, PDP'96*, pp. 179–185. IEEE Computer Society Press, 1996.
4. H. Krawczyk, P. Kuzora, M. Neyman, J. Proficz, B. Wiszniewski. STEPS — a tool for testing PVM programs. *Proceedings of SEIHPC-3 Workshop*, pp. 1–8, Spain, 1998.

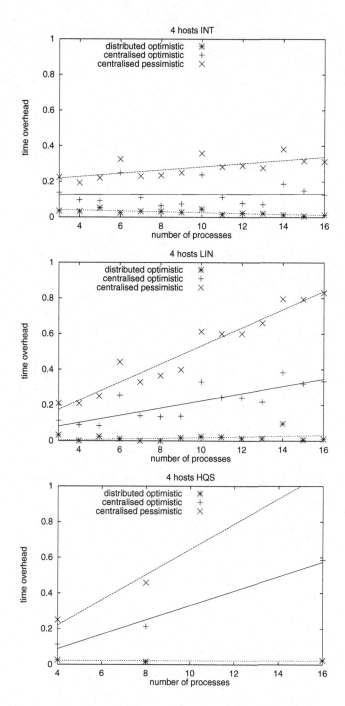

Fig. 2. Time overhead of tracing procedures

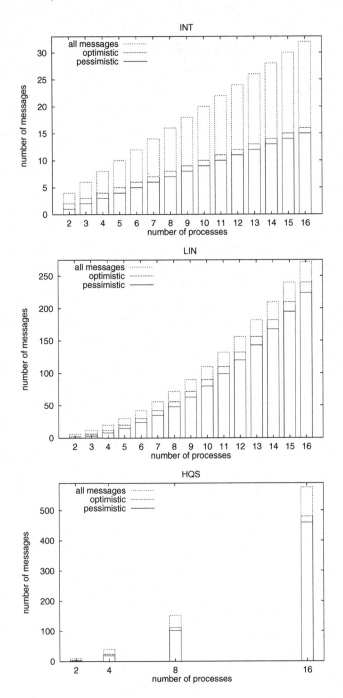

Fig. 3. Number of messages logged with optimistic and pessimistic tracing compared to the number of all processed messages

5. H. Krawczyk, B. Wiszniewski, P. Kuzora, M. Neyman, J. Proficz. Integrated static and dynamic analysis of PVM programs with STEPS. *Computers and Artificial Intelligence*, 17(5):441–453, 1998.
6. T. J. LeBlanc, John M. Mellor-Crummey. Debugging parallel programs with Instant Replay. *IEEE Transactions on Computers*, C-36(4):471–482, 1987.
7. J. Lourenço, J. C. Cunha. Replaying distributed applications with RPVM. G. Kotis P. Kacsuk, ed., *Proceedings of DAPSYS'98*, pp. 121–126, Budapest, Hungary, 1998. Universität Wien.
8. J. Lourenço, J. C. Cunha, H. Krawczyk, P. Kuzora, M. Neyman, B. Wiszniewski. An integrated testing and debugging environment for parallel and distributed programs. *Proceedings of 23rd EUROMICRO Conference*, pp. 291–298, Budapest, Hungary, 1997. IEEE Computer Society Press.
9. F. Mattern. Virtual time and global states of distributed systems. M. Cosnard et. al., ed., *Parallel and Distributed Algorithms: proceedings of the International Workshop on Parallel & Distributed Algorithms*, pp. 215–226. Elsevier Science Publishers B. V., 1989.
10. R. H. B. Netzer, B. P. Miller. Optimal tracing and replay for debugging message-passing parallel programs. *The Journal of Supercomputing*, 8(4):371–388, 1995.
11. N. Neves, W. K. Fuchs. RENEW: A tool for fast and efficient implementation of checkpoint protocols. *Proceedings of FTCS-28*, pp. 58–67. IEEE, 1998.
12. M. Neyman. Non-deterministic recovery of computations in testing of distributed systems. *Proceedings of Ninth European Workshop on Dependable Computing*, pp. 114–117, Gdansk, 1998. Technical University of Gdansk. ISBN 83-907591-1-X.
13. M. Neyman, M. Bukowski, P. Kuzora. Efficient replay of PVM programs. J. Dongarra et. al., ed., *Recent Advances in Parallel Virtual Machine and Message Passing Interface*, Lecture Notes in Computer Science number 1697, pp. 83–90. Springer-Verlag, 1999.

Scalable CFD Computations Using Message-Passing and Distributed Shared Memory Algorithms

Joanna Płażek[1], Krzysztof Banaś[1], and Jacek Kitowski[2,3]

[1] Section of Applied Mathematics FAPCM, Cracow University of Technology,
ul. Warszawska 24, 31-155 Cracow, Poland
[2] Institute of Computer Science, AGH, al. Mickiewicza 30, 30-059 Cracow, Poland
[3] ACC CYFRONET-AGH, ul. Nawojki 11, 30-950 Cracow, Poland
kito@uci.agh.edu.pl

Abstract. Two parallel programming models applied to an adaptive finite element code for solving nonlinear simulation problems on unstructured grids are compared. As a test case we used a compressible fluid flow simulation where sequences of finite element solutions form time approximations to the Euler equations.

In the first model (explicit) the domain decomposition of unstructured grid is adopted, while the second (implicit) uses the functional decomposition – both applied to the preconditioned GMRES method that solves iteratively the finite element system of linear equations. Results for HP SPP1600, HP S2000 and SGI Origin2000 are reported.

1   Introduction

Two programming models can be adopted for parallel computing – message passing and data-parallel. Usually, the first of them (explicit) offers higher parallel efficiency, while the second (implicit) – ease of programming. They reflect organization of the address space. Between two extremes, i.e. the shared address space organization and the distributed memory architecture, there is a class of virtual shared, physically distributed memory organization machines (often called Distributed Shared Memory, DSM, machines). The last one offers several typical classes, like cc-NUMA (cache coherent non-uniform memory access), COMA (coherent only memory architecture) and RMS (reflective memory systems). cc-NUMA implementations are commercialy the most popular. Examples come from HP (Exemplar with two interconnection layers), from SGI/Cray (Origin2000 with fat hypercube topology) and future SUN computing servers. The similar approach is incorporated in the present IBM RS/6000 SP computers with PowerPC604e or Power3 SMP nodes.

Since the advanced multiprocessors at present are constructed with SMP nodes the choice between the programming models is not obvious; integration of multiprocessing and multithreading would be profitable in the future.

The standard finite element procedures for solving a given problem consist in creation of element stiffness matrices and load vectors, assembling them into

J. Dongarra et al. (Eds.): EuroPVM/MPI 2000, LNCS 1908, pp. 282–288, 2000.

a global stiffness matrix and a global load vector and then solving a resulting system of linear equations. The latter task is often performed by a separate, general purpose library procedure. The parallelization of such a solver is done independently of the finite element mesh and the problem solved. Many results concerning computational mechanics have been published to date (see for example a general overview [1]).

In the reported case the solvers are built into the algorithm. They use particular data structure related to the finite element data structure and do not create a global stiffness matrix and a load vector. Instead, they proceed in the element by element manner and receive element stiffness matrices. The parallelization of such solvers is based on mesh partition and particular data handling.

In the paper we present an extension of our previous studies [2,3,4,5]. We show timing results for a CFD problem obtained on HP SPP1600, HP S2000 and SGI Origin2000 computers.

2   Algorithm for Flow Simulations

We used the following variational formulation for the stabilized finite element method [2,6]:

Find $U^{n+1} \in [H^1(\Omega_C)]^m$ satisfying the suitable Dirichlet boundary conditions and such that for every test function W the following holds:

$$
\int_{\Omega_C} W^T U^{n+1} dV + \Delta t \int_{\Omega_C} W_{,i}^T (K^{ij})^n U_{,j}^{n+1} dV
$$
$$
= \int_{\Omega_C} W^T U^n dV + \Delta t \int_{\Omega_C} W_{,i}^T (f^i)^n dV
$$
$$
- \Delta t \int_{\partial \Omega_C} W^T (f^i)^n n_i dS \tag{1}
$$

where :

- Ω_C - the computational domain, $\Omega_C \subset \mathbb{R}^l$, $l =$ 2 or 3
- n_i - the outward unit vector, normal to the boundary $\partial \Omega_C$
- U - the vector of conservation variables $(\rho, \rho u_j, \rho e)^T$, $j = 1, .., l$ (ρ, u_j and e are the density, the j-th component of velocity and the specific total energy)
- f^i - the Eulerian fluxes, $f^i = (\rho u_i, \rho u_i u_j + p\delta_{ij}, (\rho e + p)u_i)^T$, $(i, j = 1, .., l)$
- $p = (\gamma-1)(\rho e - \frac{1}{2}\rho u_i u_i)$ - the pressure (γ - the ratio of specific heats, $\gamma = 1.4$)
- $\Delta t = t^{n+1} - t^n$ - the time step length
- K^{ij} - nonlinear matrix functions representing stabilization terms and artificial viscosity

The indices i, j have range from 1 to l, the outer superscripts of functions of U refer to their actual argument (e.g.: $(K^{ij})^n = K^{ij}(U^n)$ or $(f^i)^n = f^i(U^n)$), the summation convention is used and differentiation is denoted by ','.

The problem is discretized in space using triangular finite elements with linear shape functions. For time discretization we use a version of the Taylor-Galerkin time marching scheme [7]. A sequence of solutions to one time step problem (1) constitutes a time discrete approximate solution to the Euler equations.

At each time step a stabilized finite element problem is solved with GMRES algorithm, which is one of the most successful and widely used iterative methods for nonsymmetric systems of linear equations [8,9,10]. It is preconditioned by block Jacobi iterations [11] and uses patches of elements in the finite element mesh, that define blocks within the stiffness matrix. Only these blocks are assembled during the solution procedure, overcoming the problem of distributed storage of the global stiffness matrix. Matrix-vector products in the preconditioned GMRES algorithm are performed by means of loops over patches of elements and solutions of local block problems.

In the restarted version, the number of Krylov space vectors, k, is limited to some small number (in our case $k = 10$) and the initial guess for restarts is taken as the current approximate solution.

3   Message-Passing versus Shared-Address Space in GMRES Implementation

In the message-passing programming paradigm, programmers treat their programs as a collection of processes with private local variables and the ability to send and receive data between processes by passing messages. There are no shared variables among processes. Each process uses its local variables and occasionally sends or receives data from the others.

We use this programming paradigm to create the explicit parallel algorithm in which the whole computational mesh is divided into subdomains assigned to different processor. Each processor considers only subdomain internal mesh nodes exchanging information on boundary nodes with others processors which deal with neighbouring submeshes (data locality is maintained). The subsequent steps of the GMRES algorithm are executed in such a way that except of few instructions related to global operations (e.g. calculation of vector norms, inner products) each processor performs calculations on local data. Local stiffness matrices for block problems in Jacobi algorithm are generated and assembled independently and in parallel for each subdomain.

The practical realization of this model uses PVM for message passing between different processing units. There exists one master process that controls the solution procedure and several slave processes performing in parallel the most of calculations (master-slave model).

To obtain minimal execution time for the problem the partitioning process must optimize load balance and minimize interprocessor communication. Each subdomain should contain the number of degrees of freedom proportional to the computational power of processors and minimal number of interface nodes. In our study the domain decomposition is performed with a simple mesh partition algorithm based on the advancing front [12]. Several algorithms have been tested [3]; the smallest communication overhead is observed for the algorithm which ensures vertical alignement of the subdomain interfaces. The strategy results in the smallest number of the interface nodes minimizing the communication requirements.

In the shared-address space programming paradigm (mentioned by DSM below), the program is a collection of processes accessing shared variables. The shared-address space programming style is naturally suited to (virtually) shared-address space muliprocessors.

Compilers can parallelize a code automatically, verifying loop dependencies. Such an approach results in sufficient efficiency for simple loops only. For example, a subroutine call inside a loop prevents its parallelization. To overcome those problems directives are introduced to increase degree of parallelization and to control manually many aspects of execution.

In the implicit programming model we optimize the program using compiler directives whenever a loop over blocks, nodes or individual degrees of freedom are encountered. In particular the parallelization is applied for blocks construction, computation of element stiffness matrices and assembly into block stiffness matrices, iterations of the block method.

Shared-address space computers can also be programmed using the message-passing paradigm. The local memory of each processor becomes the logical local memory and a designated area of the global memory becomes the communication buffer for message passing.

4 Results

Our implementations have been tested with an example of flow problem known as a ramp benchmark of inviscid flow [13]. A shock with Mach 10 traveling along a channel and perpendicular to its walls meets at time $t = 0$s a ramp, having an angle of 60 degrees with the channel walls. A pattern with double Mach reflection develops and a jet of denser fluid along the ramp behind the shock is observed.

Three parallel machines have been incorporated: HP SPP1600 (with 32 PA7200/120MHz processors organized in 4 SMP hypernodes and software: SPP-UX 4.2, Convex C 6.5 and ConvexPVM 3.3.10), HP S2000 (with 16 PA8000/180MHz processors in one hypernode using SPP-UX 5.2, HP C 2.1 and PVM 3.3.11) and SGI Origin2000 (with 32 R10000/250MHz processors, IRIX 6.5, SGI C 7.3 and SGI PVM 3.1.1). During the experiments we run the code on a SPP1600 subomplex consisting of 16 processors from four SMP nodes. On S2000 and on Origin2000 (mentioned by S2K and O2K respectively) no other users were allowed to use those machines.

The results refer to wall-clock execution time, T, for one time step (one finite element problem) chosen as a representation for the whole simulation, with different meshes (equal to 16858, 18241 and 73589 nodes) and with the same number of iterations (equal to 5) in the GMRES algorithm. In order to get statistically more reliable results the measurements have been collected three times from 5 subsequent time steps, since fluctuations in T of several percents were observed.

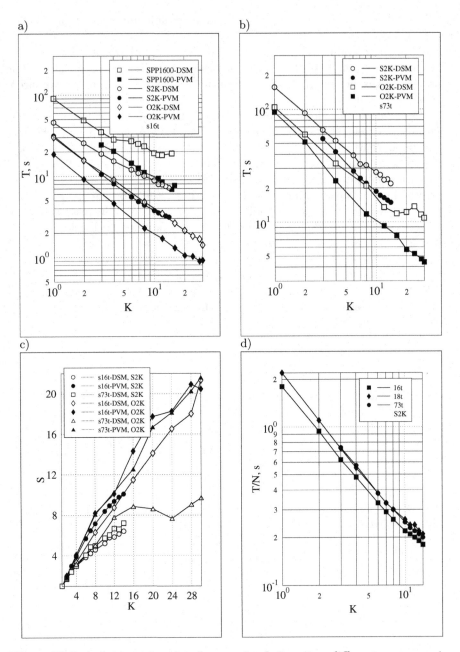

Fig. 1. Wall-clock execution time for one simulation step, different programming models and machines: (a) the mesh with $N = 16858$ nodes, (b) with $N = 73589$ nodes.
(c) Speedup for different meshes ($N = 18241$ and 73589 nodes).
(d) Scaled T for $N = 16858$, 18241 and 73589 nodes.

For a given case fixing the number of GMRES iterations we separate the problem of GMRES convergence from the problem of purely numerical efficiency of parallelization.

In Fig. 1(a) the wall-clock execution time for different number of processors, K, and for different machines as well as for different programming models is presented. Number of nodes, N, has been rather moderate, equal to $N = 16858$. The complicated architecture of SPP1600 has influenced the DSM model, while results from explicit model left undisturbed with no substantial influence of the lower bandwidth between the hypernodes. Better scalability is observed for the explicit model in comparison with DSM one, although the latter results are obtained with relative small programmer's effort. In any case PVM model turned out to be more efficient with shorter execution time. For 30 Origin2000 processors and PVM model characteristics saturation becomes evident, while staying monotonous for DSM.

Comparing results for different models no clear explanation has been found for the performance difference between explicit and implicit models for one computing node (i.e. for $K = 1$). This is probably due to distinct nodes numbering in the meshes resulting in different cache performance.

In Fig. 1(b) timings for a greater mesh consisiting of $N = 73589$ nodes are shown. Again, the difference between PVM and DSM models are not high for rather small number of processors ($K \leq 16$). The significant diffrence is obtained for $K > 16$, i.e., for O2K hypercube dimensionality, $d > 2$. No characteristics saturation is observed for PVM model due to higher computation to communication ratio. For DSM model unexpected response is found, with maximum for $K = 24$ and monotonous execution time decrease in the next K range. This feature, which could result from a complicated node architecture, needs more considerations in future.

Speedup (relative) values, S, are depicted in Fig. 1(c). Good scalability is obtained for the message-passing model, however better for Origin2000 machine. Despite of the interval $K > 16$, DSM model demonstrates higher speedup on Origin2000 than on S2000. In Fig. 1(d) we present the wall-clock execution time, T, normalized to number of mesh nodes, N. Since the characteristics are very close each other, this confirms experimentally linear computational complexity $o(N)$ of the algorithm.

5   Conclusions

The implicit programming model can bring useful and scalable parallelization of CFD applications. For cc-NUMA machines it is profitable to use it for rather small number of processors. Explicit programming gives better results in terms of scalability and execution time for the price of more complicated code structure.

From CFD study it follows that the implicit program is more sensitive to communication speed than the explicit one. Changing from one SMP node execution to multi- SMP node execution only slighty affects the performance of the explicit code, while influences significantly execution time of the implicit code.

So that we propose to use a heterogeneous model with implicit programming for a SMP node while staying with explicit one bewteen the SMP nodes. This model would be profitable also for clusters of SMP workstations.

6   Acknowledgments

The work has been sponsored by Polish State Committee for Scientific Research (KBN) Grant 8T11C 006 15. We are grateful to ACK CYFRONET-AGH for the computer time.

References

1. Idelsohn, S.R., Onate, E., Dvorkin, E.N. (eds.), Computational Mechanics. New Trends and Applications, *Proc. of Fourth World Congress on Computat.Mechanics*, June 29-July 2, 1998, Buenos Aires, CIMNE (Barcelona), 1998.
2. Banaś, K., and Płażek, J., Dynamic load balancing for the preconditioned GMRES solver in a parallel, adaptive finite element Euler code, in: J.-A. Desideri, et al., (eds.), Proc.Third ECCOMAS Computational Fluid Dynamics Conference, Sept.9-13, 1996, Paris (J.Wiley & Sons Ltd., 1996) 1025-1031.
3. Płażek, J., Banaś, K., Kitowski, J., and Boryczko, K., Exploiting two-level parallelism in FEM applications, in: B. Hertzberger and P. Sloot, (eds.), Proc.of HPCN'97 Conference, April 28-30, 1997, Vienna, *Lecture Notes in Computer Science*, **1225** (1997) 272-281 (Springer, Berlin).
4. Płażek, J., Banaś, J., and Kitowski, J., Finite element message-passing/DSM simulation algorithm for parallel computers, in: P. Sloot, M. Bubak and B. Hertzberger, (eds.), Proc.of HPCN'98 Conference, April 21-23, 1998, Amsterdam, *Lecture Notes in Computer Science*, **1401** (1998) 878-880 (Springer, Berlin).
5. Płażek, J., Banaś, K., Kitowski, J., Implementation Issues of Computational Fluid Dynamics Algorithms on Parallel Computers, in: Dongarra, J., Luque, E., Margalef, T., (eds.), Proc.of 6th European PVM/MPI Users' Group Meeting, Barcelona, Spain, September 1999, *Lecture Notes in Computer Science*, **1697** (1999) 349-355 (Springer Berlin).
6. Banaś, K., and Demkowicz, L., Entropy controlled adaptive finite element simulations for compressible gas flow, *J. Computat. Phys.* **126** (1996) 181-201.
7. Donea, J., and Quartapelle, L., An introduction to finite element methods for transient advection problems, *Comp.Meth. Appl. Mech. Eng.*, **95** (1992) 169-203.
8. Saad, Y., and Schultz, M., GMRES: a generalizad minimal residual algorithm for solving nonsymmetric linear systems, SIAM J. Sci.Stat.Comp. **7** (1986) 856-869.
9. Saad, Y., Iterative Methods for Sparse Linear Systems (PWS Pub. Comp., 1996).
10. de Sturler, E., and van der Vorst, H.A., Communication cost reduction for Krylov methods on parallel computers, in: W. Gentsch and U. Harms, eds., Proc.of HPCN'94, Conference, April 18-20, 1994, Munich, *Lecture Notes in Computer Science*, **797** (1994) 190-195 (Springer, Berlin).
11. LeTallec, P., Domain decomposition method in computational mechanics, in: J.T. Oden, ed. (North Holland, Amsterdam, 1994).
12. Farhat, C., Lanteri, S., and Simon, H.D., TOP/DOMDEC - a software tool for mesh partitioning and parallel processing, *Comput.Systems Eng.*, **6** (1995) 13-26.
13. P. Woodward and P. Colella, The numerical simulation of two dimensional fluid flow with strong shocks, *J. Computat.Phys.*, **54** (1984) 115–173.

Parallelization of Neural Networks Using PVM

Mathias Quoy[1], Sorin Moga[1], Philippe Gaussier[1], and Arnaud Revel[2]

[1] Université de Cergy-Pontoise - ETIS
6, av. du Ponceau, 95014 Cergy-Pontoise Cédex, France
quoy@u-cergy.fr, http://www.ensea-etis.fr
[2] Ecole Nationale Supérieure de l'Electronique et de ses Applications - ETIS

Abstract. We use Neural Networks (NN) in order to design control architectures for autonomous mobile robots. With PVM, it is possible to spawn different parts of a NN on different workstations. Specific message passing functions using PVM are included into the NN architecture. A graphical interface helps the user spawning the NN architecture and monitors the messages exchanged between the different subparts of the NN. The message passing mechanism is efficient for real time applications. We show an example of image processing used for robot control.

1 Introduction

Our research group develops architectures for the control of autonomous mobile robots. We take mainly inspiration from neurobiology for designing NN architectures. This work is based on a constructivist approach. We first build the architecture parts dealing with the inputs processing, and managing some low level behaviors (obstacle avoidance for instance). Like in Brooks subsumption [1], the system consists in a hierarchy of sensory-motor loops: from very fast low level sensory-motor loops (obstacle avoidance, sensor reading ...) to very time-consuming image analysis and planning procedures. In our system, data issued by these mechanisms are processed by higher level modules which may in return influence them. This architecture is integrated in the perception-action framework (Per-Ac [3]). It is composed of a reflex pathway and a learned pathway. Once learning has taken place, it may override the reflex mechanism. The inputs to the system are the image taken from a CCD camera, infra-red sensors and the direction of the north given by a compass. Each of these inputs may be processed separately. Moreover, some time consuming image processing algorithms may also be performed in parallel. Using a set of workstations, it is clearly not interesting to parallelize the network at the neuron level (one workstation per neuron !), but rather in term of computational pathways (CP) being processed in parallel. Each CP corresponds to a functional part of the global NN architecture and may run on a different workstation. The exchange of information between CPs is most of the time asynchronous. We also want to minimize the number of messages exchanged. We use PVM [1] for spawning the CPs on the workstations and for the message passing libraries [4].

---

[1] Current version used is PVM 3.4.3 for Solaris and Linux

J. Dongarra et al. (Eds.): EuroPVM/MPI 2000, LNCS 1908, pp. 289–296, 2000.

Using PVM has two interests. First, the architectures we have developed become bigger and bigger as the task being performed is more complex. So even if the computational power is increasing, we do not match the real-time needed for our robotic experiments. Second, brain computation follows different pathways in parallel and is also performed in different cortical areas. Thus, it is also interesting to preserve this parallelism in our simulations.

PVM is also used at two different levels. First, we have developed specific communication functions integrated in the global architecture indicating the kind of information sent from one NN architecture to the other (Section 2). The specific message passing algorithms described may be used in any real time application, in particular when there is a huge amount of data to deal with. Second, a process manager has been developed. This manager helps the user choosing on which workstations to run the NN architectures, and monitors all message exchanges (Section 3). In section 4, we study the performances of a message passing mechanism used in a NN architecture controlling a mobile robot. This architecture enables a robot to go where it has detected movement in its image.

2   Designing NN Architectures

We do not develop here how we construct the NN architecture for performing a particular task (indoor navigation for instance). This is the focus of numerous other papers [2, 8]. We will rather stress how PVM fits in our NN architecture. The design of a NN architecture is performed using a specific program called Leto. It has a visual interface where the user may choose between several different kinds of neurons and connect them together. Not all groups represent neurons. Some may perform specific algorithmical functions (displaying an image on screen, giving orders to the robot ...). Once designed, a Leto architecture may be saved and is run using another program called Promethe (see next section). So, it is possible to design different architectures dedicated to specific tasks. The problem is to exchange data between these different tasks. This is where PVM is used at this level. So we deal here with the design of modules that may be integrated in the NN architecture. These modules tell whom to send a message to, or who to receive a message from.

We have coded specific message passing functions using the already existing PVM routines. Our functions are implemented as algorithmical groups in the architecture. There is basically one group sending data in one NN architecture and another receiving data in another NN architecture. The data sent is the neuron values. There may be several different NN architectures running in parallel. And there may be several different sending and receiving groups in each NN architecture. So we need to define where to send and from whom to receive. This is implemented through the definition of symbolic links which must be the same for the sender and the receiver. This symbolic link is coded on the name of the link arriving to a sender or receiving group. This name is composed of two parts: the symbolic name and a number corresponding to the message passing number used by PVM. After having launched all tasks, a symbolic link table is built. This table makes the matching between a symbolic name and a PVM task identifier (tid) number. Then the relevant parts of this table are sent to the different tasks. In order for two tasks to be able to communicate, the symbolic link name and the message number must be the same [2]. Upon reception of a message, the activities of the neurons of the receiving group are the same as the ones of the sending group. Thus, from the receiving group point of view, it is as if it were directly connected to the sending group through a "real" neuronal link. The message passing functions are functionnaly invisible. The different sending and receiving functions are the following:

- *function_send_PVM*: sends the value of the neurons where it is connected to. The receiver is retrieved using the symbolic link name and the message number.
- *function_receive_PVM_block*: waits for a message (neuron values) from a sender. The sender is identified by its symbolic link and message number.
- *function_receive_PVM_non_block*: checks if a message (neuron values) has arrived from the sender. If not, execution continues on the next neuron group.

We are running our NN architectures in real time for controlling mobile robots. Depending on the task to perform, it may be very important to have access to up to date information. For instance, computing the optical flow must be performed on the most recent image data. This is not mandatory for object recognition, since it stays where it is. Nevertheless, it turns out that most computations are asynchronous. Because we have to run in real time, we do not want to wait for a task to be finished before continuing the whole computation, and we do not always know which task will run faster or slower. So in the asynchronous processing, there may be two problems: information may be missing in some parts of the architecture, because some computation is not finished yet. Conversely, some parts of the system may run much faster than others and deliver a continuous flow of redundant information. Indeed, if the sending task is running much faster than the receiving one, the receive queue will be overwhelmed with messages. Moreover, the only important message to process is the last sent.
It is easy to solve the first problem. If information has not arrived yet, the previous neuron values are used. We suppose there is a temporal coherence in the neural information (internal dynamics of the neuron [5] and use of a neural field [9]). For dealing with the second problem, we have to introduce new message passing functions:

- *function_send_PVM_ack*: sends a message only if the receiver has allowed it by sending an *ack* message. If the message has not been received, it does not send anything and execution continues on the next group of neurons.
- *function_receive_PVM_block_ack*: waits for a message (neuron values) from a sender. Once the message received, this function sends back an *ack* message to the sender.

---

[2] The message number is not mandatory. It may be chosen randomly at the symbolic link table creation. But it is easier to know it beforehand for debugging purposes.

– *function_receive_PVM_non_block_ack*: same as the previous one, but waiting is non blocking.

Thus now, a sender may only send information if the receiver is able to process it. The way we have implemented the function, the receiver sends its *ack* message just after having received a message from the sender. Thus, the sender is now allowed to send a message again. If the sender runs faster than the receiver, it sends its new message before the receiver has been able to finish its computation. So, when it comes back to the receive function, a message is present in its queue, but this message is not reflecting the current state of the sender anymore. An alternative version of the receiving function could be to send the *ack* before a blocking receive. It is now the receiver which will wait until the sender catches the *ack*, and sends its message. Thus the message received by the receiver matches now the latest state of the sender, but the sender has to wait for this message. This function is *function_receive_PVM_ack_block*. It avoids saturating the Ethernet link and loosing too much computation time in communication procedures.

3   Running NN Architectures

A NN architecture is run using a specific program called Promethe. In each NN architecture, a token is moving from neuron group to neuron group activating them sequentially. When a PVM message passing group is activated, the corresponding function described above is executed. Once all groups have been activated, running resumes on the first group (fig. 1).

We have seen that PVM is used as message passing library between tasks running NN (Promethe processes). It is now necessary to have a *task manager* (Promethe_PVM_Daemon) spawning all these tasks. In particular, this process has to build the symbolic link table and send it to the NN tasks (fig. 1). In order to achieve this, the user has to define a file (*name.pvm*) indicating: the task name, the name of the workstation where to run the NN , the name of the NN architecture. Then, each symbolic link is given with its sending and receiving task. After having built the symbolic link table, the program displays a graphical interface using Xview. We have included in this interface some helpful features such as: testing the network for the various workstations available, testing the speed of these workstations and ranking them, assigning a task to a workstation, displaying the current state of the tasks (running or waiting), and displaying in real time the messages exchanged between the various tasks. Assigning a task to a workstation may be done either as specified in the *name.pvm* file, or on the fastest workstations only, or randomly. All three options are available on line in the graphical interface. A task may also be assigned to a specific workstation by selecting the workstation's name and then clicking on the task (shown as a square in the display window). The state of the tasks and the messages exchanged are monitored by the task manager. The purpose here is not to have a complete debugging tool. It is rather thought as an help for the user. This help gives two

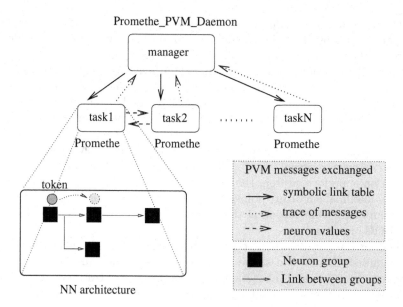

Fig. 1. Sketch of the message passing between the task manager process Promethe_PVM_Daemon and the launched Promethe tasks. Each Promethe task is a NN architecture composed of groups of neurons. A token is moving from one group to the other activating them sequentially.

informations: whether a task is running or waiting for a message, and which kind of message has been exchanged between tasks. The first information gives hints about the working load of each task, and the efficiency of the message exchanges. The second information allows to follow in real time the messages exchanged between the tasks. Each time data is sent or received, a message is issued to the manager, giving the sending and receiving tids and the message number (fig. 1). So, once all tasks are launched, the manager waits for these messages, and displays the information on screen. The manager also catches all *PvmTaskExit* signals so that it may resume its activity once all Promethe tasks are over. Monitoring the message exchanges could also have been implemented another way, the manager only waiting for any message exchanged between any tasks, and then sorting these messages depending on the message number. This supposes that all message numbers are different, which is not required if the symbolic links are different.

4   Results

We report here the performance results on a particular robotic experiment. Note that the robot [3] is also a multi-processor system (a micro controller for the speed

---

[3] Koala robot built by KTeam SA, Switzerland

control and a 68340 microprocessor for the communications with the workstations and the control of the different sensors). This system is not under the
control of PVM but it also works in an asynchronous manner.

The task of the robot is to learn to imitate a given teacher [7]. At the beginning, the robot can only use motion perception for going in the direction of the
moving object (supposed to be the teacher). If this behavior is not associated
with a negative reward, the robot also learns the static shape of the moving
object, so as to be able to move in its direction even if no motion is perceived.
This mechanism is also used to choose between different moving objects [6]. In
order to detect movements, the optical flow is computed. In parallel, an object
recognition is performed from the matching of local subimages centered around
the local maximal curvature points. These feature points correspond to the local
maximum of the convolution of the gradient image with a Difference Of Gaussian (DOG) function.

A sketch of the parallel architecture is given figure 2. Task2 performs the feature points extraction and shape recognition. Task1 performs data acquisition,
movement detection and robot movement control. These two tasks are not fully
synchronized in the sense that task1 is not waiting for the result of task2 for
continuing its computation (non blocking receive). However, task2 needs the information from task1 for its computation, because it looks for the feature points
only where movement is detected (in the case there is a moving object. In the
other case, the whole image must be processed). The data given by task1 to
task2 is a 196x144 array of bytes (image) and a 35x25x3 array of floats corresponding to where movement has been detected. Task2 is sending to task1 a
35x25x3 array of floats corresponding to the position of a recognized teacher.

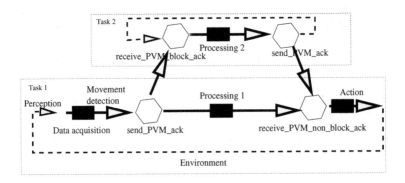

Fig. 2. Sketch of the computation done by the two tasks. Note that because the receive
in task1 is non blocking, the computation effectively executed in parallel is not always
what is marked as Processing1 and Processing2. Processing2 may be executed in task2
whereas task1 executes data acquisition and movement detection.

We have monitored the execution time in three different cases: the sequential
computation (without PVM) of the optical flow alone (will become task1), the

sequential computation of the optical flow and the teacher recognition, and the independent computation of the flow (task1) and the teacher recognition (task2). These results are given in the following table (mean-time in seconds is an average on 20 runs on SUN Sparc Ultra 10 workstations (part of a pool of workstations on a 100Mb Ethernet link). Each run corresponds to a new experiment (in particular new input data). Each task is running on a separate workstation):

time in seconds	seq. flow	seq. flow + recog.	PVM flow + recog.
seq. mean time	3.06	9.38	-
task1 mean time (0)	-	-	3.97
task2 mean time (1)	-	-	2.81
par. mean time (max)	-	-	3.97
task1 mean time acquiring data (2)	-	-	1.47
task1 mean time in PVM (sending and receiving) (3)	-	-	0.03
processing 1 (0) - (2) - (3)			2.47
task2 mean time in PVM (4)	-	-	0.32
processing 2 (1) - (4)			2.49

As expected the parallel computation runs faster than the sequential one. In average task2 runs faster than task1, mainly because of the time spent in the communications between the robot and the workstation. Thus as task2 has to wait for data from task1 in a blocking receive, the time spent in PVM functions (in particular waiting for data) is longer. Communications between the robot and the workstation is slow, so it would be particularly interesting to have a process dedicated to this task. These informations may then be dispatched to other processes.

5 Discussion

The message passing mechanism we have developed enables to use PVM for real-time applications. A message is sent only when the receiving task is ready to process it, thus reducing the network load level. Some tasks may need specific data in order to perform their computation, others may continue working even if the newest information is not available yet.
We have used PVM for parallelizing independent sub-networks composed of several groups of neurons. Some groups contain thousands of neurons. A further speed-up of our system will be the parallelization of the computation inside a group of neurons. We haven't tested yet whether PVM or threads (shared-memory) based algorithms should be used. In the later case, we would use multi-processor architectures (bi or quadra Pentiums for instance). On a bi-processor architecture, set of threads will update different subgroups of neurons and will almost divide by two the computation time devoted to a map of neurons.

This work is part of a project dedicated to the development of a *neuronal language*. Our Leto interface already allows to quickly design NN globally, ie. without specifying by hand each connection for instance. This construction is therefore made on a graphical interface: the user does not to write down his specifications in a file. The difficulty is to provide the user with enough (but not too much) different group of neurons and links between them to choose from when designing his NN architecture. By the time, we begin to have standard neuron groups and links. Moreover, some parts of the architecture are now stable and may be used without any changes for any other robotic experiments. This is the case for the image processing part for instance. A next step will be then to provide "meta-groups" of neurons (the equivalent of cortical areas) regrouping stable functional groups.

References

[1] Rodney A. Brooks. A robust layered control system for a mobile robot. *IEEE Journal of Robotics and Automation*, R.A. 2(1):14–23, March 1986.

[2] P. Gaussier, C. Joulain, J.P. Banquet, S. Leprêtre, and A. Revel. The visual homing problem: an example of robotics/biology cross fertilization. *Robotics and Autonomous Systems*, 30:155–180, 2000.

[3] P. Gaussier and S. Zrehen. Perac: A neural architecture to control artificial animals. *Robotics and Autonomous Systems*, 16(2-4):291–320, 1995.

[4] A. Geist, A. Beguelin, J. Dongarra, W. Jiang, R. Manchek, and V. Sunderam. *PVM: Parallel Virtual Machine - A users's guide and tutorial for networked parallel computing*. MIT Press, Cambridge, Massachusetts, 1994.

[5] J.A. Scott Kelso. *Dynamic patterns: the self-organization of brain and behavior*. MIT Press, 1995.

[6] S. Moga and P. Gaussier. Neural model of motion discrimination. In *ECVP98*, Oxford, England, 1998.

[7] S. Moga and P. Gaussier. A neuronal structure for learning by imitation. In F. Mondada D. Floreano, J.D. Nicoud, editor, *European Conference on Artificial life, ECAL99*, volume 1674, pages 314–318, Lausanne, september 1999.

[8] M. Quoy, P. Gaussier, S. Leprêtre, A. Revel, C. Joulain, and J.P. Banquet. A neural model for the visual navigation and planning of a mobile robot. In F. Mondada D. Floreano, J.D. Nicoud, editor, *European Conference on Artificial life, ECAL99*, volume 1674, pages 319–323, Lausanne, september 1999.

[9] G. Schöner, M. Dose, and C. Engels. Dynamics of behavior: theory and applications for autonomous robot architectures. *Robotics and Autonomous System*, 16(2-4):213–245, December 1995.

Parallel DSIR Text Indexing System: Using Multiple Master/Slave Concept

P. Laohawee, A. Tangpong, and A. Rungsawang

Massive Information & Knowledge Engineering,
Department of Computer Engineering,
Kasetsart University, Bangkok, Thailand
{g4165221,g4165239,fenganr}@ku.ac.th

Abstract. In this paper, we present another study of an improved parallel DSIR text retrieval system that can perform fast indexing of several gigabytes of text collection using Pentium-class PC-cluster. We use multiple-master/slave principle to implement this parallel indexing algorithm. In a computing node, a master process has been designed to work in conjunction with each slave process in order to utilize as much as possible the computing power during one or another process is waiting for I/O. We also present special buffering and caching techniques for boosting the computing performance. We have tested this algorithm and presented the experimental results using a large-scale TREC8 collection and investigated both computing performance and problem size scalability issue.

1 Introduction

The number of increasing web pages on the Internet, as well as all electronic textual documents in academic, business, jurisdiction, etc. continue to make us more difficult to easily access to relevant information in a reasonable time. A powerful searching or retrieval artifact like an efficient information retrieval system is thus required. In this paper we present another study of an improved parallel DSIR retrieval system [4] that can help the end-user to reach his relevant information by performing fast indexing of several gigabytes of text collection. DSIR is a vector space based retrieval model in which distributional semantic information inherently stored in the document collection is utilized to represent document content in order to achieve better retrieval effectiveness [3]. DSIR model consists of two parts, indexing and retrieval. Indexing part manipulates the text collection to be ready for searching, and retrieval part retrieves documents that match user needs.

Since, indexing method in DSIR is quite compute-intensive, a powerful single-CPU computer is still not enough to manage several gigabyte of textual database [2], we thus mainly focus here on a new DSIR indexing technique using multiple-master/slave principle. In this multiple-master/slave model, the master process has been designed to work in conjunction with each slave process to utilize as much as possible the computing power on each machine during one or another

J. Dongarra et al. (Eds.): EuroPVM/MPI 2000, LNCS 1908, pp. 297–303, 2000.

process is waiting for I/O. This principle can be called "co-operative master-slave concept" since each master and slave can co-operate to solve the dependent problems. We implemented this parallel indexing algorithm using MPI [8, 9] on Beowulf PC Pentium class machine running Linux operating system [6, 1]. During our experiments, we chose TREC8 documents as our large test collection [7]. TREC8 collection consists of more than half-million and varying length of free-text documents. We indexed FBIS (one set of documents in TREC8) collection, implemented additional caching and buffering techniques, and studied the processes' communication effectiveness of our proposed algorithm by varying both cache and buffer size. We also indexed the full version of TREC8 to study the scalability issue of our algorithm, and found that it still scale quite well as the problem size is increased.

We organize this paper in the following way. Section 2 briefly presents the DSIR indexing model. Section 3 discusses the proposed parallel DSIR indexing algorithm. Section 4 gives more detail about our experimental setup, results, and discussion. Finally, section 5 concludes this paper.

2 DSIR Indexing Model

DSIR is a vector space base retrieval model which adapts distributional semantics to alleviate the effects of polysemy and synonym found in documents. In this model, the context of words are used to characterize the meaning of documents [3]. In general, every word which is an elementary entity that holds the meaning contributes its own semantic, according to its occurrence and co-occurrence, to the whole content of the document in which it appears. The co-occurrence statistic of a word in DSIR is defined as the number of times that word co-occurs with one of its neighbors within a pre-defined boundary, called "distributional environment". Possible distributional environments can be sentences, paragraphs, sections, whole documents, or windows of k words. In DSIR computational model (See Figure 1), distributional information extracted from a collection of documents can be mapped as a matrix, called "co-occurrence matrix". Each row of the matrix represents co-occurrence statistic between an index term and its context which are assigned in the column of the matrix. Using this co-occurrence matrix, the document vector can be derived by applying Equation (1), where m_{ij} records the co-occurrence frequency between x_i and y_i extracted from the document collection, and $W(f_{ni})$ records the weighting function[5] addressing the importance of the word i in document n.

$$\overrightarrow{V}(d_n) = (\sum_{i=1}^{I} W(f_{ni})m_{i1}, ..., \sum_{i=1}^{I} W(f_{ni})m_{ij}) \tag{1}$$

3 Parallel DSIR Indexing Algorithm

DSIR indexing phase takes a large amount of computing time while the memory requirement of the algorithm is too high to be provided by a single machine. To

Co-occurrence Matrix   **Document Representation**

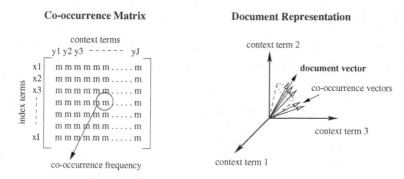

Fig. 1. Co-occurrence matrix and document representation in DSIR model.

overcome this limitation, we propose a new approach employing parallel and distributed computing using multiple master/slave principle. In this principle, each computing node consists of two processes; master process, called "Producer", and slave process, called "Consumer". The producer is responsible for computing any stuff of algorithm, and the consumer provides shared data structure, i.e. the co-occurrence matrix. This design alleviates the I/O blocking coming from the traditional single master process and several slaves' model.

During the co-occurrence matrix computation, the large co-occurrence matrix is generated. To reduce time to compute the co-occurrence statistic, the whole textual document collection is separated equally and distributed to each computing node. The consumer on each machine is assigned to host a partition of the co-occurrence matrix. Refer to Figure 1 above, the computing node i stores the co-occurrence vectors from rows $(i-1)I/NP$ to iI/NP, where I is a number of index terms and NP is the number of computing machines. The co-occurrence data in each machine is computed by the producer, while the update of co-occurrence matrix partition is done by the consumer.

To explain more clearly, the producer first extracts co-occurrence statistic from a local sub-collection, then identifies and sends this data to the consumer at its corresponding destination machine. The destination machines can be determined by consulting co-occurrence routing table. This table provides mapping between co-occurrence vectors and its host nodes. As for the consumer, it collects the incoming co-occurrence data and updates the co-occurrence vectors in its partition. To avoid the problem of I/O blocking, this algorithm employs MPI asynchronous communication.

After the co-occurrence matrix is constructed, the document vectors can be derived. During this phase, the producer reads a document from its local sub-collection, then converts it to a set of terms. Refer to the equation (1), as the co-occurrence matrix is located in each computing node, the producer send those terms to the corresponding consumers so that the portions of the final vector are computed. Finally, the producer gathers the portions of the final vectors from consumers to produce the required document vector.

3.1   System Tuning

In co-occurrence matrix computational process, there are a large amount of global messages transmitted to update remote co-occurrence partition. To reduce the number of communications, all of the co-occurrence statistics of documents are buffered until some thresholds are reached. This threshold can be the boundary of a document or multiple documents, then distributed to each consumer instead of element-by-element send.

To avoid a large number of remote co-occurrence matrix access, the producer caches some parts of each co-occurrence matrix in main memory. For the effectiveness of cache performance, only high document frequency parts of the co-occurrence matrix are cached. This can be done in the following way. First, index and context terms in the co-occurrence matrix are sorted by their document frequency in decreasing order. Second, co-occurrence vectors of index terms are distributed to each computing node using simple round-robin method. Then the co-occurrence vectors of high document frequency index terms which locate in the top rows of a partition are cached.

4   Experimental Results

In this section, we present the results concluding from two sets of experiments. For the first experimental setup, we study the computing performance between before and after using the buffering technique on the co-occurrence matrix computation process, and the caching technique on the indexing process. For the second experimental setup, we examine the scalability issue of our implementation by using a full set of half million-page TREC8 documents. All of experiments are performed on a cluster of 16 Intel Celeron 466MHz processors, each is equipped with 128MB of RAM and simple 10GB IDE drive. All computing nodes are connected via 100Mbps Ethernet switch.

4.1   Effect of Using Buffering and Caching Techniques

To study the effect of the buffering and caching technique in our multiple producer/consumer model, we use FBIS 140317 documents to be our test collection. We choose 20000 index terms and 2500 context terms, yielding the co-occurrence matrix of 20000 by 2500 elements. Several curves from Figure 2 and Figure 3 conclude the results from these experiments.

We can discuss these results into two parts. For the co-occurrence matrix computational process, a speedup factor is decreased when we test on two computing node. Since the co-occurrence matrix is divided and scattered to several consumers, there are many update data traveling between producer and host consumers via the network. Updating the co-occurrence matrix via network takes a large amount of time more than single machine takes to access the whole matrix in main memory. Thus the most of computational time is wasted for data traveling back and forth in the network. The speedup factor starts to increase while

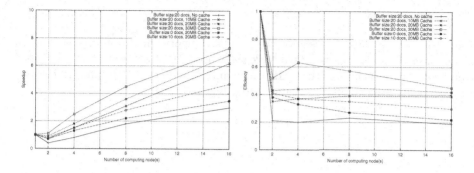

Fig. 2. Co-occurrence matrix computational process with caching and buffering technique.

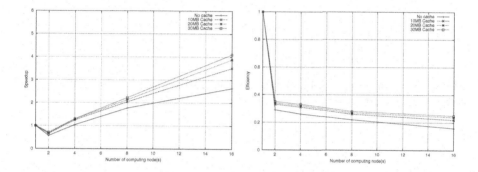

Fig. 3. Document vectors derivation process with caching technique.

the efficiency curve slightly decreases when we add more computing nodes into the system. Moreover, when larger buffer and cache size have been employed, we can achieve a higher speedup factor. This result shows that both buffering and caching technique help very much to reduce the network traffic between several consumers.

For the document vector derivation process, the caching technique has only a slightly effect on the speedup factor, even though larger size of cache has been added to the system. After examination closely what the problem occurs with the computing performance when increasing more cache size, we discover the fact that the producer must wait for a long time to gather large size of messages of document vector portions computed by the corresponding host consumers in order to derive the final document vector. Sending and receiving a large portion of messages via network is the main defect (of the message-passing library itself, perhaps) that causes the inefficiency of our caching technique proposed here.

4.2   Scalability

To study the scalability issue of the proposed algorithm, we set up the experiments in the following way. We took the whole TREC8 as our test collection, and reran experiments with 20MB cache and 20 buffer size. Results from these experiments are depicted in Figure 4 and Figure 5.

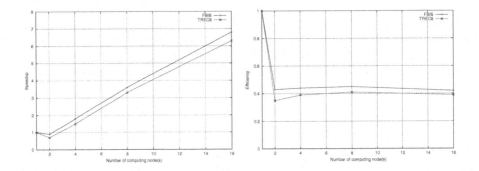

Fig. 4. Problem size scalability when using TREC8 as the test collection in co-occurrence matrix computation process.

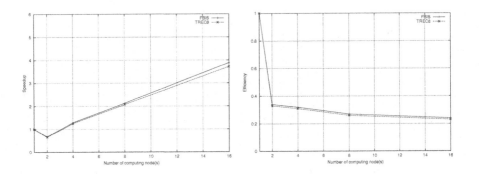

Fig. 5. Problem size scalability when using TREC8 as the test collection in document vectors derivation process.

The results show that our proposed algorithm still scales quite well when the problem size has been increased. This result show that multiple master-slave principle can assist to solve a large compute-intensive problem like large-scale text retrieval.

5   Conclusion

This paper proposes another parallel DSIR text indexing algorithm using multiple master/slave model, and presents experimental results using a large TREC8 collection. We illustrate that parallel and distributed computing technique like PC-cluster can be used to build an efficient tool for indexing a large text collection. In particularly, we have found that designing a fine grain parallel algorithm, i.e. co-occurrence matrix computation and document vector derivation, in DSIR model is not easy to achieve for a perfect speed-up due to the problem of computing too much inherently global data in the DSIR model itself. However, this problem can be alleviated by using caching and buffering technique. We also found that co-operative master/slave computing technique can be used to increase computing performance, and we believe that it is suitable for solving a large compute-intensive problem like information retrieval. We anticipate to ameliorating our parallel DSIR indexing algorithm and testing it with several million web-page documents in the next future.

Acknowledgement

We thank to MIKE staffs for their help and fruitful comments, especially N. Bunrupantunad, A. Laohakanniyom, J. Malawong, T. Supatwattana, J. Chaiwattanakulkit.

References

[1] T.E. Anderson et al. A case for nows. *IEEE Micro*, Febuary 1995.

[2] A. Rungsawang. Dsir: The first trec-7 attempt. In *Proceeding of the Seventh Text REtrieval Conference*. NIST Special publication, September 1998.

[3] A. Rungsawang and M. Rajman. Textual information retrieval based on the concept of the distributional semantics. In *Proceeding of the 13th International Conference on Statistical Analysis of Textual Data*, December 1995.

[4] Tangpong A. Rungsawang A. and Laohawee P. Parallel dsir text retrieval system. In *Recent Advances in Parallel Virtual Machine and Message Passing Interface proceeding/6th European PVM-MPI User's Group Meeting*, volume 1697, pages 325–332. Springer, September 1999.

[5] Robertson S. and Jones S. Relevance weighting of search terms. *American Society Information Science*, May-June 1976.

[6] P. Uthayopas. Beowulf class cluster: Opportunities and approach in thailand. In *First NASA workshop on Beowulf class computer systems*. NASA JPL, October 1997.

[7] E. Voorhees and D. Harman. Overview of the Eigth Text REtrieval Conference (TREC8). In *The Eight Text REtrieval Conference (TREC8)*. NIST, 2000.

[8] Marc Snir. Steve Otto. Steven Huss-Lederman. David Walke. and Jack Donggarra. *MPI:The complete Reference*, volume 1. The MIT Press, 1996.

[9] Barry Wilkinson and Michael Allen. *Parallel Programming:Techniques and applications using networked workstations and parallel computers*. Prentice hall, 1999.

Improving Optimistic PDES in PVM Environments [1]

Remo Suppi, Fernando Cores, Emilio Luque

Computer Science Department – Universitat Autònoma de Barcelona – Spain
Remo.Suppi@uab.es Fernando@aows10.uab.es E.Luque@cc.uab.es

Abstract. The implementation issues and results of a technique named Switch Time Warp (STW) for improving Optimistic Parallel Discrete Event Simulation (PDES) in PVM environments. The STW mechanism is used for limiting the optimism of the Time Warp method. The idea of the STW consists of attempting to adapt the execution speeds of the different LP dynamically in order to minimise the number of rollbacks, and as a consequence, reducing the simulation time. The proposed method achieves significant time/performance improvements for rollback reduction in PDES.

1 Introduction

The main objective of this paper is to describe the development and the evaluation of a tool designed to build distributed discrete event simulators based on Switch Time Warp algorithm [9][11]. This tool will have to demonstrate the validity of the algorithm proposed in [9] and at the same time is intended to be a step previous to building a flexible simulation environment that allows concrete problems within the field of the high performance simulation to be solved.

The simulation is one of the fields that requires most processing time and therefore parallel simulation is outlined as a useful tool to give response to given problems in an acceptable time.

Parallel simulation is also economically justified by the possibility of distributing the task between machines connected in a network (cluster). It is possible to develop high performance simulators taking advantage of normal (modest) machines incorporating some tools like PVM [8] to create a cluster-based parallel machine, i.e. PC-Linux cluster.

The problem of simulating the behaviour achievement of complex systems promises to be one of the problems that present us with the greatest range of possibilities in the forthcoming years. Problems such as air traffic control, the behaviour of telephony interconnection nets, meteorological predictions, behaviour of populations, distribution of information, etc. [5] can all require the obtention of information from parallel discrete event simulation.

---

[1] This work has been funded by the CICYT under contract TIC-98-0433

J. Dongarra et al. (Eds.): EuroPVM/MPI 2000, LNCS 1908, pp. 304-312, 2000.

2 Parallel Discrete Event Simulation (PDES)

The concept of a discrete event simulator can be defined as a model of a physical system that changes state only in discrete time instants and that it is controlled by events, i.e, the system observation is only accomplished during the occurrence instant of an event. Discrete event simulation is interesting since it does not imply greater complexity in obtaining an events model from a physical system. It is only necessary to extract the actions and the state changes that occur in the system.

2.1 Describing PDES Using an Example

To clarify the above observation we will consider an example of a physical system in predicting its behaviour. In this particular case we are interested in knowing the development of a population of wolves and goats obliged to live together. This system is within the prey-predator category. The wolf is a natural predator of the goats and therefore the goats are condemned to extinction. But the number of goats is much higher that the number of wolves and therefore they may not necessarily be wiped out. Once the physical system is identified, it is necessary (analysis phase) to obtain and define the events. In this case the conclusion is that there are basically 6 events that can be associated to an occurrence probability:

Event	Description	Probability
E1	A goat is born	0.1
E2	A wolf is born	0.08
E3	A goat dies (natural)	0.096
E4	A wolf dies (natural)	0.054
E5	A goat is eaten by a wolf	0.2
E6	Wolves die through insufficiency of food (goats).	0.00001

With this discrete event model it is necessary to build a simulator that will reproduce the behaviour of the physical system through these events. Moreover the following equations will be necessary to simulate the evolution of the populations:
1. ΔC = Goats that are born - Goats that die
2. ΔLL = Wolves that are born - Wolves that die
3. $C(t_n) = C (t_{n-1}) + \Delta C (t)$ ($C(t_n) = $ *Number of goats at t_n*)
4. $LL(t_n) = LL (t_{n-1}) + \Delta LL (t)$ ($LL(t_n) = $ *Number of wolves at t_n*)
5. Goats that die = goats that die of natural death + goats that are eaten
6. Wolves that die = wolves that die of natural death + wolves that die through lack of food

The variable t defines the current simulation instant (t_n is the virtual time at the instant n). The previous model proposed is very simple since it studies the interaction of two species. But if the goal is to study the evolution of a set of species, for example a model that includes 100 species, considering that in some degree all of them are predators, the problem becomes very complex. This situation would imply 10200 possible events to try for each simulation instant (100 for birth, 100 for natural deaths and 10000 for depredation). This, obviously, implies a temporary complexity of the problem and is intractable within a reasonable time. From here emerges the need for accelerating the simulation process. The Parallel Discrete Event Simulation (PDES) is the solution to this problem because it allows us to increase the computation power by using parallel/distributed systems. The idea is to divide the problem (events) into a set of partitions and to assign each one of these to a processor of the parallel/distributed system. These partitions will be linked by event exchange (timestamped messages in the distributed system). From the discrete event model described, a Parallel Discrete Event Simulator can be built. For this it is necessary to divide the discrete event simulator into a set of tasks (logical processes: LP's) so that each LP simulates a part of the model.

In our example, we can built a logical process "goats" that process the events generated by the goats (birth, death or depredation) and a "wolf process" that accomplishes the same task with the events generated by the wolves. It will also be necessary to have an interface of communication between the two processes to process those events generated by a process and consumed by the other (depredation). To profit from the availability of distributed systems, in simulation speed, it would be necessary to distribute the processes to a different processors.

Each LP processes external events (generated by others LPs) as well as internal events (generated by the internal/local processing of the events). Each event can change the local state of the system and / or to generate one or more new events. The global state of the system is defined in terms of the different local states of the LP's that form the simulation. The PDES can be seen as a set of interrelated processes where each one simulates a subspace of the space-time of the problem.

The main problem of the PDES is that depending on the distribution of LP's it should be able to assure that the simulated system is causal. The Local Causality Constraint (LCC) says: *A discrete event simulation that consists of a set of LP's interrelated through timestamped messages fulfills the causality principle if (only if) each LP processes the events in a non-decreasing order of time, i.e., the future cannot affect the past [2]*. The causality problem does not occur in the sequential simulator. In a PDES simulator it is necessary to assure that the processes act in synchronised form. We can consider for example that the wolves' process (of the previous example) will be implicitly slower than the goats' process. The wolves' process (slower) will have advanced to t_1 in their local time (local virtual time LVT) and the goats' process (faster) will have evolved to t_2 ($t_2 > t_1$). If at this time the wolf process generates an external event (E5 -A goat is eaten by a wolf-), this event will have to be processed by the goats' process in instant t_1 and not in t_2. The goats' process must comeback up to time t_1, and to cancel all the actions produced between t_1 and t_2. In this situation the principle of Local Causality Constraint (LCC) is unfulfilled.

As it is impossible to solve beforehand what the relative execution speed between the logical processes will be, a synchronisation mechanism is necessary. This synchronisation gives two different algorithm families in PDES: conservative and optimistic algorithms.

The conservative algorithms are those that strictly observe the causality principle. The quantity of parallelism that can be extracted from the conservative algorithms is very limited and it is generally because other types of algorithms (optimistic), which present a greater profit, are preferred.

Optimistic algorithms do not adhere strictly to the "LCC law", and for this reason, they can produce causality errors, but the algorithms have mechanisms to detect these errors and cancel their effects. In an optimistic algorithm, a LPi will remain blocked only if it does not have either input message or internal events to process. In other cases it will choose the event with the smallest timestamp. If at some subsequent time an event with a smaller time arrives, it will produce a causality error. At such a moment the algorithm will have to return to a sure state and to annihilate the effects produced from this state to the last event processed. This situation of returning to a sure state forces the algorithm to keep the old states in memory. This is one of the weak points of the algorithm. The Time Warp (TW) is the most referenced implementation of optimistic algorithms [5][2].

The TW algorithm is an optimistic mechanism based on the virtual time of each process. Each process LPi has its own local virtual clock (LVT). A causality error is detected when a process LP receives a message that contains a smaller timestamp than the LVT. In this situation the rollback mechanism is activated. This mechanism consists of returning to a sure state and annihilating the effects of the events processed from this state until the arrival of the event that produced the error. The principal problems of the TW that affect the speed of the simulation are: a) Lost of simulation work (rollbacks). b) Annihilation messages (anti-messages) sent to remove the previous incorrect messages. c) Spread of the annihilation messages if the destination process has already processed the wrong message (rollback chains).

3 Switch Time Warp Algorithm

In a TW mechanism the relative execution speeds of the different LP's cannot be controlled and the problem that some LP's have greatly progressed with respect to another can emerge. In this situation, the interrelation between low-high speed processes will generate rollback. An incorrect LP's speed balancing will generate a higher number of rollbacks and the processes will lose a lot of time in processing them; the speed profit introduced by the algorithm can therefore be very poor.

Several approaches have been developed to solve this problem: the Moving Time Window [10], the Breathing Time Window [13], the Adaptive Time Wrap Concurrency Control Algorithm [1], the Probabilistic Cost Expectation Function Protocol [3], or the PADOC Simulation Engine [4].

The idea of the proposed algorithm "Switch Time Warp (STW)" [9][11] consists of attempting to adapt the execution speeds of the different LP dynamically in order to minimise the number of rollbacks, and as a consequence, reducing the simulation time. Our model is based on the general case, where the number of LPs required for a simulation (n) do not match the number of processors available to run the simulator (p) with $n>>p$. In this case, the maximum simulation speed can be achieved by a full occupation of the available processors time, performing correct simulation work.

Our proposal includes a process manager (local scheduler) in each processor to locally monitor the dynamic behaviour of the LPs allocated in it. The main task of this manager is to optimise the CPU-time occupation by balancing the relative execution time of those LPs involved in *rollbacks*.

Once a certain threshold value for the number of rollbacks and anti-messages (anti-messages are sent to undo the incorrect work carried out by a process that a rollback executes) is detected in an LP, the process manager will try to adequate the relative speed of the implied processes. The manager will slow down the fastest LP involved in this high generation of rollbacks (assigning it less CPU time so as not to further advance its LVT), and spend that processing capability to accelerate slower LPs. The threshold value is the point at which we have to decide when it is necessary to limit the optimism of the TW. A detailed description of the STW algorithm can be found in [9].

4 Implementation Issues

The algorithm for STW is similar to the TW mechanism. The difference is that a new set of function calls have been added in order to compute the necessary values for evaluating whether the process runs in an optimistic/over-optimistic state. These functions are locally executed on the node, which add a fixed computing overhead to all the processes The overhead added by this process is very low for the effective utilisation-rate improvement obtained (4.5% (max) compared to the execution time of the TW) .

The STW has been implemented for Unix™ systems (SunOS 5.x) using PVM libraries [8] and STLv3 (Standard Template Library). PVM (Parallel Virtual Machine) facilitates work with an heterogeneous distributed machine. In our design of the STW mechanism, using PVM library, we associate a Unix process for each LP in our PDES scheme. This LP is a node in the distributed simulation application and communicates with other LP's using the PVM library functions. Figure 1 shows the STW processes hierarchy where the arrows indicate the precedence of the processes' creation. All the processes, except the "father" process, are created by the PVM spawn primitive and are controlled as a PVM group in each processor. The "father" process creates all the STW schedulers from the user configuration. In each processor, the STW scheduler creates the LPs that will execute the simulated application.

An important part of the implementation of the SWT mechanism has been the integration of the STW-scheduler with the CPU process-scheduler provided by the operating system. In our case (SunOS 5.x) the OS supports three types of scheduling classes for processes: Real-Time (RT), System (SYS) and Time-Sharing (TS). The LPs processes are executed in the TS class (and we assume that there are no processes in the RT class). The STW scheduler (that operates in highest priority TS class) oversees the behaviour of all LP processes and changes the priority of the process that run in an over-optimistic state (having an optimism greater that the threshold value). As the LP's receive the time slice proportional to the priority, the penalised process will receive less CPU time. With this new CPU time, "optimism" will be reduced and the STW scheduler will change (or not) the priority level for this.

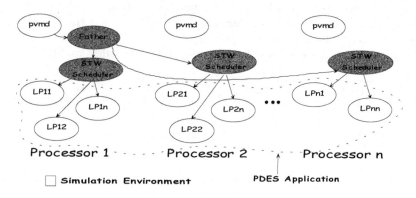

Fig. 1. STW Processes Hierarchy

5 Case Study and Results

To validate and evaluate the performance improvement obtained by the proposed STW method, we carried out a Ring Service Queuing (RQS) experiment, using two different environments: simulation and real execution. By simulation, a PDES including the STW has been simulated to run on a sequential simulator. In real execution a PDES including STW has been implemented for Unix and PVM as described in the previous section.

The RQS application is described in terms of a set of logical processes (Fig. 2). A RSQ graph has a set of nodes that receives input messages, generates internal events and sends output messages. This simple application presents large simulation problems under optimistic algorithms due to the high quantity of rollbacks and rollback chains that are produced.

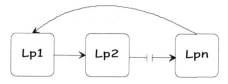

Fig. 2. Ring Service Queuing Model

5.1 Simulation

The simulation approach can be suitable in order to make some tests with a higher number of LP and processors. For this task, we used the **P**arallel **& D**istributed Algorithm-**A**rchitecture **S**imulator (PandDAAS) developed by the UAB [13]. In Pand-DAAS the distributed simulation is specified by an application graph (LP's) whose distributed execution is simulated in the sequential simulator PandDAAS.

By simulation we analysed RSQ applications from 10 to 500 LP (in the 500 LP graph, $15*10^6$ events have been processed). Table 1 shows the results for both methods in function of the time used by distributed simulation. We can verify that in all cases the STW method notably reduces the execution time of the simulation.

Number of Processes	TW Simul. Time (virtual time)	STW Simul. Time (virtual time)	Simulation Time Improvement (%)
10	13,567	11,807	15
50	96,657	59,373	53
100	256,092	165,802	46
500	26,455,566	13,843,024	91

Table 1. STW & TW Simulation Time & STW improvement (simulated)

5.2 Real Execution

For the analysis in a real environment (SolarisOS & PVM), we used RSQ applications with 2, 8, 16 and 20 logical processes (LP) using a pool of Sun SPARCStation. The average improvement of STW is 19,5% for 20 LP.

Table 2 illustrates the execution behaviour (1st & 2nd rows), the rollback reduction (3rd row) and the execution time improvement (4th row) for the RQS experiment of 2, 8, 16 and 20 LPs for STW and TW methods. We can observe that in the RQS experiment for 2 and 8 processes, the TW execution time is better than the STW (1st and 2nd columns), but the quantity of rollback messages has been reduced to 24.8% and 30.3% respectively. This situation arises due to the fixed overhead that introduces the calculation if a process is or is not in an over-optimistic state.

For 16 and 20 LP's it can be observed that the STW notably reduces the number of rollback messages (3rd and 4th columns). This reduction implies that, under the STW, the simulation has an execution time better than that for the TW. The execution time improvement increases with the number of LPs.

	2 LP	8 LP	16 LP	20 LP
TW Execution Time (seconds)	333	1,554	3,626	8,461
STW Execution Time (seconds)	372	1,573	3,146	7,079
Rollback Reduction (%)	24.8	30.3	36.4	42.9
Execution Time Improvement STW vs TW (%)	-10.5	-1.2	15.3	19.5

Table 2. Real execution of Time Warp and Switch Time Warp

6 Conclusions and Future Work

An improved method (STW algorithm) for optimistic PDES and its implementation using PVM has been presented and evaluated. To overcome rollback overhead in the TW mechanism, a solution based on the idea of "limiting the optimism" by distributing CPU time has been implemented. We have carried out the implementation of a dynamic adaptation of event processing capability (LP speed), based on balancing the implied LP relative speed (STW mechanism). An RQS application has been analysed using simulation and real execution. By simulation, potential improvement has been evaluated (91 % with respect to the TW for 500 LP's). The average improvement of STW is 19,5% in RSQ application for 20 logical processes executed under PVM in a pool of Sun SPARCstation. The differences between the simulation results and the real results can be attributed initially to the PVM communication model (all messages are centralised by the PVM daemon and this daemon is not present in simulation runs). In this sense, a change of communication model is necessary to obtain better results. The possibilities are the use of direct PVM communication method, or the use of another communication library with a different communication model (i.e. MPI [7]).

Future work is divided in two lines: a) Improvement of the real simulation environment: we need to make extensive tests to analyse the influence of the communication model. b) Mapping of the processes: The STW has a limit to when all process in a processor can be penalised, since the slowest processes are assigned to other processors. In this case, a load balancing technique is necessary.

The authors wish to thank to Pere Munt i Duran for his contribution in the development and implementation of the STW algorithm under PVM.

References

1. Ball, D., and Hoyt, S., The adaptive Time-Warp concurrency control algorithm. Proc. SCS Multiconference on Distributed Simulation 22 1 (1990) pp. 174-177.
2. Ferscha A., Parallel and Distributed Simulation of Discrete Event Systems. Handbook of Parallel and Distributed Computing. McGraw-Hill (1995).
3. Ferscha A., Lüthi J., Estimating Rollback Overhead for Optimism Control in Time Warp. Proc. 28th Simulation Symposium, IEEE Press (1995) pp. 2-12.
4. Ferscha A., Probabilistic Adaptive Direct Optimism Control in Time Warp. Proc. 9th Workshop on Parallel and Distributed Simulation (1995) pp. 245-250.
5. Fujimoto. R., Parallel Discrete Event Simulation. Com. ACM 33 10 (1990) pp. 30-53.
6. Lin, Y-B., Lazowska, E., Optimality considerations of "Time Warp" parallel simulation. Proc. SCS Multiconference on Distributed Simulation 22, 1 (1990) pp. 29-34.
7. MPI: a message passing interface standard. 94239, Univ. of Tennessee (April 1994).
8. PVM User's Guide. University of Tennessee. ORNL/TM 1287 (September 1994).
9. Serrano M., Suppi R., Luque E., Rollback reduction in optimistic PDES. Technical Report - University Autonoma of Barcelona (1999).
10. Sokol L.M., Briscoe D.P., and Wieland. A.P., MTW: a strategy for scheduling discrete simulation events for concurrent execution. Proc. SCS Multiconference on Distributed Simulation 19, 3 SCS International (July 1988) pp. 34-42.

11. R. Suppi, M. Serrano, F. Cores, E. Luque. STW. Switch Time Warp. A model for Rollback Reduction in Optimistic PDES. Parallel Computing '99 (Parco99). 1999. Proceedings will be published by Imperial College Press.
12. Steinmann J, Breathing TW. 7th Workshop P&D Simulation, IEEE (1993) pp. 109-118.
13. PandDAAS - Parallel & Distributed Architecture-Algorithm Simulator - User's Guide, Caos, University Autonoma of Barcelona. www.caos.uab.es. (1999)

Use of Parallel Computers in Neurocomputing

Szabolcs Payrits, Zoltán Szatmáry, László Zalányi, and Péter Érdi

KFKI Research Institute for Particle and Nuclear Physics of the Hungarian
Academy of Sciences, Department of Biophysics, P.O. Box 49,
H-1525 Budapest, Hungary
quador@rmki.kfki.hu, szaki@sunserv.kfki.hu, zala@rmki.kfki.hu,
erdi@rmki.kfki.hu
http://www.rmki.kfki.hu/biofiz/cneuro/cneuro.html

Abstract. Large-scale simulation of brain activity is based on a general theory within the frameork of statistical field theory. The theory and algorithm developed is now implemented to a cluster. By extending the computational capacity the simulation of normal and pathological cortical activity propagations became possible.

1. Neural Simulations

1.1 Neurodynamic System Theory

Dynamic system theory offers a conceptual and mathematical framework to analyze spatiotemporal neural phenomena occurring at different levels of organization, such as oscillatory and chaotic activity both in single neurons and in (often synchronized) neural networks, the self-organizing development and plasticity of ordered neural structures, and learning and memory phenomena associated with synaptic modification.

There are two basic strategies to learn more about integrated neural mechanisms. The inverse method start with activity data and results in data on functional connectivities among neural structures to be involved. Most of the inverse methods serve information about the static relationship of structural connectivities. The direct method, namely simulations based on physiologically realistic models of anatomical structures supplemented with hypothesis on the structural connectivites among substructures, serves simulated activity data to be compared by those derived from experimental techniques. *Simulators* are the proper methods to *test hypotheses* on the Functional Networks and the *mechanism* of *activity generation* and *propagation* through different brain regions [1].

1.2 Neuro-Simulators: A Short Survey

There are many neuro-simulators, see eg:
Neural Modeling Software
http://www.hirn.uni-duesseldorf.de/~rk/cneuroeu.htm

J. Dongarra et al. (Eds.): EuroPVM/MPI 2000, LNCS 1908, pp. 313-321, 2000.

They can be categorized into two classes:

1.2.1 **Conductance-based simulators** are proper tools for simulating single cell and small network dynamics. NEURON and GENESIS are the most extensively used softwares. Detailed single cell modeling had a renaissance after intracellular measuring methods were used for recording membrane potentials, and there was a hope to record even in different compartments of a single cell. We may consider this technique, as microscopic, which cannot be extened to make large-scale simulations.

1.2.2 **Neural Network based simulators** are generally artificial NN oriented, or they can be used for brain simulation without having the chance to incorporate realistic data. http://www.geocities.com/CapeCanaveral/1624/

2. Neurodynamical (Population) Model: Short History and Present Status

2.1 Brief History

There is a long tradition to try to connect the "microscopic" single cell behavior to the global "macrostate" of the nervous system, analogously to the procedures applied in statistical physics. Global brain dynamics is handled by using continuous (neural field) description instead of the networks of discrete nerve cells.

Ventriglia constructed a neural kinetic theory [2]. Having been motivated by this approach, a substantially improved new theory, algorithm and software tool were established in the Budapest Computational Neuroscience Group [3].

Our goals were:
- to give a general theory within the framework of statistical field theory and
- a computational model to simulate large-scale neural population phenomena and to monitor also the behavior of the underlying "average single cell"
- to prepare the simulating software
- to adopt the model for simulating different cortical population phenomena.

For the population behavior a *diffusion* model is defined which enables cells that are initially in the same state to be dispersed among different states. The model is equipped with some important features. Single Cell Model is integrated into the Population Equation. Continuum Model is Discretized and Scaled.

3. The Equations

The main partial differential equation describing the propagation of the population activity in the state space is the following :

$$\frac{\partial g_s(r,u,X,t)}{\partial t}+$$

$$+\frac{\partial}{\partial u}(\varepsilon_s(r,u,X,t)\,g_s(r,u,X,t))+\frac{\partial}{\partial X}(\eta_s(u,X)\,g_s(r,u,X,t))-$$

$$-\frac{D_u}{2}\frac{\partial^2 g_s(r,u,X,t)}{\partial u^2}-\frac{D_X}{2}\frac{\partial^2 g_s(r,u,X,t)}{\partial X^2}=$$

$$b_s(r,u,X,t)-n_s(r,u,X,t)$$

Where g is a probability density function (PDF) describing the activity at a given neural tissue point r, and at time t. The other two variables are random variables of the PDF, u stands for membrane potential and X stands for calcium concentration of the cell. This two variables constitute a two-dimensional probability density function for every point of the neural tissue and for every time point.
The calcium influx into the cell is:

$$\eta_s(u,X)=-\beta X-BI_{Ca}(u)$$

and the electric current

$$\varepsilon_s(r,u,X,t)=-\frac{1}{C_s}\sum_i I_s^{(i)}(u,X)-\frac{1}{C_s}\sum_{s'} I_{s's}^{syn}(r,u,t)$$

The $I_s^{(j)}$ currents are the currents generated by the membrane channels, and $I_{s,s'}$ is the synaptic current between population s and s', and defined as

$$I_{s's}^{syn}(r,u,t)=-\gamma_{s's}(r,t)(u-E_{s's})$$

Where γ is the post-synaptic conductance. This term includes the interaction between the points of the neural issue, so if the activity of a cell is high, it will cause other cells' membrane potential to rise, as follows:

$$\gamma_{s's}(r,t)=\int_{R_{s'}}\phi_{s'}(r')\int_0^{infinite}a_{s'}(r',t-t'-d_{s's}(r',r))A_{s's}(k_{s's}(r',r),t')dt'dr'$$

where we integrate on the whole space of the neural issue and $a_s(r,t)$ is the activity of population s at position r at time t, $\phi_{s'}$ is the density of the cells in the population at given position, $d_{s's}$ stands for the delay of the impact between two positions, $k_{s's}$ is the connection strength between the positions. If we excite a synapse, the effect of this excitation can be measured for a while on the postsynaptic cell, and the amount of this effect is a function of time and descibed by function $A_{s's}$.

g_s	PDF function of population s
r	location in real space
t	time
u	membrane potential
χ	calcium concentration
ε_s	electric current into the population s
η_s	calcium influx to the population s
b_s	ratio of the cells in population s returning from firing
n_s	ratio of the cells in population s which are going to fire
C_s, β, B	constants
$I_s^{(j)}$	input currents generated by the membrane channels
$I_{s,s'}$	synaptic current between population s and s'
γ	postsynaptic conductance function
$\phi_{s'}$	cell density function of the population s'
a_s	activity of the population s
$d_{s',s}$	delay of the inpact between two position
$k_{s',s}$	connection strenght between two position
$A_{s',s}$	synaptic current function

4. Discretization, Implementation

The discretization was done by having a uniform lattice regarding to the position in the neural tissue.. We also have a uniform lattice for the probability density function by variables u and χ .

The discretization of the equation describing the electric and calcium currents is simply done by sampling the function at the given discrete values of the variables.

The only remarkable problem arises when we would like to solve the partial differential equation at discrete points. We try to do that by playing upon the fact that

$g_s(r, u, \chi, t)$ is a probability density function and our purpose is to preserve at least the first two moments of it. Therefore we get a restraint on timestep and lattice resolution, as this amounts depend on each other.

The implementation is done in C++, having a class for every important object in the simulation, so every part of the program can be easily changed if necessary [4].

- class AlphaFunction describes the functions representing the synapses
- class Cell describes the properties of one cell.
- class ConnectionFunction defines the $k_{s',s}$ functions mentioned above
- class DensityFunction defines the $\phi_{s'}$ function above
- class Element implements the dynamics of one point in the neural issue
- class Grid implements the whole neural lattice
- class Pipe calculates the effect of the excitations a cell gets, it corresponds to the function $y_{s',s}$

5. How to Paralellize This Problem ?

The question is whether if it is possible to change the architecture of the program above to make it suitable for a distributed environment [1]. The most time-consuming piece of the program is the approximation of the partial differential equation describing the probability density functions g, and it is apparent that the dynamics of one point of the neural issue is relatively independent from the other points, the only influence of a point on an other one is through the function y .

The simplest and trivial change is to split the Element objects, having the interface on the main node, and doing the actual calculation on other machines. There is one more advantage of having a main node, for the user interface is much easier to implement this way.

We selected the PVM environment, for we have different kind of platforms working on, even though the same operating system on every machine.

We had one main process implementing all the classes but the actual calculation in the Element class, and in the constructor of the Element class we started a PVM child process, setting the inputs and getting the ouputs via PVM messages. In the destructor, we destroyed the PVM process. This way the parallelization is totally transparent, it is unseen for any object using the Element objects, it was needless to modify those part of the program.

6. Performance and Optimalizations

Given the implementaion above we achieved very poor performace. The utilization of the total processing power of the machines was pretty low, typically between 20 and 40 percent, depending on the resolution of the neural lattice, and the usage of the main node was 100%.

One of the main reasons of it was that only moving the Element objects into PVM children was not sufficient, for by using big lattices the number of connecton functions (y) grew quadratically. The calculation of the connections requires some processing power, which - because of the delay of a synaptic excitation is several timesteps long - at big lattices slows down the main node. Therefore we had to move not only the calculation of the activity function, but also the calculation of the connection function to the distributed environment, actually moving the Pipe classes to the PVM children.

We assumed that after this change we exploited the processing capabilities of the available machines, but we got only 60-80% processor time useage, even though the useage of the main node's processor time remained pretty low, about 10-20 percent.
It turned out that because of the asymmetrical architecture, while the main node routed the excitation data and did miscellenous calculations, user interface processing, the child processes ran idle. One way to avoid this would have been to transformed the architecture symmetrical, not having main process and implementing everything in PVM children.
As this would have made the implementaion more complex, and we would have lost the advatage of the transparency of the parallelization, we wanted to avoid dropping the asymetric architecture. We have rather chosen to implement an *asynchronous* architecture. It means that the child processes doesn't calculate the probability density function of the actual timestep, but the PDF at a *later* time point, therefore it is not needed to wait for the results of the calcuations done on the main node. The following figure is to illustrate the difference:

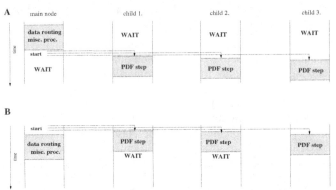

Fig.1. Time chart for synchronous and asynchronous architecture

We selected to calculate the following timestep in the child processes. The restraint, that every connection between the neural field's points has to be at least one timestep long, enables us this 'in advance' processing.

Given these two optimalizations, the processor time utilization climbed up to nearly 100%, typically above 95% not dependig on the discretization level.

8. Results

8.1 Hardware

We had the following hardware environment available for the simulations:

8.1.1 Sun Ultra 30
        UltraSparc II 250Mhz processor
        128 Mbyte RAM
        100 Mbit Ethernet adapter
        Linux 2.2 kernel

8.1.2 Linux cluster
        16 discless machines with 366 Mhz Intel processors
        128 MB RAM per machine
        Connected via 100 Mb Ethernet switch
        Linux 2.2 kernel
        Only visible node from outside is the main node, other nodes can be
        accessed through PVM [6],[7]

The results of our simulations on neural cortical structures [5] - performed by the above described cluster system - can be found on our web page at: http://www.rmki.kfki.hu/biofiz/lmate/duke/. The figures below show the increase in performance when multiple nodes are used in the calculations. Clearly, the time required for calculation drops inversely with the number of nodes applied. When the ratio of speedup is plotted against of the number of applied nodes an almost linear performance increase is observable.

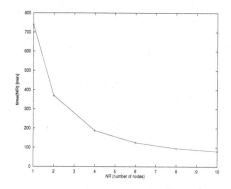
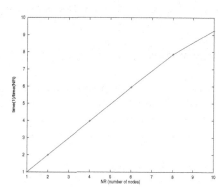

This boost in performance was achieved by the application of a cost-efficient cluster machine, which is comparable in performance with some multiprocessor architectures and is available for the fracture of their price. The table below shows the performance advantage of the cluster compared to the Sun Ultra 30.

Number of grids	Real time computing in seconds		Sun/cluster
	Linux cluster	Sun Ultra 30	running time fraction
8	26,6	211,55	7,95
18	54,66	546,8	10
32	76,86	921,5	11,98

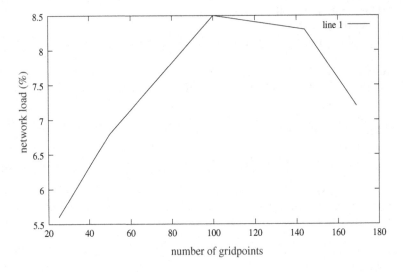

The computational efficiency could be decreased by the slow communication between the nodes. The figure below demonstrates low, 7-8% utilization of the communication capacity in reasonable discretization level.

9. Conclusions

Cluster systems and parallelization based on message-passing protocols are cost-effective solutions for neural simulations, as this simulations can be typically split into good separatable parts.

Acknowledgements

This work was supported by the National Science Research Council (OTKA T 025500 and OTKA T 025472).

References

1. Arbib, M., Érdi, P., Szentágotai, J.: Neural Organization: Structure, Function and Dynamics. MIT Press (1997)

2. Ventriglia, F.:.Kinetic Approach to Neural Systems.Bull. Math. Biol. **36** (1974) 534{544
3. Barna, G., Gröbler, T., Érdi, P.: Statistical model of the Hippocampal CA3 Region II. The Population Framework: Model of Rhythmic Activity in the CA3 Slice. Biol. Cybernetics **79** (1998) 308{321
4. Szatmáry, Z.: An Application of Statistical Neural Tissue Model on Clustermachine.   M. S. Thesis. Technical University of Budapest (2000)
5. http://www.dnaco.net/kragen/beowulf-faq.tex
6. http://www.cacr.caltech.edu/research/beowulf/tutorial/tutorial.html
7. http://beowulf-underground.org/doc_project/index.html
8. Kötter, R., Sommer, F. T.: Global Relationship between Anatomical Connectivity and Activity Propagation in the Celebral Cortex. Phil. Trans. R. Soc. Lond. **B 355** (2000) 127{134

A Distributed Computing Environment for Genetic Programming Using MPI

Francisco Fernández[2], Marco Tomassini[1], Leonardo Vanneschi[1], and Laurent Bucher[1]

[1] Computer Science Institute, University of Lausanne,
1015 Lausanne, Switzerland
[2] Dpto. Arquitectura y Tecnología de Computadores,
Universidad de Extremadura, Cáceres, Spain

Abstract. This paper presents an environment for distributed genetic programming using MPI. Genetic programming is a stochastic evolutionary learning methodology that can greatly benefit from parallel/distributed implementations. We describe the distributed system, as well as a user-friendly graphical interface to the tool. The usefulness of the distributed setting is demonstrated by the results obtained to date on several difficult problems, one of which is described in the text.

1 Introduction

Genetic Programming (GP) is a new evolutionary computing approach aimed at solving hard problems for which no specific algorithm works satisfactorily. GP is an heuristics based on the principles of biological evolution where individuals are selected for survival and reproduction according to their adaptation to the environment. GP considers the evolution of a population of computer programs which can potentially solve a given problem. Specific operators are defined in order to implement program mutation, crossover and selection. By defining a fitness measure to be attached to each individual in the population and by biasing the evolution towards fitter individuals, the iterative use of these operators drives the process towards programs that solve better and better the problem at hand. The GP approach was proposed by Koza at the end of the 1980s [5] and is now developing rapidly both in academia and industry. Individual programs in GP are expressed as parse trees using a restricted language that fits the problem to be solved. This language is formed by a user-defined *function set F* and *terminal set T* chosen such that it is thought to be useful *a priori* for the problem at hand.

As an example, suppose that we are dealing with simple arithmetic expressions in three variables. In this case suitable function and terminal sets might be defined as: $F = \{+, -, *, /\}$ and $T = \{A, B, C\}$. Some possible GP trees arising from these sets are shown in Figure 1, where the genetic operation of crossover (to be explained later) is also illustrated.

Evolution in GP is as follows. An initial random population of trees (programs) is constructed. A fitness value is assigned to each program after actual

J. Dongarra et al. (Eds.): EuroPVM/MPI 2000, LNCS 1908, pp. 322–329, 2000.

execution of the program (individual) and genetic operators are applied to selected individuals in order to produce new ones. The population size usually stays constant: new fitter individuals replace bad individuals. This cycle goes on until a satisfactory solution has been found or another termination criterion, such as maximum computing time, is reached. The aim in GP is to discover a program that satisfies a given number m of predefined input/output relations: these are called the *fitness cases*. For a given program p_i its fitness $f_j(p_i)$ on the j-th fitness case represents the difference between the output g_j produced by the program and the correct answer G_j for that case. The total fitness $f(p_i)$ is the sum of the errors over all m fitness cases: $f(p_i) = \sum_{k=1}^{m} \| g_k - G_k \|$. A better program will thus have a lower fitness under this definition, and a perfect one will score 0 fitness.

The crossover operation starts by selecting a random crossover point in each parent tree and then exchanging the sub-trees, giving rise to two offspring trees, as shown in Figure 1. Mutation is implemented by randomly removing a subtree at a selected point and replacing it with a randomly generated subtree.

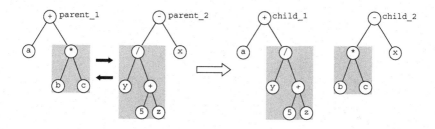

Fig. 1. Example of GP trees and of the crossover operation.

Although artificial evolution by GP has been cast as a sequential process for descriptive purposes, such evolution is intrinsically parallel. Genetic programming evolution is a robust but slow process. Hence, parallel execution is a welcome solution to reduce computing time. Parallel and distributed GP settings may also bring advantages from the algorithmic point of view. There are few studies in the field: early ones are [1], where a today obsolete Transputer-based parallel computer is used and [6]. Initial work by our group based on PVM with more restricted features and without graphical monitoring tools is described in [3]. Here we present a new and richer implementation of our distributed GP system using MPI. The present environment features a graphical user interface whose aim is both to make its use more intuitive for novices and to allow expert users to closely monitor the evolutionary process.

In section 2 we describe general modeling issues in parallel and distributed genetic programming. Section 3 gives details on our implementation of distributed GP. Following that, we describe the graphical user interface and monitoring tool.

Finally, a sample appplication to a difficult problem is commented and we offer our conclusions.

2   Distributed Genetic Programming

Genetic programming can be readily parallelized by introducing multiple communicating populations, in analogy with the natural evolution of spatially distributed populations. This model is called *island* or coarse-grain. Subpopulations may exchange information from time to time by allowing some individuals to migrate from one subpopulation to another according to various patterns. The main reason for this approach is to periodically reinject diversity into otherwise converging subpopulations. As well, it is hoped that to some extent, different subpopulations will tend to explore different portions of the search space. Within each subpopulation a standard sequential genetic programming evolutionary algorithm is executed between migration phases. The most common replacement policy is for the migrating n individuals to displace the n worst individuals in the destination subpopulation. The subpopulation size, the frequency of exchange, the number of migrating individuals, and the migration topology are new parameters of the algorithm that have to be set in some empirical way [1, 7].

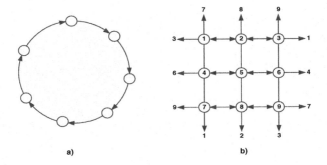

Fig. 2. Two commonly used distributed GP topologies: a) the "ring" topology, b) the "mesh" topology. Arrows represent message exchange patterns.

A few migration topologies have been used: the "ring", in which populations are topologically disposed along a circle and exchanges take place between neighbouring subpopulations and the "grid" where "meshes of islands", possibly toroidally interconnected, communicate between nearest neighbours. These topologies are illustrated in Figure 2. One possible drawback of these *static* topologies is that some bias might be introduced by the constant exchange pattern. *Dynamical* topologies, where destination nodes change during time seem more useful for preserving diversity in the subpopulations. We have used with success a "random" topology, where the target subpopulation is chosen randomly at each migration phase ([3] and see next section).

The performance increase in terms of computing time can be modeled as follows. The sequential GP runtime T^{seq} of a population of P individuals is determined by the genetic operators and by the fitness evaluation. Selection, crossover and mutation take time $O(P)$ since all these operators act on each individual and perform a transformation independent of the program size. The fitness calculation is the most important part and its complexity $T_{fitness}$ is $O(PCm)$: each individual is evaluated m times and each evaluation takes on average C arithmetic or logical operations. Here C is the average program complexity (i.e. the number of nodes in the tree structure) and m is the number of fitness cases. The total sequential time is thus $T^{seq} = gT_{population} + gT_{fitness}$, where g is the number of generations.

Consider the island model where N populations of P/N individuals each are equally distributed on a system of N machines. Now the genetic operators take time $O(P/N)$ while fitness evaluation is $O((P/N)Cm)$. The only overhead is given by the communication of migrating individuals which takes time $O(k(P/N)C)$. Here $k \sim 0.05$ is an empirical constant which represents the fraction of migrating individuals; thus, communication time is small with respect to the other terms.

Finally, if we consider an asynchronous island model where migration takes place with non-blocking primitives, the communication time is almost completely overlapped with computation and can be neglected to first approximation. Therefore, $T^{par}_{fitness} = (1/N)T^{seq}_{fitness}$ and $T^{par}_{population} = (1/N)T^{seq}_{population}$, giving nearly linear speedup. Of course, the preceding argument only holds for dedicated parallel machines and unloaded clusters and does not take into account process spawning, message latency time and distributed termination. Nevertheless, GP is an excellent candidate for parallelization as shown by the results presented here and in [1, 6, 2].

3   MPI Implementation

The implementation of the tool described in this work can be divided into two components: a parallel genetic programming *kernel* implemented in C++ and with MPI message passing, and a graphical *user interface* written in Java. The parallel system was designed starting from the public domain GPC++ package [8]. Here we present the kernel and its parallelisation strategy, while the graphical monitoring tool is described in the next section.

The computation can be basically thought of as a collection of processes, each process representing a population for the specific genetic programming problem. The processes/populations can be evolved in parallel and exchange information using the MPI primitives. The messages exchanged by these processes are groups of GP individuals and the communication happens through another process called the *master* that runs in parallel with the others and that implements a given communication topology. The master also sends termination signals to the other processes at the end of the evolution. In this configuration, each process/population executes the following steps:

While termination condition not reached **do in parallel** for each population

- Create a random population of programs;
- Assign a fitness value to each individual;
- Select the best n individuals (with $n \geq 0$) and send them to the master;
- Receive a set of n new individuals from the master and replace the n worst individuals in the population;
- Select a set of individuals for reproduction;
- Recombine the new population with crossover;
- Mutate individuals;

And the master process executes the following steps:

For each population **do**

- Receive n individuals;
- Send them to another population according to the chosen topology;

Before sending the individuals to the master, each population packs these trees into a message buffer. The master receives the buffer and directly sends it to another population. In this way, the data can be exchanged between processes with only one send and receive operation, and the packing and unpacking activities are performed by the population managing processes. The user can parameterize the execution by setting the value of n, the number N of individuals in each population and the communication topology among others. The comunication between the processes/populations and the process/master is *synchronous* in the sense that all the processes/populations wait until they have received all the n new individuals before going on with the next iteration.

One important feature of the system is that it allows to easily model several communication topologies, such as those depicted in Figure 2. The communication paths in these mesh and ring topologies are implemented by the master process.

To implement the random topology, the master, each time it receives a block of individuals from a population calculates a random number between 1 and the total number of processes and sends the block to the population whose MPI process ID corresponds to that number (the process ID of the master is 0). In order to promote fairness, a second constraint that is enforced by the system is that each population must receive a block of individuals before an exchange cycle is finished.

4   Graphical User Interface and Monitoring Tools

Most evolutionary computation environments do not feature a graphical user interface (GUI). This is inconvenient since parameter setting and other choices have to be done in old-style file-based fashion, which is obscure and difficult for the beginners to work with. Even the experienced researcher may benefit from a more user-friendly environment, especially if she wishes to closely monitor the

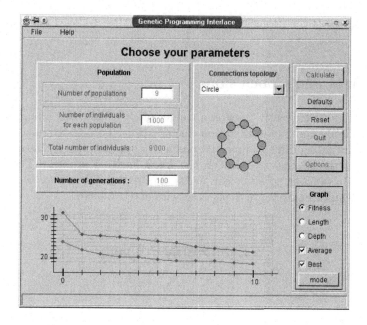

Fig. 3. The monitoring graphical user interface.

complex evolutionary process since this might shed light into the nature of the evolution itself.

Our GUI is written in standard Java and it was designed so as to be clean and easy to use. It communicates with the computation kernel through bi-directional channels and also starts the distributed computation. Information is displayed on a window featuring the actions that the user can follow, an example of which is given in Figure 3. The following is a succint description of the actions and the information available to the user. The parameters for the run can be entered using the text fields for that purpose and if some parameter is not provided the system warns the user. Pre-defined standard default parameter settings are also proposed. Some less important parameters, which also have default values, can be set from a second window that appears by clicking the "options" button. Run-time quantities such as best and average fitness, average program complexity and size of the trees can also be calculated and displayed at any time during the run. The example in Figure 3 shows a graph of the average and best fitness for the population as a whole. The interface can also display the tree corresponding to the best current solution in raw or simplified form. The topology can be chosen from a list in the panel "connection topology" and an icon on the window shows the type selected ("ring" in the Figure). Facilities for end-of-run calculation of several useful statistics are also provided. We plan to add the possibility of examining statistics for each single node by clicking on the corresponding icon or by using a node number in a list. Color codes can also be useful for representing different states of the evolution process or to visualize nodes that are receiving or sending messages.

5   Results and Conclusions

The environment currently runs on a cluster of PCs under the Linux operating system, as well as on Sun workstation clusters. It has been tested on a number of problems, including difficult financial prediction applications [2]. In this section, we describe the results obtained on the *Even Parity 5* problem. The boolean *even-k-parity function* of k boolean arguments returns *True* if an even number of its Boolean arguments are *True*; otherwise it returns NIL.

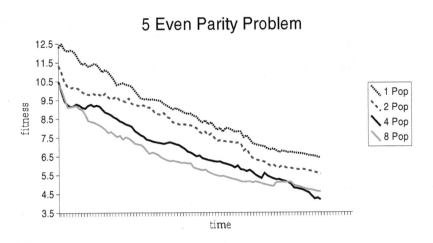

Fig. 4. Convergence results for the 5 Even Parity Problem, with 3200 individuals subdivided into 1, 2, 4, 8 populations.

Measurements have been performed on a population of 3200 individuals, on 2 populations of 1600 individuals each, on 4 populations of 800 individuals each and on 8 populations of 400 individuals each. The other key parameters of the runs were: random communication topology, maximum number of generations= 100, crossover rate= 0.95, mutation rate= 0.1, tournament selection. Figure 4 shows the average fitness as a function of the evolution time for the four implementations. Since GP is a stochastic algorithm, these curves represent averages over twenty different runs. These results show clearly that the distributed setting gives faster convergence toward the optimal solution (fitness = 0). In particular, we note that the 4- and 8-populations cases show faster convergence than the single population or 2-populations cases. One might be led to believe that further partitioning of the populations is always beneficial.

However, we have shown elsewhere [4] that for many problems there is a convenient total number of individuals and of subpopulations that gives the most cost-effective results for a given predetermined computational cost. Thus, it is not useful to keep adding individuals or to distribute them into more smaller populations above a certain limit.

Although there are also time savings due to parallel execution (see section 2), we did not measure speedup data since the cluster of workstations employed for the experiments was always in use for many other processes as well.

Currently, the system is being used on real-life machine learning applications, especially in the field of finance. As well, we use the system to perform experimental studies of distributed GP on several classical benchmark problems. This is a part of a longer term project whose aim is a better understanding of the dynamics of multi-population GP by way of experiment and by theoretical modeling. In the future, we plan to extend the capabilities of the system towards totally asynchronous execution and to a geographically enlarged metacomputing framework.

References

[1] D. Andre and J. R. Koza. Parallel genetic programming: A scalable implementation using the transputer network architecture. In P. Angeline and K. Kinnear, editors, *Advances in Genetic Programming 2*, pages 317–337, Cambridge, MA, 1996. The MIT Press.

[2] B. Chopard, O. Pictet, and M. Tomassini. Parallel and distributed evolutionary computation for financial applications. *Parallel Algorithms and Applications*, 2000. (to appear).

[3] F. Fernández, J. M. Sánchez, M. Tomassini, and J. A. Gómez. A parallel genetic programming tool based on pvm. In J. Dongarra, E. Luque, and Tomás Margalef, editors, *Recent Advances in Parallel Virtual Machine and Message Passing Interface*, volume 1697 of *Lecture Notes in Computer Science*, pages 241–248. Springer-Verlag, Heidelberg, 1999.

[4] F. Fernández, M. Tomassini, W. F. Punch III, and J. M. Sánchez. Experimental study of multipopulation parallel genetic programming. In Riccardo Poli, Wolfgang Banzhaf, William B. Langdon, Julian F. Miller, Peter Nordin, and Terence C. Fogarty, editors, *Genetic Programming, Proceedings of EuroGP'2000*, volume 1802 of *LNCS*, pages 283–293. Springer-Verlag, Heidelberg, 2000.

[5] J. R. Koza. *Genetic Programming*. The MIT Press, Cambridge, Massachusetts, 1992.

[6] M. Oussaidène, B. Chopard, O. Pictet, and M. Tomassini. Parallel genetic programming and its application to trading model induction. *Parallel Computing*, 23:1183–1198, 1997.

[7] T. Starkweather, D. Whitley, and K. Mathias. Optimization using distributed genetic algorithms. In H.-P. Schwefel and R. Männer, editors, *Parallel Problem Solving from Nature*, volume 496 of *Lecture Notes in Computer Science*, pages 176–185, Heidelberg, 1991. Springer-Verlag.

[8] T. Weinbrenner. Genetic Programming Kernel version 0.5.2 C++ Class Library. *University of Darmstadt*.

Experiments with Parallel Monte Carlo Simulation for Pricing Options Using PVM

Adrian Rabaea and Monica Rabaea

Department of Computer Science and Numerical Methods
"Ovidius" University of Constantza
Blvd. Mamaia 124, 8700 Constantza, Romania
{arabaea,mrabaea}@univ-ovidius.ro

Abstract. Pricing options often requires use of Monte Carlo methods in financial industries. We describe and analyze the performance of a cluster of personal computers dedicated to Monte Carlo simulation on the evaluation of financial derivatives. Usually, Monte Carlo simulation (MCS) requires too much computer time. This requirement limits most of MCS techniques to use supercomputers, available only at supercomputer centers. With the rapid development and low cost of PCs, PC clusters are evaluated as a viable low-cost option for scientific computing. The free implementation of PVM is used on fast ethernet based systems. Serial and parallel simulations are performed.

1   Introduction

Among the different numerical procedures for valuing options, the Monte Carlo simulation is well suitable for the construction of powerful pricing models. It is especially useful for single variable European options where, as a result of a non-standard pay-out, a closed-form pricing formula either does not exist or is difficult to derive. In addition, the price of complex options is sometimes difficult to explain intuitively and a simulation can often provide some insight into the factors that determine the pricing.

The commonly used Monte Carlo simulation procedure for option pricing can be briefly described as follows: firstly simulate sample paths for the underlying asset price; secondly compute its corresponding option payoff for each sample path; and finally, average the simulated payoffs and discount the average to yield the Monte Carlo price of an option.

An option is a contract that gives you the right to buy or sell an asset for a specified time at a specified price. This asset can be a "real" asset such as real estate, agricultural products, or natural resources, or it can be a "financial" asset such as stock, bond, stock index, foreign currency, or futures contract. Essentially, by buying the option, you transfer your risk to the entrepreneur selling you the options.

Therefore, an option is a contract between two parties: a buyer and a seller (or option writer). The buyer pays to the seller a price called the premium, and

J. Dongarra et al. (Eds.): EuroPVM/MPI 2000, LNCS 1908, pp. 330–337, 2000.

in exchange, the option writer gives to the buyer the right to buy or sell some underlying securities at some specified price for some specified period of time.

An option to buy is a call option, and an option to sell is a put option. The specified price is called the strike or exercise price, and the option's life is called the time to maturity or time to expiration. If the right to exercise is "any time until maturity" then the option is called an American option. If the right to exercise is "at time of maturity" then the option is called an European option.

2   The Black-Scholes Model

We denote by $S(t)$ the stock price at the time t. In the certainty case, the stock price at the time of the option's maturity T, equals the future value of the stock price $S(0)$ when continuously compounded at the risk-free interest rate r, $S(T) = S(0)e^{rT}$. One way to think about this is that the future value is the end result of a dynamic process. That is, the stock price starts at $S(0)$ at the present time 0, and evolves through time to its future value.

The formal expression that describes how the stock price moves through time in the certainty case is: $dS/dt = rS$ (this says that the rate of change of the stock price over time is proportional to the stock price at time t). The expression above describes the dynamic stock price process in a world with certainty. We can rewrite the equation as: $dS/S = rdt$. In this form, r is the instantaneous rate of stock's return (r is also called the drift rate of the stock price process).

If instantaneous return is r, its logarithm is a continuously compounded return. For the case of no uncertainty, the drift rate for the logarithm of this process is the same, but in an uncertain world this is not the case.

In a world with uncertainty and risk-averse investors, we expect that the instantaneous return from the stock, noted μ, will exceed the instantaneous risk-free rate of return (i.e. $\mu > r$). We must add a source of randomness to the instantaneous rate of return which has statistical properties that capture the fact that observed stock prices vary, and that a typical stock price path has variance which increases with time.

Black and Scholes [2] assume a model for stock price dynamics that is formally described as geometric Brownian motion. This model has the following form:

$$\frac{dS}{S} = \mu dt + \sigma dW \quad , \quad t \in [0, T] \tag{1}$$

where the parameters μ and σ are constant with respect to t and S. Here there are two factors that affect the instantaneous rate of return on a stock. The first one is the time. Over the period of time dt, the stock's return changes by the amount μdt. The second factor is uncertainty. The sensitivity to this source of uncertainty is captured by the term σ which is the volatility coefficient for the stock price. The net effect of adding the term σdW to the certainty model is to create a stochastic path for stock prices around the certainty path. Uncertainty in the model is added to let the model better satisfy properties exhibited by real world stock price.

Let $f(S, t)$ denote the value of any derivative security (e.g. a call option) at time t, when the stock price is $S(t)$. Using Ito's lemma,

$$df = \sigma S \frac{\partial f}{\partial S} dW + \left(\mu S \frac{\partial f}{\partial S} + \frac{1}{2} \sigma^2 S^2 \frac{\partial^2 f}{\partial S^2} + \frac{\partial f}{\partial t} \right) dt$$

and assuming that there are no arbitrage opportunities on the market, we get the following parabolic partial differential equation (PDE)):

$$\frac{\partial f}{\partial t} + rS \frac{\partial f}{\partial S} + \frac{1}{2} \sigma^2 S^2 \frac{\partial^2 f}{\partial S^2} - rf = 0 .$$

This is called the Black-Scholes partial differential equation. Its solution, subject to the appropriate boundary condition for f, determines the value of the derivative security. For an European call option, the boundary condition is

$$f(S, T) = \max\{0, S(T) - K\} ,$$

where K is the strike price and T is the time to expiration.

The solution of the above PDE is given by the Black-Scholes formula :

$$C = SN(d_1) - Ke^{-rT} N(d_2) , \tag{2}$$

where

$$d_1 = \frac{\log(S/K) + (r + \sigma^2/2)T}{\sigma\sqrt{T}} , \qquad d_2 = d_1 - \sigma\sqrt{T}$$

and N is the cumulative standard normal distribution.

Therefore, there are five parameters which are essential for the pricing of an option: the strike price K, the time to expiration T, the underlying stock price S, the volatility of the stock σ, and the prevailing interest rate r.

In some cases, the type of option is so complicated (for example, in (1) μ or σ are random) that the solution of the PDE is very difficult to be found. When this is the case, it is nearly always possible to obtain the option price by an approximation using an appropriate - maybe computationally intensive - numerical method. The standard methods are discussed in [3].

3   Monte Carlo Simulation

Usually, for solution of financial problems, the Monte Carlo Simulation (MCS) methods are used (e.g. to value European options and various exotic derivatives). But, because such kind of problems are very complicated, the MCS algorithms becomes too computational "expensive". On the other hand, due to the inherent parallelism and loose data dependencies of the above mentioned problems, Monte Carlo algorithms can be very efficiently implemented on parallel machines and thus may enable us to solve large-scale problems which are sometimes difficult or prohibitive to be solved by the other numerical methods. For implementing Monte Carlo method to price European options, the following procedure is used:

- for the life of the option, simulate sample paths of the underlying state variables in the pricing model,
- for each path, calculate the discounted cash flows of the option
- take the sample average of the discounted cash flows over all sample paths.

For pricing European calls, we have to compute $E(S(T)-K)^+$, where $(S(T)-K)^+ = \max\{S(T) - K, 0\}$. Then, we compute the call value C by

$$C = \exp(-rT)E(S(T) - K)^+ . \tag{3}$$

As we already have mentioned in Section 2, the assets follow a geometric Brownian motion and the stock price $S(t), t \in [0, T]$ are log-normally distributed. For a given partition $0 = t_0 < t_1 < ... < t_N = T$ of the time interval $[0, T]$, a discrete approximation to $S(t)$ is a stochastic process $\tilde{S}_t$ satisfying

$$\tilde{S}_{k+1} = \tilde{S}_k \exp((r - \frac{1}{2}\sigma^2)\delta t + \sigma\sqrt{\delta t}Z_k) , \tag{4}$$

for $k = 0, 1, ..., N - 1$ (where we used the subscript k instead of the time step subscript t_k), with $\delta t = t_{k+1} - t_k = T/N$, and initial condition

$$\tilde{S}(0) = S(0) , \tag{5}$$

where

- $Z_0, Z_1, ..., Z_{N-1}$ are independent standard normal random variables, and
- $\sigma\sqrt{\delta t}Z_k$ represents a discrete approximation to an increment in the Wiener process of the asset.

The call price estimate is then computed using the discount formula (3). After repeating the above simulation for a large number of time steps, the initial call value is obtained by computing the average of estimates for each simulation. The disadvantage of the Monte Carlo simulation for European options is the need of a large number of trials in order to achieve a high level of accuracy.

4   Cluster Architecture

Clusters of computers (workstations) constructed from low-cost platforms with commodity processors are emerging as a powerful tool in computational science. These clusters are typically interconnected by standard local area networks, such as switched Fast Ethernet. Fast Ethernet is an attractive option because of its low cost and widespread availability. However, communication over Fast Ethernet incurs relatively high overhead and latency. But, for our above described problem, the communication requirements are insignificant.

We used a cluster of 10 PCs, each of them having Compaq Deskpro Intel 200MHz Pentium-MMX processor, with 64MB of RAM. For the Fast Ethernet networking we used a 3Com Fast EtherLink XL 10/100Mb TX (Ethernet NIC 3C905B-TX) PCI network cards and a 3COM Super Stack II Baseline 10/100 Switch 3C16464A switch.

The Windows 95 distribution was used. Three years ago, this cluster costed $10,000 but with the current depreciation of computer hardware it is now much cheaper.

5   Parallel Implementation

The Monte Carlo method for pricing derivatives is an ideal candidate for the use of PVM software. As stated above, the Monte Carlo can take up to hours to run. Using PVM ([1], [5]), this disadvantage can be eliminated.

We implemented parallel Monte Carlo simulation on a cluster described in Section 4 before under PVM and we applied master/slave approach. As we have already mentioned in the above Section 4, the MCS for pricing option allowed us to have minimal communication, i.e. to pass to each processor only the parameters:

- $S0$ = initial underlying stock price,
- K = strike price,
- σ = volatility of the stock,
- r = prevailing interest rate,
- δt = length of interval in uniform N-period partition for time T,
- T = time to expiration,
- $NSIMP$ = number of Monte Carlo simulations per processor,

to run the algorithm in parallel on each processor by computing the option's value for $NSIMP$ simulations and, at the end, to collect the results from slaves without any communication between sending the parameters and receiving the call value. The only communication is at the beginning and the end of the algorithm execution which allows us to obtain very high efficiency for our parallel implementation.

This algorithm was implemented using the PVM MASTER/SLAVE model. The MASTER program is responsible for sending/receiving parameters to/from slaves and computing the final value. Each SLAVE receives from the MASTER program the parameters it needs for computation, computes and sends back the results.

There is a worker process (task) per node (processor); the master process can either share a node with a worker process or run on a dedicated node.

M. The MASTER program
    1. The MASTER process send to all SLAVE processes the parameters: $S0$, K, σ, r, δt, T, $NSIMP$ which are necessary for calculating C;
    2. The MASTER process receives from each SLAVE process the computed value of C ;
    3. The MASTER process computes the final option price.

S. The SLAVE program
    1. Each SLAVE process receives parameters from the MASTER process for computing initialization;
    2. The SLAVE process performs its local computation (to evaluate C, using (3), (4) and (5)) ;
    3. The SLAVE process sends the results back to the MASTER process.

6   Numerical Tests

We performed a simulation study using the Black and Scholes model. The Monte Carlo option price for a given $NSIMP$ and p processors can be computed according to above algorithm.

The numerical tests were made on a cluster of 10 PC, under PVM, for $r = 0.07$, $S0 = 100.00$, $K = 95.00$, $\sigma = 0.20$ and $T = 0.25$. The theoretical value computed according to (2) is $ST = 8.056$. We tested the methods in the European case because the true price can be analytically determined.

For $\delta t \in \{10^{-2}, 10^{-3}\}$ we generated Monte Carlo option price estimates. These prices were computed with $10^1, ..., 10^6$ sample paths in order to examine the impact caused by different numbers of sample paths. For each test we priced options and computed the *error = theoretical value - Monte Carlo simulation value*. The numbers in Table 1 and Table 2 represent the errors for $\delta t = 0.001$ and $\delta t = 0.01$, respectively. The first column in both tables indicates the number of simulation steps per processor.

Table 1. Errors for Monte Carlo Simulation using $\delta t = 0.001$

p NSIM	1	2	3	4	5	6	7	8	9	10
10^1	-3.700	+1.312	-2.322	-0.950	-0.474	+0.909	+0.650	+0.197	-0.998	-1.811
10^2	-0.889	-0.273	-0.306	-0.327	-0.004	+0.179	-0.398	+0.018	-0.271	+0.283
10^3	+0.041	+0.113	-0.060	-0.135	+0.114	+0.052	+0.065	+0.088	-0.135	+0.078
10^4	+0.059	-0.037	+0.043	-0.049	+0.031	+0.004	+0.005	+0.000	-0.039	-0.022
10^5	+0.008	+0.026	+0.007	-0.004	-0.007	+0.009	+0.004	+0.002	-0.016	+0.003
10^6	+0.005	+0.005	-0.000	-0.004	-0.004	-0.004	-0.007	+0.006	-0.001	+0.001

Table 2. Errors for Monte Carlo Simulation using $\delta t = 0.01$

p NSIM	1	2	3	4	5	6	7	8	9	10
10^1	-2.970	-2.168	+0.006	+0.158	-1.853	-0.400	-1.038	+0.030	-1.718	-0.743
10^2	-0.830	-0.200	+0.557	+0.302	+0.273	-0.170	+0.568	-0.377	+0.252	+0.239
10^3	-0.021	-0.120	-0.195	-0.248	+0.228	-0.082	+0.006	-0.044	-0.080	-0.145
10^4	+0.044	+0.051	+0.045	-0.005	+0.061	-0.007	-0.011	-0.009	-0.055	+0.000
10^5	-0.014	-0.031	-0.014	+0.004	+0.000	-0.000	-0.012	-0.028	+0.004	-0.007
10^6	+0.003	+0.005	+0.007	+0.003	-0.002	-0.004	+0.002	-0.000	+0.004	+0.000

We can observe that the error decreases when the number of sample paths increases. Unfortunately, in the same time we have to observe a disadvantage of the Monte Carlo simulation for European options. This consists in the large number of trials necessary to achieve a high level of accuracy.

In all tests we used the *gasdev* routine for generating random deviates with a normal distribution (Box-Muller method) and the pseudo random generator *ran2* as the source of uniform deviates (the long period random number generator of L'Ecuyer with Bays-Durham shuffle and added safeguards) [4]. The results are sensitive to the initial seed. Figure 1 shows the results of Monte Carlo simulation obtained with randomly chosen initial seeds.

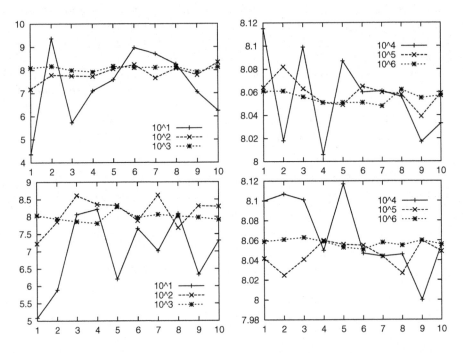

Fig. 1. Computed option price with respect to number of processors, using MCS method for $10^k, k = 1, ..., 6$ sample paths (upper: $\delta t = 0.001$, down: $\delta t = 0.01$)

Theoretically, we can obtain an arbitrary degree of accuracy. But, from a practical view point, higher is the level of accuracy, bigger will be the computational effort for the MCS algorithm. This is, of course, due to the well-known fact that the standard error of Monte Carlo estimate is inversely proportional to the square root of the number of simulated sample paths.

The quality of the random number generator is essential. We used pseudo random generator. This random generator often requires a very large number of simulation repetitions to minimize errors. It is possible to use quasi random generators that are designed simply to fill the space in an interval more uniformly than uncorrelated random points.

In a more formal sense, using quasi random generators we can reduce the error associated with a simulation from $\mathcal{O}(1/\sqrt{N})$ to $\mathcal{O}(1/N)$.

The parallel efficiency E, as a measure that characterizes the quality of the parallel algorithm, is defined as: $E = \frac{T_1}{pT_p}$, where T_p is the value of the computational time for implementation the algorithm on a system of p processors. The parallel efficiency and the percentages of work, random generation and latency, in all Monte Carlo repetitions, are given in Table 3.

Table 3. Computing time and efficiency for 10,000 simulations and $\delta t = 0.001$

Time in seconds	% random generator	% work	% latency	efficiency
13	62 %	37 %	1 %	99 %

We observe that a substantial computing time is used to generate random numbers. The time required to perform 10.000 sample paths depend on the latency of the network; it is variable because the network is a shared resource. But, when network is "free", the latency is very small.

7   Conclusions

The problem of pricing options by parallel Monte Carlo numerical methods is considered. Numerical tests were performed for a number of PCs using PVM on a cluster of personal computers.

This study describes an application of parallel computing in the finance industry. Options are continuously growing more complex and exotic, and for an increasing number of pricing problems, no analytical solutions exist. This is where the advantage of Monte Carlo methods appears.

Parallel models are required for performing large scale comparisons between model and market prices. Parallel models are useful tools for developing new pricing models and applications of pricing models.

In our parallel implementation we calculated one price of the call option. To compute this price by Monte Carlo simulation we need more computational power. Using p processors the execution time is p times small.

References

1. Beguelin, A., et al: A Users' Guide to PVM Parallel Virtual Machine, Oak Ridge National Laboratory, U.S. Department of Energy Contract, DE-AC-05-84OR21400.
2. Black, F., Scholes, M.: The pricing of Options and Corporate Liabilities, Journal of Political Economics 81, 1973, 637-659
3. Hull J.: Options, Futures, and Other Derivative Securities, Prentice-Hall, 1993
4. Press, W., Teukolsky, S., Vetterling, W., Flannery, B.: Numerical Recipes in C, Second Edition, Cambridge University Press, 1992
5. Scott, S. L. ,Fischer, M., Geist, A.: PVM on Windows and NT Clusters, EuroPVM-MPI98, Lecture Notes in Comp. Science, Springer Verlag, 1998

Time Independent 3D Quantum Reactive Scattering on MIMD Parallel Computers

Alessandro Bolloni, Stefano Crocchianti, and Antonio Laganà

Dipartimento di Chimica
Università di Perugia
via Elce di Sotto, 8
06123 Perugia (Italy)

Abstract. An exact three dimensional quantum reactive scattering computational procedure (APH3D) aimed at calculating the reactive probability for atom diatom chemical reactions has been parallelized. Here, we examine the structure of the parallel algorithms developed to achieve high performances on MIMD architectures.

1   Introduction

A key goal of modern chemical investigation is the rationalization of molecular processes, since this is the base for modeling several technological and environmental applications. Among these, of great importance are those leading to chemical reactions. Although the formalism for treating exactly reactive processes is fully established since long time, its complex algorithmic formulation and its computationally intensive numerical implementation have strongly limited advances in this field even for elementary atom diatom reactions [1]. Therefore, an active line of research is the investigation on how, for this class of problems, innovative numerical approaches can be designed and related computational procedures can be implemented on parallel architectures. To guarantee the portability of the code, use was made of the MPI paradigm.

Goal of this paper is to illustrate the advances of a project aimed at implementing a parallel version of a full dimensional quantum reactive scattering computational procedure for atom diatom systems. In section 2 the mathematical foundations and the algorithmic structure of the related codes are presented. In section 3 the modifications needed for a parallel organization of the programs are illustrated. In section 4 performances of their parallel implementations are discussed.

2   Mathematical Foundations and Algorithmic Structure

From a mathematical point of view, the reactive scattering problem can be reconducted to the integration of a 9 dimensional differential equation, once that the motion of the electrons has been decoupled (Born Oppenheimer approximation[2]).

J. Dongarra et al. (Eds.): EuroPVM/MPI 2000, LNCS 1908, pp. 338–345, 2000.

By taking advantage of the invariance of the center of mass motion and the constance of both the energy E and the total angular momentum $\mathbf{J}$ (J is its quantum eigenvalue and M its projection on the z axis of the space fixed coordinate frame), the equation defining the n-th partial wave of the system Ψ^{JMpn} of parity p in three dimensions can be reduced to:

$$\hat{H}\Psi^{JMpn} = E\Psi^{JMpn} \tag{1}$$

In equation (1) $\hat{H}$ is the Hamiltonian operator that, in terms of the Adiabatically adjusting Principal axis Hyperspherical (APH) coordinates [3] [4] [5], can be partitioned as follows:

$$\hat{H} = \hat{T}_\rho + \hat{T}_h + \hat{T}_r + \hat{T}_c + V(\rho, \theta, \chi) \tag{2}$$

with ρ being the hyperradius, θ and χ the internal hyperangles, and $\hat{T}_\rho, \hat{T}_h, \hat{T}_r, \hat{T}_c$ the various terms of the kinetic operator describing its radial, angular, rotational and Coriolis components, respectively. The $V(\rho, \theta, \chi)$ term is the potential energy function describing the interaction between the three atoms generated by solving the (separated) electronic problem at various nuclear geometries.

Equation (1) is solved by expanding the partial wave Ψ^{JMpn} as products of the Wigner rotational functions $\hat{D}^{Jp}_{AM}$ depending on the Euler angles (α, β, γ) (these angles describe the spatial orientation of the coordinate system integral with the plane formed by the three particles, and Λ is the projection of $\mathbf{J}$ on the z axis of these Body Fixed coordinates), of the surface functions Φ depending on the θ and χ hyperangles (at fixed value of the hyperradius) and of functions $\psi(\rho)$ depending on ρ and carrying the scattering information:

$$\Psi^{JMpn} = 4\sum_{t,\Lambda} \rho^{-\frac{5}{2}} \psi^{Jpn}_{t\Lambda}(\rho)\Phi^{Jp}_{t\Lambda}(\theta, \chi; \rho_\epsilon)\hat{D}^{Jp}_{\Lambda M}(\alpha, \beta, \gamma). \tag{3}$$

To perform the numerical integration the hyperradius interval is partitioned into several small sectors. For each sector ϵ the surface functions $\Phi^{Jp}_{t\Lambda}(\theta, \chi; \rho_\epsilon)$ are computed at the sector midpoint ρ_ϵ by solving the eigenvalue $(\varepsilon^{Jp}_{t\Lambda})$ equation:

$$\left[T_h + \frac{15\hbar^2}{8\mu\rho_\epsilon^2} + \hbar^2 GJ(J+1) + \hbar^2 F\Lambda^2 + V(\rho_\epsilon, \theta, \chi) - \varepsilon^{Jp}_{t\Lambda}(\rho_\epsilon)\right]\Phi^{Jp}_{t\Lambda}(\theta, \chi; \rho_\epsilon) = 0 \tag{4}$$

where μ is the reduced mass of the system, G and F are coefficients depending on the mass and the geometry of the triatom. Equation (4) is solved by applying the *Analytic Basis Method* [6] that expands the surface functions in terms of a basis set of analytic functions centered on each arrangement channel.

The substitution of expansion (3) into equation (1) leads to the following set of coupled differential equations:

$$\left(\frac{\partial^2}{\partial\rho^2} + \frac{2\mu E}{\hbar^2}\right)\psi^{Jpn}_{t\Lambda}(\rho) = \frac{2\mu}{\hbar^2}\sum_{t'\Lambda'}\left\langle \Phi^{Jp}_{t\Lambda}\hat{D}^{Jp}_{\Lambda M}|\hat{H}_i|\Phi^{Jp}_{t'\Lambda'}\hat{D}^{Jp}_{\Lambda'M}\right\rangle\psi^{Jpn}_{t'\Lambda'}(\rho) \tag{5}$$

with $\hat{H}_i$ being:

$$\hat{H}_i = \hat{T}_h + \hat{T}_r + \hat{T}_c + \frac{15\hbar^2}{8\mu\rho^2} + V(\rho, \theta, \chi). \qquad (6)$$

The set of coupled equations (5) is then solved by propagating the solution matrix using the *Logarithmic Derivative Method* [7]-[10] from a small value of ρ to a large asymptotic one. There, a mapping of the solution matrix into Delves coordinates [3] and from Delves into Jacobi coordinates is performed. Then, the scattering matrix **S** is determined by imposing asymptotic boundary conditions.

The related computational procedure (APH3D) is articulated into two large programs (ABM and LOGDER) and other few small ones. ABM is the program devoted to the calculation of surface functions and related eigenvalues. LOGDER is the program devoted to the propagation of the solution matrix. Remaining programs perform all the transformations necessary to evaluate **S**. Recently, the problem of parallelizing ABM was tackled [11][12] and partially satisfactory results were obtained. Yet, the work of parallelizing simultaneously both ABM and LOGDER was not considered before.

3   The Parallel Implementation

The serial version of ABM consists of two nested loops: the outer loop runs over the sector index; the inner loop runs over the values of the projections Λ.

For each sector, the program determines the value of the hyperradius at the sector midpoint (ρ_ϵ), integrates equation (4) and calculates the coupling matrix that is then stored on disk. The scheme of the ABM program is therefore:

```
Read input data
Calculate quantities of common use
LOOP on sector index
    Calculate ρₑ
    LOOP on Λ
        Construct the basis set at ρₑ
        Solve equation (4) to generate surface function at ρₑ
        IF(not first sector) then
            Calculate overlaps with surface functions at ρₑ₋₁
            Store on disk overlap matrix
        END if
    END loop on Λ
    Calculate the coupling matrix
    Store on disk the coupling matrix
END loop on sector index
```

As apparent from the above scheme, the computational feature inhibiting parallelization (provided that the calculation of the surface functions fits into the node memory) is the calculation of the overlap integrals between surface functions of the current sector and those of the previous one. To do this, the eigenvectors of the surface functions of the previous sector need to be used to evaluate those surface functions at the grid points of the present sector. This difficulty can be overcome by assigning statically blocks of sectors to each node and repeating the calculation of the surface functions of the previous sector only for the first sector of each block [11].

In a recent paper [12] we discussed the superiority of adopting a dynamical scheduling of the work load. To do this, however, the calculation of the surface functions of the preceeding sector needs to be repeated at each ρ value. In the improved version of ABM needs to be repeated only the calculation of the basis set for the preceeding sector, thus avoiding the solution of the Schrödinger equation for this sector. The resulting structure of the master process is:

```
Read input data
Send input data to all slaves
LOOP on sector index
    Calculate ρ_ε
    Call MPI_SEND(ρ_ε)
END loop on sector index
```

while the slave process is :

```
Recv input data
10 Call MPI_RECV(ρ_ε)
Calculate ρ_ε
LOOP on Λ
    Construct the basis set at ρ_ε
    Solve equation (4) to generate surface functions at ρ_ε
    Store on disk eigenvalues and eigenvectors
    Call MPI_BARRIER
    IF(not first sector) then
        Construct the basis set at ρ_ε-1
        Read eigenvectors at ρ_ε-1
        Compute overlap integrals
        Store on disk the overlap matrix
    END if
END loop on Λ
Calculate the coupling matrix
Store on disk the coupling matrix
GOTO 10
```

In the above scheme, when the slave process is assigned a task to perform, it computes the primitive basis set for the current sector, from which eigenvalues and surface functions at ρ_ϵ are calculated by solving equation (4). Related eigenvectors are stored on disk. Surface functions for the previous sector are reconstructed by retrieving from disk (where they are written by the node performing the calculation for the previous sector) related eigenvectors without solving again equation (4). To prevent attempts to read not yet stored information, nodes are synchronized before reading from disk in order to ensure that related writing operations have been completed. This is accomplished by defining an MPI communicator that groups together all the slaves and by putting an MPI_BARRIER. After reading the necessary information from disk, sector calculations are completed by evaluating the coupling matrix.

Another aspect that has been considered for the optimization of the parallel model is the management of output files. In the sequential version of the program only two files (one for the whole coupling matrix and one for the whole overlap matrix) containing the information of all sectors are generated. In the parallel program writing operations of the various sectors are decoupled by associating an individual file to each sector.

The serial version of LOGDER consists of two nested loops: the outer loop runs on the energy values at which propagation must be performed, the inner loop runs on sectors. For each sector the propagator integrates one step forward the set of coupled differential equations given in (5):

```
Read input data
LOOP on energy E
    LOOP on sectors
        Calculate ρ_ε
        Call the propagator
    END loop on sectors
    Store the solution matrix
END loop on energy E
```

At the end of the propagation through all the sectors, the solution matrix is stored on disk for use by subsequent programs, and the propagation for another energy is started.

The most natural way of parallelizing LOGDER is to adopt a *task farm*[13] at the level of the loop on energy. Accordingly, the scheme of the master process is:

```
Read input data
Send input data to all slave
LOOP on energy E
    Call MPI_SEND(E)
END loop on energy E
```

The process sketched above reads and broadcasts the input data to all slave processes. Then the work is assigned to the workers by sending the current energy value. The scheme of the slave process is:

```
Recv input data
10 Call MPI_RECV(E)
LOOP on sectors
    Calculate ρ_ε
    Call the propagator
```

```
END loop on sectors
Store the solution matrix
GOTO 10
```

The slave process receives firstly the input data and then receives the energy value E for which the propagation has to be performed. At the end of the propagation, the slave process stores on disk the solution matrix and gets ready to receive the next energy value.

4   Performance Measurements

Performances of the parallel versions of ABM and LOGDER where measured on the Cray T3E/1200 256 at CINECA (Bologna, Italy) using as input parameters those of the $Li + FH$ reaction. The total angular momentum was set equal to zero ($J = 0$), the hyperradius was subdivided into 230 sectors and the surface functions were expanded using a basis set of 277 functions.

Elapsed times (in seconds) measured for ABM on various machine configurations are shown in figure 1. In figure 2 the related speedup calculated using an estimate of the sequential time obtained by extrapolating the time measured for parallel runs to a single processor run (18203 s) is plotted.

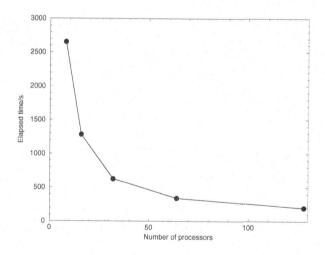

Fig. 1. Elapsed time measured for ABM.

As is apparent from figure 2, the program scales well, despite the fact that it is impossible to evenly distribute 230 sector calculations among the considered numbers of processors (elapsed times measured here are about 5 times smaller than those reported in ref. [12]).

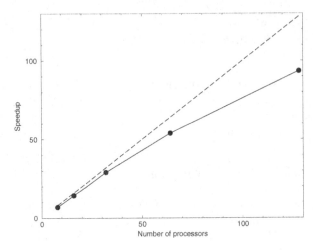

Fig. 2. Limit (dashed line) and measured speedup (solid line) for ABM.

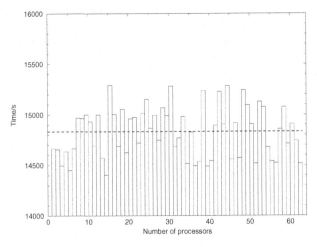

Fig. 3. Elapsed time measured for LOGDER.

The performance of the parallel version of LOGDER was measured by carrying out calculations for 126 energies on 64 nodes (individual node elapsed times are plotted in figure (3)). In this figure the mean node elapsed time is also given as a dashed line. As apparent from figure (3), the work load is almost evenly distributed among the nodes since the deviation of the individual node elapsed time from the mean value varies between +3.09% and -2.89%. The (small) imbalance is mainly due to the fact that, during the propagation, each slave process has to read 3 files from disk for each sector. This causes competition among the various processors and generates inefficiences depending on the disk I/O speed.

5   Conclusions

The parallelization of complex computational procedures such as those devoted to full dimensional quantum reactive scattering calculations is a rather intriguing task. The study reported in this paper shows that to achieve high speedups the parallelism has to be kept at high level (coarse granularity) and in some cases calculations have to be repeated to decouple existing order dependencies. This is the case of ABM for which, to remove order dependencies of the sequential code the calculation of the surface functions has to be repeated and one has to manage several files stored on disks (this introduces a dependence from the speed of the disks). However, in our tests the performance of the program is not significantly penalized by this, owing to the high disk speed of the Cray machine used.

The parallelization of LOGDER showed more natural since a dynamical assignment of the work load can be adopted if the whole propagation (having a strict sequential nature) can be assigned to a single node.

6   Acknowledgments

Thanks are due to CINECA for providing access and computing time on the Cray T3E. AB acknowledges a fellowship from INFN (PQE2000 project). SC acknowledges a fellowship from the University of Perugia. Financial support from ASI and MURST is also acknowledged.

References

1. A. Laganà, Comp. Phys. Comm., **116** (1999) 1-16.
2. M. Born, J. R. Oppenheimer, *Ann. der Physik*, **84**, (1927) 457-484.
3. R. T. Pack, G. A. Parker, J. Chem. Phys., **87** (1987) 3888-3921.
4. G. A. Parker, R. T Pack, A. Laganà, B. J. Archer, J. D. Kress, Z. Bačic in *Supercomputer algorithms for reactivity, dynamics and kinetics of small molecules*, A. Laganà Ed. (Kluwer, Dordrecht 1989), 271-294.
5. G. A. Parker, A. Laganà, S. Crocchianti, R. T Pack, J. Chem. Phys., **102** (1995) 1238-1250.
6. G. A. Parker, R. T Pack, J. Chem. Phys., **98** (1993) 6883-6896.
7. B. G. Wicke, D. O. Harris, J. Chem. Phys., **64** (1976) 5236-5242.
8. B. R. Johnson, J. Chem. Phys., **67** (1977) 4086-4093.
9. B. R. Johnson, J. Chem. Phys., **69** (1979) 4678-4688.
10. G. A. Parker, J. C. Light, B. R. Johnson, Chem. Phys. Lett., **73** (1980) 572-575.
11. A. Laganà, S. Crocchianti, G. Ochoa de Aspuru, R. Gargano, G. A. Parker, Lecture Notes in Computer Science, **1041** (1995) 361-370.
12. A. Bolloni, A. Riganelli, S. Crocchianti, A. Laganà, Lecture Notes in Computer Science, **1497** (1998) 331-337.
13. S. Pelagatti, *Structured development of parallel programs*, Taylor&Francis (London, 1998).

FT-MPI: Fault Tolerant MPI, Supporting Dynamic Applications in a Dynamic World

Graham E. Fagg and Jack J. Dongarra

Department of Computer Science, University of Tennessee,
104 Ayres Hall, Knoxville, TN-37996-1301, USA.
Fagg@cs.utk.edu

Abstract. Initial versions of MPI were designed to work efficiently on multi-processors which had very little job control and thus static process models, subsequently forcing them to support dynamic process operations would have effected their performance. As current HPC systems increase in size with higher potential levels of individual node failure, the need rises for new fault tolerant systems to be developed. Here we present a new implementation of MPI called FT-MPI[1] that allows the semantics and associated failure modes to be completely controlled by the application. Given is an overview of the FT-MPI semantics, design and some performance issues as well as the HARNESS g_hcore implementation it is built upon.

1. Introduction

Although MPI is currently the de-facto standard system used to build high performance applications for both clusters and dedicated MPP systems, it is not without it problems. Initially MPI was designed to allow for very high efficiency and thus performance on a number of early 1990s MPPs, that at the time had limited OS runtime support. This led to the current MPI design of a static process model. While this model was possible to implement for MPP vendors, easy to program for, and more importantly something that could be agreed upon by a standards committee.

The MPI static process model suffices for small numbers of distributed nodes within the currently emerging masses of clusters and several hundred nodes of dedicated MPPs. Beyond these sizes the mean time between failure (MTBF) of CPU nodes start becoming a factor. As attempts to build the next generation Peta-flop systems advance, this situation will only become more adverse as individual node reliability becomes out weighted by orders of magnitude increase in node numbers and hense node failures.

---

[1] FT-MPI and HARNESS are supported in part by the US Department of Energy under contract DE-FG02-99ER25378.

J. Dongarra et al. (Eds.): EuroPVM/MPI 2000, LNCS 1908, pp. 346-353, 2000.

The aim of FT-MPI is to build a fault tolerant MPI implementation that can survive failures, while offering the application developer a range of recovery options other than just returning to some previous check-pointed state. FT-MPI is built on the HARNESS meta-computing system [1].

2.   Check-Point and Roll Back verse Replication Techniques

The first method attempted to make MPI applications fault tolerant was through the use of check-pointing and roll back. Co-Check MPI [2] from the Technical University of Munich being the first MPI implementation built that used the Condor library for check-pointing an entire MPI application. In this implementation, all processes would flush their messages queues to avoid in flight messages getting lost, and then they would all synchronously check-point. At some later stage if either an error occurred or a task was forced to migrate to assist load balancing, the entire MPI application would be rolled back to the last complete check-point and be restarted. This systems main drawback being the need for the entire application having to check-point synchronously, which depending on the application and its size could become expensive in terms of time (with potential scaling problems). A secondary consideration was that they had to implement a new version of MPI known as tuMPI as retro-fitting MPICH was considered too difficult.

Another system that also uses check-pointing but at a much lower level is StarFish MPI [3]. Unlike Co-Check MPI which relies on Condor, Starfish MPI uses its own distributed system to provide built in check-pointing. The main difference with Co-Check MPI is how it handles communication and state changes which are managed by StarFish using strict atomic group communication protocols built upon the Ensemble system [4], and thus avoids the message flush protocol of Co-Check. Being a more recent project StarFish supports faster networking interfaces than tuMPI.

The project closest to FT-MPI known by the author is the unpublished Implicit Fault Tolerance MPI project by Paraskevas Evripidou of Cyprus University. This project supports several master-slave models where all communicators are built from grids that contain 'spare' processes. These spare processes are utilized when there is a failure. To avoid loss of message data between the master and slaves, all messages are copied to an observer process, which can reproduce lost messages in the event of any failures. This system appears only to support SPMD style computation and has a high overhead for every message.

3.   FT-MPI Semantics

Current semantics of MPI indicate that a failure of a MPI process or communication causes all communicators associated with them to become *invalid*. As the standard provides no method to reinstate them (and it is unclear if we can even *free* them), we are left with the problem that this causes MPI_COMM_WORLD itself to become invalid and thus the entire MPI application will grid to a halt.

FT-MPI extends the MPI communicator states from {valid, invalid} to a range {FT_OK, FT_DETECTED, FT_RECOVER, FT_RECOVERED, FT_FAILED}. In essence this becomes {OK, PROBLEM, FAILED}, with the other states mainly of interest to the internal fault recovery algorithm of FT_MPI. Processes also have typical states of {OK, FAILED} which FT-MPI replaces with {OK, Unavailable, Joining, Failed}. The *Unavailable* state includes unknown, unreachable or "we have not voted to remove it yet" states.

A communicator changes its state when either an MPI process changes its state, or a communication within that communicator fails for some reason. The typical MPI semantics is from OK to Failed which then causes an application abort. By allowing the communicator to be in an intermediate state we allow the application the ability to decide how to alter the communicator and its state as well as how communication within the intermediate state behaves.

3.1.1 Failure Modes

On detecting a failure within a communicator, that communicator is marked as having a probable error. Immediately as this occurs the underlying system sends a state update to all other processes involved in that communicator. If the error was a communication error, not all communicators are forced to be updated, if it was a process exit then all communicators that include this process are changed. Note, this might not be all current communicators as we support MPI-2 dynamic tasks and thus multiple MPI_COMM_WORLDS.

How the system behaves depends on the communicator failure mode chosen by the application. The mode has two parts, one for the communication behavior and one for the how the communicator reforms if at all.

3.1.2 Communicator and Communication Handling

Once a communicator has an error state it can only recover by rebuilding it, using a modified version of one of the MPI communicator build functions such as MPI_Comm_{create, split or dup}. Under these functions the new communicator will follow the following semantics depending on its failure mode:

SHRINK: The communicator is shrank so that there are no holes in its data structures. The ranks of the processes are **changed**, forcing the application to recall MPI_COMM_RANK.

BLANK: This is the same as SHRINK, except that the communicator can now contain gaps to be filled in later. Communicating with a gap will cause an invalid rank error. Note also that calling MPI_COMM_SIZE will return the size of the communicator, not the number of valid processes within it.

REBUILD: Most complex in that it forces the creation of new processes to fill any gaps. The new processes can either be places in to the empty ranks, or the communicator can be shrank and the processes added the end. This is used for applications that require a certain size to execute as in power of two FFT solvers.

ABORT: Is a mode which effects the application immediately an error is detected and forces a graceful abort. The user can not trap this, and only option is to change the communicator mode to one of the above modes.

Communications within the communicator are controlled by a message mode for the communicator which can be either of:

NOP: No operations on error. I.e. no user level message operation are allowed and all simply return an error code. This is used to allow an application to return from any point in the code to a state where it can take appropriate action as soon as possible.

CONT: All communication that is NOT to the effected/failed node can continue as normal. Attempts to communicate with a failed node will return errors until the communicator state is reset.

The user discovers any errors from the return code of any MPI call, with a new fault indicated by MPI_ERR_OTHER. Details as to the nature and specifics of the error is available though the cached attributes interface in MPI.

3.1.3 Point to Point verses Collective Correctness

Although collective operations pertain to point to point operations in most cases, extra care has been taken in implementing the collective operations so that if an error occurs during an operation, the result of the operation will still be the same as if there had been no error, or else the operation is aborted.

Broadcast, gather and all gather demonstrate this perfectly. In Broadcast even if there is a failure of a receiving node, the receiving nodes still receive the same data, i.e. the same end result for the surviving nodes. Gather and all-gather are different in that the result depends on if the problematic nodes sent data to the gatherer/root or not. In the case of gather, the root might or might not have gaps in the result. For all gather which typically uses a ring algorithm it is possible that some nodes may have complete information and others incomplete. Thus for operations that require multiple node input as in gather/reduce type operations any failure causes all nodes to return an error code, rather than possibly invalid data. Currently an addition flag controls how strict the above rule is enforced by utilizing an extra barrier call at the end of the collective call if required.

4.   FT-MPI Usage Example

Typical usage of FT-MPI would be in the form of an error check and then some corrective action such as a communicator rebuild. A typical code fragment is shown below, where on an error the communicator is simply rebuilt and reused:

```
rc= MPI_Send (----, com);
If (rc==MPI_ERR_OTHER)
     MPI_Comm_dup (com, newcom);
     com = newcom;  /* continue.. */
```

Some types of computation such as SPMD master-slave codes only need the error checking in the master code if the user is willing to accept the master as the only point of failure. The example below shows how complex a master code can become. In this example the communicator mode is BLANK and communications mode is CONT. The master keeps track of work allocated, and on an error just reallocates the work to any 'free' surviving processes. Note, the code checks to see if there are surviving worker processes left after each death is detected.

```
rc = MPI_Bcast ( initial_work....);
if(rc==MPI_ERR_OTHER)reclaim_lost_work(...);

while ( ! all_work_done) {
  if (work_allocated) {
    rc = MPI_Recv ( buf, ans_size, result_dt,
                    MPI_ANY_SOURCE,   MPI_ANY_TAG, comm, &status);
    if (rc==MPI_SUCCESS) {
                          handle_work (buf);
                          free_worker (status.MPI_SOURCE);
                          all_work_done--;
                        }
    else {
          reclaim_lost_work(status.MPI_SOURCE);
          if (no_surviving_workers) { /* ! do something ! */ }
        }
  } /* work allocated */

  /* Get a new worker as we must have received a result or a death */
  rank=get_free_worker_and_allocate_work();
  if (rank) {
    rc = MPI_Send (... rank... );
    if (rc==MPI_OTHER_ERR) reclaim_lost_work (rank);
    if (no_surviving_workers) { /* ! do something ! */ }
  } /* if free worker */

} /* while work to do */
```

5.   FT_MPI Implementation Details

FT-MPI is a partial MPI-2 implementation in its own right. It currently contains support for both C and Fortran interfaces, all the MPI-1 function calls required to run both the PSTSWM [6] and BLACS applications. BLACS is supported so that SCALAPACK application can be tested. Currently only some the dynamic process control functions from MPI-2 are supported.

The current implementation is built as a number of layers as shown in figure 1. Operating system support is provided by either PVM or the C Harness *g_hcore*. Although point to point and collective communication is provided by the stand alone SNIPE_Lite communication library taken from the SNIPE project [4].

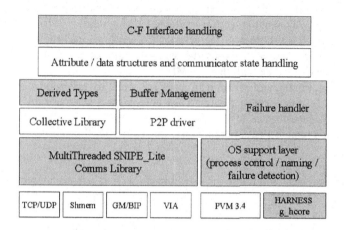

Fig. 1. Overall structure of the FT-MPI implementation.

A number of components have been extensively optimised, these include:

- Derived data types and message buffers. Particular attention has been paid in improving sparse data set and numeric representation handling.
- Collective communications. They have been tuned for both optimal topologies (ring verse binary vs binomial trees) as well as dynamic re-ordering of topologies.
- Point to point communication using a multi-threaded SNIPE_Lite library that's allows separate threads to handle send and receives so that non-blocking communications still make progress while not within any MPI calls.

It is important to note that the failure handler gets notification of failures from both the communications libraries as well as the OS support layer. In the case of communication errors this is usually due to direct communication with a failed party fails before the failed parties OS layer has notified other OS layers and their processes. The handler is responsible for notifying all tasks of errors as they occur by injecting notify messages into the send message queues ahead of user level messages.

6. OS Support and the Harness g_hcore

When FT-MPI was first designed the only Harness Kernel available was an experiment Java implementation from Emory University [5]. Tests were conducted to implement required services on this from C in the form of C-Java wrappers that made RMI calls. Although they worked, they were not very efficient and so FT-MPI was instead developed using the readily available PVM system.

As the project has progressed, the primary author developed the g_hcore, a C based HARNESS core library that uses the same policies as the Java version. This core allows for services to be built that FT-MPI requires.

The g_hcore library and daemon process (g_hcore_d) has good performance compared to the Java core especially in a LAN environment when using UDP, with remote function invocation times of 400uSeconds compared to several millisecond for Java RMI between remote JVMs running on Linux over 100Mb/Sec Ethernet.

Current services required by FT-MPI break down into three categories:

1. Meta-Data storage. Provided by PVM in the form of message mboxes. Under the g_hcore as a multi-master master-slave replicated store.
2. Process control (spawn, kill). Provided using pvm_spawn and pvm_kill for PVM, and fork-exec and signal under the g_hcore_d.
3. Task exit notification. pvm_notify and pvm_probe under PVM, and via the spawn service under g_hcore catching Unix sigchild and broken sockets.

7. FT-MPI Tool Support

Current MPI debuggers and visualization tools such as totalview, vampir, upshot etc do not have a concept of how to monitor MPI jobs that change their communicators on the fly, nor do they know how to monitor a virtual machine. To assist users in understanding these the author has implemented two monitor tools. HOSTINFO which displays the state of the Virtual Machine. COMINFO which displays processes and communicators in colour coded fashion so that users know the state of an applications processes and communicators. Both tools are currently built using the X11 libraries but will be rebuilt using the Java SWING system to aid portability. An example displays during a SHRINK communicator rebuild operation is shown in figure 2, where a process (rank 1) has just exited.

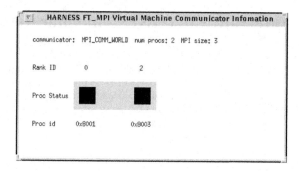

Fig. 2. COMINFO display for an application with an exited process. Note that the number of nodes and size of communicator do not match.

8. Conclusions

FT-MPI is an attempt to provide application programmers with different methods of dealing with failures within MPI application than just check-point and restart. It is hoped that by experimenting with FT-MPI, new applications methodologies and algorithms will be developed to allow for both high performance and the survivability required by the next generation of terra-flop and beyond machines.

FT-MPI in itself is already proving to be a useful vehicle for experimenting with self-tuning collective communications, distributed control algorithms and improved sparse data handling subsystems, as well as being the default MPI implementation for the HARNESS project.

9. References

1. Beck, Dongarra, Fagg, Geist, Gray, Kohl, Migliardi, K. Moore, T. Moore, P. Papadopoulous, S. Scott, V. Sunderam, "HARNESS: a next generation distributed virtual machine", Journal of Future Generation Computer Systems, (15), Elsevier Science B.V., 1999.
2. G. Stellner, "CoCheck: Checkpointing and Process Migration for MPI", In Proceedings of the International Parallel Processing Symposium, pp 526-531, Honolulu, April 1996.
3. Adnan Agbaria and Roy Friedman, "Starfish: Fault-Tolerant Dynamic MPI Programs on Clusters of Workstations", In the 8th IEEE International Symposium on High Performance Distributed Computing, 1999.
4. Graham E. Fagg, Keith Moore, Jack J. Dongarra, "Scalable networked information processing environment (SNIPE)", Journal of Future Generation Computer Systems, (15), pp. 571-582, Elsevier Science B.V., 1999.
5. Mauro Migliardi and Vaidy Sunderam, "PVM Emulation in the Harness MetaComputing System: A Plug-in Based Approach", Lecture Notes in Computer Science (1697), pp 117-124, September 1999.
6. P. H. Worley, I. T. Foster, and B. Toonen, "Algorithm comparison and benchmarking using a parallel spectral transform shallow water model", Proccedings of the Sixth Workshop on Parallel Processing in Meteorology, eds. G.-R. Hoffmann and N. Kreitz, World Scientific, Singapore, pp. 277-289, 1995.

ACCT: Automatic Collective Communications Tuning

Graham E. Fagg[*], Sathish S. Vadhiyar, and Jack J. Dongarra

Computer Science Department,
University of Tennessee,
104 Ayres Hall,
Knoxville, TN-37996-1301,
USA
fagg@cs.utk.edu

Abstract. The performance of the MPI's collective communications is critical in most MPI-based applications. A general algorithm for a given collective communication operation may not give good performance on all systems due to the differences in architectures, network parameters and the buffering scheme of the underlying MPI implementation. In this paper, we discuss an approach in which the collective communications are tuned for any given system by conducting a series of experiments on the system. We also discuss a dynamic topology method that uses the tuned static topology shape, but re-orders the logical addresses to compensate for changing run time variations. A series of experiments were conducted comparing our tuned MPI_Bcast to various native vendor MPI implementations. The results obtained were encouraging, and show that our implementations of collective algorithms can significantly improve the performance of current MPI implementations.

1. Introduction

This project grew out of an attempt to build efficient collective communications for a new fault tolerant MPI implementation known as HARNESS FT-MPI [9], but as it developed was found to be applicable to other current MPI implementations. This project differs from at least two different efforts that have been made in the past to improve the performance of the MPI collective communications for a given system. They either dealt with the collective communications for a specific system or tried to tune the collective communications for a system based purely on mathematical models or both. Lars Paul Huse's paper on collective communications [2] studied and compared the performance of different collective algorithms on SCI based clusters. MAGPIE by Thilo Kielman et. al. [1] optimizes collective communications for clustered wide area systems. Though MAGPIE tries to find the optimum buffer size and optimum tree shape for a given collective communication on a given system, these optimum parameters are determined using a performance model called the *parametrized LogP* model. Mathematical models based on few network parameters in the system do not adequately take into account the overlap in communication that occurs in collective communications.

J. Dongarra et al. (Eds.): EuroPVM/MPI 2000, LNCS 1908, pp. 354-361, 2000.

In this paper, we discuss an approach in which the optimum algorithm and optimum buffer size for a given collective communication on a system is determined by conducting experiments on the system. This approach follows the strategy that is used in efforts like ATLAS [7] for matrix operations and FFTW [6] for Fast Fourier Transforms. The experiments were conducted in several phases. In the first phase, the best buffer size for a given algorithm for a given number of processors is determined by evaluating the performance of the algorithm for different buffer sizes. In the second phase, the best algorithm for a given message size is chosen by repeating phase1 with a known set of algorithms and choosing the algorithm that gives the best result. In the third phase, phase1 and phase2 is repeated for different number of processors.

The large number of buffer sizes and the large number of processors significantly increase the time for conducting the above experiments. While testing different buffer sizes, only values that are power of 2 and multiples of the basic data type are evaluated. Similarly, the experiments are conducted for only "useful" number of processors. Work is under way to reduce the number of experiments and still achieve good optimization of the collective communications.

In Section 2, we examine the different algorithms that are available in our repertoire. In Section 3, we describe the machines we used, the experiments conducted on the machines, and analysis of the results. In Section 4, we discuss the dynamic topology method that reorders the processes within a given topology for communication and methods for reducing the total search space examined. In Section 5, we present some conclusions. Finally in Section 6, we outline the future direction of our research.

2.   Algorithms for Collective Communications

The first crucial step in our effort is to develop a range of competitive algorithms for efficient collective communications over different topologies and network infrastructures. In this section, we describe the different algorithms used in our experiments.

Developing competent algorithms for broadcast, scatter and gather is significant since the other collective communication operations can be implemented with the combination of these three collective operations.

- Sequential tree: In this topology, the root sends the messages successively to all the other processors. If there are n processors, this algorithm takes n-1 steps to complete. Since the latencies are not chained, this algorithm gives good performance in wide-area networks.
- Chain tree: In the chain tree, the root sends to process 1 and process N-1 receives from N-2. Process $r \in [1 \ldots N-2]$ receives from r-1 and sends to r+1. Though process N must wait for N-1 time steps for the reception of the message, the pipelined nature of the algorithm gives successive operations high throughput.
- Binary tree: Each node but the root receives from one node, and all sends to up to two other nodes. This algorithm takes at most $O(\log_2 N)$ steps to complete.
- Binomial tree : The definition of the binomial tree as given in the paper by Laurs Paul Huse is "In $s \in [1 \ldots Ln]$ steps, process 0 in all groups send to $r_x = \lfloor (2+maxr)/2 \rfloor$ which receive from 0. All groups with more than two processes are

then split in $\Phi = [0...r_x-1]$ and $\Psi = [r_x ...maxr]$ and new ranks $r' = r-r_x$ assigned to Ψ."

In most cases, the binomial tree algorithm gives better performance than the binary tree.

3.   Experimental Setup and Results

The experiments consist of many phases. In the first phase, we determine the best segment size for a given message size for a given algorithm for a collective operation. The segment sizes are powers of two, multiples of the basic data type and less than the message size. Having conducted the first phase for all the algorithms, we determine the best algorithm for a collective operation for a given message size. Message sizes from the size of the basic data type to 1MB were evaluated. This forms the second phase of the experiments. Though we have conducted the experiments on only eight processors, the third phase of the experiments would be to evaluate the results on a set of different number of processors. The number of processors will be power of two and less than the available number of processors. Our current effort is in reducing the search space involved in each of the above phases and still be able to get valid conclusions. The experiments were conducted on multiple systems including:

- 143-MHz UltraSPARC systems using 100 Mbps Ethernet
- dual processor (300/450 MHz) and single processor (450/600 MHz) Linux/NT machines connected by 100Mbit Ethernet, Giganet and Myrinet interconnections
- 34 node IBM SP2 system consisting of two eight way SMP high nodes and 32 thin nodes running AIX 4.2.

Figure 1 shows the results on the Intel machines with eight processors running Linux and interconnected by 100Mbs Ethernet. Because of the Fast Ethernet link, the overhead associated with the communication dominates the *gap* times [3]. Since in binary and ring algorithms, a processor communicates with only few other processors, these algorithms are able to utilize the gap values more efficiently than the other algorithms. Hence these algorithms combined with message segmenting help in improving the performance over the default MPICH. The MPICH default binomial algorithm does not give a good performance on the Intel machines since a processor does not immediately send the next segment of a message to another processor as soon as the first segment is sent.

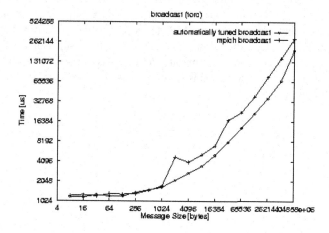

Fig. 1. Broadcast performance for an Intel Linux Cluster.

Experiments were also conducted on the IBM SP2 system using both its Power2 thin nodes and its SMP high nodes. The MPI collective algorithms were implemented on top of the IBM vendor MPI. The performance of the collective algorithms on the IBM thin nodes are shown in figure 2.

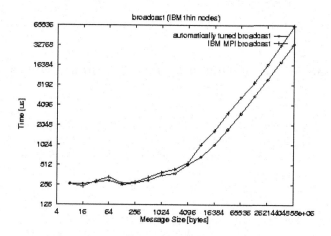

Fig. 2. Performance of the IBM SP2 thin nodes.

The superior performance of the communication adapter results in very small gap values. Hence the binary and the ring algorithms combined with message segmentation give better performance than the IBM MPI algorithm for message sizes larger than 8K bytes.

Figure 3 show the results on high node 8-way SMPs. IBM MPI sends and receives take place through the communication adapter. This results in large gap values for communication between nodes on a SMP. These gap values are utilized by the overlap in communication in binomial algorithms. This results in superior performance over IBM MPI which tries to use the same algorithm for communication on both thin and high nodes. Thus different algorithms have to be used on the same system for different memory models.

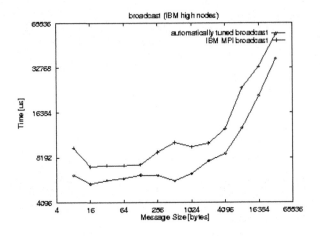

Fig. 3. Performance on the IBM high SMP nodes.

4.   Dynamical Reordering of Topologies and Reduced Search Space

Most systems rely on all processes in a communicator or process group entering the collective communication call synchronously for good performance, i.e. all processes can start the operation without forcing others later in the topology to be delayed. There are some obvious cases where this is not the case:

The application is executed upon heterogeneous computing platforms where the raw CPU power varies (or load balancing is not optimal).

The computational cycle time of the application can be non-deterministic as is the case in many of the newer iterative solvers that may converge at different rates continuously.

Even when the application executes in a regular pattern, the physical network characteristics can cause problems with the simple logP model, such as when running between dispersed clusters. This problem becomes even more acute when the system latency is so low, that any buffering, while waiting for slower nodes, drastically changes performance characteristics as is the case with BIP-MPI [8].

4.1 Dynamic Methodology

This method is a modification of the previous tuned method, where we use the tuned topology as a starting point, but the behavior of the method is varied between actual uses of the collective operations at run-time.

The method forces all the non-root nodes to send a small start-acknowledge (SACK) message to the root node, which the root uses to builds a mapping from communicator rank to logical address within the chosen topology dynamically. Each process, after having sent its SACK, then receives its own topology information via the root directly or by piggy backing the information on a user data message depending on the MPI operation being performed. This information can be split into multiple messages such as from whom do they receive from, and whom do they send to, as the information *becomes available.* i.e. a process might not be a leaf node in the tree topology but still receive all their data before knowing whom to send to.

Figure 4 demonstrates this methodology. Case 1 is where all processes within the tree are ready to run immediately and thus performance is optimal. In Case 2, both processes B and C are delayed and initially the root A can only send to D. As B and C become available, they are added to the topology. At this point we have to choose whether to add the nodes depth first as in Case 2a or breadth first as in Case 2b. Currently breadth first has given us the best results. Also note that in CASE 1, if process B is not ready to receive, it effects not only its own sub-tree, but depending on the message/segment size, it is possible that it would block any other messages that A might send, such as to Ds sub-tree etc. Faster network protocols might not implement non-blocking sends in a manner that could overcome this limitation without effecting the synchronous static optimal case, and thus blocking send are often used instead.

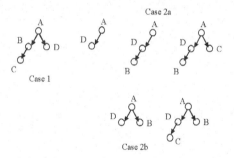

Fig. 4. Re-ordered topologies of a message tree

Currently we are testing the cost of overhead incurred in using this technique for different network infrastructures. We are also exploring the conditions needed for the automatic use of this technique during the course of the computation. Initial results have been promising, especially for large messages and network interfaces with very low latency, that rely on the receivers to have already posted receives to allow DMA message transfers. Worst case results have been equivalent to the overhead for *n*-1 small message send/receives. Best case has been within a few percent of optimal where no re-ordering on the same example has produced multiples of the optimal wall clock times, although this varies with the operation, number of processors, data size and level of initial synchronization.

4.2   Reducing the Search Space

Initial efforts for reducing the search space needed to get a close to optimal result are focused around using domain specific knowledge such as the shape of time verses segment size function as shown in figure 5. In this case we have significantly reduced total time by using hill decent algorithms that start at the maximal segment size rather than a linear search across all possible segment sizes.

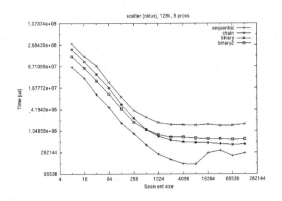

Fig. 5. Shape of scatter operation for various segment sizes.

5.   Conclusion

The optimal algorithm and the optimal buffer size for a given message size depends on a given configuration of the system including the gap values of the networks, memory models, the underlying communication layer etc. The optimal parameters for a system can be best determined by conducting experiments on the system. Our results show that the optimal parameters obtained from the experiments gave better performance than some native MPI implementations which implement a single algorithm irrespective of the system parameters. The randomness of our results for a given system also show that a generalized mathematical model will often not be able to give optimal performance.

We have also shown that during application execution, dynamically altering the mapping between rank and position within a topology can yield additional benefits in terms of performance.

6.   Future Work

The research is still in its preliminary stage of development. More competent algorithms for other collective communications have to be implemented. One of our primary goals in the future will be to conduct less experiments and still be able to obtain optimal performance for a given message size and a given number of processors. When complete, ACCT will be released as a standalone (MPI Profiling) library that can be used to improve any currently available MPI implementation.

7.   References

[1] Thilo Kielmann, Henri E. Bal and Segei Gorlatch. Bandwidth-efficient Collective Communication for Clustered Wide Area Systems. *IPDPS 2000*, Cancun, Mexico. (May 1-5, 2000)

[2] Lars Paul Huse. Collective Communication on Dedicated Clusters of Workstations.

[3] David Culler, R. Karp, D. Patterson, A. Sahay, K.E. Schauser, E. Santos, R. Subramonian and T. von Eicken. LogP: Towards a Realistic Model of Parallel Computation. In *Proc. Symposium on Principles and Practice of Parallel Programming* (PpoPP), pages 1-12, San Diego, CA (May 1993).

[4] R. Rabenseifner. A new optimized MPI reduce algorithm. http://www.hlrs.de/structure/support/parallel_computing/models/mpi/myreduce.html (1997).

[5] Marc Snir, Steve Otto, Steven Huss-Lederman, David Walker and Jack Dongarra. MPI- The Complete Reference. *Volume 1, The MPI Core, second edition* (1998).

[6] M. Frigo. FFTW: An Adaptive Software Architecture for the FFT. *Proceedings of the ICASSP Conference*, page 1381, Vol. 3. (1998).

[7] R. Clint Whaley and Jack Dongarra. Automatically Tuned Linear Algebra Software. *SC98: High Performance Networking and Computing.* http://www.cs.utk.edu/~rwhaley/ATL/INDEX.HTM. (1998)

[8] L. Prylli and B. Tourancheau. "BIP: a new protocol designed for high performance networking on myrinet" In the PC-NOW workshop, IPPS/SPDP 1998, Orlando, USA, 1998.

[9] Beck, Dongarra, Fagg, Geist, Gray, Kohl, Migliardi, K. Moore, T. Moore, P. Papadopoulous, S. Scott, V. Sunderam, "HARNESS: a next generation distributed virtual machine", Journal of Future Generation Computer Systems, (15), Elsevier Science B.V., 1999.

Author Index

Albada, G.D. van, 27
Almeida, F., 104
Astaloš, J., 225

Badia, R.M., 39
Baiardi, F., 80
Baliś, B., 242
Banaś, K., 282
Bauzá, M., 113
Bolloni, A., 338
Bolton, H.P.J., 88
Booth, S., 176
Borensztejn, P., 113
Bubak, M., 242
Bucher, L., 322
Butler, R., 168

Cassirer, K., 18
Chiola, G., 129
Chiti, S., 80
Ciaccio, G., 129
Cores, F., 304
Cotronis, J.Y., 192
Crocchianti, S., 338

Domokos, G., 64
Dongarra, J.J., 346, 354
Dózsa, G., 258
Drótos, D., 258

Érdi, P., 313
Espinosa, A., 47

Fagg, G.E., 346, 354
Fernández, F., 322
Fernández, G.J., 113
Fink, T., 208
Frisiani, A., 152
Funika, W., 242

Gaussier, P., 289
Geist, A., 1

Giné, F., 233
Girona, S., 39
González, D., 104
González, J.A., 96
Groenwold, A.A., 88
Gropp, W.D., 160, 168
Guérin Lassous, I., 72
Gustedt, J., 72

Hendrikse, Z.W., 27
Hernández, P., 233
Hluchý, L., 225, 250
Hunzelmann, G., 10
Huse, L.P., 56

Imamura, T., 200
Iskra, K.A., 27

Jacobo-Berlles, J., 113

Kitowski, J., 282
Koide, H., 200
Kouniakis, C., 192

Labarta, J., 39
Laganà, A., 338
Laohawee, P., 297
León, C., 96
Lérida, J., 233
Livny, M., 3
Lovas, R., 258
Luque, E., 47, 233, 304
Lusk, E., 5, 168

Margalef, T., 47
Mazzocca, N., 266
Mejail, M., 113
Mierendorff, H., 18
Migliardi, M., 152
Moga, S., 289
Moreno, L.M., 104
Mori, P., 80

Morvan, M., 72
Mourão, E., 176

Neyman, M., 274
Nguyen, G.T., 250
Nitsche, T., 145

Overeinder, B.J., 27

Payrits, Sz., 313
Pedroso, H., 184
Petcu, D., 216
Piccoli, F., 96
Płażek, J., 282
Printista, M., 96

Quoy, M., 289

Rabaea, A., 330
Rabaea, M., 330
Rak, M., 266
Reussner, R., 10
Revel, A., 289
Ricci, L., 80
Roda, J.L., 96
Rodríguez, C., 96, 104
Roy, R., 121
Rungsawang, A., 297

Samba, G., 121
Sande, F., 96

Schutte, J.F., 88
Schwamborn, H., 18
Silva, J.G., 137, 184
Silva, L.M., 137
Sloot, P.M.A, 27
Solsona, F., 233
Steen, P.H., 64
Sterling, T., 7
Sunderam, V., 152
Suppi, R., 304
Szatmáry, Z., 313
Szeberényi, I., 64

Takemiya, H., 200
Tangpong, A., 297
Távora, V.N., 137
Tomassini, M., 322
Tourancheau, B., 9
Träff, J.L., 10
Tran, V.D., 250
Tsiatsoulis, Z., 192
Tsujita, Y., 200

Vadhiyar, S.S., 354
Vanneschi, L., 322
Varin, E., 121
Villano, U., 266

Wismüller, R. 242

Zalányi, L., 313

Lecture Notes in Computer Science

For information about Vols. 1–1835
please contact your bookseller or Springer-Verlag

Vol. 1836: B. Masand, M. Spiliopoulou (Eds.), Web Usage Analysis and User Profiling. Proceedings, 2000, V, 183 pages. 2000. (Subseries LNAI).

Vol. 1837: R. Backhouse, J. Nuno Oliveira (Eds.), Mathematics of Program Construction. Proceedings, 2000. IX, 257 pages. 2000.

Vol. 1838: W. Bosma (Ed.), Algorithmic Number Theory. Proceedings, 2000. IX, 615 pages. 2000.

Vol. 1839: G. Gauthier, C. Frasson, K. VanLehn (Eds.), Intelligent Tutoring Systems. Proceedings, 2000. XIX, 675 pages. 2000.

Vol. 1840: F. Bomarius, M. Oivo (Eds.), Product Focused Software Process Improvement. Proceedings, 2000. XI, 426 pages. 2000.

Vol. 1841: E. Dawson, A. Clark, C. Boyd (Eds.), Information Security and Privacy. Proceedings, 2000. XII, 488 pages. 2000.

Vol. 1842: D. Vernon (Ed.), Computer Vision – ECCV 2000. Part I. Proceedings, 2000. XVIII, 953 pages. 2000.

Vol. 1843: D. Vernon (Ed.), Computer Vision – ECCV 2000. Part II. Proceedings, 2000. XVIII, 881 pages. 2000.

Vol. 1844: W.B. Frakes (Ed.), Software Reuse: Advances in Software Reusability. Proceedings, 2000. XI, 450 pages. 2000.

Vol. 1845: H.B. Keller, E. Plöderer (Eds.), Reliable Software Technologies Ada-Europe 2000. Proceedings, 2000. XIII, 304 pages. 2000.

Vol. 1846: H. Lu, A. Zhou (Eds.), Web-Age Information Management. Proceedings, 2000. XIII, 462 pages. 2000.

Vol. 1847: R. Dyckhoff (Ed.), Automated Reasoning with Analytic Tableaux and Related Methods. Proceedings, 2000. X, 441 pages. 2000. (Subseries LNAI).

Vol. 1848: R. Giancarlo, D. Sankoff (Eds.), Combinatorial Pattern Matching. Proceedings, 2000. XI, 423 pages. 2000.

Vol. 1849: C. Freksa, W. Brauer, C. Habel, K.F. Wender (Eds.), Spatial Cognition II. XI, 420 pages. 2000. (Subseries LNAI).

Vol. 1850: E. Bertino (Ed.), ECOOP 2000 – Object-Oriented Programming. Proceedings, 2000. XIII, 493 pages. 2000.

Vol. 1851: M.M. Halldórsson (Ed.), Algorithm Theory – SWAT 2000. Proceedings, 2000. XI, 564 pages. 2000.

Vol. 1852: T. Thierauf, The Computational Complexity of Equivalence and Isomorphism Problems. VIII, 135 pages. 2000.

Vol. 1853: U. Montanari, J.D.P. Rolim, E. Welzl (Eds.), Automata, Languages and Programming. Proceedings, 2000. XVI, 941 pages. 2000.

Vol. 1854: G. Lacoste, B. Pfitzmann, M. Steiner, M. Waidner (Eds.), SEMPER — Secure Electronic Marketplace for Europe. XVIII, 350 pages. 2000.

Vol. 1855: E.A. Emerson, A.P. Sistla (Eds.), Computer Aided Verification. Proceedings, 2000. X, 582 pages. 2000.

Vol. 1856: M. Veloso, E. Pagello, H. Kitano (Eds.), RoboCup-99: Robot Soccer World Cup III. XIV, 802 pages. 2000. (Subseries LNAI).

Vol. 1857: J. Kittler, F. Roli (Eds.), Multiple Classifier Systems. Proceedings, 2000. XII, 404 pages. 2000.

Vol. 1858: D.-Z. Du, P. Eades, V. Estivill-Castro, X. Lin, A. Sharma (Eds.), Computing and Combinatorics. Proceedings, 2000. XII, 478 pages. 2000.

Vol. 1860: M. Klusch, L. Kerschberg (Eds.), Cooperative Information Agents IV. Proceedings, 2000. XI, 285 pages. 2000. (Subseries LNAI).

Vol. 1861: J. Lloyd, V. Dahl, U. Furbach, M. Kerber, K.-K. Lau, C. Palamidessi, L. Moniz Pereira, Y. Sagiv, P.J. Stuckey (Eds.), Computational Logic – CL 2000. Proceedings, 2000. XIX, 1379 pages. (Subseries LNAI).

Vol. 1862: P.G. Clote, H. Schwichtenberg (Eds.), Computer Science Logic. Proceedings, 2000. XIII, 543 pages. 2000.

Vol. 1863: L. Carter, J. Ferrante (Eds.), Languages and Compilers for Parallel Computing. Proceedings, 1999. XII, 500 pages. 2000.

Vol. 1864: B. Y. Choueiry, T. Walsh (Eds.), Abstraction, Reformulation, and Approximation. Proceedings, 2000. XI, 333 pages. 2000. (Subseries LNAI).

Vol. 1865: K.R. Apt, A.C. Kakas, E. Monfroy, F. Rossi (Eds.), New Trends Constraints. Proceedings, 1999. X, 339 pages. 2000. (Subseries LNAI).

Vol. 1866: J. Cussens, A. Frisch (Eds.), Inductive Logic Programming. Proceedings, 2000. X, 265 pages. 2000. (Subseries LNAI).

Vol. 1867: B. Ganter, G.W. Mineau (Eds.), Conceptual Structures: Logical, Linguistic, and Computational Issues. Proceedings, 2000. XI, 569 pages. 2000. (Subseries LNAI).

Vol. 1868: P. Koopman, C. Clack (Eds.), Implementation of Functional Languages. Proceedings, 1999. IX, 199 pages. 2000.

Vol. 1869: M. Aagaard, J. Harrison (Eds.), Theorem Proving in Higher Order Logics. Proceedings, 2000. IX, 535 pages. 2000.

Vol. 1872: J. van Leeuwen, O. Watanabe, M. Hagiya, P.D. Mosses, T. Ito (Eds.), Theoretical Computer Science. Proceedings, 2000. XV, 630 pages. 2000.

Vol. 1873: M. Ibrahim, J. Küng, N. Revell (Eds.), Database and Expert Systems Applications. Proceedings, 2000. XIX, 1005 pages. 2000.

Vol. 1874: Y. Kambayashi, M. Mohania, A M. Tjoa (Eds.), Data Warehousing and Knowledge Discovery. Proceedings, 2000. XII, 438 pages. 2000.

Vol. 1875: K. Bauknecht, S.K. Madria, G. Pernul (Eds.), Electronic Commerce and Web Technologies. Proceedings, 2000. XII, 488 pages. 2000.

Vol. 1876: F. J. Ferri, J.M. Iñesta, A. Amin, P. Pudil (Eds.), Advances in Pattern Recognition. Proceedings, 2000. XVIII, 901 pages. 2000.

Vol. 1877: C. Palamidessi (Ed.), CONCUR 2000 – Concurrency Theory. Proceedings, 2000. XI, 612 pages. 2000.

Vol. 1878: J.P. Bowen, S. Dunne, A. Galloway, S. King (Eds.), ZB 2000: Formal Specification and Development in Z and B. Proceedings, 2000. XIV, 511 pages. 2000.

Vol. 1879: M. Paterson (Ed.), Algorithms – ESA 2000. Proceedings, 2000. IX, 450 pages. 2000.

Vol. 1880: M. Bellare (Ed.), Advances in Cryptology – CRYPTO 2000. Proceedings, 2000. XI, 545 pages. 2000.

Vol. 1881: C. Zhang, V.-W. Soo (Eds.), Design and Applications of Intelligent Agents. Proceedings, 2000. X, 183 pages. 2000. (Subseries LNAI).

Vol. 1882: D. Kotz, F. Mattern (Eds.), Agent Systems, Mobile Agents, and Applications. Proceedings, 2000. XII, 275 pages. 2000.

Vol. 1883: B. Triggs, A. Zisserman, R. Szeliski (Eds.), Vision Algorithms: Theory and Practice. Proceedings, 1999. X, 383 pages. 2000.

Vol. 1884: J. Štuller, J. Pokorný, B. Thalheim, Y. Masunaga (Eds.), Current Issues in Databases and Information Systems. Proceedings, 2000. XIII, 396 pages. 2000.

Vol. 1885: K. Havelund, J. Penix, W. Visser (Eds.), SPIN Model Checking and Software Verification. Proceedings, 2000. X, 343 pages. 2000.

Vol. 1886: R. Mizoguchi, J. Slaney /Eds.), PRICAI 2000: Topics in Artificial Intelligence. Proceedings, 2000. XX, 835 pages. 2000. (Subseries LNAI).

Vol. 1888: G. Sommer, Y.Y. Zeevi (Eds.), Algebraic Frames for the Perception-Action Cycle. Proceedings, 2000. X, 349 pages. 2000.

Vol. 1889: M. Anderson, P. Cheng, V. Haarslev (Eds.), Theory and Application of Diagrams. Proceedings, 2000. XII, 504 pages. 2000. (Subseries LNAI).

Vol. 1890: C Linnhoff-Popien, H.-G. Hegering (Eds.), Trends in Distributed Systems: Towards a Universal Service Market. Proceedings, 2000. XI, 341 pages. 2000.

Vol. 1891: A.L. Oliveira (Ed.), Grammatical Inference: Algorithms and Applications. Proceedings, 2000. VIII, 313 pages. 2000. (Subseries LNAI).

Vol. 1892: P. Brusilovsky, O. Stock, C. Strapparava (Eds.), Adaptive Hypermedia and Adaptive Web-Based Systems. Proceedings, 2000. XIII, 422 pages. 2000.

Vol. 1893: M. Nielsen, B. Rovan (Eds.), Mathematical Foundations of Computer Science 2000. Proceedings, 2000. XIII, 710 pages. 2000.

Vol. 1894: R. Dechter (Ed.), Principles and Practice of Constraint Programming – CP 2000. Proceedings, 2000. XII, 556 pages. 2000.

Vol. 1895: F. Cuppens, Y. Deswarte, D. Gollmann, M. Waidner (Eds.), Computer Security – ESORICS 2000. Proceedings, 2000. X, 325 pages. 2000.

Vol. 1896: R. W. Hartenstein, H. Grünbacher (Eds.), Field-Programmable Logic and Applications. Proceedings, 2000. XVII, 856 pages. 2000.

Vol. 1897: J. Gutknecht, W. Weck (Eds.), Modular Programming Languages. Proceedings, 2000. XII, 299 pages. 2000.

Vol. 1898: E. Blanzieri, L. Portinale (Eds.), Advances in Case-Based Reasoning. Proceedings, 2000. XII, 530 pages. 2000. (Subseries LNAI).

Vol. 1899: H.-H. Nagel, F.J. Perales López (Eds.), Articulated Motion and Deformable Objects. Proceedings, 2000. X, 183 pages. 2000.

Vol. 1900: A. Bode, T. Ludwig, W. Karl, R. Wismüller (Eds.), Euro-Par 2000 Parallel Processing. Proceedings, 2000. XXXV, 1368 pages. 2000.

Vol. 1901: O. Etzion, P. Scheuermann (Eds.), Cooperative Information Systems. Proceedings, 2000. XI, 336 pages. 2000.

Vol. 1902: P. Sojka, I. Kopeček, K. Pala (Eds.), Text, Speech and Dialogue. Proceedings, 2000. XIII, 463 pages. 2000. (Subseries LNAI).

Vol. 1904: S.A. Cerri, D. Dochev (Eds.), Artificial Intelligence: Methodology, Systems, and Applications. Proceedings, 2000. XII, 366 pages. 2000. (Subseries LNAI).

Vol. 1906: A. Porto, G.-C. Roman (Eds.), Coordination Languages and Models. Proceedings, 2000. IX, 353 pages. 2000.

Vol. 1908: J. Dongarra, P. Kacsuk, N. Podhorszki (Eds.), Recent Advances in Parallel Virtual Machine and Message Passing Interface. Proceedings, 2000. XV, 364 pages. 2000.

Vol. 1910: D.A. Zighed, J. Komorowski, J. Żytkow (Eds.), Principles of Data Mining and Knowledge Discovery. Proceedings, 2000. XV, 701 pages. 2000. (Subseries LNAI).

Vol. 1912: Y. Gurevich, P.W. Kutter, M. Odersky, L. Thiele (Eds.), Abstract State Machines. Proceedings, 2000. X, 381 pages. 2000.

Vol. 1913: K. Jansen, S. Khuller (Eds.), Approximation Algorithms for Combinatorial Optimization. Proceedings, 2000. IX, 275 pages. 2000.

Vol. 1917: M. Schoenauer, K. Deb, G. Rudolph, X. Yao, E. Lutton, J.J. Merelo, H.-P. Schwefel (Eds.), Parallel Problem Solving from Nature – PPSN VI. Proceedings, 2000. XXI, 915 pages. 2000.

Vol. 1918: D. Soudris, P. Pirsch, E. Barke (Eds.), Integrated Circuit Design. Proceedings, 2000. XII, 338 pages. 2000.

Vol. 1923: J. Borbinha, T. Baker (Eds.), Research and Advanced Technology for Digital Libraries. Proceedings, 2000. XVII, 513 pages. 2000.

Vol. 1924: W. Taha (Ed.), Semantics, Applications, and Implementation of Program Generation. Proceedings, 2000. VIII, 231 pages. 2000.

Vol. 1926: M. Joseph (Ed.), Formal Techniques in Real-Time and Fault-Tolerant Systems. Proceedings, 2000. X, 305 pages. 2000.

Vol. 1931: E. Horlait (Ed.), Mobile Agents for Telecommunication Applications. Proceedings, 2000. IX, 271 pages. 2000.